The Emergence of
Social Security in Canada

Comments on previous editions:

'Provides many valuable insights surrounding the complexities of social policy developments within the changing economic, political, and social conditions throughout Canada.'

—The Social Worker

'Indispensable as background ... a proficient and superb chronicle.'

—Canada Public Policy

'Should be mandatory reading for those interested in social policy.'

—Canadian Public Administration

Dennis Guest

The Emergence of
Social Security in Canada
Third Edition

UBCPress / Vancouver

Printed in Canada on acid-free paper ∞
ISBN 0-7748-1551-X

National Library of Canada Cataloguing in Publication Data

Guest, Dennis, 1923-
  The emergence of social security in Canada

  Includes bibliographical references and index.
  ISBN 0-7748-0551-X

  1. Public welfare – Canada – History. 2. Social security – Canada – History. I. Title.

HV105.G83   361.6'2'0971   C79-091179-5

Canadä

UBC Press gratefully acknowledges the financial support for our publishing
program of the Government of Canada through the Book Publishing Industry
Development Program (BPIDP), and of the Canada Council for the Arts, and
the British Columbia Arts Council.

UBC Press
The University of British Columbia
2029 West Mall
Vancouver, BC V6T 1Z2
604-822-5959 / Fax: 604-822-6083
E-mail: info@ubcpress.ca
www.ubcpress.ca

Contents

Figures and Tables

Preface to the Third Edition

The first edition of this book was written during the 1970s, building upon a PhD dissertation written at the London School of Economics in the 1960s. Beginning a third edition, more than a quarter of a century later, it is appropriate to ask if the five major themes in the development of Canadian social security, identified in the first edition, are still pertinent to a discussion of substantial, if not radical, changes occurring in Canadian social security policy in the late 1990s.

The debate over the relative merits of a *residual* (market oriented) versus an *institutional* (solidaristic) concept of social security has been more pointed in the 1980s and 1990s than at any time since the Second World War. The residual approach has been actively advanced by those who advocate a much smaller role for government, and who support cuts in public spending and in the civil service, as well as policies of deregulation, privatization, and decentralization (even though the Canadian public voted decisively against more decentralization when they rejected the 1992 Charlottetown Accord). All these policies are promoted as the only way to deal with both global competition and serious and growing unemployment. Residual social policies in provincial social assistance programs and serious cuts in health care and social services, led by the federal government's draconian cuts in transfer payments, have appeared in most parts of the country. Adding to the support for residual policies in Canada is the influence of the United States, where a wellspring of residual ideas has turned into a flood under the influence of New Right Republicanism, confirming the view of the world community that the United States is *the* 'welfare state laggard' among advanced industrialized nations, and, many would say, has the dysfunctional society to prove it.[1] Fortunately, several nations of the European Community provide a salutary reference point for the advantages of an institutional approach to social security.

Similarly, Canada's success in establishing a defensible *social minimum* of income for a majority of elderly and retired Canadians and a defensible (indeed, highly creditable) social minimum of health care for all Canadians only magnifies the country's failure to muster the political will to improve on these minimums and ensure a reasonable standard of living for all Canadians.

Defining the *causes of poverty* and its phantom offspring, 'dependency,' has been a growth industry in the 1990s, employing scores of well-financed academics in search of the precise mix of incentives and disincentives to prevent safety 'nets' from becoming 'hammocks.' At the same time, attempts to develop answers to tangible problems, such as child poverty, are left largely in the hands of voluntary committees or other interest groups.

The growth of *participatory citizenship*, another theme introduced in Chapter 1, has languished for lack of government support. Social security programs that confer rights to benefits or services are personally empowering. It can be argued that one unanticipated consequence of the system of social rights subsumed under the term 'welfare state,' including such extensions of individual rights as freedom of information legislation, human rights statutes, and the appointment of ombudsmen, is a population less deferential to authority and with a greater propensity to demand accountability from public and private sector officialdom. The rejection of the Charlottetown Accord in the national referendum of 1992 might be one manifestation; the public chastising of a large cable company because of its negative billing practices[2] represents another small but significant redistribution of power, traceable, I would argue, to the sense of personal security and empowerment linked to social security measures. The serious recessions of the early 1980s and early 1990s, compounded by jobless economic growth, downsizing, and increasing restrictions on such key programs as unemployment insurance, have created widespread social insecurity and thus impaired the environment in which citizen participation flourishes best.

Finally, *constitutional issues* continue to be a significant factor in shaping Canadian social security legislation, even though the BNA Act was consigned to history and reborn as the Constitution Act, 1867, with the significant addition of the Charter of Rights and Freedoms in 1982. The division of power and responsibilities between the two levels of government has become even more contentious in the 1990s with the growth of Québécois nationalism, and I have tried to pay more attention to this aspect. I have also revised and condensed some of the earlier material, including developments in the 1940s, 1960s, and 1970s.

Readers of the first two editions of this book have suggested additional themes for a third edition, such as First Nations issues, immigration and social policy, and gender and social policy. These, indeed, are significant gaps in my account of Canadian social security history. Fortunately, there are many scholars who are making up for these deficiencies to the edification of us all. For example, on the First Nations issues, a recent book by Frank J. Tester and Peter Kulchyski[3] provides heretofore largely unknown information on how social security programs were administered in Canada's far north. It came as a shock to learn that universal family allowances were administered to the Inuit as a form of needs-tested welfare benefit from 1945 to 1951, and that no elderly Inuit were able to qualify for old age pensions from 1927 to 1950 because they lacked date of birth records.

The thoughtful suggestions from readers prompt me to say that if I had the opportunity to write another history of Canadian social security, I would base it on three themes of redistribution: redistribution of income and wealth, of essential services, and of power. Such a framework would, I think, capture all of the significant elements that have eluded me on these previous attempts.

Preface to the Second Edition

In 1942, Sir William Beveridge said in his book *Pillars of Security* that no satisfactory scheme of social security could be devised except on three assumptions:

(a) Children's allowances, paid both when the responsible parent is earning and when he is not earning.
(b) Comprehensive health and rehabilitation services for prevention and cure of disease and restoration of capacity for work, available to all members of the community.
(c) Maintenance of employment, that is to say, avoidance of mass unemployment.[1]

I find it of some interest, historically, that during the first half of the 1980s, the period covered in this second edition, Canadians have engaged in intense policy debate on the issues of medicare, family allowances, and unemployment. A fourth topic, the inevitable consequence of the demographics of ageing, aggravated by inflation – that is, the adequacy of Canada's old age pension system – was another major social issue.

The first edition of this book was concerned with the building and development of social security in Canada with a focus on the pre-World War Two era and with the tensions existing within that process between the residual and institutional concepts of social policy. In this second edition, the story appears to be mainly about the erosion of social security and the efforts to shore up its structure. The residual-institutional tensions remain.

Preface to the First Edition

One of the fundamental distinctions between life today in an urbanized, industrialized society and life in a predominantly agricultural, rural-based society such as Canada was at the time of Confederation is the critical importance for the individual and family of a regular and adequate cash income. In 1867, the year of Confederation, a majority of Canadians earned their livelihood in one of three ways: farming, fishing, or logging. These three primary industries and some mining were the main support of a small group of manufacturing and service industries. Many, if not most, of the necessities of life were produced on the family farm or obtained by barter. The chief causes of income interruption – illness, injury, premature death of the breadwinner, and old age – were handled within the family group or with the support of neighbours and other members of the then small, closely knit communities. However, the processes of industrialization and urbanization, which had already begun at the time of Confederation and which were to accelerate sharply at the turn of the century, severely eroded this independence and weakened these informal systems of social security. As a consequence, Canadians were forced to devise alternative means of meeting the age-old risks to livelihood as well as to develop measures to deal with new and emerging risks that arose out of Canada's successful progress toward an urban-industrial society.

In discussing social security programs it is customary to speak of universal risks to income – universal in the sense that all citizens in an industrialized nation may be exposed to them. It is possible to conceptualize these risks in a number of ways. We may categorize risks as either natural or man-made. The former are exemplified by extreme old age, illness, disability, and childbearing. The latter include those that have their source wholly or predominantly within social and cultural factors, as in the case of unemployment, underemployment, discrimination, compulsory retirement, the delayed entry of young people into the labour market, and 'an infinite variety of subtle cultural factors ranging from the "right" union ticket to the possession of an assortment of status symbols' – all of which may inhibit to a greater or lesser degree the earning power of individuals, thus impairing their standard of living and that of their dependants.[1]

Alternatively we may categorize risks to income as (a) risks that threaten the *continuity of income*, such as unemployment, sickness and disability (which may be temporary or long term), death or absence of the bread-winner, pregnancy and childbearing (for women who are wage earners supporting families in part or completely), and old age or retirement; and (b) those risks that pose a threat to the *adequacy of income*, such as family size, the costs of medical and hospital care, shelter costs, low earnings (including low wage rates, intermittent, seasonal, or casual employment), and inflation.[2]

Efforts to maintain income and ensure its adequacy in the face of these universal risks have given rise to a variety of government actions. One of the most significant forms of public initiative in this area, and one to which increasing attention has been paid since the end of the Second World War, is that of maintaining a healthy economy and full employment.[3] Secondly, once people are in the labour force, governments act to protect jobs through the imposition of tariffs and to protect the worker from exploitation through minimum wage legislation and the legalization of labour unions and collective bargaining. A third form of government action involves the efforts made to encourage individuals to make provision against threats to their social security through personal savings or insurance. The stimulation of savings institutions, the development of public annuity schemes, and the granting of tax concessions for retirement and other types of savings plans are examples. A fourth category of government initiative, the focus of this study, is the enactment of social security measures. This has as its objective a redistribution of income in favour of persons whose normal sources of income have been temporarily or permanently interrupted and the removal or a lessening of the burden of some commonly experienced charges on income – charges that, in the absence of such aid, would pose a serious threat to the individual's or family's standard of living.

In what follows, the developments in Canada's social security system are traced from the pre-Confederation era to the present day, but with a major focus on events between 1914 (marking the beginning of the modern era in social security) and the closing years of the Second World War. The war years of 1939 to 1945 stand out as a clear divisional period in the history of Canadian social security. The socioeconomic consequences of the war, cou-pled with the depression that preceded it, breached once and for all a num-ber of barriers that had impeded social security developments up to that time. The war mobilized Canadian personnel at every level and stimulated sentiments and demands about the peace to follow. Under the stress of the war, and the vision of peace to follow, the bases for planning were sharply altered: social security programs, from this point on, reflected some new realities and introduced concepts and policies radically different from those existing in the prewar years. This is not to say that antagonistic value systems and deeply held prejudices concerning the nature of poverty did not continue to play a significant role in shaping events after the Second World War. But they were opposing views now, not a general consensus. An examination of the historical roots of Canadian social security policy, with the war and other milestones to mark the way, will, by illuminating the past, help us to chart our course in the years ahead with more intelligence and optimism.

Acknowledgments

I owe a great deal to other students of Canadian social policy who offered constructive criticism of drafts of this book in one or more of its editions: Glenn Drover, Brigette Kitchen, Jack MacDonald, Christine McNiven, Leonard Marsh, Michael Mendelson, Hugh Shewell, Richard Splane, and Frank Tester. My thanks as well to the readers for UBC Press and the Social Science Federation of Canada, who were particularly helpful with respect to the first edition. Thanks to Trudy Cowan and Pat McGechaen, who typed the first edition.

A special vote of thanks to Joan Guest for her editorial assistance on all three editions.

Finally, I would like to pay tribute to the memory of Richard Titmuss of the London School of Economics, who helped to shape my ideas on social policy, and to the memory of Leonard Marsh, the unsung architect of Canada's social security system.

The Emergence of
Social Security in Canada

1

The Emergence of Social Security in Canada: Major Themes

The Shift from a Residual to an Institutional Concept of Social Welfare

It is possible to identify five major themes in Canadian social security history. The first of these involves the development of alternatives to the traditional means of distributing income, goods, and services.[1] In the nineteenth century, and well into the twentieth, it was commonly held that the family and the private market were the two 'normal' channels of help for individuals and families faced with the loss of income or an income that was inadequate to cope with certain non-discretionary items of expenditure. If a situation occurred that interrupted the income of an individual or family, the appropriate course of action was to seek alternate sources of income – another job, borrowing, seeking credit – or, where these measures failed, to ask the help of a relative. If for some reason these two avenues of help were closed, then and only then would a social welfare agency step into the breach to offer aid on a temporary and emergency basis until the individual's capacity for self-support was regained. In the 1920s in Canada, a head of a household who found himself unemployed and unable to secure another job would be expected to meet his living expenses by drawing on his savings, seeking help from his relatives, having recourse to some agency within the private market – a bank, a finance company, a pawnshop – or by prevailing upon his creditors to carry him until he was able to meet his commitments. If these normal avenues of help were not open to him, he would be forced to apply to his municipality for aid. More often than not, he would be referred to some charitable agency for temporary help, as municipal departments of public assistance were the exception rather than the rule in the 1920s. Applying for 'relief,' as it was commonly referred to, was a demeaning and stigmatizing experience because it was widely regarded as clear evidence of personal incompetence and failure. Any help given was of a gratuitous nature, there being no thought of a right to assistance. This minimal, temporary type of service, offered at the discretion of the social welfare agency, meeting need only after evidence had been presented that all other avenues of help had been explored, was typical of what has been termed a *residual* concept of social security. This concept played a major role in shaping policy and programs in Canada up to the 1940s.

The idea of limiting social security organizations to a role residual to those of the private market and the family has gradually given way to the view that social security organizations must be designed as a first line of defence. This approach, referred to as the *institutional* concept of welfare, has resulted from the growing recognition that because of the nature of social organization in an urban-industrial society, the risks to an individual's social security are part of the social costs of operating a society that has provided higher standards of living for more people than ever before in our history. This being the case, it is argued that society should not allow the costs of its progress to fall upon individuals and families, but should protect and compensate people who experience more than their fair share of the costs. Under this institutional conception of social security, the individual whose income is terminated by reason of unemployment (to continue the earlier illustration) must be protected by a public program that maintains his income, or a reasonable portion of it, until he is reemployed. Recourse to such help, as in the case of unemployment insurance, carries no stigma. Furthermore, the claimant for unemployment insurance, having fulfilled the conditions necessary to make his claim, receives his benefit as a right and not as a gratuity. Additionally, having established the fact that he is experiencing the risk insured against, he is assumed to be in need, and the benefits are paid to him without the searching and often humiliating inquiry into personal circumstances that typify help under the residual concept of social security.

The intrusion of social security organizations into the operation of the private market has, throughout the history of social security in Canada, brought into conflict opposing systems of values and beliefs. In essence, the private market, which has been the paramount institution in society for the distribution of income, goods, and services, has been challenged by the development of alternative institutional arrangements that utilize other criteria to determine the distribution of income, goods, and services, such as need, contractual rights, and the status of age, residence, and citizenship.[2] A residual role for social security programs harmonizes with the laissez-faire theory of government – the 'least government is the best government.' It is supported by those values of an individualistic, free enterprise philosophy that stress self-reliance, the duty incumbent upon families to care for their own, and the threat to freedom inherent in the extension of government activities, particularly where these directly affect the lives of individuals and families. The whole system of beliefs encapsulated in the term 'Protestant ethic' are also aligned with this limited conception of social security.

The private market, it is claimed, operates with a rough kind of justice by rewarding work, foresight, and thrift. Normally, the individual and his or her family may claim their fair share of needed goods and services through the market system if they exercise these desirable traits. More importantly, if people are lax, improvident, and foolish, they are punished by their inability to obtain the goods and services they need. Where such behaviour leads to a request for help from some public welfare agency, the residual concept of social security continues the punishment by providing assistance in a manner that stigmatizes and degrades the recipient. Thus, the market system and the residual social security system combine to act as powerful motivating forces to teach the habits of industry and thrift, which, it is suggested, enhance the prosperity of the individual, the family, and the community.

The institutional concept of social security organizations considers social security programs to be the primary defence against adversity and rejects the argument that hard work, thrift, and foresight are virtues likely to be found wanting in the poor and dependent. It dispenses with moralizing about the shortcomings of the person in need and delineates instead clearly defined social responsibilities for the universal risks to human welfare that characterize life in an industrial society. In effect, this view represents an extension of the concept of responsibility urged by proponents of the residual role from family to community. The duty incumbent upon families to care for their own is not denied. Indeed, proponents of social security will argue that such programs strengthen and support families in meeting their obligations. But there is a duty on the part of a civilized society to see that the costs and benefits of industrial progress are shared by all and that the protection of the most vulnerable members of the community – the aged, children, the disabled, workers who have been made redundant by rapid social change – are first priorities in policy and programming. Opponents of this approach have argued that shielding the individual from the exigencies of life saps independence and results in continuing and growing demands for support from the state. Thus, the welfare state is linked by some to an increase in dependency and, eventually, a weakening of the economy.[3]

The conflict over an institutional as opposed to a residual role for social security programs has been a significant and recurring theme in the history of Canadian social security. The forces supporting a residual role were most influential in the years prior to 1940, but the shift to the institutional role was unmistakable at the close of the Second World War. Nevertheless, in every major social security issue since 1945 these two viewpoints have had their adherents, and both sides have been influential in shaping policy decisions. Since the mid-1970s, however, proponents of the residual approach have increasingly dominated the social policy debate.

The Social Minimum

Essential to this study is the 'social minimum' concept and the attempt to establish it for Canadians. This concept has been described by one Canadian scholar as 'the realization that in a civilized society, there is a certain minimum of conditions without which health, decency, happiness and a "chance in life" are impossible.'[4] It is an idea that has evolved over the past century, reflecting changes in the public conscience, in national income and productivity, and in the breadth of economic democracy. The roots of the concept of a social minimum lie in the first British minimum wage laws, the early Factory Acts, the concern about child labour, the Poor Law Commission of 1909 in the United Kingdom, and the surveys of poverty and the conditions of labour in London, New York, Pittsburgh, Chicago, and elsewhere at the turn of the century. The development of a 'social minimum' in health, housing, education, and social welfare generally arises from a mixture of motives. Altruism, the belief in the perfectibility of man, and the pursuit of social justice all play their part. But support comes as well from those concerned about property rights, public order, and the well-being of the elite and powerful.[5]

Redefining the Causes of Poverty and Dependency

Closely related to the search for a social minimum is a third element in the history of social security in Canada – the process of defining and redefining the causes of poverty and dependency. It was part of the folklore of Canadian life in the nineteenth and well into the twentieth century that Canada was a land of opportunity for all who were willing to work. The social security measures that other industrialized nations were undertaking at this time were, it was claimed, not required in Canada. The amount of unavoidable poverty worthy of charitable concern was relatively negligible and could be handled by the existing private philanthropic agencies. Therefore, government action was unnecessary. Challenging this complacency was difficult in the face of an almost total absence of data on unemployment rates, income statistics, housing conditions, and other social indicators. The wall of prejudice that concealed the true nature and extent of poverty in Canada was gradually pierced by the march of events, the unremitting labour of dedicated individuals and groups of concerned citizens, and the work of civic, provincial, and federal committees established to investigate pressing social issues. Through these efforts, the causes of poverty were redefined, prejudicial attitudes toward the poor were challenged, and the groundwork was laid for public action.

The Growth of Participatory Citizenship

A fourth and most recent theme in Canadian social security history is the increasing amount of public interest in the form, content, and operation of social security programs. As such programs have been developed to cover larger sections of the population and as benefits have increasingly become a matter of right based upon age and citizenship, as in the case of family allowances and old age pensions, or a contractual element, as with contributory insurance, Canadians have begun to take a proprietary interest in the operation of these programs – and quite properly so. Interest in adequate appeal procedures, in citizen representation on policy and planning boards, militancy on the part of client groups calling for better service, more adequate benefits, and greater accountability by public officials – all of these are recent manifestations of this proprietary interest. They are developments in responsible government and participatory citizenship.

The Influence of the BNA Act on Social Security Developments

Finally, and inescapably, a major theme in Canadian social security history must be the impact that Canada's 'constitution,' the British North America Act of 1867, has had on its development.

The BNA Act, which brought about a political union of New Brunswick, Nova Scotia, Canada East, and Canada West, was propelled by political and economic pressures. Politically, British North America felt threatened by jingoistic elements in the United States who urged the American annexation of the vast lands controlled by the Hudson's Bay Company in what is now western Canada. Business leaders in the two Canadas, as well as English railway promoters, hoped that by integrating the western lands into a larger British North American union, the encroachment of the Americans and their 'republicanism' would be stopped and western development would provide a much-needed stimulus to the sagging economies of the Canadas and the Maritimes. With the end of the American Civil War, the relative prosperity which that conflict had engendered in British North America came to an end. There were additional setbacks: Britain had, in 1846, terminated its preferential trade agreements with her colonies; and in 1866 the United States had suddenly abrogated the Reciprocity Treaty, a trading arrangement that was favourable to Canadian products. Technological change in the form of the steamship caused a slow but steady decline in the shipping industry of Nova Scotia and New Brunswick, which was based on the wooden sailing ship. All of the colonies were burdened by the costs of rail- and canal-building ventures that had not yielded the expected economic returns. Accordingly, political union, to be followed by an aggressive program of western development and the building of a national economy, was seen as an answer to the economic plight of the eastern provinces, lessening their dependence upon both the United States and Britain.

Some colonial leaders, notably John A. Macdonald, favoured a unitary state (following the British model) in preference to a federation (the American model). But Canada East, Nova Scotia, and New Brunswick objected to such centralization, and a federal scheme was adopted. However, the Fathers of Confederation were anxious to avoid what they considered the errors and excesses of the American federal system, particularly the emphasis on states' rights – a policy linked clearly in those years to the calamitous Civil War. It was to this end that the British North America Act was drafted: its aim was to make the central government clearly and unequivocally the most important and powerful. The senior level of government was given all of what were then considered the significant governmental roles together with the most important sources of taxation, leaving the provinces with what were perceived as relatively minor responsibilities and, correspondingly, with minor sources of tax revenue.

Thus, the decision was made to give the federal government control over defence, criminal law, regulation of trade and commerce, banking, currency, weights and measures, interprovincial transportation and communication, immigration, and other areas related primarily to economic development. The provinces, on the other hand, were given exclusive powers to pass laws in relation to the administration of justice, municipal institutions, and the establishment and maintenance of prisons, hospitals, asylums, and charitable institutions. The dominion government was given special jurisdiction over certain classes of individuals and institutions, such as Natives, war veterans, and federal prisons.

The general rule established by the division of powers in the BNA Act was that health and welfare concerns, as we now know them, were the sole responsibility of the provinces and their municipalities. In 1867 health and welfare were minor governmental concerns:

> The Fathers of Confederation, when they drafted the British North America Act, were not dealing with a modern industrial society of workers living in towns, dependent on wages, and linked by effective communications across the whole country. Their concept of welfare, inherited largely through their forebears in Great Britain and the United States, or pre-revolutionary France, was related to a 'settled people' in relatively self-sufficient localities. Welfare services as such were scarcely mentioned and apparently relegated to the jurisdiction of the provinces, and by them in most cases unthinkingly assumed to be largely municipal and local matters.[6]

Not only were the Fathers of Confederation dealing with a primarily rural society (only three cities in Canada – Montreal, Toronto, and Quebec – had a population of more than 30,000 in 1867, and four-fifths of the population lived in rural areas), but the 1860s, at least for colonial legislators, marked the high tide of laissez-faire philosophy in government, which restricted its role to that of preserving law and protecting the rights of property. 'Within this framework of order provided by public authority, individuals were expected to work out their own destiny unrestrained and unassisted by governments. There was a general conviction, widely confirmed by contemporary example, that Providence helps those who help themselves.'[7] In this respect, the British North America Act was 'in harmony with current British precept and example.' More properly, it might have been said, it was in harmony with *conventional* British practice and example, as from the end of the 1840s onward, the necessity for state intervention was increasingly, if reluctantly, recognized in Britain.[8]

It is generally conceded by historians that the Fathers of Confederation intended the dominion government to hold the residual power in all matters not explicitly granted to the provinces.[9] To this end the Dominion was given the power to make laws for 'the Peace, Order and good Government of Canada in relation to all Matters not coming within the Classes of Subjects of this Act assigned exclusively to the Legislatures of the Provinces.' The intentions of Macdonald and his colleagues were frustrated by the presence, among the subjects of provincial jurisdiction listed in Section 92, of two vaguely worded areas of responsibility: 'Property and Civil Rights in the Province' and 'Generally all Matters of a merely local or private Nature in the Province.' For more than twenty years following Confederation, the judicial committee of the Privy Council interpreted the BNA Act in accordance with the division of powers as envisaged by the men who designed it. But gradually the judicial committee shifted its position when it divided the dominion powers into two distinct parts – general and enumerated. It then argued that the enumerated powers were the most significant and that the general power, the 'Peace, Order and good Government' clause, was merely a supplementary grant of power to the dominion government and of lesser importance than the enumerated powers. Once this position had been taken, the dominion government's general power to legislate was downgraded, and the interpretation of federal and provincial powers became a competition between the relative significance of the enumerated powers under Sections 91 and 92. Because the powers of the provinces included the two vaguely worded sections mentioned above, the provinces enjoyed a considerable advantage. There were few, if any, questions brought before the judicial committee that did not touch on 'property and civil rights,' for example. The more important question of whether the issue was one of national importance and therefore requiring action by the federal government lost out when the general power to legislate was relegated to secondary importance to the enumerated powers.

Thus it was that while the need for health and welfare provisions on a nationwide basis grew with Canada's increasing industrialization, the responsibility for initiating and paying for these services was, by judicial interpretation, left firmly in the care of the provinces, which lacked the necessary finances to carry out the responsibility. The impasse that developed because of the incongruity between legislative responsibility and financial capability was one reason for the delay in the establishment of vital programs of social security in Canada. Insofar as the constitutional dilemma was concerned, advances in social welfare legislation had to wait upon one of three developments: a provincial government's willingness and ability to finance needed measures; an amendment to the BNA Act to permit federal entry into an area of jurisdiction otherwise assigned to the provinces; or the development of stratagems to secure federal financial help without appearing to violate the provisions of the BNA Act.

2
The Colonial Inheritance

The policies and programs of modern social security legislation in Canada have roots extending back to the late sixteenth century in England and France. The migration of the United Empire Loyalists to British North America in the latter part of the eighteenth century introduced policies and practices for dealing with poverty and its related problems based on legislation passed by a Tudor parliament in 1601 and later adapted to life in the thirteen American colonies. At a time when the Elizabethan poor law was being transplanted into New England, the colonists of New France were drawing upon the traditions of their homeland in developing programs to meet problems of poverty and human need. This early history requires a brief examination for the light it throws on later developments.

When Nova Scotia, New Brunswick, and the provinces of Canada came together in 1867 to form the Dominion of Canada, each province had already established a system of poor-relief practices, each of which differed from the others.

Elizabethan Poor Law in the Maritimes
In Nova Scotia and New Brunswick, poor relief bore the strong stamp of the Elizabethan poor law legislation of 1601, a consequence of the British influence in the founding of Halifax in 1749 and the impact of the Loyalist migration from the American colonies in 1783. The core of the Elizabethan poor law was the assumption of public responsibility for the relief of the dependent poor, financed and administered by the smallest unit of government, the parish, but answerable to the central government in London. This policy marked a final break with the earlier practice of attempting to relieve the distress of the poor and destitute through voluntary subscriptions to a poor-relief fund coupled with harsh punishments to discourage vagrancy and begging. In affirming a public, tax-supported system for the relief of destitution, the march toward the welfare state had begun. When the Tudor parliament of 1597-8 redrafted the poor laws, they defined the

causes of poverty as they understood them and laid down specific policies and programs as remedies.[1] The parish authorities were required to provide for those members of their parish who were too old, sick, or disabled to support themselves – the 'impotent poor.' They were also asked to provide work for the able-bodied unemployed and to punish those deemed able to work but unwilling to do so. Local authorities were, in addition, empowered to provide for the children of parents too poor to care for them by placing such children in apprenticeships so that they might eventually become independent of public aid.[2]

Relief for the impotent poor was to be provided in 'abiding houses' or almshouses. Such congregate care came to be known as 'indoor relief,' as opposed to 'outdoor relief,' help given to people in their own homes. The latter form of help was much preferred by the poor because the typical almshouse, or 'poorhouse' as it was commonly called, was an object of fear and loathing to all but the most desperately poor. The administrative problems and expense of operating a poorhouse often led the parish to limit help to 'outdoor relief.' There was, however, a continuing demand for some type of full-time care to meet the needs of the sick, the old and feeble, the mentally ill and mentally disabled, and the abandoned and orphaned children and infants. Thus, there was continual pressure for institutions to be built.

Providing work for the able-bodied unemployed was a central concern and obligation of the parish under Elizabethan poor law. This was to be accomplished within an institution that came to be called the 'workhouse' or, more euphemistically, the 'house of industry,' where, it was hoped, the able bodied would learn or retain the habits of industry and help to offset the cost of their keep. As an alternative, the poor could be provided with materials for spinning and weaving to work on at home. Children were to be trained in regular work habits through the apprenticeship system, although the English experience demonstrated that many of these apprenticeships were little more than 'thinly disguised slavery' in cotton mills, mines, and, in what is probably the most infamous chapter of child exploitation in English history, the employment of pauper children as chimney sweeps.[3]

Theoretically, the Elizabethan poor law called for careful differentiation between one category of poor and another: almshouses for the old and sick, workhouses or work materials for the able-bodied poor, houses of correction or even the common jail for those who refused to work, and apprenticeships for the children of the poor. In practice, however, and in the interests of keeping the poor law tax to a minimum, parish authorities cut corners by attempting to meet the needs of all the poor and destitute in one facility, and the poorhouse became a home to the dependent and destitute of all ages and conditions – the sick, the mentally ill, the mentally disabled, infants and children, tramps and vagrants. Thus, one of the most depressing institutions ever devised by humans began to proliferate. In its manifest function, that of providing efficient and humane care for the destitute, the poorhouse failed miserably.[4] But it had as a latent function the role of disciplining the labour force, and in this respect it was undoubtedly successful. The individual clung to his or her job when the only alternative to work, no matter how onerous or ill paid, was a choice between starvation or the parish workhouse with its penal atmosphere, the risk of contagion from infectious diseases, and the ignominy of being labelled a 'pauper.'

Nova Scotia in 1763 and New Brunswick in 1786 passed poor law legislation modelled on the Elizabethan statute. The responsibility for the relief of the poor fell on the parish in New Brunswick and the township in Nova Scotia, supplemented by the occasional provincial grant to meet an extraordinary emergency – a fire, an outbreak of typhoid fever or cholera, or other unusual conditions.[5] The application of the Elizabethan system, with its most characteristic feature, congregate care for the destitute, was slow to develop in the frontier conditions of late-eighteenth-century Nova Scotia and New Brunswick. England in 1601 was a populous country with well-established communities, whereas British North America was sparsely populated and communities were raw, underdeveloped, financially insecure, and had a highly mobile population (given the movement of immigrants from Europe and the settlers coming in from the American colonies). Under these conditions, aberrations in the poor law system developed, as in New Brunswick where small, impoverished rural parishes instituted the practice of contracting out the care of their poor to the lowest bidder, rather than pay the cost of building and operating their own poorhouses. Some rural parishes extended this practice to include the holding of annual public auctions of paupers. In 1884 one overseer of the poor in the Parish of Sussex, Kings County, New Brunswick, described these public auctions as a 'hard and unpleasant duty' and a 'stigma' on the people of Kings County. It was also unpleasant for those who were auctioned off. Reports of inquests into the deaths of paupers being cared for under this system provide evidence of wilful neglect and physical abuse. Although widely condemned, the practice of auctioning off the care of destitute people continued in some rural parishes in New Brunswick until the end of the nineteenth century.[6]

By the mid-nineteenth century, public institutions for the care of the poor and destitute were operating in larger centres, such as Saint John, supplemented by 'outdoor relief' at the discretion of officials.[7]

Describing the poorhouses of New Brunswick in the early nineteenth century, James Whalen says:

The almshouses of the nineteenth century provided little separation of the inmates except by the broad classification of sex, and the unclassified nature of these establishments must have had a demoralizing influence on many inmates and in particular the children. Since no public hospitals existed in the province prior to 1865, most almshouses served as both hospitals for the sick and shelters for the destitute at the same time. The danger of this situation, especially during epidemics hardly needs to be explained.[8]

The English poor law model was never copied in Prince Edward Island owing to the relative absence of municipal government outside of Charlottetown and Summerside and to the island's limited size and population. Poor relief and related measures tended to be administered by the provincial government from Charlottetown both in the colonial period and following the province's entry into Canada.[9]

In the case of Newfoundland, where municipal organization was retarded by the British government's policy in the eighteenth century of discouraging settlement, a tradition of provincial government responsibility for such necessary services as roads, marine works, and poor relief was established. The Colonial Office in London also provided grants on an ad hoc basis in response to natural disasters and petitions from philanthropic societies. When grants from the legislative assembly in St. John's or the Colonial Office were not forthcoming, the inhabitants relied on the help of family, friends, and neighbours and upon the help of voluntary charitable organizations.[10]

Poor Relief in Upper and Lower Canada

In Upper Canada, legislation was passed in 1792 that introduced the main body of English civil law into the new province but specifically and pointedly excluded a poor law. The reasons for this action are a matter for conjecture, but it has been suggested that the political leaders of the day may have been reflecting a popular sentiment opposed to direct taxation in an economy where the great majority had little in the way of a cash income. Furthermore, giving responsibility to local government for poor relief may have been seen as strengthening local as opposed to centralized government, thus fostering the despised 'republican' tendencies that had nourished the American Revolution.[11]

The rejection of the Elizabethan poor law system by Upper Canada meant that 'there was an absence of public responsibility for the poor for many years after the decision was taken. The immediate effect of the rejection ... was to shift the responsibility for the poor from the public authority to the individual, the family and private philanthropy.'[12] However, as Richard Splane's history of social welfare in Ontario indicates, this initial abdication of public responsibility for the poor did not eliminate the need to deal with the problems posed by the vagrant, the offender, the insane, and the destitute of all ages and conditions. The result was a gradual, if reluctant, assumption of public responsibility for certain categories of need and a sharing of responsibility with voluntary charity organizations for others. The same session of the Upper Canada legislature that rejected the poor law took steps to establish local jails in the interest of law and order. The jails became a type of poorhouse, a catchall for a variety of social problems – the homeless poor, the insane, offenders both petty and serious, young and old. Dissatisfaction with this situation led to the first provincial institution in Upper Canada, the Kingston penitentiary, built during the 1830s to move long-term offenders from local to provincial control. This was followed by the establishment of a provincial asylum for the insane in the 1850s (although the mentally ill could still be found in local jails as late as the 1890s). As early as the 1830s, public funds were used to provide quarantine hospitals for the victims of epidemics of such diseases as cholera, an action motivated as much by self-interest as by charitable impulse. Public funds were also made available to assist the destitute immigrant and, in emergencies, the unemployed. The relative absence of public services during this period acted as a stimulus for voluntary activity, and as charity organizations established their programs, they found it necessary to seek government grants to assist them in meeting the pressing needs uncovered by their activities. They, in turn, came to accept government monitoring and regulation as a quid pro quo for the public monies received.

The pattern of poor relief was different again in Lower Canada. Here the French Catholic tradition of assigning responsibility for the health, education, and welfare of the community to the church prevailed after initial experimentation with additional forms of help. The French government, for example, eager to promote settlement in the colony, was active in safeguarding the welfare of the French colonists. Furthermore, lay management and initiative in programs to assist the poor were part of the history of early poor-relief policies in New France.[13] On balance, however, the French Canadians took the view that a secular poor-relief system lacked the scope, influence, and permanence of a charity operated by a religious institution. Institutions for the sick, the orphaned, the elderly, and for the education of the young were built and operated by religious orders. This type of help was supplemented by 'a system of weekly licensed begging, combined with congregational and monastic alms-giving in Quebec and Montreal.'[14] After the Conquest, and following the immigration of English-speaking settlers into Lower Canada and the growing urbanization with its attendant social problems, the Protestants in Lower Canada as well as the Catholic majority began to establish separate institutions for various categories of poor and dependent persons.[15]

When those who framed the BNA Act gave the provinces exclusive powers to legislate in all matters pertaining to 'The Establishment, Maintenance and Management of Hospitals, Asylums, Charities and Eleemosynary Institutions in and for the Province, other than Marine Hospitals,'[16] they did so in the belief that such responsibilities would be assigned by the provinces to their local municipalities where colonial tradition dictated they belonged. By this time provincial governments were playing an increasingly important role in social welfare matters, financially and administratively, as the social welfare history of Ontario indicates. Notwithstanding this trend, it was believed at the time of Confederation that provincial responsibilities in social welfare would diminish over time as municipal governments developed to the point where they could carry their welfare responsibilities unaided.[17] As new provinces entered Confederation, they followed colonial tradition by delegating responsibility for 'poor relief' and other types of care for indigent persons to their municipalities, although the English poor law model of making such programs mandatory was never replicated outside of New Brunswick and Nova Scotia.[18] In the case of the four western provinces, where municipal organization was rudimentary when it existed at all, it was necessary for provincial governments to arrange for such services as the costs of institutional care for the indigent elderly, paupers' funerals, and emergency poor relief in unorganized areas of the provinces. Where municipalities were organized, the new western provinces followed the colonial tradition by transferring responsibility for health and welfare concerns to the local governments.

The Role of Private Philanthropy

Another legacy from the colonial period was the proliferation of private charity organizations, often organized around religious or ethnic loyalties. The Catholic-Protestant dichotomy in private charity organizations was particularly evident in eastern Canada from the 1830s on.[19] Following the Napoleonic Wars, an increasing number of immigrants from the British Isles came to British North America, and for many the conditions were very hard, particularly in the winter months when work was scarce and living costs were high. Public relief, where it existed, was likely to be meagre at best and often administered in a harsh and degrading manner. To save the 'worthy poor' from the humiliation of accepting public relief, to supplement inadequate public provision, or to provide help where municipalities were unwilling to do so, charitably disposed citizens would band together to provide the poor with the basic necessities. The resulting fragmentation in effort not only impeded a more comprehensive and non-partisan approach to poor relief but also helped to conceal the magnitude of the problems faced. This fragmentation occurred 'despite attempts ... by the most public-spirited citizens to promote the comprehensive, non-partisan relief of the urban poor, on the ground that "we are but a part of one great human family." '[20] Furthermore, the ad hoc nature of many charitable organizations, which waxed and waned depending on the economic conditions, the season of the year (winter being a particularly active time for charities), or the advent of such calamities as typhoid epidemics, fostered a crisis-oriented approach to community services. On a more positive note, growth in the number of voluntary organizations working with the poor provided the opportunity for citizen participation in a critical aspect of social affairs.[21]

Attitudes and Ideologies

Attitudes toward poverty and the poor in the colonial period are also part of our inheritance. The values of individualism and free enterprise flourished naturally in the frontier society of British North America. It was widely held that the chance to build a better life in the New World was open to all. In the preindustrial era, when the 'clearing and cultivation of land was the chief occupation of most Canadians,'[22] many achieved little more than the life of a subsistence farmer. But these men and women and their families, owning their land, possessed a highly prized sense of independence. Maintaining this independence was the minimum condition for a sense of self-respect. Poverty was common enough in colonial times, but to be dependent upon public or private charity was quite another matter. Dependency carried with it the despised label of 'pauper' and was widely regarded as a sign of personal failure if not moral obloquy. It was something to be avoided at all costs. The same attitude prevailed in French Canada. Poverty-stricken French Canadians in this period were noted for the stoicism with which they endured their plight rather than accept the status of a dependent person, which they equated with personal disgrace.[23]

Our forebears recognized that some poverty was unavoidable. As the Elizabethans had done before them, the colonists of British North America defined the 'honest poor' as those who were unable to work by reason of age, disability, or sickness and the able bodied who could not find employment. The case for the unemployed was particularly strong during the long winter months when economic activity slowed, although sympathy for this latter group did not prevent employers from taking full advantage of the surplus of labour during the winter by slashing wage rates by one-quarter to one-half.[24] In coastal towns a third category, the impoverished immigrant, was also considered a legitimate recipient of charity.[25] Although these categories aroused public sympathy, it should not be assumed that help was generously extended. Arrangements for meeting the most pressing needs were haphazard at best, and the welfare of even the most worthy recipients was sadly neglected.[26]

The apathy toward the condition of the poor in British North America may be related to the view, commonly held, that poverty was the result of some personal failing or character flaw. Certain elements of Protestant theology provided support for this view by interpreting success as evidence of godly living and of God's grace. The corollary was, of course, that poverty was an indication of a sinful life and of divine retribution. Therefore, such help as was extended to the poor was often accompanied by unsolicited and largely irrelevant advice on how the poor might regain God's grace through the exercise of those human qualities that he apparently admired and rewarded. The poor were urged to appreciate the values of thrift, hard work, self-help, and self-discipline. Biblical tracts pointing the way to spiritual salvation were popular items for distribution to the poor. A particular danger for the poverty-stricken, according to conventional wisdom, was addiction to strong drink, which in a government report of 1849 was blamed for one-half of the crime, two-thirds of the insanity, and three-fourths of the paupers in the Province of Canada.[27] Perhaps it is not surprising that in a society where the liberal, individualistic values dominated, where the life and living conditions of the colonists owed so much to personal effort and initiative, individualistic explanations of poverty should abound. This, too, is part of our colonial inheritance.

Political ideologies that have helped to shape Canada's social security system also have their roots in the colonial era. Some Canadian scholars have utilized the historical insights of Louis Hartz, who has analyzed the ideological development of new societies founded by Europeans in terms of their 'point of departure' from the mother country.[28] Thus, French Canada and Latin America were 'feudal fragments' reflecting the 'feudal or tory values of the organic, corporate, hierarchical community' of Catholic, pre-Enlightenment France and feudal Spain and Portugal. Somewhat later chronologically, the United States, English Canada, and Dutch South Africa were 'bourgeois fragments' reflecting the liberal individualism of their founders. Australia, later still, is seen as the one example of a 'radical fragment' founded by men and women imbued with the working-class ideologies of mid-nineteenth-century Britain.

Hartz and some Canadian writers have argued that Canadian and American political ideologies are similar in most important aspects.[29] Others take the view that there are important and crucial differences in the ideological development of Canadian society.[30] Those who see these distinctions point to the emergence of a socialist party in Canada with a political strength unmatched by any similar party in the United States. The growth of socialist ideology in Canada relates in part to the presence of both Tory and liberal values in Canadian history. The ideology of socialism combines the feudal or Tory tradition of concern for the group aspects of human life with the liberal values of maximizing individual freedom and liberty. This produces a set of ideas that emphasizes the notion of equality of condition through cooperative, collective action, displacing the liberal emphasis on equality of opportunity with its connotation of competitive struggle. According to Hartzian theory, American society lacks a Tory heritage, and therefore this gap in its ideological spectrum inhibits the development of a viable socialist party in the United States.

The strength of Tory values in Canadian history can be traced to the 'feudal fragment' of French Canada, with its heritage of collectivist endeavour, and to the imprint of Tory British military officers and government officials who took charge after the conquest of New France and whom Lower describes as 'tory and feudal.'[31] Even more significant was the influx of Loyalists from the American colonies following the American Revolution in the late eighteenth century (in actuality, prerevolutionary American whigs with a 'tory touch').[32] Added to this was the significant number of British immigrants who came to British North America between 1815 and 1850, many of whom held Tory notions of social hierarchy.

Christian and Campbell provide a useful summation of Canada's ideological inheritance and its uniqueness on the North American continent:

> In the first place we have identified three distinct ideological approaches to politics which in one way or another have been available for 'export' to Canada: liberalism, organized around the two concepts of individuality and liberty; toryism, built upon collectivism, and hierarchy or privilege; and socialism, sharing the tory's collectivism, but seeking to replace privilege by equality. Second, we have seen that all three have found a place in the Canadian political culture, though not of equal strength. Third, we have seen how this ideological diversity – the existence of tory and socialist elements in a dominant liberalism, sharply distinguishes Canada within North America. [33]

While stressing the significance of Tory traditions in Canadian history, the domination of liberal ideology in the realm of politics, economics, and ethics, particularly in the last half of the nineteenth century, is acknowledged by all. But the influence of Tory values and the subsequent development of socialist ideology have been sufficient to leave their imprint upon Canadian history, not least of all upon the history of its social security system.

3
Saving for a Rainy Day: Social Security in Late-Nineteenth-Century and Early-Twentieth-Century Canada

The first thirty years of Confederation, up to the end of the nineteenth century, witnessed the completion of an all-Canadian transcontinental railway, the promotion of large-scale immigration, the opening of western Canada to settlement, and the fostering of Canadian industry by means of protective tariffs. These developments reflected three goals generally recognized and accepted by Canadians of the time: to settle the country's vast and sparsely inhabited western regions; to promote a strong, integrated, and varied economy; and to make Canada 'the homeland of a prosperous and contented people.'[1]

The progress of this 'National Policy,' as it was termed, was initially slowed by an economic depression that lasted, with only brief periods of respite, from 1873 until the end of the century. Despite the economic setbacks, the processes of urbanization and industrialization began to accelerate, and the face of Canada was changed, unalterably, within a few years. The imposition in 1879 of a series of protective tariffs by the federal government to protect and stimulate the development of secondary industry set the stage for a rapid growth of towns and cities.[2] The factory system in Canada, according to contemporary observers, 'sprang into existence almost at one bound' as a result of the 1879 legislation.[3]

A statement made by J.S. Woodsworth in 1908 succinctly described the rapid urbanization that had taken place in Canada and that was continuing even more rapidly in the first decade of the twentieth century: 'Canada is leaving the country for the city ... The population of Ontario more than doubled from 1851 to 1901, but the population of Toronto increased over six times during the same period. The population of the Province of Quebec was almost twice as large in 1901 as in 1851, but that of Montreal was over four and one-half times as large. Manitoba is an agricultural Province, and yet one-quarter of the entire population is resident in the city of Winnipeg alone.'[4]

By the 1880s the social and economic consequences of rapid industrialization in a competitive, free enterprise economy began to accumulate, most noticeably in the towns and cities. The working and living conditions of the industrial worker became an early focus of attention spurred on by an increasingly militant and articulate labour movement.

Royal Commission on the Relations of Labour and Capital, 1887

A series of federal investigations into industrial conditions in 1882 and again in 1885 reported the exploitation of children in factories and the unsanitary and dangerous working conditions for many workers.[5] Macdonald, faced with an election in 1887 and anxious to maintain the working-class support that he had won in 1872 with the passage of the Canada Trade Unions Act,[6] appointed a royal commission 'to enquire into and report on all questions arising out of the conflict of labor and capital.'[7] The commissioners were, almost to a man, supporters of Macdonald's Conservative Party, but this did not prevent a split from developing along class lines within the commission between the labour representatives and those who took a more paternalistic and conservative view. The result of the split was the publication of two reports, the *First Report,* the more conservative of the two, and the *Second Report,* reflecting a pro-labour, albeit conservative, viewpoint. Both reports were unanimous in their condemnation of certain aspects of the factory system; both urged repeal of, or change in, certain laws that oppressed the working man, woman, and child; and both acknowledged, although with differing degrees of emphasis, that labour organizations had a legitimate role to play in society. As Kealey notes, it takes a close examination of the two reports to observe the differences.[8]

The 'Labor Commission,' as it came to be known, travelled extensively through eastern Canada over a period of seven months and heard testimony from nearly 1,800 witnesses representing both workers and management. Of interest to the student of Canadian social security programs is the evidence presented as to how people coped with the common exigencies of life in an urban, industrial society, given the almost total absence of social security programs. The record reveals for the most part a pattern of grim exploitation of men, women, and children: long hours of work (fifty-four to sixty hours a week was commonplace), low pay (which was quite callously reduced in winter months by many manufacturers), dangerous and unhealthy workplaces, and chronic unemployment and underemployment for many as trade recessions and the immutable law of supply and demand worked through the economic system.

From a twentieth-century perspective, the most striking impression received from reading the testimony of workers and employers, apart from the absence of social security protection, is the powerlessness of the working classes. Factories and workplaces as described by witnesses read more like places of detention than employment. It was not uncommon for factory hands to be locked into their factories during working hours – one consequence, perhaps, of the many young children employed.[9] Employers and their supervisors acted like martinets. Many physically disciplined their child employees, some to an extent that shocked the commissioners and earned their strong condemnation. Employers imposed fines for being late, for breakage, for substandard work, and in some concerns, for laughing and talking. The *Second Report* commented: 'Of all the mean pitiless exactions which labor has to suffer from, this is the vilest. A young woman will work hard from Monday morning until Saturday evening for a paltry pittance of three or four dollars, and when pay day comes find that the sum of 25 or 50 cents, or even one dollar, has been deducted for some trifling breach of rules, or because of the petty spite of the overseer.'[10]

This practice was generally imposed upon women and children, as they were said to be more passive in their acceptance of these impositions than men. However, evidence taken in Nova Scotia from miners indicated that their pay was unfairly docked for short weight, and the practice of docking men's pay for being late for work was common in many industries.[11]

Attempts by workers to redress the imbalance of power by forming unions were met with intimidation and blacklisting. The typical attitude of management of the day toward unions is revealed in the following exchange between the superintendent of the Toronto Street Railway and a commissioner:

Q. Is there any objection on the part of the street railway company to men belonging to a secret society of any kind? A. We have no objection to men belonging to anything except labor organizations.
Q. Are the men in your employ required to sign a paper previous to entering your employment? A. They are.
Q. What is the nature of that agreement? A. That they will not join any labor organization while in the employ of the company.
Q. And if a man joins such an organization, what is the result? A. It is optional with us whether we keep him on or not.[12]

With respect to the adequacy of wages, the commissioners noted that 'the testimony taken sustains a belief that wages in Canada are generally higher than at any previous time, while hours of labor have been somewhat reduced. At the same time, the necessaries and ordinary comforts of life are lower in price than ever before, so that the material condition of the working people who exercise reasonable prudence and economy has been greatly bettered, especially during the past ten years.'[13]

The *Second Report*, from the labour faction, repeated this testimonial to Macdonald's administration almost word for word.[14] No attempt was made to relate wages paid to the cost of living except to note that women's wages, which were generally set at half that paid to a man, were not high enough to enable a young woman to live independently from her family. The *Second Report* contained the general comment that 'all wage earners in subordinate positions' earn 'barely enough to supply sufficient of the necessaries of life' for the proper maintenance of wife and family.'[15]

Both reports mentioned the high cost of rental accommodation and noted that yearly increases in rents, common at the time, imposed 'a serious burden on ... people struggling for a living.'[16] The *Second Report* added: 'No matter how great the increase, how serious the exaction, the landlord is all powerful; there is no appeal from his decision.'[17] The answer to the housing problem, according to the *First Report,* was for the worker to own his own home. In view of the low level of wages and the rising costs of land in cities, this was a naive recommendation. Even with home ownership, the worker was still at a disadvantage in many communities. The *First Report* noted that 'in most cities, if not all, the homes of the comparatively poor are, in proportion to their value, more highly taxed for municipal purposes than those of wealthy people.'[18] Both reports observed that the blight of overcrowded tenements, which had so disfigured large American and European cities by this time, 'was only found in a few instances' in Canada. Given less prominence, however, in an appendix to the *First Report* was the following statement: 'It is undeniable that workers are badly lodged in houses badly built, unhealthy and rented at exorbitant prices.'[19] The sanitary condition of workers' dwellings led the commissioners to recommend a general tightening of municipal sanitation laws, which were found to be 'in large measure inoperative' owing to 'their indefiniteness, the apathy of inspectors, the influence of landlords, or the helplessness of the tenant.'[20]

The evidence presented to the commission vividly illustrated the need for a law covering compensation for work-related injuries or death (not to mention regulations pertaining to industrial safety).[21] The following exchange between a commissioner and an official of a cotton mill in Cornwall, Ontario, is one example:

Q. Have you had any accidents in the mill? A. We have.

Q. Would you state the nature of the accidents? A. Well the only thing that I remember was a man falling into the vat; that was on account of a staging of his own putting-up falling into the vat.

Q. He lost his life? A. He died a few days afterwards.

Q. Is any provision made by the company to aid the families of operatives who are injured or lose their lives – was any recompense made to the widow of this man? A. Yes; we recompensed her considerably ... We gave her one month's pay, and paid the funeral expenses – in fact, I believe we gave her $100 – paid the doctor's bill; paid everything of that sort – the grocer's bill, even.[22]

Evidence was taken as well from several youngsters who testified they had lost fingers, arms, and legs working with dangerous machinery. The following testimony of a former employee of a mill in Ottawa reports the results of a serious accident and the discretionary nature of any help offered the injured workman:

Q. Did you lose your arm and leg in the same accident? A. Yes sir; I fell in a hole, and the axle of the wheel crushed my arm and leg.
Q. How old were you? A. Twelve years – going on thirteen.
Q. How old are you now? A. I am going on nineteen years.
Q. What is your business now? A. I have none at all.
Q. Did your boss do anything for you? A. Well, he gave me $10 over and above the wages he owed me, and then they got up a collection and raised $25 for me.
Q. Was the subscription made up among the workingmen? A. Yes, sir.
Q. Who paid for the medicines and the doctor's fees? A. I did, sir, but I rather think that the boss paid the hospital dues for the time I was there. I was sixteen days in hospital.[23]

The following evidence was taken from an Ottawa logger, known in the nineteenth century as a 'shanty-man':

Q. Are any precautions taken by these men or their employers while they are in the shanties in case of accident? Suppose a man is cut – supposing he receives a severe cut, is anybody there to attend his wounds? A. Yes; it is done this way. One man has to dress the other, and the man that is cut or is sick is charged for his time and he loses his pay.
Q. Supposing you are injured, supposing you receive a severe cut in the middle of the month, is your time stopped at once? A. Yes; the moment that you are wounded your time is stopped.[24]

A Nova Scotia miner was asked: 'In the case of sickness or in the case of the death of a cutter or a laborer, would any assistance be rendered by the mining company except the doctor's attendance? A. Not as I know of; they are not in the habit of doing anything like that.'[25]

The only form of income protection that a worker had would be from membership in a union or some type of fraternal organization or benefit society (the latter two types of organizations proliferated in the latter part of the nineteenth century). Only the most stable members of the working class would be able to take advantage of these forms of help since membership in a union at this time was restricted to a few skilled trades, and regular premium payments to a fraternal organization or benefit society were difficult to maintain for workers in low-paid, unskilled, or seasonal work. Members of the cigar makers union, for example, were paid $5 per week for sixteen weeks in case of sickness or injury (average earnings of cigar makers at this time being about $8 or $9 per week). If the worker was still unable to work after sixteen weeks, his benefit was reduced to $3 and then finally to $2. When a member died, a lump sum benefit was paid, ranging from $200 to $500, depending upon the length of time he had been a member.

If a worker could not call upon a benefit society in time of need, there was nothing to stave off complete destitution except municipal poor relief, where it existed, or emergency aid from a church or voluntary charitable agency. The *Second Report*, in commenting on the value of trade unions, said: 'In nearly all of these societies benevolence forms a prominent part of their work – the caring for the sick and injured, and the providing for the families of deceased members by their insurance departments.'[26]

Some companies assisted their employees in forming and operating benefit plans. The Springhill Mine in Nova Scotia, for example, contributed to a benefit fund as well as arranging for a check-off system for members' contributions. At Springhill the minimum contribution was 30 cents a month, for which a worker would be eligible, in the case of sickness or injury, to receive $2.50 a week for twenty-six weeks (a miner's rate of pay averaged from $1.40 to $1.65 per day). If a miner wished to contribute a higher premium of 50 cents a month, he could qualify for benefits of $4 a week. In the case of death of a member, a lump sum benefit of $60 was paid.[27] These benefit schemes covered a worker whether or not his sickness or injury was work related. When workers' compensation laws did arrive, they covered only work-related injury, disease, or death – a much narrower range of protection.

Some companies required their workers to join a company benefit scheme through which the employees were forced to pay the costs of expensive private insurance against sickness, accident, or death. The commissioners were particularly critical of the Grand Trunk Railway, which, in addition to compelling its employees to pay 80 per cent of the cost of their own benefit scheme, required that they waive any rights to sue the company for compensation in cases of injury or death due to company negligence.[28] This was at a time when railroads were coming under increased criticism for their poor industrial safety record.

The commissioners who signed the *First Report* recommended that the federal government establish an annuity system that would enable Canadian workers to save for their old age. This would 'remove from many the fear of dependence upon relatives or upon charity in their declining years.'[29] Such a scheme, they maintained, could be operated without expense to the government. This recommendation was predicated on one of the most cherished beliefs of those nineteenth-century Canadians who lived well above the poverty line – that much poverty in old age, or at any other time of life, could be avoided by application of thrift. But the possibility of saving for one's old age, given the low wages and the unemployment, particularly during the winter months, was an illusion that would impede progress toward old age pension legislation for years to come.

The Labor Commission made a number of recommendations to improve the lot of the average industrial worker in Canada. But the sense of urgency that should have animated its report was muted by preliminary comments that cast an unwarranted rosy glow over industrial conditions generally. Of all the recommendations made touching on issues that cried out for change, only one was acted upon – the proclamation of Labour Day as a national holiday in 1894. Kealey suggests that the Macdonald government used the question of possible infringement on provincial jurisdiction as a convenient excuse for its failure to take action on the report's recommendations.[30]

Added to the problems of the industrial worker in Canada were the social problems created by the neglected child, the delinquent, the mentally ill and mentally disabled, the growth of slums, the incidence of poverty, crime, disease, and infant mortality. These and other social ills generated 'a great outpouring of concern' as the nineteenth century drew to a close.[31] The public discussion that took place at this time had as its theme the proper relationship between government and the citizen. In the latter part of the nineteenth century, Canadian public opinion underwent 'a rapid and marked transformation.' The doctrines of laissez faire and of individualism were being challenged by notions of social justice, by a concern for the well-being of the group and of the wider interests of the community as a whole.

The Establishment of Social Minima

One aspect of this shift of opinion was an attempt, however ill-defined, to establish some concept of a social minimum for Canadians living in a society where they were virtually unprotected from the effects of rapid social change and the costs of industrial progress. Efforts to establish social minima invariably spring from a variety of motives. The agitation for free public schools, for example, was supported by those whose strongest motivation was the belief that education was of value for all children and should be their right.[32] But public education, as far back as the colonial period, had been advocated on the grounds that providing a minimum of education for all would increase law and order in the community – an argument judged to have more general appeal than one based on purely religious or moral views.[33] Moving children off the streets and into schools was also seen as a measure of social control – a means of combating juvenile delinquency. But it was the industrial revolution that most propelled the notion of compulsory education for all children into action. Industry came to recognize that it not only required a workforce with a minimum of education but that the school experience prepared the child for the discipline of the factory. 'By the end of the nineteenth century,' according to Anthony Platt, 'the working class had imposed upon them a sterile, authoritarian education system which mirrored the ethics of the corporate workplace and was designed to provide an increasingly refined training and selection mechanism for the labor force.'[34]

In the 1870s, primary schooling became free in Ontario, British Columbia, and Manitoba. Prince Edward Island had free education in 1852. Nova Scotia provided elementary and secondary education as early as 1864. But in each of these provinces the opportunity afforded by free schools was not fully realized until attendance was made compulsory some years later. Free public libraries, an informal extension of public education, began to be established in Canada in the 1880s; by 1900 they were fairly common in the larger Canadian cities and towns.

The idea of a social minimum in health began with the entry of governments into the field of public health, initially at the municipal level on an ad hoc basis to combat outbreaks of cholera, smallpox, and typhoid, followed by the development of provincial boards of health over the opposition of tax-conscious citizens and those who believed that death rates were fixed by God. One of the first provincial boards of health was set up in Ontario in 1882. In Nova Scotia, a Department of Public Health, succeeding an earlier Central Board of Health, was established in 1904. New Brunswick created a full-time cabinet post for health in 1918, and this example was followed by several other provinces. After pressure from the provincial governments, a federal Department of Health was established in 1919.

In an attempt to establish certain socially desirable minima for factory workers, seven bills were introduced into the dominion parliament between 1880 and 1886 aimed at regulating working conditions. The need for such regulation was undeniable, and considerable public support was created. But none of the bills passed, some having been withdrawn under pressure from employers' groups (although they were supported by manufacturers who wished to eliminate the competition of the sweatshops). Other bills were successfully challenged on the ground that they were beyond the constitutional powers of the federal government.[35]

The extension of the franchise can be seen as another aspect of the social minimum – a minimum of political democracy and power-sharing. In 1867 the newly formed Dominion began by using the provincial franchises for federal elections, which, by and large, linked voting rights to the ownership of property. This effectively disenfranchised a sizeable segment of the population. In the 1850s, for example, fewer than half of the adult males in Hamilton, Ontario, owned or rented enough property to vote in elections for the legislative assembly.[36] Women were denied the right to vote even if they met the property qualifications.[37] The discrimination against women voting was partially rectified during the First World War when Manitoba became the first province to grant them a vote in provincial elections. Other provinces quickly followed; by 1919 all except Prince Edward Island and Quebec had granted women the right to vote provincially.[38] The federal government moved toward giving women the vote when, in 1917, it enfranchised women members of the armed forces, notably nurses, along with all other serving members. Later that same year, close female relatives of men serving in the armed forces overseas were permitted to vote federally. Finally, in 1920, the federal government passed the Dominion Elections Act that established universal suffrage for men and women in federal elections, though it still excluded significant groups of Canadians – registered Natives, Canadians of Chinese, Japanese, and East Indian parentage (unless they had served in the armed forces), and members of certain religious sects who were exempt from military service.

Extending the franchise to women was more than a matter of simple social justice. It was also part of the strategy of the prohibitionists, who, realizing the close relationship between the women's suffrage and the prohibition movements, assumed that if women were given the vote they would overwhelmingly endorse prohibition. At the federal level, the government, by extending the vote to close female relatives of men serving overseas in 1917, hoped to win their electoral support for its controversial conscription policy. Somewhat the same mixture of expediency and principle was evident in trade union pressure to prohibit child labour and thereby eliminate a source of downward pressure on wages.

Having secured the vote, even in a restricted form, it was possible for most skilled workers to press for recognition of their right to unionize. Until 1872, when unions were legalized, breaking an employment contract was a criminal conspiracy. Between that date and 1900, industrial workers became free of many legal restraints on union activity, although in disputes involving management and labour the application of the law was said to have had a 'peculiarly one-sided impact.'[39] At the turn of the century, as Canadian unions slowly gained strength, they agitated for legislation that had a wider application than the issue of wages and working conditions and that expressed a social minimum concept. Thus, in 1898 the Trades and Labour Congress of Canada passed resolutions in favour of free compulsory education, the reduction of the working day to eight hours, six days a week, the government inspection of all industries, minimum wages based on local conditions, public ownership of all utilities, and the abolition of child labour for children under fourteen. The impact of these resolutions was negligible; prior to the First World War Canadian unions were weak and few in number, owing to the mobility of labour, its heterogeneous nature, and the active resistance of employers.[40]

Herbert Ames: Pioneer Social Researcher

By the 1890s social reform had become a multifaceted public issue. Proposals for reform in the field of housing, sanitation, town planning, public health, factory legislation, child welfare, corrections, civic politics, and a host of other related subjects were brought to the public's attention by the press, the work of concerned individuals, voluntary organizations, and social movements.

A leading example of individual effort was the work of Sir Herbert Brown Ames, a well-to-do Montreal manufacturer who typifies the 'tory touch' in Canada's ideological development.[41] As a member of Montreal's social and business establishment, he accepted the class divisions that existed but felt that his position in society carried with it a responsibility for the welfare of the industrial classes. With an enlightened self-interest, he viewed society as an organic whole, noting that 'honest thinkers in every land are coming more and more to realize what is meant by the interdependence of society, when those who study city life are each day more fully persuaded that ordinary urban conditions are demoralizing and that no portion of the community can be allowed to deteriorate without danger to the whole.'[42]

During the autumn and early winter of 1896, Ames launched a study of the 'ordinary urban conditions' to be found in a square mile of Montreal's working-class district, containing 38,000 homes as well as factories and other working establishments. He organized a house-to-house survey, modelled on the pioneering work of Charles Booth in London,[43] gathering information on employment and family incomes, with a particular focus on housing conditions – the degree of overcrowding, sanitary arrangements, and rentals charged.

His work, published in 1897, provides an invaluable glimpse into the life of a representative segment of Montreal's working class just before the turn of the century. The information gleaned from the survey permitted Ames to challenge some of the conventional attitudes toward poverty and its causation: 'As to the causes of poverty, chief among them is insufficient employment. Few are the families where nothing is earned, although there are such subsisting more or less worthily upon charity. Almost without exception each family has its wage earner, often more than one, and upon the regularity with which the wage earner secures employment depends the scale of living for the family.'[44]

Ames then proceeded to deal with the argument that he knew his readers would raise: that the effects of irregularity of employment could be met by the worker practising thrift and 'saving for a rainy day' while employed. Referring to some of the poorer families in his survey, he wrote: 'With most of the wage-earners of these families the program for the year is as follows: Work upon the wharves in summer and odd jobs of any sort during five long winter months. When spring arrives, overdue rent and debt at the corner grocery have so mortgaged the coming summer's earnings that saving becomes impossible.'[45]

This view, backed up by his research, served to refute the complacent attitude of another member of Montreal's establishment, William C. Macdonald, the tobacco manufacturer, who ten years previously in an appearance before the Labor Commission was asked about his company's policy of reducing wages in the winter:

> Q. Does not the cost of living, to working people, increase during the winter? Do they not have to pay much larger sums in the winter than in the summer season? A. Oh, yes.
>
> Q. Is it not a hardship to them to have their wages reduced at the time they need it more than in summer? A. That will depend on how they provide for rainy days. When they have good wages they should save for the short period.[46]

Ames selected a smaller sample of 323 families classified as 'the poorest of the poor' for closer examination. One of his areas of inquiry involved asking the poor families to assign a cause for their poverty:

> With 109 families, or 34 per cent the reply was 'irregularity of work.' The wage earners were not without vocations but their employment was intermittent and often work ceased altogether for considerable periods. With 87 families or 28 per cent the answer was that the wage earners had no work whatsoever, nor did there seem to be any immediate prospect of getting any. With 27 families, or 9 per cent, old age had unfitted and with a like number sickness had prevented the workers from earning the requisite support. Out of these 323 families, among the poorest of the poor, 62 per cent claimed to be able to better their condition were employment regular and abundant. That a certain percentage of the answers given did not state the real facts of the case is quite probable. Few are the families that will admit to a stranger that drink, crime or voluntary idleness is the cause of their misery, though in 7 per cent of the cases visited drunkenness was clearly at the bottom of the trouble. Still it is the belief of the investigator that the undeserving among the poor form a far smaller proportion than is generally imagined.[47]

Here again, Ames was questioning the conventional wisdom that defined poverty very largely in terms of personal inadequacy. As if anticipating a chorus of protest from his readers, he supported his findings by quoting similar studies from the United States, where, in Ames's words, 'want of employment was believed to be the cause of distress in as many cases as sickness, intemperance, and shiftlessness combined.'[48]

Ames helped Canadians to redefine the causes of poverty. His research demonstrated that the problem was very largely rooted in economic and social arrangements. His proposals for remedying the problems he uncovered included winter works programs at minimum wages for those who could work,[49] the enforcement of higher standards in housing construction, sanitation, and town planning,[50] as well as the building of low-rental accommodation under private, philanthropic auspices.[51] The very poor, those whom Ames called 'the submerged tenth,' who were unable to work through illness, old age, or for other reasons, could, he thought, be left to private charity.

Ames's research is remarkable for its early attempt to define a poverty line (another expression of the social minimum) and to estimate the incidence of poverty existing in Montreal in 1897. Ames estimated that families with less than $5 per week of income could not make proper provision for a growing family. Families below this level he classified as 'poor,' and they comprised between 11 and 12 per cent of the population surveyed.[52] At the other end of the economic spectrum were the families with incomes of not less than $20 per week or $1,000 a year. These were the 'well to do' of the area, comprising 15 per cent of the total sample, made up of proprietors, managers, professionals, storekeepers, and a few families where the combined income of several workers produced this standard of living.[53] The remaining 73 per cent of the population, comprising the 'real industrial class,' had family incomes averaging $10 per week.[54]

Ames's poverty line of $5 per week for a family of five was not supported by any survey of average family expenditure; but modern investigators, using the Department of Labour's family budget survey developed in 1926 and calculating back to 1900, have estimated that basic necessities for a family of five at that time would have cost $9.64 per week, and the cost for the total needs of the same family would have been $13.77.[55] Using the figure of $9.64 as the poverty line for a family of five, a recent investigator, Terry Copp, suggests that the great majority of Montreal's working-class population – the 73 per cent that made up what Ames called the 'real industrial class' – lived at the poverty level or fractionally above it. Many families at this level of income would have had little or no margin of income left for savings, unforeseen expenditures, or investment in personal development.

The Urban Reform Movement

The work of Ames was part of a larger movement of urban reform that developed in Canada in the 1880s.[56] Initially, the movement was sparked by newspapers known as 'the peoples' journals,' which published articles and stories on the social pathology of city life in the United States, Britain, and Canada, in all its fascinating and sometimes lurid manifestations.

These reports so magnetized the reading public that by the end of the century, any paper that had a regard for its circulation had to 'pay at least lip service to the cause of urban reform.'

The urban reform movement in Canada, with theoretical and practical underpinnings derived from both European and American experience, encompassed a bewildering variety of causes: public control of utilities, including street railways; improvements in the health and moral character of cities; the promotion of a larger measure of social justice; campaigns for town planning, the provision of parks and playgrounds, and other public amenities; and pleas for 'purity in government,' a reference to corruption in the political arena.

Running through the spirited public debates that the movement stimulated was the common theme of the interdependence of city people and the organic nature of the urban community – arguments that nourished collective solutions to social problems. Prior to the turn of the century, however, voluntary effort in dealing with social problems was still preferred to encouraging a public response, particularly by the more conservative and influential segment of the community. Consequently, voluntary organizations to combat a wide variety of social ills sprang up on every side. The founding of the Toronto Humane Society in 1887 is a case in point. It evolved out of a series of articles written by Joseph J. Kelso, a young court reporter for the Toronto *Globe*, on the plight of neglected, abused, and delinquent children and on cruelty to animals in that city. The society, pledged to protect both animals and children from cruelty, soon found that it could not operate on behalf of children without the legal authority to do so and without some public financial commitment. They obtained both by successfully petitioning the Ontario provincial legislature to pass An Act for the Protection and Reformation of Neglected Children (1888), and later, in 1893, to pass a more advanced piece of child welfare legislation that emphasized even more strongly a public responsibility and a public role through the appointment of a superintendent of neglected and dependent children. However, this public concern for the welfare of neglected children was to be expressed through the use of voluntary children's aid societies, the first of which had been formed in Toronto in 1891. Thus, voluntarism and collectivism were combined to provide what Kelso and his friends hoped would be an effective as well as an economical service for neglected and dependent children.[57]

The urban reform movement signalled the growing strength of collectivist thought in Canada and the ebbing of the laissez-faire tide. This trend was reflected in an address given to the Canadian Club of Ottawa in 1914 by the mayor of Toronto, H.C. Hocken.[58] He spoke of 'a new spirit in municipal government' that involved a growing public responsibility for a variety of human services and regulatory agencies. He noted 'with astonishment' the increases in public expenditure by his city over the five-year period from 1909 to 1913 and cited a number of municipal services operating in 1913 that had not existed five years earlier. They included public health nurses to combat the infant mortality rate, inspection of milk supplies, food outlets, and food processors, and dental clinics for poor children. The city had also established a minimum wage for civic employees and had instituted a number of programs to deal with the unemployment situation, which was particularly bad in the years 1913 and 1914. Municipal government, the mayor said, had ceased to be a matter of construction and maintenance of sewers, sidewalks, and roads: 'the problems we have to deal with now are problems affecting human welfare, problems of prevention, the problems looking to the betterment of the people of cities.'

The Social Gospel Movement

Coinciding with the urban reform movement was the social gospel movement, strongly influenced by American and British examples, which surfaced in Canada in the 1890s. It represented an attempt by the Protestant religions, principally the Methodists, Presbyterians, and Anglicans, to apply the teachings of Christ to the economic and social problems of the day.[59] This appealing and apparently simple idea had its radical, conservative, and middle-of-the-road adherents. The conservatives tended to support government legislation to promote the good of society by suppressing evil, specifically by campaigning for prohibition, Sunday blue laws, and the repression of prostitution and gambling. The more radical element saw an affinity between Christianity and socialism and were prepared to support the implications of this linkage. They urged that cooperation replace competition as a motivating force in society, in effect advocating an overturning of the capitalist system. A majority took a middle road, favouring a broad program of liberal reform measures, leading ultimately to the welfare state.

Canadians had attended three notable interdenominational conferences in the United States on social problems in 1887, 1889, and 1893. In 1902 the Methodist Church in Canada set up a standing committee to deal with social problems. In its policy statements, the church became increasingly critical of the social and economic system, and in 1906, at its Seventh General Conference, it issued a strong denunciation of capitalism, denouncing it for its vast private fortunes coexisting with poverty wages, sweated labour, and child labour. It called for the regulation of the economic system according to the principles expressed in the Golden Rule and the Sermon on the Mount.[60]

In 1907 the Moral and Social Reform Council of Canada was organized, including representatives of the Anglican, Methodist, Presbyterian, and Baptist Churches as well as the Trades and Labour Congress of Canada. It was this alliance that succeeded in having the federal government enact the Lord's Day Act in 1906, which prohibited the sale of articles and the employment of persons in industrial and commercial work on Sunday (works of necessity and mercy were excepted). From labour's point of view, this act was an expression of one type of social minimum – that of restricting weekly hours of labour.

As the churches became more active in programs of social reform and community action, they set up departments of social service to run and coordinate their expanding social welfare and social reform activities.[61] The secretaries and other personnel of these departments invariably spearheaded the more radical thrusts of the social gospel movement that developed in the first two decades of the twentieth century. In 1913 the Moral and Reform Council of Canada changed its name to the Social Service Council of Canada; in March of 1914, five months before the outbreak of the First World War, the council called its first national congress on social problems.

The Social Service Congress, 1914

Delegates from all parts of the country, including representatives from the three levels of government, but lacking any representation from business or industry, assembled in Ottawa to hear speakers on a wide selection of topics. They included, among others, the relationship of the church to industrial life, child welfare, the problems of the city and the country, commercialized vice and the white slave traffic, immigration, political purity, and temperance.

The right, centre, and left wings of the social gospel movement were each represented from the speaker's platform. However, the enthusiasm for this first large and impressive gathering cast a patina of unity over the congress. Those on the left denounced capitalism, referring to it as 'an evil tree that bears evil fruit';[62] they urged closer links between labour and the church[63] and called for a more equitable distribution of wealth.[64] Speakers on the right took more traditional positions on such issues as the weekly day of rest and 'the fitting employment of its hours,' and the problems of prostitution, drinking, and gambling.[65] It is important to note, however, that many prohibitionists were in the vanguard of social reform. The elimination of the sale of liquor was, for many of them, a first step in a broad program of social reconstruction. The mainstream of the movement was well represented by those calling for measures of reform and regulation in aid of various categories of people or for the extension of existing social services.[66]

The 1914 congress is noteworthy for its evidence of a growing appreciation for social security programs, specifically the use of social insurance to protect people against work injury, old age, and unemployment. Proponents of these measures displayed a knowledge of European and American developments in this field, and they were considerably less tolerant of the conventional objections to providing an income to people in need. Speaking on pensions for widows left with the care of children, Rose Henderson, a Montreal delegate, made the point in these terms:

> 'We must be careful not to pauperize,' say some comfortable wiseacres. We pension Royalty, noblemen, statesmen, judges, civil servants, industrial magnates, army and naval officers, all in receipt of good salaries during their lives. Is there any reason why our widowed mothers with young children should not be pensioned? Thirty-three bishops and archbishops in the House of Lords in England draw large pensions for practically doing nothing but opposing progressive measures introduced for the amelioration of the lot of the poor. Would anyone suggest that these noble lords were being pauperized by their pensions?[67]

The 1914 congress was a display case of religiously motivated social reform thought in Canada, just prior to the First World War. It was part of the great 'outpouring of concern' by Canadians in reaction to the social disorganization, the squalor, the poverty, and the oppression of labour that accompanied Canada's move into the industrial age. The delegates left the congress more confident than ever that it was possible to reconstruct Canadian society on Christian principles. The social gospel movement was in the ascendancy. But, five months away, the horror of the First World War was waiting to shatter its dreams and aspirations.

Government Annuities Act of 1908

One of the resolutions passed at the Social Service Congress of 1914 was a request to the federal government to institute a system of old age pensions. This action reflected the growing concern for the elderly in Canada, which had been raised periodically from various public forums from the 1880s on.[68] In 1886 the Royal Commission on the Relations of Labor and Capital had congratulated the federal government on encouraging working people to save from their surplus earnings in post office and government savings banks but went on to urge the creation of a government annuity system, 'under which working people and others might make provision for old age by periodical or occasional payments of small sums.'[69] In 1891 an Ontario Royal Commission on the Prison and Reformatory System decried the numbers of homeless elderly who were lodged in local jails on charges of vagrancy because there was no other place for them. It was recommended that each county in Ontario be required to operate a poorhouse for the reception and care of homeless people. This view of how poor, elderly people should be treated would be deemed archaic within the next decade.[70] At the beginning of the century, the Canadian trade union movement was asking for public pensions in line with programs adopted by other industrialized nations, notably Germany (1889), Denmark (1891), New Zealand (1898), Australia (1901 and 1908), and Britain (1908). By 1900 the only initiative taken by the federal government was to extend the hours of post office savings departments on Saturday evenings from 7:30 to 9:00 pm.[71] The question of pensions for cabinet ministers received more prompt attention. In 1905 privy councillors who had been head of a department for five years or over were granted a retirement pension of $3,500 per annum, and this legislation was made retroactive to include all former cabinet ministers with the required years in office.[72] This action may have helped to prompt the Trades and Labour Congress of Canada to call for a system of public pensions at its annual convention in 1905. The issue of old age pensions was first raised in the House of Commons in 1906; between that date and 1914, when the war's emergency deflected parliamentary energies, two special committees of the House studied the question, but the federal government was not sympathetic to the idea. Pensions for cabinet ministers were condoned, but pensions for average Canadians were characterized as a 'socialist experiment.'[73] To forestall such experiments, the federal government introduced a system of government annuities in 1908.

In an era in which the residual concept of social welfare was dominant, one might have expected the government to call for tenders from the private market in setting up such a scheme. However, it was widely appreciated that premiums for endowment policies offered by private insurance companies were beyond the financial means of most working-class Canadians. In any case, the government was in a poor position at this time to recommend that Canadian workers seek income protection for their old age from the private sector. In 1906 a federal Royal Commission on Life Insurance, sparked by a similar investigation of irregularities in the insurance business in New York state, revealed instances of mismanagement of funds, financial irregularities, and what one Toronto newspaper called 'disclosures of the most barefaced and brazen dishonesty.'[74] The result of the commission's hearings and report was a considerable fall in public confidence in private insurance companies. Thus, a compromise between public and private provision emerged: a scheme of government-operated annuities was offered to the public as a means of overcoming the deficiencies in the private market. Individual contracts could be started with an initial premium of $10. Payments did not have to be made monthly or yearly, although regular contributions were encouraged. There was no cancellation of the contract because of failure to keep up with payments. One source of serious criticism of private insurance that had come to light was the millions of dollars in unearned profit that had accrued from lapsed policies. It was recognized, however, that failure to make regular payments to the government annuity would result in very small pension incomes.

A Canadian researcher who made a detailed study of the Government Annuities Act of 1908 concluded that

> this Act had many excellent features. Public administration offered security of funds, confidence, freedom from forfeiture, and elasticity in making payments. As a long-term investment the inducements offered were superior to those offered by private companies. But could it become an effective instrument for achieving security in old age on the part of the average workman? Could any voluntary scheme actually meet the income maintenance problems involved? For skilled workers regularly employed, and for middle-class people, an additional outlet for savings devoted solely to the building up of an old age annuity might become an attractive prospect. But for the average factory worker it was expecting too much in terms of discipline and sacrifice. His surplus, if any, was small, and there were too many current risks demanding accessible savings to make it possible for him to tie up regular sums for a distant prospect. The whole Act insofar as it was intended to serve the needs of workingmen was based on misconception of their way of life.[75]

A random sample of annuity contracts examined in 1915 indicated that 'purchasers were mainly people in the lower-paid professions (notably teachers and clergy), clerks, skilled tradesmen, farmers and small businessmen. Labourers accounted for only 4 percent of sales.'[76] Between 1908 and the beginning of the Old Age Pensions Act in 1927, only 7,713 annuities were issued, leaving the vast bulk of ageing, needy Canadians dependent upon families, friends, or organized charity, often in the form of indoor relief.

Public Assistance at the Turn of the Century

One aspect of the social minimum concept in Canada prior to the First World War was the form of public aid to people in financial need. Up until the war, the only type of public assistance available was that provided on an emergency basis by municipalities or by private charities acting as their agents, and generally referred to as 'outdoor relief.' Most of the help given was assistance in kind – that is, in the form of grocery hampers, secondhand clothing, and orders for fuel. Very little cash was provided, in keeping with the prevailing view that poverty was intimately related to, among other human frailties, a chronic inability to budget properly. Such help that was provided, whether in cash or in kind, was given as emergency aid with little in the way of assistance on a regular, continuing basis.

The amount and form of help given to the dependent poor were conditioned by the famous (or infamous) English poor law principle of *less eligibility*. This principle, first enunciated by the Poor Law Reform Commission of 1834, decreed that in Britain the standard of living provided by the municipality for its dependent poor must be at a less favourable standard than that which the lowest-paid labourer could earn for himself and his family. While not given formal recognition in Canada, the principle of less eligibility pervaded the administration of public assistance to the poor from the outset, resulting in meagre subsistence-level handouts, which for long-term dependencies (as in the case of a mother left to care for a family of small children) became a threat to the health of the individuals and families assisted.

An extension of the less eligibility belief that also infiltrated into Canada from England was the workhouse test. This had the dual aim of detecting fraudulent claims for assistance as well as implementing less eligibility as a principle. As it was not always thought possible to provide assistance in amounts less than that of the lowest-paid independent wage earner, as that class of labourer might well be at a bare subsistence level, the condition of the recipient of welfare was made less favourable by providing assistance in an unpalatable form – indoor relief. The offer of help conditional upon entry into one of the poor law institutions was called the 'workhouse test.' People who refused to accept this form of help were considered to have fraudulently asked for assistance. Those who accepted it were clearly those in most desperate need and therefore the proper subjects for charity.

As Canada approached the end of the nineteenth century, there was increasing 'uneasiness at the idea of building large institutions, named after the most lavish contributor to house people who needed care,'[77] and outdoor relief became more common. The workhouse test now became the work test, which meant that an applicant for public assistance, unless he had a medical certificate excusing him from work, could be required to saw cordwood or break rock as a condition for receiving help. In 1915, for example, the House of Industry in Toronto required an applicant for relief to break up a crate of rocks weighing 650 pounds.[78] Once again it was held by welfare administrators and those responsible for policy that such a requirement separated the genuine case of hardship from the fraudulent, as well as making the conditions of life for the assisted poor 'less favourable' than for the unassisted. The amount of help provided as outdoor relief, following the less eligibility concept, was so minimal that the recipient was often forced to supplement this aid by applying to private individuals and charitable organizations for additional help. In effect, public aid had to be supplemented in many cases by begging. In the larger cities, particularly during the winter months or during periods of economic recession, an array of charitable agencies would spring up as a result of public concern for the poor. This in turn resulted in a movement, at about the turn of the century, to organize the various charities and introduce a more systematic approach to relief-giving as a means of avoiding duplication of effort and cutting down on fraudulent application – the latter subject generating, then as now, more interest than it deserved.

Attitudes toward the poor and explanations of the causes of poverty in the decade prior to the First World War appear to have changed very little from what they were in the nineteenth century, the research of H.B. Ames notwithstanding. The Associated Charities of Winnipeg, formed in 1908, stated in their first annual report that, although they had 'no exact record,' they were satisfied that intemperance was an important contributing factor in 80 per cent of cases of destitution.[79] In a 1912 report this same organization, in explaining its function to the public, revealed a characteristic view of poverty held by charitable agencies: 'If material assistance was all that was needed, if the families seeking it could in all cases be relied upon to use it in such a way that they would quickly become self-supporting the work of this department would be easy. Unfortunately, the large majority of applications for relief are caused by thriftlessness, mismanagement, unemployment due to incompetence, intemperance, immorality, desertion of the family and domestic quarrels. In such cases the mere giving of relief tends rather to induce pauperism than to reduce poverty.'[80]

As long as this definition of poverty prevailed, a limited, residual approach to social welfare seemed to many to be justified. It was only when the causes of poverty began to be decisively redefined that a foundation for changes in the social security system was laid. These changes came about as a result of a host of socioeconomic forces unleashed by industrialization. The first of these developments was the workers' compensation movement.

4

The First Stage of the Modern Era: Workers' Compensation in Ontario

The story of the evolution of workers' compensation in Canada, touching as it does the constitutional area of 'property and civil rights,' falls within the jurisdiction of the provinces, and thus the student of social policy faces not one but ten stories. However, Ontario's story is the most significant. The Ontario Workmen's Compensation Act of 1914 was Canada's first piece of social insurance[1] providing compulsory income protection against one of the major risks to the continuity of income in an industrial society – work-related sickness, disability, or death. Furthermore, this scheme involved the payment of benefits in cash, and, later, medical and rehabilitative services, as a right and not as an act of charity. Here we have the emergence of a program with a clear institutional concept at a time when the residual concept of social security held undisputed sway. Such a development requires an explanation.

Prior to the Ontario act, the worker's only avenue for securing compensation for work-related sickness or injury from his place of employment was through the courts. In the interpretation of the common law, the courts heavily favoured the rights of property over the rights of injured workers or their heirs. Employers could marshal three defences in law that effectively shielded them from liability for accident claims in a majority of cases: the rules of 'contributory negligence,' of 'common employment,' and of 'assumption of risk.' These legal defences meant that the injured employee or his heirs could not recover damages (or the claim was substantially reduced) if it could be shown that the victim was in any way responsible for the accident, or that the accident was caused by the actions of a fellow employee, or that the accident resulted from one of the normal or assumed risks of the particular job.

The gross inequity of these interpretations of the common law did not begin to register in the public mind until the incidence of industrial death, disease, and injury began to climb. This occurred as a result of the application of steam and then, at the turn of the century, of electrical energy to the industrial processes, which required people to work in close proximity to machinery that was heavier, faster, and infinitely more dangerous to life and limb. These risks were aggravated by a lack of managerial responsibility linked to absentee ownership, which characterized the larger industrial enterprises, by the attempt to maximize profits without regard to the welfare of the worker, and by the absence of industrial safety programs.[2]

Factory Acts and Employers' Liability Acts

Public indignation and concern over the mounting toll of death and disablement began to manifest itself in Canada in the 1880s, partly as a result of federal inquiries such as the Royal Commission on the Relations of Labor and Capital (discussed in Chapter 3), and partly from the agitation of trade unionists and other groups. Initially, provincial governments responded by passing Factory Acts to require the use of safety equipment, limit the hours of work, and restrict the employment of children. Ontario in 1884 was the first province to pass such an act.[3] However, Factory Acts did not answer the equally pressing issues of the worker's loss of income owing to work-related accidents and the sense of financial insecurity that working people, particularly those in hazardous occupations, must have endured for themselves and their families. Ontario again led the way in 1886 by passing legislation of a type known as an 'employers' liability act,' modelled on British legislation of 1880.[4] Other provinces followed suit between 1891 and 1911. The effect of this type of legislation was to diminish the usefulness of the common law as a defence against claims for damages by injured workers or their heirs. Employers' Liability Acts still required the worker to prove negligence on the part of the employer, but now the worker was helped with his or her claim by the fact that in certain well-defined circumstances the traditional defences would no longer hold. Specifically, the common law defences of 'assumed risk' and 'common employment' were substantially weakened.[5]

These changes in the common law faced the employer with the greater likelihood of large damage suits as well as the expense of court actions. The labour-management bitterness that ensued from legal battles was another cost to be reckoned with. The number of workers who took their employers to court began to escalate both as a result of their improved chances of winning their cases and because of the growing strength of unions and fraternal societies that assisted their members in carrying their claims for compensation through the courts. Insurance companies, with greater frequency, settled claims for damages out of court rather than face the possibility of more costly judgements awarded by the courts. This in turn raised accident liability insurance rates. Employers began to realize that a pooling of the risks from accident claims would increase their business costs by a modest but predictable amount; this was to be preferred to the existing arrangement that left the individual employer open to large and unpredictable costs arising out of accident liability suits.

For their part, the workers could not afford the delays and costs of litigation unless they were strongly supported by a union or fraternal society. Working people were looking for a system that would provide them with a just and speedy settlement. Models for such legislation had emerged in Europe by the turn of the century, specifically in Germany and England.

A New Principle from Britain

In 1897 Britain introduced the Workmen's Compensation Act, replacing the Employers' Liability Act of 1880. An entirely new principle was introduced by this act: under the old legislation the worker was required to prove negligence by the employer, whereas with the new act 'the criterion was injury (or disease or death).'[6] This stimulated interest in Canada and particularly in Ontario. The provincial government commissioned James Mavor, a University of Toronto economics professor, to report on the new English compensation law and its possible application to Ontario. Mavor submitted his report in 1900, recommending that the existing 'employers' liability' type of legislation be retained because the English compensation system, if adopted, would throw the whole cost of insuring against industrial accidents upon industry. The government accepted Mavor's arguments and took no further action for a decade.

Quebec Workmen's Compensation Act of 1909

The same year that Mavor presented his report to the Ontario government, the chief factory inspector for Quebec, Louis Guyon, attended two international conferences in Paris dealing with work accidents, social insurance, and the legal protection of working people.[7] He returned to Quebec with a detailed knowledge of European compensation legislation and a determination to reduce the industrial accident rate as well as bring into being a more just compensation system in Quebec. He was assisted in his campaign by the fact that from 1893 manufacturers and industries in Quebec were required to report all accidents. Although Guyon estimated that at least one in three went unreported, the statistics that were available revealed a rising toll of death and disablement. According to Terry Copp, support for Guyon's campaign from Quebec trade unions was halfhearted, but he persisted, and in 1907 the provincial government established a Commission on Labour Accidents.[8] Some employers expressed opposition to any change in the law covering compensation, but the Quebec branch of the Canadian Manufacturers' Association supported the principle of the worker's right to compensation unless negligence could be proved. Spokespersons for labour asked for a system of compulsory insurance. The result of these hearings was the Quebec Workmen's Compensation Act of

1909, which established a procedure for claims and a schedule of payments for various grades of disability, except in those cases where it could be shown that the worker's negligence had caused the accident. The weaknesses of this legislation were that it was not compulsory, there was no independent board established to administer it (the administration was under the jurisdiction of the Supreme Court and the Circuit Court of Quebec), and the defence of 'contributory negligence' was upheld. It was still within the power of the court to reduce the amount of compensation if the accident was the result of the 'inexcusable fault' of the worker.[9]

The introduction of the Quebec Compensation Act spurred interest in the same subject in Ontario. As in the case of Quebec, compulsory reporting of accidents was required from 1886, and the statistics compiled added weight to the demands for a better measure of protection.[10] In contrast to Quebec, in Ontario it was the trade unions that led the agitation for change, and in 1910, after considerable pressure by labour, the province established a Commission of Inquiry under Chief Justice William Meredith.

Initially, business interests in Ontario reacted negatively to the idea of paying the costs of a form of no-fault insurance, particularly at a time when the conventional wisdom attributed 95 per cent of industrial accidents to worker negligence.[11] However, the Canadian Manufacturers' Association, having had time to study the implications of the Quebec legislation, saw that a scheme that would stabilize costs and spread the risk of liability insurance would be a marked improvement over the existing arrangement. At the same time, the employer would be spared the ill will between himself and his employees that litigation fostered. At the hearings before the commission, therefore, the CMA proposed replacing the existing liability insurance with 'some form of accident insurance, whereby those who are injured in the course of their employment would receive a reasonable compensation without having to have recourse to legal process.' On this point both labour and management were in agreement. While business was generally unanimous in favouring a compensation law, there was disagreement on the details of the plan. Would the new scheme be modelled on German legislation by which industries were grouped according to the degree of accident risk, thereby providing a form of collective liability, but using private insurance carriers? Or would the British legislation of 1897 be copied, which made employers individually liable (again, private insurance carriers were used)? A third model, state insurance, which bypassed the private market in favour of a state-owned and state-controlled organization, was operating in Norway and was soon to be enacted by the State of Washington. It was this last model that was eventually favoured by the Canadian Manufacturers' Association. Canadian labour representatives did not take a strong stand on whether the insurance carrier should be a private or a government insurance plan. They were much more concerned to contest the demand of industry that labour make a contribution to the cost of a compensation scheme. Labour argued that the pain, suffering, and loss of income suffered by the injured worker was more than a sufficient contribution.

Chief Justice Meredith submitted his final report in 1913, together with a draft of a proposed Workmen's Compensation Act. His plan contained elements of the German, English, and state insurance systems.[12] The Ontario government convened a meeting of industry and labour in January of 1914 to discuss the pending legislation. Labour was generally favourable to Meredith's draft bill, although it was critical of a seven-day waiting period, the scale of benefits, and the fact that the rule of 'contributory negligence' had not been completely repudiated. Industry, while supporting the principle of compensation, attacked the benefit levels as 'preposterous' and the provision of pensions for slight permanent disability as 'unfair to industry.' It continued to press for a contribution from the worker toward the cost of the plan, and maintained that because of compensation the worker's right to sue his employer under the common law should be abolished. Industry was also critical of the administrative structure, terming it too complex and unworkable.

Michael Piva's research indicates that labour was taken aback by the virulence of industry's attack on the bill. Labour appeared to go on the defensive – it became conciliatory and did not press its demands for improved benefit levels as vigorously as it might have. Labour representatives agreed to give up their right to sue the employer under common law if the worker's right to compensation was automatic and not the result of a court proceeding. They said that they would support the bill even though they felt the scale of compensation was too low.

Ontario Workmen's Compensation Act, 1914

The government introduced the Workmen's Compensation Act in March of 1914 (an election year in Ontario), and Piva argues that 'labour it would appear, had won on every point.' Labour did win its demand that the worker not contribute to the cost of the plan. However, benefit scales remained as they were in the draft legislation. Compensation did become automatic, but a waiting period of seven days was required before any benefits were paid, and there were no benefits if the compensation board was satisfied that the accident had been caused by the serious and wilful misconduct of the worker. This last stipulation was modified to the extent that in the case of death or serious injury, benefits would be received regardless of the cause of the accident. The administrative organization as recommended by Chief Justice Meredith remained intact. The Ontario Workmen's Compensation Act of 1914 was hailed as one of the most advanced pieces of compensation legislation in North America. It marked the beginning of a workers' compensation movement in Canada, as workers in other provinces demanded and eventually won similar protection.[13]

The Ontario act was fundamentally different from the employers' liability type of act that preceded it. The new legislation embodied the doctrine of liability without fault, which meant that compensation for injury or death was to be paid as a right without the necessity of a lengthy court procedure to determine negligence. This doctrine was grounded in a new awareness that developed at this time that work injuries were one of the costs of industrial progress, which simple justice dictated must not fall on the individual worker. Although the costs of compensation were, in the first instance, placed upon industry, Chief Justice Meredith noted in his report that, ultimately, the cost was paid by the general public in terms of higher costs for manufactured goods and services.[14]

In effect, a redefinition of dependency had occurred. I have already noted that prior to Crystal Eastman's study of work-related injuries in Pittsburgh steel mills, the conventional wisdom of the day attributed 95 per cent of industrial accidents to employee carelessness. Undoubtedly the same kind of thinking existed in Canada, but it is clear that in the first two decades of the twentieth century a shift of opinion occurred, and the conditions of industry were now seen as the primary and significant source of the accident rate.

Evaluating the Ontario Workmen's Compensation Act of 1914

Ontario workers benefited from this new piece of legislation in a number of ways. They were protected from income interruption resulting from all accidents sustained at work and from certain work-related diseases. The act assured the worker of receiving benefits regardless of his employer's financial position. Furthermore, in sharp contrast to the prevailing system of poor relief, these benefits were paid in cash and as a right. They came in regular, periodic instalments for as long as the disability lasted, although for slight but permanent disability a lump sum payment could be made with the board's permission. Within a few years after the passage of the original legislation, the worker was given more protection by the addition of a full range of medical and rehabilitative services. It was also possible for injured workers to have their cases reopened if they suffered a recurrence of disability or if an individual's condition worsened. In return for these advantages, the worker gave up the right to sue the employer for damages under the common law.

The new act's adequacy as a piece of social security legislation may be judged in part by the degree to which the program facilitated the meeting of its qualitative goals.[15] The two primary goals of the new legislation, as outlined by Chief Justice Meredith, were to ensure the worker certainty of entitlement to compensation and to prevent the disabled worker from becoming financially dependent upon family, friends, or the wider community.

Certainty of entitlement was augmented in this instance by taking the administration of compensation cases out of the courts, where claims procedures were lengthy and uncertain, from the worker's point of view, and placing them under the jurisdiction of a three-man board where decisions were rendered quickly. Entitlement is also directly linked to a program's inclusiveness – the degree to which a program covers the population at risk. The tendency in early workers' compensation legislation was to cover only occupations considered dangerous. The Ontario act moved past this point but stopped well short of comprehensive coverage. Several important occupational groups were excluded from protection – farming, wholesale and retail establishments, and domestic service. The commissioner noted 'there is no logical reason why all should not be included,' but he nevertheless doubted whether public opinion would accept a more comprehensive scheme. It is reasonable to wonder whose 'public opinion' was in mind.[16]

The adequacy of the new act must be viewed in relation to its goal of preventing dependency. It can be argued that by setting benefit rates at 55 per cent of the claimant's average earnings, and given the low wage levels that were all too common, this percentage of income protection would not be an effective bulwark against dependency. The fact that benefit rates were set at this marginal level indicates the strength of the notion that higher benefit rates would seriously impair the incentive to work (although the irony of relating this concern to people already in the labour force seldom occurred to those who expressed concern over the work-incentive issue). The waiting period of seven days before any benefits, other than medical, were provided was another limitation on the plan's adequacy and inclusiveness. According to the American Accident Table, a one-week waiting period excludes 47 per cent of temporary disability cases from benefits.[17]

While the compensation benefits for temporary and permanent disability were wage related – the rates were proportional to the worker's average wages – the benefits for widows and orphans of men killed in industrial accidents or who died from a work-related disease were provided at a flat rate. Flat-rate benefits provide a uniform payment for all persons in defined categories, and in this case widows or disabled widowers were to receive $20 per month and $5 per month for each child with a maximum payment of $40 to a family.[18] The maximum limit on pensions to widows and orphans meant that a mother received support for no more than four children. The failure to vary the allowances for children in relation to their ages was another serious defect. With these meagre allowances it is difficult to see how the goal of preventing dependency would be met.[19] The Ontario Workmen's Compensation Act made no specific mention of an appeal procedure except to provide the opportunity for any weekly or other periodical payment to a worker to be reviewed at the request of either the employer or the employee. Despite its name, the act covered both male and female employees, adults and children.[20]

For administrative purposes, the act divided employers into two groups. The larger group comprised those who paid a contribution into a fund, administered by the board, from which accident claims were paid. A much smaller group, consisting in the main of large utilities and the railroads, were individually liable, at the board's direction, to pay for compensation and medical aid. The board was given extensive powers, equivalent to the Supreme Court, which gave it the right to compel witnesses to appear as well as to demand documents, papers, and other things pertinent to a case. The board's decision was final and could not be challenged. Undoubtedly the board's authority materially assisted in establishing public confidence in a new and still somewhat controversial program.

The Workmen's Compensation Act was of considerable benefit to employers. The majority were no longer individually liable for damages. Instead they became part of a collective insurance system that provided cheaper coverage than could be obtained from private insurance companies. Smaller businesses no longer faced the risk of financial ruin through lawsuits, and costs of accident compensation and accident insurance, which up to the passage of the new act were unpredictable and rising, now became predictable and stabilized. Labour-management relations were improved by the cessation of the adversarial system that had been used to settle accident claims.

However, one unintended consequence of the workers' compensation movement was that it obscured a larger and more serious risk to the continuity of income – sickness and disability unrelated to the workplace. It has been estimated that time lost from work as a result of occupationally related disability comprises only 10 per cent of the total of all time lost as a result of sickness and disability.[21] It was this wider form of protection that was needed to prevent dependency related to sickness and disability. One may conclude, as Roy Lubove does, that compensation laws met the employers' needs more completely than those of the wage earner, whose real need was for a comprehensive measure to protect him from the risk of earning loss arising from disability or disease regardless of the cause. Canada had to wait a further fifty-seven years for this important piece of social security legislation to be enacted.

In the years prior to the First World War, health and welfare problems were, in the main, the responsibility of the municipality or of some local philanthropic organization. The war and the advent of the various provincial Workmen's Compensation Acts marked the beginning of greater provincial intervention in the health, welfare, and social security fields. From this point on, people began to turn to the senior levels of government in their requests for solutions to social problems that heretofore had been regarded as matters of purely municipal or county concern.

The introduction of the Ontario Workmen's Compensation Act with its modern focus, conferring rights to benefit, resulted in a hairline crack appearing in the residual mould of Canadian social security provision. However, the values supporting the more restricted role for social security remained influential and were to dominate social security developments for another quarter of a century.

5
The Social Impact of the First World War

The war produced profound changes in Canada's social and economic structure. The economy, which had faltered badly in 1913 and 1914, throwing thousands of Canadians out of work and exposing them to the haphazard mixture of grudging municipal relief and private charity, quickly revitalized as orders for munitions and foodstuffs for Allied armies poured in. As a result of the war, the productive capacity in all sectors of the economy increased dramatically.[1] Politically, the effects of the war brought about the beginnings of new political parties with clearly defined class interests. The two old-line federal parties had, since Confederation, experienced some success in uniting the diverse interest groups in Canada behind various versions of a 'national policy.' The war shattered this tenuous unity as farm and labour groups developed as a political force. A significant focus for discontent was the fact that the sacrifices demanded of all in the interests of the war effort were, in reality, falling on some segments of society while others reaped huge profit and advantage. This resentment was to find dramatic expression in the immediate postwar years in the Winnipeg General Strike of 1919 and the electoral successes of the United Farmers' parties in Ontario (1919), Alberta (1921), and Manitoba (1922), and in the election of sixty-five Progressives and two Labour members to the House of Commons in 1921.

Wartime efforts and mobilization contributed to the further decline of the laissez-faire philosophy of government. The hitherto unprecedented emergency of the First World War gave many Canadians their first inkling of how government could mould their lives. In addition to directing the use of economic resources and encouraging the production of certain materials and foodstuffs necessary for the war effort, the government engaged in rationing of vital supplies, took action against hoarders, and, of signal importance for income security plans in the future, imposed a federal income tax on personal income. The government also became the sole support of hundreds of disabled soldiers, their wives and children, and the widows and orphans of the men killed in battle. From developments such as these, Canadians began to see that government had a variety of positive roles to play other than being merely a 'night watchman,' protecting property and maintaining law and order.

The sacrifices demanded of average Canadians provoked a call for a new social order with the return of peace. Farmers' groups, organized labour, women's organizations, the churches, and political parties all developed their agendas for change.[2] But the hope of reform-minded Canadians that the federal government would use as much energy in providing for the welfare of Canadians as it had in prosecuting the war began to fade at the war's end. The Parliament in Ottawa quickly revealed its predilection for relying on the institutions of the family and the marketplace to meet social welfare needs.

The Mothers' Pension Movement

A number of socioeconomic forces combined during and immediately following the First World War in Canada to produce a 'mothers' pension' movement. Widowed mothers with small children to support had long been traditional and 'worthy' targets for charitable agencies. However, they were only one segment of the larger, one-parent family problem that included separated, deserted, and divorced mothers, women whose husbands were in prison or hospitalized, families where the father was seriously incapacitated, and unmarried mothers.

The problem of the one-parent family became more acute as the processes of industrialization shattered the informal social security system that grew out of a settled, rural life and the support of the extended family and long-time friends and neighbours. The anonymity of city life weakened the informal sanctions operating in small, closely knit communities to reduce the incidence of family breakup and to remind husbands and wives of their responsibilities to one another and to their children. By drawing more women into the labour force, industrialization broke down the conventional male-female roles, while the economic security of the breadwinner, now increasingly both male and female, was made dependent upon the state of a labour market that fluctuated unpredictably. Divorce became more common, as did desertion (the poor man's divorce), leaving many women and children without financial support.[3]

As the most innocent victims of family breakup are children, it is not surprising that at the turn of the century in Canada, as the pace of industrialization accelerated, there also developed a renewed concern for the welfare of children. The early answer to the problem of children left stranded by family breakup was institutional care – orphanages, refuges, industrial schools, or various forms of apprenticeship. These programs of child care came under severe criticism at the momentous White House

Conference on Children called by President Roosevelt in 1909. The conference's first, and justly famous, recommendation declared that a child should not be removed from home for reasons of poverty alone.[4] This emphasis on the importance of preserving a child's home whenever possible provided the stimulus for a mothers' pension movement in the United States that 'swept across the nation after 1911,' and unquestionably helped to fuel the demand for similar legislation in Canada.[5]

The arguments for an income maintenance program for mothers left with the care of young children was strengthened by the fact that private charities in Canada, just prior to the war, began to coordinate their efforts to prevent costly duplication of services and to introduce a more systematic and effective program of aid. From these early 'associations of charities' came the first rudimentary measurement of the extent to which the one-parent family was coming to the attention of charity organizations. During the month of February 1915, for example, the Associated Charities of Winnipeg reported that of 703 families assisted, nearly one-quarter required help because of the father's absence.[6]

The mobilization of soldiers in 1914 created the need for dependants' allowances and pensions for the widows and orphans of men killed in battle. The reasonableness of these arrangements for servicemen and their families naturally served to highlight similar categories of need among the civilian population.

Another factor that focused attention on the one-parent family during the First World War was a heightened concern for the health of the newborn infant (a common phenomenon in wartime when large numbers of a nation's adult population face the risk of being killed). In the October 1918 issue of *Social Welfare,* one writer reflected, with unconscious irony, on how successful the city of London, England, had been in reducing infant mortality: 'Its Public Health Board has reduced the infant mortality rate lower than many other cities of the world. Had the rest of Great Britain been as diligent and as successful in conserving the lives of infants during the years from 1872 to 1899, Great Britain today would have had 1,600,000 males of military age to call upon. What a vast army she could have thrown into the world conflict in Flanders had she but saved the lives of these children.'[7] In the same issue, another writer noted that Ontario's infant mortality rate compared unfavourably with that of England and Wales. The article continued: 'That Ontario, in her comparative youth, should pay in 1917 an infant mortality rate 16 higher in the 1,000 than England is execrable; that she pays it needlessly makes the offence a crime. Criminal it is at any time but with the nation losing 13,031 men in 1916, and 22,608 in 1917, by the deaths in the overseas forces, it is suicidal.'[8]

The tragic loss of life in the war (61,326 killed, 172,950 wounded) was compounded by the influenza epidemic of 1918 that took an estimated

30,000 lives, many of them young parents. The country's anguish at this double blow was an additional element contributing to an increased concern for children and a sympathy for mothers left alone to raise a family.

The changing status of women, particularly during the First World War, undoubtedly contributed to the evolution of mothers' pensions. During this era, as already noted in Chapter 3, the right to vote was extended to women federally in 1918, and between the years 1916 and 1920 seven provinces gave women the vote. It is hardly a coincidence that provincial schemes of mothers' pensions in five of those provinces should follow in such short order the granting of the franchise to women.

Many of those who campaigned for mothers' pensions wished to see legislation that would emphasize the pension concept, thereby reducing the discretionary element in the program's administration. By giving the needy mother a strong claim on a benefit related to her status as a mother with dependent children, rather than relating the assistance to a condition of indigence, it was hoped that much of the stigma associated with traditional poor relief would be diminished.[9] This idea was nourished by the development of federal war service pensions and social insurance benefits for widows and orphans under provincial workers' compensation laws. There was much discussion about 'the state's obligation,' the 'rights of children,' and the rights of the dependent mother.[10] There was a growing conviction that 'the care of the fatherless child must be looked after in some other way than by charity or outdoor relief.'[11] However, the pension concept was opposed by private charity organizations in Canada. Essentially, the opposition was similar to that encountered by the mothers' pension movement in the United States from the established private charitable agencies, which had a long history of opposition to any expansion of public welfare.

Canadian opposition to the concept is implicit from an attempt made in Toronto in 1914, a few months before the outbreak of the war, to establish a project that would demonstrate the need for a provincial system of mothers' pensions. The Local Council of Women, after listening to the appeal of a delegation of charity-assisted mothers, applied to the Social Service Commission of Toronto for permission to solicit funds from the public for this purpose. The money collected was to be used to provide a small but regular income for a selected group of needy mothers in the hope that after a year's successful demonstration, the provincial government would make some permanent arrangement.

The Social Service Commission, a board composed largely of representatives of private charitable organizations in the city charged with the coordination and administration of poor relief in Toronto, gave the idea a lukewarm reception. It set out a number of conditions that had the effect of limiting the scope of the demonstration project, and the plan failed to develop any momentum. The scheme was dropped a few months after its inception by the need to collect money for the Patriotic Fund, established to assist the dependants of servicemen and others affected by the war.[12]

The arguments advanced by private charitable agencies against the mothers' pension movement were based on their long-established position that public authorities should restrict themselves to maintaining various types of institutions for such groups as the mentally ill, the mentally disabled, delinquents, criminals, and so on, leaving the provision of what was termed 'family relief' to the voluntary sector. Behind this opposition to any expansion of public welfare lay the deeply held conviction that unless the dispensing of outdoor relief was carefully controlled, the initiative and independence of the poor would be undermined. The mothers' pensions concept not only represented a major expansion of outdoor relief, but it created the expectation among poor families headed by women that they were entitled to receive help. The private agencies felt that this popularizing of the concept of public aid encouraged dependency and was not the basis for a financially responsible program.[13]

Those who supported mothers' pensions argued that families were breaking up for the lack of a regular, assured income. It was impossible, they said, for a mother to be both a breadwinner and a homemaker, a convincing argument at a time when the ten-hour workday was commonplace. They also maintained that the conservation of family life was a responsibility of government, a collectivist notion that raised the hackles of those committed to the tenets of stern individualism.

The crux of the conflict between the private charity agencies and the supporters of mothers' pensions came down to this: the voluntary charity establishment, both in the United States and Canada, refused to define the one-parent family problem as primarily one of lack of income. Wedded to individualistic explanations of poverty, the leaders of private charitable organizations held that the problem was not so much economic as personal. A request for financial aid was a sign of personal inadequacy at best, with the possibility of more serious pathology lurking in the background. For this reason, the emphasis on relief-giving had to be on a rehabilitative process – a restoring of the individual's capacity for independence through counselling, support, and personal influence.[14] The corollary of this position, which developed in the 1920s, was that financial support was ineffective, if not dangerous, unless accompanied by skilled, professional social work investigation and supervision.

The supporters of mothers' pensions, on the other hand, defined the problem more in terms of mass poverty arising from a complex of social and economic conditions quite beyond the control of the individual family. The problem was one that only the resources of government could handle (private agencies were always complaining about deficits); therefore, government action was required. The expansion of public welfare in this instance did not rule out the need for rehabilitative casework in some instances, but economic assistance 'had to be dispensed as one element in a broad plan of social treatment.'

With the many socioeconomic changes engendered by the war, and with the determined and effective lobbying of women's organizations, labour groups, and others, mothers' pensions became politically popular in Canada between 1916 and 1920. By 1920 even the Social Service Commission of Toronto had joined with a large delegation to petition the Ontario government for legislation to assist dependent mothers.[15] Outright opposition to the idea would have been politically risky for the private agencies (the opposition of American private agencies to mothers' pensions, early in the century, brought them an unprecedented amount of public criticism). However, where they could safely lobby against the legislation, they did so; and where they could not prevent a measure from being brought in, they endeavoured to have it framed in a manner that reflected the traditional practices of private charity administration, essentially a residual concept of social welfare. The history of mothers' pensions in British Columbia is illustrative.

Mothers' Pensions in British Columbia

In 1918 a large delegation, composed principally of representatives of various women's groups but including the mayors of Vancouver, New Westminster, and Chilliwack, travelled to Victoria to petition the government to establish a system of mothers' pensions. Premier John Oliver, who a year earlier had treated a much smaller delegation in a cool and non-committal manner, was too good a politician not to be impressed by the size of this second delegation. He called them 'the most businesslike and representative delegation that had ever appeared before government.'[16] However, he delayed taking action until November 1919, when he established a commission to report on the feasibility of such a program. Public hearings were held throughout the province, and submissions were received from a wide cross section of the community. The following quotation from the commission's report provides evidence of the degree of public support for mothers' pensions:

> The need for mothers' pensions was drawn very forcefully to the attention of the Commission by the various witnesses who testified at its hearings in all parts of the province. State assistance for indigent mothers of young children was endorsed by seventy-seven women's organizations, twenty-four fraternal societies, thirty-four labour organizations, six other organizations, ten ministers of the gospel, thirteen doctors, four insurance agents, and forty-six private individuals. Witnesses everywhere welcomed the idea of granting pensions to those mothers who, through no fault of

their own, found themselves unable to support their children and educate them to become useful citizens. No witness anywhere appeared before the Commission in opposition to the principle of mothers' pensions. Regrets were expressed on all sides that the subject of mothers' pensions had not been investigated long ago. Widespread demand was made for the immediate crystallizing into legislation of recommendations along the lines set out in this report. A profound conviction was shown by the public spirited citizens for progressive legislation in keeping with the spirit of the times.[17]

The commission's report was tabled at the 1920 session of the British Columbia legislature, and the necessity for mothers' pensions 'was so strongly emphasized that a "Mothers' Pension Act" was passed on April 17, 1920.'[18] An important element in this statute's rapid progress through the legislature was the impending provincial election in which the women of the province would be voting for the first time.

The 1920 Mothers' Pension Act of British Columbia did not bestow a non-discretionary pension on women left with children to support. It did, however, make it easier and less stigmatizing for mothers to apply for a small, assured monthly income for themselves and their children under the age of sixteen. At a time when numerous Canadians were drawing war service pensions from the federal government or provincial pensions from workers' compensation programs, the use of the term 'pension' to describe the benefits of what was really a public assistance measure encouraged women in need of financial assistance to apply. This was one of the goals of the mothers' pension movement – the lessening of the charity stigma that was part and parcel of relief-giving up to this time.[19] The pension concept was enhanced when, after the first six months of operation, the administration of the act was transferred from the Superintendent of Neglected Children to the Workers' Compensation Board. Many women had objected to the association of their allowance with the Superintendent of Neglected Children.[20] The administrative move to the Workers' Compensation Board enabled the recipients of mothers' pensions to benefit from the medical and legal services of the board. Although these services were extended on a 'charity basis,' in that arrangements were made for services to be performed without a fee or at a reduced fee, the fact that they were arranged through the Workers' Compensation Board may have helped to diminish the charity aspect of the service.[21]

The Mothers' Pension Act uncovered a significant amount of poverty in British Columbia, far more than had been anticipated. The commission's report recommending the legislation estimated that 258 widows and 593 children would be possible entrants into the scheme within the first year and that even this figure might be reduced with careful screening. No estimate was given of other one-parent family situations that might require assistance, and one is left wondering why projections of the program's costs were made only on the basis of widows and their children. However, even the estimated number of needy widows was well short of the mark. On the strength of this incomplete evidence, the commission suggested that about 235 families might qualify for coverage at an average cost per family of $55 per month, with the total cost of the program estimated at $155,100.[22]

Even before the act was proclaimed in July 1920, applications began 'to pour into the office from all parts of the Province,' indicating the incidence of poverty in one-parent families and the appeal of the pension concept to the public mind. The act covered indigent mothers, with one or more children under sixteen, who were widows or deserted wives; wives of men who were inmates of asylums or penal institutions; mothers whose husbands were unable to support their families because of illness or accident; and 'any other person whose case, in the opinion of the Superintendent, is a proper one for assistance under the provisions of this Act.'[23] This latter clause provided the administrators with the necessary leeway to extend the program's benefits to other single parents, such as divorced women, unmarried mothers, or foster mothers.

The act was proclaimed in July 1920, and by November 1,182 applications had been placed on file and more were being received daily. Of that number, 636 pensions were granted by 30 November 1920, nearly three times the estimate made by the commission, and at a cost of $287,110.17. By 1924-5, a year of economic recession in British Columbia, the total cost of mothers' pensions was $437,572, covering 847 families; by the end of the decade, 1929-30, the total cost had risen to $777,916, covering 1,370 families, an increase of 62 per cent over the 1924-5 figure.[24] These costs were carried entirely by the provincial government. However, the strict means test and other more restrictive eligibility clauses of the act meant that many more needy families were denied help. In the relative prosperity of the 1920s, the unanticipated costs of the program went unremarked, but when the Depression struck, the Mothers' Pension Act came under hard scrutiny.

The Attack on the Pension Concept

The provincial government in 1931, reeling from the drastic effects of the economic slump and under pressure from the business community to cut government spending, asked the Canadian Council on Child and Family Welfare to review the operations of the act. The council, founded in 1920, was a voluntary agency supported by federal subsidies. It was established 'to serve as a national clearing house for child welfare, to issue professional guidance materials, to inform public opinion, and to formulate briefs for legislation.'[25] As such, it was frequently called upon by private and public agencies to offer advice in child and family welfare issues, and by 1930 it had developed into Canada's most influential voice on social welfare matters.

The council, and particularly its able executive director, Charlotte Whitton, were the repositories of the traditional private charity agency attitudes about the role of government in social welfare and the nature of poverty and its treatment. Consequently, the council was basically antago- nistic to the development of mothers' pensions in any other form except that which would prevent what it considered to be the harmful effects on the human character of 'undiscriminating paternalism,' Reviewing the role of mothers' pensions in British Columbia, the Whitton inquiry noted: 'There is a grave danger of the development, as a matter of course, of a general tendency to reliance on social aid that the inquiry regards with grave disquiet as destructive of personal effort, and self-dependence, and so disruptive of the very basis of initiative, enterprise, and strength of char- acter that must be the greatest resource of any people.'[26] This belief espoused a highly discriminatory form of public assistance that owed more to English poor law concepts than to modern ideas of social security.

The private agency view that lack of money was perhaps the least of the problems facing one-parent families was reiterated by Whitton in her report to the provincial government:

> Mothers aid [Whitton declined to use the term 'pension'], properly admin- istered, is much more than a mere means for supplying a stated amount of material wants. It is a question not only of whether aid is given, or how much is given, but how it is given. Service must precede and accompany it, to the end that the family itself realizes that it, and each of its members, no less than provincial funds, must honestly and sincerely participate in the whole plan, which is the development of initiative, and self-reliance and independence at the earliest possible date, and to such degree and strength as to avoid future dependency.[27]

The council's antagonism toward the pension concept and the implied expansion of public welfare that it represented can be taken from the fact that Whitton made much of the disparity between the commission's esti- mate in 1920 of possible enrolment under the plan and the actual number of families granted pensions after the first year. She blamed the pensions concept of the program for costs she said were 'difficult to justify': 'There is abundant evidence in the files and records of the British Columbia sys- tem to indicate that the confusion of "pension" and "allowance" pay- ments in the designation of the legislation has led to the application, enrolment, and payments in respect to large numbers of mothers and fam- ilies in whose cases the dictates of child protection and sound social work would require cancellation of allowance, and provision for the care of the children under other guardianship and custody.'[28] The point at issue here was the fact that British Columbia's Mothers' Pension Act had departed from the canons of private agency practice by the liberality of its coverage and by not making provision for skilled social work supervision.[29] Whitton suggested that too many people were receiving assistance who with 'careful supervision' might have been dealt with in other ways. These 'other ways' came down to emphasizing individual and family responsibility – an attempt to shore up the residual concept of social welfare. Rather than provide an assured, minimum income to destitute mothers and their children, it was better to pass laws to pursue and punish deserting husbands; better to pressure people to care for their destitute relatives; better to insist that penitentiaries pay inmates a wage that could be allocated for the support of their families; better that divorced husbands be made to live up to their obligations; better that unmarried mothers give up their children for adoption. But until all deserting and divorced husbands had been rounded up, until relatives assumed their family responsibilities, until prison labour paid wages to support a prisoner's family (still not a reality in the 1990s), and until unmarried mothers could be counselled into giving up their children for adoption, who would meet the living costs of the families concerned? Their only resource was the hit-and-miss system of poor relief, the inadequacies of which had prompted the movement for mothers' pensions in the first place.

The confusion created by the 'pension concept' could be cleared up, Whitton suggested, by changing the public's perception of the program from a pension concept to a public assistance measure. It was recommended that the act's name be changed to the Mothers' Allowances Act and its objective stated as 'a measure to provide allowances to *certain* mothers in respect to their *dependent* children.'[30] Furthermore, the administration should be transferred from the Workers' Compensation Board to the Superintendent of Welfare.

Other recommendations received and accepted by the provincial government (grateful to have a rationale for cutting back on services to mothers and their children from such an impeccable source) included raising the residence qualification – a favourite poor law device for denying people help – and requiring that the municipality pay 50 per cent of the cost of allowances to recipients within their borders – another remnant of poor law administration.

Whitton had charged, with justification, that municipalities were 'unloading' their family welfare cases on the provincial program to avoid having to pay their share of local relief costs. Municipalities used various devices to do this, including political pressure and, a common tactic, lowering the assessment on the mother's property so that she might meet the rigid means test.[31] There was no evidence that anyone other than needy mothers and their children were placed on the program, but the fact that municipalities had evaded their responsibilities by the use of 'highly questionable subterfuges' was, in Whitton's view, indefensible.[32] It confirmed an opinion, long held by private charitable organizations, that public welfare was subject to political pressure and susceptible to abuse.

The impact of the council's report was a significant cutback in services to poverty-stricken mothers and their children. Mothers with only one child were refused help in most cases and had to either seek employment (not the easiest task in the Depression) or live on municipal relief. As municipal relief rates were generally lower than those paid under the Mothers' Pension Act, living standards were even more depressed for the families concerned. A cut in benefit rates was ordered; it had been tacitly recommended by the council's report, which, with unflattering intent, described the British Columbia Mothers' Pension Act as providing 'the most generous mothers' allowances in North America.'[33] Existing pensions were reviewed, resulting in a demand for refunds exceeding $4,000 from beneficiaries. A shifting of half the cost of benefits to the municipalities together with a 'considerable tightening up on the examination of applications' reduced the overall cost of mothers' pensions to the province by 39.5 per cent in 1934-5.[34]

The opposition of the Canadian Council on Child and Family Welfare to a widening of social security protection in British Columbia in 1931 marked the continuation of a traditional commitment by private welfare agencies to the values of individualism and localism. The council had, from its outset, demonstrated its willingness to ignore the relevance of income security measures to the field of child welfare and to impede their implementation. In 1925, for example, the council sponsored a conference on child welfare at which a 'comprehensive five-year program of effort' in the child welfare field was outlined. Plans of action relating to health, child labour, care of problem children, mental hygiene, education, recreation, and legislative proposals were considered. Conspicuous by its absence was any mention of mothers' pensions despite the fact that only five of Canada's nine provinces had such programs.[35]

The council continued to impede the implementation of provincial mothers' pensions acts under the aggressive leadership of Charlotte Whitton. In her annual report to the council in May 1933, Whitton noted that New Brunswick had passed a Mothers' Allowance Act in 1930 but had not brought it into force, and that in Quebec a royal commission had recommended a system of mothers' allowances: 'In both provinces, when consulted, your executive director since 1929-30 has repeatedly urged non-adoption of this legislation until and unless preceded by more centralized child protection and general family relief services and supervision of a centralized provincial nature.'[36] Thus, the council continued to press the traditional private charity viewpoint that financial aid, without social work supervision, was worse than no aid at all. The consequences of the council's position for mothers and children in New Brunswick, for example, can be appreciated by the following description of poor-relief practices in Moncton, New Brunswick, in 1938: 'The only relief policy that can be stated as such appears to be – "Get by with giving the least possible relief and give it with the implication that it will not be repeated." ... Apparently the amount for food varies from a $2.00 order for one week for a family of two, up to a maximum of $4.00 a week for the largest families.'[37]

Evaluating the Program

The focus of mothers' pensions (or mothers' allowances as they were called in some, and eventually all, provinces) was one of concern for dependent children. 'This being the case,' wrote A.E. Grauer in 1939, 'some of the differences between provinces regarding qualifications for allowances are beside the point as they hinge upon the condition of a parent when obviously the need of the child is the same regardless of technicalities relating to the parent.'[38] British Columbia's program, as an example, covered, among other situations, a mother whose husband was in a tuberculosis sanatorium, a mental hospital, a prison, or was totally incapacitated. Ontario's legislation was similar, but in Nova Scotia none of these situations was recognized.

Residence requirements varied from province to province, ranging from no specific period of time in Alberta, one year in Saskatchewan, two years in Ontario and Manitoba, three years in British Columbia, New Brunswick, Nova Scotia, and Prince Edward Island, and five years in Quebec.

Other eligibility requirements that served to exclude rather than include mothers and children were the mother's nationality, her character, and the amount of personal and real property she owned. In British Columbia an applicant in 1920 had to be a British subject. Even being born in British Columbia did not insure coverage; Native mothers were excluded,[39] and if a woman married an alien she lost her citizenship. An actual case illustrates how such eligibility requirements prevented otherwise eligible families from receiving help: 'In 1926 Mrs. M. married an American, had two children by him and was subsequently deserted. Mrs. M. was denied entry into the United States as she was classified as a Canadian. She was therefore without a country having lost her Canadian citizenship through marriage. She was ineligible for the mothers' pension as she was not a British subject. Being without funds when her husband deserted her this woman had to depend on charity for an existence.'[40]

Applicants for mothers' pension had to be of good character – a throwback to poor law concerns about distinguishing between worthy and unworthy applicants. It was common practice to require the applicant to furnish two letters of reference, and other inquiries would be made as to her standing in the community. This provision frequently disqualified needy mothers, as the following case illustrates:

A woman with three children, one of whom was crippled, was granted a pension after the death of her husband. Three years later she remarried and her pension ceased forthwith. Although she had married her second husband in good faith, it turned out to be a bigamous union. Her second husband was jailed and on his release disappeared from the scene. With no means of support, the woman reapplied for a mothers' pension but was told that in view of her bigamous marriage she was not a 'fit and proper person' to receive a pension.[41]

The most difficult eligibility test of all was the means test. In British Columbia an applicant was required to have less than $500 in cash or liquid assets and real property valued at less than $1,500. Other provinces were more lenient in this respect.[42]

Not only did the degree of inclusiveness vary from one province to another, but substantial differences prevailed in the allowances provided, differences that could not be defended by reference to variations in the cost of living from one region to another. The adequacy of allowances was seldom sufficient to raise the family above the poverty level. At the outbreak of the Second World War, it was found that mothers' allowances compared unfavourably in amount to the allowances granted to wives and children of men in the armed forces (see Table 5.1).

The federal government's allowances for servicemen's dependants provided a defensible standard of living based on a cost of living study conducted by the Toronto Welfare Council.[43] It is of interest to note that the rationale for providing soldiers' dependants with an adequate living allowance (above subsistence but requiring economy in budgeting) was 'to save the soldier from financial anxiety and relieve him, if possible, from home worries so that he might be an efficient fighting man.'[44]

The Public Assistance Method

It has long been argued that the public assistance method saves tax dollars by limiting aid to those who can demonstrate need, and that greater flexibility is possible because benefits can be tailored to individual circumstances. However, these advantages must be weighed against the disadvantage of the searching inquiry into personal affairs with the risk of a serious invasion of personal privacy, which precedes the granting of help and may even accompany receipt of it. Moreover, the flexibility of public assistance is attenuated when, as was common to mothers' allowances, maximum payments per family, regardless of the number of children, are laid down in the legislation.[45] When a searching inquiry into an applicant's financial situation is coupled with meagrely defined maximum allowances (a consequence of the less eligibility principle), the suspicion is raised that the inquiry is not, whatever welfare administrators may believe, an operation designed to assist

Table 5.1

Comparison of mothers' allowances with armed forces allowances, 1943

Armed forces allowances for mother and one child (per month)	Mothers' allowances for mother and one child (per month)						
	BC	AB	SK	MB	ON	PQ	NS
$67.00	$42.50	$47.50 or $45.00[a]	$10.00	$33.00	$35.00[b]	$25.00[c]	$15.00[d]

[a] Depending on the age of the children.
[b] $35 paid in cities; $30 in towns; and $25 in rural areas.
[c] $25 paid in cities; $20 in towns; and $15 in rural areas.
[d] This is a minimum figure. An individual budget was calculated in each case, but with a maximum of $80.

Source: L.C. Marsh, *Report on Social Security for Canada* (Ottawa 1943), 25.

the applicant but rather to disqualify the individual or family by discovering hidden resources or other impediments to eligibility for benefits.

The most serious drawback to the public assistance method, however, is that the applicant approaches the welfare authorities as a *supplicant* for help rather than as a *claimant* for benefits. The weakness of this position is demonstrated by the control that may be exerted over the recipient's life by welfare administrators as a condition of the receipt of benefits. The report by the Canadian Council on Child and Family Welfare on the administration of mothers' pensions in British Columbia in 1931 recommended the following intrusions into the personal lives and autonomy of the program's recipients:

(a) Families receiving allowances may not move from a city to a rural area or from a rural area to a city without the written consent of the administration.

(b) No male boarders other than members of the beneficiary's immediate family shall be allowed in the home of a mother under allowance.

(c) That as a condition of granting or continuing the allowance in the case where the father is incapacitated that they may be required to accept institutional care, where the cause of the disability is a disease which is or is likely to be a menace or danger to the health of the children in the home.[46]

It is significant that social workers are not generally employed to administer social insurance benefits, war pensions, or benefits under Canada's more recent universal programs. This is not to say that some recipients of other types of income maintenance programs, or any Canadian, could not benefit from the help of a skilled social worker. The services of a social worker might be made available on the request of the recipients rather than imposed upon them when their only need is for financial assistance.

Programs that depend on provincial initiative have inevitably produced an uneven development of services across the country. The mothers' pension movement resulted in five provinces passing legislation by 1920. In Nova Scotia and New Brunswick, commissions were established to investigate the issue. The Nova Scotia commission, established in 1919, came to the conclusion in 1920 that it could not reliably estimate the costs involved and, in effect, recommended no action be taken. This ended the matter until the 1930s, when the Depression forced the province to help its municipalities with local relief costs. To this end, a limited program of mothers' allowances was passed in 1930 with the province carrying 100 per cent of the costs. The New Brunswick commission recommended a mothers' allowances act early in the 1920s, but no action was taken until 1930, when an act was passed but not implemented. It was finally brought into operation in 1943. Prince Edward Island did not bring in a Mothers' Allowance Act until 1 July 1949.

Quebec did not provide a system of mothers' allowances until 1937, despite repeated petitions on the subject and the recommendation of a provincial royal commission on social insurance (1930-3). The Taschereau regime (1920-36) 'eschewed all forms of state intervention,' and it was left to the Union Nationale Party under Maurice Duplessis, which toppled Taschereau, to bring in legislation, the cost of which was carried entirely by the province.[47]

The provincial programs of financial assistance to needy mothers that developed in Canada during the First World War and that were adopted in five provinces within the space of four years (1916-20) were the first modern public assistance[48] programs in Canada. They represented a significant departure from traditional poor-relief practices that had existed from colonial times. For one category of dependent poor, a new social minimum had been established. Canadians from Ontario to British Columbia by 1920 had decided that the haphazard system of municipal and private charity would no longer suffice for mothers with dependent children. Here, for the first time, was a continuing program of financial aid to one segment of the poor, administered and financed by the provincial government, although some provinces did require a municipal contribution.[49]

These programs represented a successful attack on the traditional idea that welfare concerns were purely local in character and therefore the responsibility of municipalities or local charity. They also questioned the conventional wisdom that only the private charity organization was capable of doing family and child welfare work. The status of public welfare was raised by the development of mothers' pensions from an ad hoc, poorly administered function of government to a point where specially trained staff were recruited and a centralized system of administration was developed with money appropriated from provincial treasuries to pay for the program. With improved, centralized administration, there was a reduction in the capricious discretionary power of local officials, which had characterized so much of poor-relief administration up to this time.

6

The 1920s:
No Priorities for Welfare

The 1920s began with a short, sharp recession in 1921 and 1922 and ended with the onset of the longest and most catastrophic economic depression in Canada's history. The time between, however, was one of remarkable economic growth and prosperity for all of Canada except the Maritimes.[1] The age of steel and steam, which had helped to open the west in the prewar era, now gave way to the age of alloys, to hydroelectric power, and to the internal combustion engine. These technological advances promoted the development of Canada's mineral wealth, notably in the Pre-Cambrian Shield, where rich deposits of mineral ore and hydroelectric resources lay side by side. Once developed, the hydroelectric plants enabled vast new areas of forest to be exploited by the pulp and paper industry. Western wheat production increased to meet the demands of war-ravaged Europe, and a series of bumper crops, combined with good prices and lowered production costs, brought prosperity to the prairie provinces, while British Columbia's market for minerals and lumber expanded with the opening of the Panama Canal.

The development of the automobile produced new jobs and large capital investment in factories, repair and service facilities, the petroleum industry, and in road building. There was a vast increase in public expenditure on utilities electrical systems, telephones (government operated in the three prairie provinces), water and sewage systems, as well as on public buildings of various kinds. All of the services that had been forestalled by the war's emergency were now being initiated.

The levels of government that carried most of the weight of public expenditure on services were the provinces and their municipalities. The federal government, after leading the country through the war, now appeared reluctant to take on any more new commitments or to offer the leadership that had characterized it in the prewar era. The national goals that the dominion government had set for itself – the opening and settlement of the west, the uniting of the country by the transcontinental railways – had been accomplished. Furthermore, the demands on government for roads, public utilities, educational facilities, institutions, and services were clearly the responsibility of the provinces by the terms of the British North America Act. The federal government offered some help to new provincial undertakings through conditional grants[2] – provincial employment services, a program of venereal disease control, aid to technical and agricultural education, and highway construction were examples of such joint undertakings. However, the Liberal government under Mackenzie King had terminated most of these grants by the end of the 1920s. The policy of the federal government during this time was, according to Donald Creighton, 'to avoid new commitments, reduce the burden of old obligations and return, as far as possible, to pre-war finance.'[3]

The vacuum created by the cautious federal attitude was filled by the provincial governments who 'plunged eagerly into a wide range of government activities' buoyed up by new and lucrative sources of tax funds such as motor licences, gasoline tax, and liquor taxes. Between 1921 and 1930 public welfare expenditures for all governments rose 130 per cent, and three-fourths of this expenditure was borne by the provinces and municipalities.[4] Despite the rise in expenditure on public welfare, less than one-fifth of provincial-municipal revenues was being spent on these vital areas.

This neglect was all the more critical because the much vaunted prosperity of the 1920s was, for many Canadians, perhaps a majority, an illusion. In 1925 the Canadian Brotherhood of Railroad Employees calculated the price of a budget for a family of five that would maintain health and decency. The average cost, based on prices in ten Canadian cities, was $2,203.37. The average wage rate in the same year was $1,440 for all classes of labour, although this figure did not take account of losses as the result of unemployment, accidents, strikes, or other causes. Wages in principal occupations in 1925 varied from $1,000 to $2,000 in the building trades; from $950 to $1,400 for civic employees; $700 to $1,600 for factory workers; and from $900 to $2,500 (a small group) for railroad workers.[5] A study prepared in the 1930s concluded that in 1929, the last year of prosperous times prior to the Depression, a majority of Canadians were living below a bare standard of decent livelihood.[6] A more recent analysis of working-class incomes in Montreal in the late 1920s found that, even at the peak of prosperity at the end of the decade, the average income for adult male workers in occupations that accounted for at least 67 per cent of the labour force fell well below the minimum income ($1,590) required to support an average family.[7]

Agendas for Change
During the war, when the enormity of the price being paid in lives and human misery penetrated the clouds of patriotic fervour that had enveloped the country in 1914, a demand arose for a better world once peace was achieved. Farmers' groups, organized labour, women's organizations, the churches,

business and industry, politicians and political parties, governmental commissions, and international bodies contributed their agendas for change.[8]

Farmers issued their New National Policy in 1918, aimed chiefly at dismantling Canada's system of protective tariffs.[9] Organized labour, badly split between its left- and right-wing factions, endorsed socialism, industrial unionism, and the six-hour day[10] on the one hand, or, on the other, concerned itself primarily with the bread and butter issues of trade unionism – wages, working conditions, and the acceptance by management of collective bargaining.[11] The Social Service Council, the reforming arm of Protestantism in Canada, continued to promote a program of social reform in the tradition of the social gospel movement. In 1918 the council quoted, with approval, the postwar agenda of the British Labour Party with its call for an assured national minimum of livelihood for all.[12]

The war 'energized and united women as never before.'[13] Where formerly women had to push themselves forward to gain a foothold in many areas of society, the war meant that their help was 'suddenly required everywhere.' Encouraged by this acceptance and by their success in winning the vote in six provinces and federally by 1918, women's groups campaigned for an end to sexual stereotyping and discrimination.[14]

In 1919 the Liberal Party held a convention in Ottawa to pick a successor to Sir Wilfrid Laurier and to develop a party platform in preparation for the next federal election. A platform was adopted, 'so forward-looking in its proposals that some would not be implemented for twenty-five years,'[15] and a new leader, W.L. Mackenzie King, was chosen. The resolution on labour and industry passed at the convention contained the following statement on the party's social security goals: 'So far as may be practicable having regard for Canada's financial position, an adequate system of social insurance against unemployment, sickness, dependence in old age, and other disability which would include old age pensions, widows' pensions, and maternity benefits, should be instituted by the Federal Government in conjunction with the Governments of the several provinces.'[16]

Mackenzie King had contributed his ideas for a new postwar society in his book *Industry and Humanity,* published in 1918. King was to claim in later life that his book contained the blueprint for the social security provisions that Canada eventually adopted. His book does lay out the rationale for a system of social insurance protection against the common risks to income interruption, and he supported the British Labour Party's concept of a national minimum. However, King was assailed with doubts as to the possible adverse effects of social security protection on the habits of thrift and industry.[17] King's book reveals that he could intellectualize about the need for social security protection, but he fails to convey any sense of commitment.

On the international scene, the International Labour Organization, established in 1919 as a companion body to the League of Nations, had as two of its chief goals the reduction of poverty and human distress and the improvement of working and living conditions in all countries of the world. It began by formulating universal standards in working and related conditions to which member nations were expected to subscribe (one of its first efforts involved the eight-hour day). It soon became a clearinghouse for information and research in the labour field, including social security programs.

Royal Commission on Industrial Relations, 1919

The year 1919 brought widespread labour unrest, as a result of rapid inflation in the cost of living (see Figure 6.1), which wages and rising levels of unemployment with the scaling down of the wartime economy aggravated by demobilization. Employer opposition to unions stiffened with the rise in unemployment; strikes and lockouts were numerous and widespread. The federal government, in April 1919, established a Royal Commission on Industrial Relations to inquire into labour unrest. The commission's report arrived on the government's desk just as the most momentous labour dispute in Canadian labour history, the Winnipeg General Strike, was coming to an end.

Figure 6.1

Annual average percentage change in the consumer price index, 1915-25

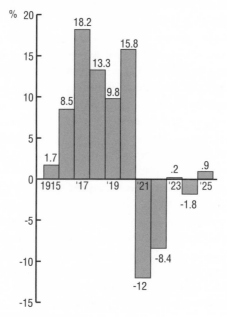

Source: Statistics Canada (see Appendix Table A2).

The commission, which had travelled from coast to coast to hear submissions from interested parties, identified the chief causes of social unrest in Canada as unemployment and the fear of unemployment; the high cost of living in relation to wages and the desire of the worker for a larger share of the product of his labour; the desire for shorter hours of labour; the denial of the right to organize and the refusal to recognize unions; lack of confidence in constituted government; insufficient and poor housing; restrictions upon the freedom of speech and press; ostentatious display of wealth; and the lack of equal educational opportunities.[18]

The commission's recommendations, conservative but not reactionary, were another contribution to the ferment for social change. The commission recommended the regulation of public works to relieve unemployment and to help build housing; the payment of a living wage; an eight-hour day and a weekly day of rest; the right to bargain collectively; the establishment of industrial councils; the fixing of minimum wages for women, girls, and unskilled labour; better educational opportunities; and state insurance against unemployment, sickness, disability, and old age. The commission was not unanimous in its recommendations. Two commissioners contended, with reference to the social security recommendations, that existing local institutions and charities were capable of meeting what little poverty existed in Canada and that old age pensions or unemployment insurance 'might seriously affect the ambition of the worker.' Fifteen years later, in the throes of the Depression, the irony of such views would be vividly demonstrated.

The federal government convened a meeting of management, labour, and representatives of the general public in September 1919 to consider the recommendations of the royal commission. At this meeting the postwar agenda of business and industry was revealed as a stand-pat position. Employers refused to make any concession on two of the most important questions from labour's standpoint – collective bargaining and the eight-hour day. The social security recommendations were dealt with innocuously by a recommendation that a 'Board or Boards, be appointed to enquire into the subjects of State Insurance.'[19]

All the talking and planning on 'reconstruction,' on 'making Canada a home fit for heroes,' produced infinitesimal results.[20] Infinitesimal, that is, when contrasted with the hopes and aspirations of groups such as the Methodist General Conference of 1918, which called for an end to the commercial and industrial methods based on individualism and competition and a transference of 'the whole economic life from a basis of competition and profits to one of cooperation and service.'[21]

Following the war, the mood in Canada was a desire to 'get back to normal' (a sharp contrast to the feeling that was to prevail at the end of the Second World War). This conservative reaction, fuelled by the Russian

Revolution and, for some, its Canadian counterpart, the Winnipeg General Strike, was mirrored in the federal government's failure to utilize the sense of national purpose that had developed during the war to carry forward with postwar reconstruction. The federal election of 1921, which produced a Liberal minority government under Mackenzie King, further weakened any resolve the government might have had to deal with national problems. Instead, the government relaxed most of its wartime powers and turned the country's domestic problems over to the provinces, their municipalities, and the marketplace.

Social Reform in the 1920s

Some of the social reform movements that were building prior to the war were checked – the social gospel movement and the urban reform movement both languished in the 1920s – while other movements were stimulated by the war. As a result of the large number of psychiatric casualties in the armed forces, for example, interest in mental health and the care of the mentally ill received a new impetus,[22] as did the care and treatment of blindness.[23] The high percentage of Canadians found unfit for military duty, coupled with the death of over 60,000 young Canadians in France, helped to promote a greater interest in health matters generally and in child welfare in particular.[24] A federal Department of Health was established in 1919, federal grants-in-aid were offered to the provinces to combat venereal disease, and the Canadian Council on Child Welfare was formed in 1920.

   In the social welfare field, the profession of social work, emerging out of the liberal individualism of private charitable agency values and practices, was, generally speaking, an additional conservative force at this time.[25] The social gospel movement, which had had strong links with private charitable agencies before the war, found its missionary zeal in social reform out of step with the increasing professionalism of social work. Although the break was not an abrupt one, the Protestant churches and other groups that had pushed for broad programs of social reform through the Social Service Council separated from 'professional' social work, and the social reform element in Canadian life was thereby diminished and weakened.

   Five risks to the economic security of the individual and family generated attention in the 1920s. Only two, retirement or old age and low wage rates, resulted in a program of any consequence; two risks, unemployment and family size, foundered on the rocks of conventional wisdom. The fifth, housing costs, resulted in a limited program that was characterized by insufficient planning, generally poor administration, and conflicting goals.

Unemployment: No Longer a Novelty

As the pace of industrialization quickened in Canada just prior to the 1900s, unemployment 'ceased to be a novelty.'[26] Business recessions had occurred from 1873 to 1879, 1884 to 1887, 1893 to 1896, and again from 1914 to 1915. People began to see that unemployment, even in a new and developing country, was caused by forces beyond the individual's control. This view clashed with the older notion, more appropriate to a rural, preindustrial Canada, that unemployment was evidence of an unwillingness to work. In the 1890s a Canadian speaking to a meeting of the National Conference on Charities and Correction revealed this dichotomy of view when she referred to that 'perplexing mass of poverty that is, to so great an extent, the result of scarcity of work, but also too often of shiftlessness, improvidence, laziness and intemperance.'[27] In the 1890s there was little perception that one might cause the other.

It was not until the recession of 1914-15 that an official inquiry into the causes and possible remedies of recurring unemployment was launched in Canada by the province of Ontario.[28] This inquiry noted that 'personal causes of unemployment have received, heretofore, a disproportionate amount of attention,' and went on to argue for a system of public works during recessions; the appointment of a Provincial Labour Commission to administer a system of free public employment bureaus and to control private employment offices, where the commission found evidence of chicanery; the development of vocational training and guidance; the extension of the school-leaving age; and the need to develop an adequate system of statistics on the extent and nature of unemployment. With regard to the problem of income maintenance for the unemployed, the commissioners took a more conservative view and recommended that voluntary associations, generally trade unions, should receive some government assistance and encouragement to operate their own unemployment benefit scheme for their members. For workers who were not fortunate enough to have this type of protection (and this was the overwhelming majority), a better coordination of charitable activities was recommended. No criticism was made of the degrading conditions that accompanied the receipt of municipal poor relief. The British system of unemployment insurance that began in 1911 was studied by the commissioners, but they considered that a compulsory system of state insurance would be inadvisable owing to the absence of a government-operated chain of employment bureaus and the lack of necessary statistical data on which to assess the probable degree of risk and its resulting cost.

The wartime boom served to postpone action on the unemployment question until 1918, when the federal government passed the Labour Coordination Act by which the senior level of government, through conditional grants, encouraged the establishment of public employment bureaus. This measure was brought about by the imminent demobilization of the army and the expected flood of job applicants on the labour market. It also reflected the forlorn hope that the risk of unemployment could be appreciably minimized by organizing the labour market through the use of employment bureaus.

In 1919 the National Industrial Conference had recommended that consideration be given to the advisability of state insurance against unemployment, as well as sickness, invalidity, old age, and widowhood. The government's only immediate response was to announce in the 1921 Speech from the Throne that the Department of Labour was surveying systems of unemployment insurance and old age pensions.[29]

The recession of 1920-1 raised the issue of unemployment relief again. The severity of the unemployment problem at this time, coupled with the fact that many of its victims were returned soldiers and workers released from war industry jobs, brought the federal government reluctantly into the picture. The Conservative government authorized federal relief grants to the provinces in 1921 for both public works and direct relief. In making these grants, the federal government emphasized that it was under no constitutional obligation to do so. 'Unemployment relief,' the federal government stated, 'always has been and must necessarily continue to be, primarily a municipal responsibility, and in the second instance the responsibility of the province.'[30] When the Liberal government took office later that year, it assumed the same stance in relation to aiding the provinces with the costs of unemployment, stating: 'The Minister concurs in the view that unemployment relief is fundamentally a municipal and provincial responsibility; that the abnormal economic and industrial conditions now existing and arising in a measure out of the late war alone afford justification for action on the part of federal authorities.'

Once again the economic recovery that took place in 1923 and that led into a buoyant economic climate until the crash of 1929 forestalled any permanent arrangements for meeting the income needs of the unemployed, although federal aid for unemployment relief amounting to one-third of the cost, with the provinces and municipalities sharing the balance, continued each year during the 1920s except for 1925 and 1928. So limited was the public welfare administrative structure in Canada at this time (only Manitoba and Ontario had departments of public welfare by 1928) that federal aid was frequently disbursed by private agencies. Assistance was given in kind, rarely in cash, and questions of adequacy were only just beginning to be raised.

The provinces, taking their cue from the federal position, tended to delegate responsibility for unemployment relief to their municipalities. An observer of public welfare in Ontario at the end of the 1920s noted that 'unemployment relief on the part of the Ontario government is regarded as an extraordinary measure, not a permanent policy, and is available only in times of special stress.'[31]

With the concept of local responsibility for unemployment relief being trumpeted from Ottawa and the provincial capitals, there was little effective demand for a reallocation of responsibilities or for permanent measures to protect the unemployed. Those who argued for plans to meet future unemployment crises, as one social worker noted, 'were unpopular indeed.'[32]

This reluctance to come to grips with the effects of unemployment can be traced in part to prevailing notions about the nature of unemployment and its remedies. It was held by some that unemployment was not a serious problem in Canada, but rather the problem was one of unequal distribution of labour. Hence, the emphasis was on establishing public employment offices to direct men and women to available jobs. It was still commonly argued that public provision to relieve the poverty of the unemployed would destroy their incentive. A representative of the Canadian Manufacturers' Association told a parliamentary committee investigating unemployment, sickness, and disability insurance in 1928 that 'It is infinitely preferable that a man who is out of work should bestir himself and look for a new job, rather than sit down and twirl his hands and look for unemployment relief.'[33] Another time-honoured argument in support of the status quo was the contention that wages were sufficiently high in the prosperous 1920s to permit a thrifty man to put aside something as protection against a spell of unemployment.

The parliamentary committee reported that unemployment insurance was an inevitable development, and it endorsed the principle of a compulsory, contributory plan similar to that recommended nearly a decade earlier by the Royal Commission on Industrial Relations (1919). The report noted that legal opinion had established that responsibility for such legislation, under the terms of the BNA Act, rested with the provinces but that this would not prevent the dominion government from contributing a grant-in-aid in support of a provincial scheme. It was recommended that the matter be referred to the provinces for action. But events and attitudes ruled otherwise. The general prosperity of the late 1920s, the conventional attitudes concerning unemployment and its remedies, and the aggressive touting of the virtues of free enterprise whenever the topic of social insurance was raised obscured the need for some permanent system of income protection against unemployment.

Minimum Wage Legislation

Provincial minimum wage legislation developed in Canada toward the close of the First World War and during the 1920s. The seemingly rapid adoption of this principle came about because of the example set by other British dominions, Australia specifically, and by certain American states – Massachusetts, Oregon, and California.[34] It was also pushed by Canadian labour unions, whose strength increased from 143,000 in 1915 to 378,000 in 1919.[35] The movement gained some support from those employers who were prepared to pay a fair wage and who feared the competition from business rivals who reduced their production costs by paying low wages.

Beginning in 1918, minimum wage legislation was directed at the most exploited group in the labour force – women and girls. Men were expected to bargain with their employers, but later amendments to these provincial acts included male employees within the scope of minimum wage laws.[36]

Minimum wage legislation, an expression of the social minimum concept, did little to assure that workers would be lifted out of poverty. The minimum wage structure was related to a bare subsistence living for a worker and a family of four or five in the case of a male employee, and for a single person with no dependants in the case of a female employee. The history of the Ontario minimum wage legislation of 1920 illustrates how minimal the standard was. The goal of the Ontario legislation was that the minimum wage should provide a 'living wage.' A budget for a single, independent woman was established for the city of Toronto; some small variations were allowed in other centres in Ontario depending upon the size of the community. The budget for Toronto was set at $653.25 per annum – which amounted to $12.56 per week.[37] This contrasts with a minimum cost of living budget prepared by the Dominion Civil Service Commission in 1919 based on studies of prices conducted by the Department of Labour and on similar studies made in the United States. The Civil Service Commission's minimum budget for a person without dependants was $903 per annum or over $17 per week.[38]

Even with minimum wage legislation, it was possible for employers to evade the law by such stratagems as paying the minimum wage but requiring longer hours of work,[39] or by paying male employees at less than the minimum wage required for females. The lack of adequate inspection to enforce the law made evasion comparatively easy. With the important exceptions of mothers' pensions and old age pensions, minimum wage legislation was the sole evidence of a welfare state in Canada in the 1920s.

Old Age Pensions

Old age pensions were the chief contribution to modern income maintenance legislation in Canada made during the 1920s. The agitation for old age pensions, as noted in Chapter 3, began early in the twentieth century with the issue being raised in the House of Commons for the first time in 1906. Between 1908 and 1914 two special select committees of the House of Commons were appointed to consider the subject, with no decisive recommendations resulting. The issue was briefly debated at the beginning of the war when the question of soldiers' pensions was being considered. Labour leaders called for pensions for the 'soldiers of industry,' but no action was taken. The Canadian response, as discussed in Chapter 3, was to establish a system of government annuities.

The agitation for an old age pension scheme continued despite the passage of the Government Annuities Act of 1908, which of course could do nothing at all for those already old and in need. The Liberal convention of 1919 promised to take action on old age pensions. The Trades and Labour Congress of Canada at its 1921 convention called for old age pensions, unemployment insurance, and sickness and disability insurance. The time seemed propitious for legislation to be enacted. However, no action was forthcoming from the government, a result, in part, of the federal emphasis upon retrenchment of public expenditure at the war's end, until the House of Commons appointed a special committee in 1924 to investigate a system of old age pensions for Canada.[40] The committee reported in 1925 and recommended a non-contributory scheme of $20 per month for persons aged seventy years or older, subject to a strict means test, with costs to be shared equally between the provinces and the federal government. Reading the proceedings of the committee's meetings, it is evident that considerations of cost overshadowed their deliberations. In those pre-Keynesian days, the federal government, faced with heavy debt charges incurred by the war as well as a hitherto unprecedented bill for veterans' pensions and allowances, was reluctant to commit itself to any new and expensive programs. Setting the pensionable age at seventy rather than at sixty-five, as was common in other English-speaking countries, and fixing the maximum pension at $20 per month rather than at a suggested and more defensible figure of $30 or even $40 per month were cases in point.[41] The lack of statistical data on income distribution in Canada permitted the committee to indulge in the fantasy of viewing the pension as a supplement to other savings rather than an adequate pension in itself.[42]

Why was a contributory plan not considered? Bryden suggests that the administrative complexities of such a plan seemed insurmountable in 1924.[43] Mackenzie King put forward additional objections to a contributory program when he pointed out that such a plan would not help the present generation of old people. He went on to describe the proposed pension bill as 'the first necessary step to bring about that larger measure of contributory social insurance which is one of the great needs of our time.'[44] He was also aware that a contributory scheme launched by the Dominion alone would require a constitutional amendment – a difficult hurdle in view of hostility to the plan expressed from Quebec sources.[45] Of the two options facing Canada in 1925 – the non-contributory type of plan and the contributory or social insurance type – the former promised to raise fewer political and social hackles than the latter. Public opinion was generally in favour of pensions for the elderly poor at this time, but the concept of social insurance was alien to many. Canada was neighbour to the greatest exponent of free enterprise in the world, and talk of social insurance was met with the standard fears: it would impair the individual's sense of thrift; it would penalize industry and raise the price of manufactured goods; and it would build a large government bureaucracy that could not be expected to operate without waste and inefficiency.[46]

Despite the recommendations of the parliamentary committee in 1925, there was no mention of old age pension legislation in the speech from the throne on 8 January 1926. Nor was there any indication that the subject had been considered by the government. The only province that showed real interest in the special committee's recommendations was British Columbia. The spokespersons for other provinces either expressed perfunctory interest or were hostile to what they considered federal interference in a provincial concern.

But the issue was raised with determination by two Labour members from Winnipeg, J.S. Woodsworth and A.A. Heaps, at a time when King was desperately trying to hang on to power following the 1925 federal election that left the Liberals with only 99 seats in a 245-seat Commons.[47] King had to count on the support of the 24 Progressives, which could not always be relied upon, 4 Independents, and the 2 Labour members to counter the 116 Conservatives. Woodsworth and Heaps sent identical letters to King and the Conservative leader Arthur Meighen asking whether they had plans for the current session with respect to provision for the unemployed and old age pensions. Meighen's reply was noncommittal, but King, anxious for legislative allies, arranged to draft an old age pensions bill immediately. The bill was introduced, and the measure, which closely followed the recommendations of the 1925 committee's report, was passed without strenuous debate. The Senate, on the other hand, not having to face the electorate and holding more traditional views, turned the measure back, claiming that such pensions were a provincial responsibility, and expressed fears for the 'solidarity of family ties' if the care of the elderly were to be assumed by the state. The numbers of young men who had been killed or disabled in the war, thereby robbing some of the aged of family members upon whom to depend, weakened this argument, and some of the advocates did not fail to point this out. However, the measure was reintroduced the next year in response to continued public pressure, Liberal senators were brought into line by party whips, and the measure became law.

Under the provisions of the Old Age Pensions Act of 1927, the dominion government agreed to reimburse each province participating in the scheme to the extent of one-half of the provincial expenditure for old age pensions. The dominion legislation laid down the standards of eligibility for pensions, the maximum amounts of pension payable, and residence requirements. However, there was sufficient ambiguity in the wording of the regulations to permit provincial interpretation, which led to some marked differences in the administration of the act from one province to another. By extending help in the form of conditional grants, the federal government was able to sidestep the constitutional issue that would have arisen if the Dominion had itself embarked upon the administration of a means-tested program in each province.[48]

British Columbia was the first province to pass the enabling legislation and signed its agreement with the dominion government in September 1927; by 1929 the five provinces west of Quebec were participating. The act was amended in 1931 by the Conservatives under R.B. Bennett to increase the dominion contribution from 50 to 75 per cent of the cost of pensions (excluding administrative costs), and by 1936 the remainder of the provinces and the Northwest Territories were taking part in the scheme.[49]

Thus, it took nine years for the old age pension system to become national in character. But it 'was the first area of social need that became politically attractive at the national level.'[50] It was also the dominion government's first major entry into the field of social welfare on other than an emergency basis. A significant aspect of the act was its departure from traditional poor law practice of restricting help to indigents. Instead, the act permitted pensions to be paid to old people whose yearly income was less than a stipulated amount ($365 a year or below); pension and outside income combined could not exceed this amount. This meant that the eligibility procedure centred on a 'means test' rather than on an exhaustive examination of the applicant's needs, means, and even lifestyle, a procedure that was the sine qua non of traditional welfare administration. This new approach has been termed a type of 'income-conditioned pension,' and its introduction at this time advanced the concept of pensions as a right and decreased the feelings of dependency on the part of the applicant.[51]

Evaluating the Old Age Pensions Act of 1927

The Old Age Pensions Act remained in operation from 1927 to 1952, when new legislation was introduced. During its years of operation, the program's inclusiveness and adequacy were unduly limited by the rules and regulations governing eligibility. Leonard Marsh's review of Canada's social security system in 1942 noted the following administrative practices that either made it difficult for old people to qualify for a pension or prevented them from receiving the maximum pension:

(a) The requirement that a recipient be a British subject;

(b) The residence requirements, both federal and provincial;

(c) Means testing in terms of the applicant's personal income, personal property qualifications, and even the assumption of income from property when in fact such income did not exist;

(d) The principle 'zealously adhered to' in certain provinces of the responsibility of children for the maintenance of their elderly parents to the point of assuming that income was actually forthcoming from children even in cases where it was not;

(e) The scaling down of allowances below the amount permissible by the statute on the grounds that the pensioner did not require even that amount of pension.[52]

The equity of the act was more apparent than real. Ostensibly each province was subject to the same regulations, and an interprovincial board was set up to promote as much uniformity in the administration of the act as possible. However, equity was compromised by the fact that the original regulations were drafted in a way that placed 'extensive discretion' in the hands of provincial pension authorities. Added to this, the federal government had no authority to supervise the administration of provincial pension schemes other than to audit provincial claims for the federal share of pension costs.

Even in such apparently straightforward matters as determination of age and residence there was little uniformity. But it was in the critical area of the means test that the greatest attrition of the principle of equity occurred. Variations were found from province to province as to what income would be excluded for the purpose of calculating the pension; the treatment of earnings, contributions from children, and regulations dealing with real and personal property and recoveries from estates varied. Attempts to rectify this situation in 1937 by the Inter-Provincial Board only resulted in a more restrictive and rigid interpretation of the act. It was not until the regulations were revised in 1947 and 1948 that a better balance was struck between national uniformity and flexibility.[53]

The provision of an appeals procedure for pensioners who felt they had been unjustly dealt with was not provided for in the act and regulations. This matter was left entirely to the provinces, and the most common method of handling this issue was to make provincial pension authorities the final court of review, thereby excluding the law courts from the appeal process. Pensioners were permitted to appeal the handling of their case to the Pension Board either on their own or with the assistance of a friend. But as the essential element of an appeal procedure is that appeals must be heard by an independent and disinterested body, the appeals system was a sham. Joseph Laycock is right in observing that a system of 'due process' would have enhanced the notion of a pension as a right.[54]

With regard to the issue of administrative efficiency, Laycock argues that the administration of social services in Canada 'has usually been maintained at a higher level when services have been under the full control of either federal or provincial governments.' Much has been written on the administrative difficulties of divided jurisdiction in Canadian federal-provincial relations:

The Rowell-Sirois Commission was keenly aware of the administrative problems of conditional grants. Hesitations and delays in implementing public policies are inevitable when decisions either of a broad or of a routine nature can be made only with the agreement of two levels of government. No adequate techniques for resolving conflicts between two levels of government are available, and disputes which can be expeditiously resolved at relatively junior levels if the matters were the exclusive concern of one government may complicate the work of officials of senior appointment or Cabinet ranks. The procedural burdens, particularly those imposed on auditing officials, are considerable.[55]

The problems of divided jurisdiction aside, administrative problems were exacerbated by the failure of the federal government to share in the costs of administration. The cost-sharing agreement applied to the costs of pensions alone. This same penurious attitude was passed on by provincial authorities toward their municipalities, where much of the processing of applications and other routine pension administration were carried out.

The lack of concern for administrative efficiency was mirrored in personnel practices by provincial pension authorities. In the early years of the scheme, staff selection was largely a matter of political patronage. It follows, of course, that few standards were set as to education or training for work in the pension field. High turnover of staff, low pay, and lack of job security characterized the early years of the program's administration. As the program developed, however, the need for some standards in staff selection and in personnel practices became obvious. Provinces such as British Columbia led the way by hiring professional social workers as field workers.

The three most notable achievements of Canada's first old age pension scheme (as analyzed by Laycock) were

(1) Despite the limitations imposed on nationwide social security planning by the BNA Act, the Old Age Pensions Act of 1927 achieved national coverage by 1936.

(2) There was a strong element of national uniformity notwithstanding the variations in the interpretation of the act from one province to another. The national coverage and the elements of national uniformity focused the interest in pensions on the national capital and encouraged Canadians to see social security issues as national rather than purely local concerns.

(3) The pension scheme, by virtue of the federal-provincial agreements (and the difficulty in altering the agreements by either party), achieved a degree of stability from the beginning that enhanced the program's worth, particularly during the Depression of the 1930s when many government programs had to be severely curtailed.

Family Allowances

The first indication of official interest in family allowances in Canada occurred when the subject was investigated by a parliamentary committee of the federal government in 1929.[56] Conflicting evidence was presented to the committee. The chief proponent of family allowances, Father Leon Lebel, SJ, of Quebec, already known in that province for his interest in the subject, argued that the inadequacy of the average industrial wage was leading to a drop in the birthrate and to a loss of population by emigration to the United States. Because of the importance of children as future citizens and members of the labour force, a voluntary system of family allowances, paid by employers and modelled upon the French system, should be instituted. This would make it possible for couples to have larger families and would discourage emigration. His chief opponent was Charlotte Whitton, executive director of the Canadian Council on Child and Family Welfare, who said that passage of such a piece of legislation was an admission that wages in Canada were substandard and could not be improved. Her objections did not end there. She felt that parental responsibility would be undermined and that the cost of the scheme would be excessive.[57] Whitton's arguments were supported by two other members of Canada's fledgling social work profession. Mildred Kensit, a child-welfare worker from Montreal, told the parliamentary committee that family allowances would encourage the increase in the family size of an undesirable class of people – referring to the people in receipt of low wages – who, she said, were 'frequently physically and mentally unfit.' Robert E. Mills, director of Toronto's Children's Aid Society, said that the question of family allowances had been discussed at a large meeting of social workers in Toronto and that a resolution opposing such a scheme had been passed without a single dissenting voice. He went on to say that family allowances would be an unwarranted interference with the freedom and initiative of the individual. All three argued for more services for children, but financial grants to parents were seen as posing a very great danger. Furthermore, the official organ of child welfare workers in Canada, *Canadian Child Welfare News,* had described the concept of family allowances three years earlier as '*entirely foreign* to present Canadian and United States practice'[58] (italics added).

Some spokespersons for organized labour saw family allowances as a threat to their right to demand higher wages; at the annual meeting of the Trades and Labour Congress in 1929, a resolution was passed opposing the introduction of family allowances on this ground. However, the All-Canadian Congress of Labour recommended the idea to delegates at their third annual convention in 1929, 'as a step toward a more equitable distribution of income.'[59]

The parliamentary committee decided, in the face of conflicting evidence and in the absence of any broad public support, that the matter required further study and that the question of dominion-provincial jurisdiction would have to be settled before any action could be taken.

In 1930 the province of Quebec established a Social Insurance Commission to conduct a broad inquiry into Quebec's social welfare problems. In 1932, as part of its study, the commission called for evidence on the issue of family allowances, and once again Whitton and Lebel gave testimony in much the same vein as before the parliamentary committee. In their report the commissioners said: 'We are here face to face with a system exclusively European, adapted to low wages and it is very difficult to predict what would be the results of its application here.' The commissioners noted that the proponents of family allowances countered the suggestion that wages were generally higher in Canada than in Europe with the concession that allowances be paid beginning with the third child. This did little to allay the fears of the commissioners, who suggested that Father Lebel's plan for a voluntary system of family allowances, paid by the employer, would place Quebec industry at a disadvantage and would cause a movement of population from the farming communities into the towns. The commissioners' final argument in their rejection of family allowances was that such schemes ran the risk of turning the family into a state institution. They concluded their statement by offering 'a tribute to those who have consented to bear the heavy burden of a large family.'[60]

Apart from these brief flurries of interest in family allowances in the late 1920s and early 1930s, the subject was a dead issue in Canada until the Second World War era.[61]

Housing

The Royal Commission on Industrial Relations of 1919 identified the scarcity and bad quality of housing in Canada as one of the chief causes of social unrest. Wartime priorities had reduced the number of houses built in Canada during the 1914-18 period, which merely aggravated the existing shortage of suitable dwellings, a problem that had occupied Canadians in many parts of Canada prior to the war.[62]

In 1919 the federal government developed a limited housing scheme by establishing a fund of $25 million to be lent to the provinces on the basis of 25 per cent participation, the provinces in turn making loans to their municipalities. Not all provinces participated, and the results varied from municipality to municipality. A later government study outlined the shortcomings of the program: 'The housing scheme of 1919 was launched before adequate machinery and techniques of administration had been developed. Dependence was placed upon the municipal organization and, except in Winnipeg, the commissions established to supervise the housing program were in the main negligent and inefficient.'[63] This scheme did not assist the lowest income groups, whose shelter needs were the most pressing. Winnipeg, a city that operated a more or less successful program of home building, built 712 middle-class homes of five or six rooms from 1920 to 1923. Help under this scheme was limited to those who could invest a small equity. The provision of low-rental accommodation and the elimination of slum conditions were not attempted. Furthermore, the generally poor performance of municipal housing commissions undoubtedly strengthened the argument of those who were opposed to government intervention in the housing field. The timing of this particular venture indicates that it was launched primarily as a device to combat the high unemployment that developed in the immediate postwar period. If the central goal had been housing, the planning and direction might have been more adequate. As with all other social welfare matters, however, the weakness of municipal government was a paramount barrier to innovation.

7
The Depression Decade: Cracking the Residual Mould

The Great Depression of the 1930s was a time when even 'provident and thrifty' people endured the humiliation of 'going on relief.' It was a time of mass unemployment and seriously depressed standards of living. At the bottom of the depression in 1933, nearly one-quarter of the labour force was out of work and seeking jobs, and an estimated 15 per cent of the population was in receipt of relief. By 1939, when economic conditions had improved somewhat, at least one-third of the Canadian people could not afford a diet considered nutritionally adequate by health authorities.[1]

Some regions of the country suffered greater hardships than others. Owing to a combination of circumstances – the disastrous fall of wheat prices from $1.60 a bushel in 1929 to 38 cents in 1931 and a series of successive crop failures caused by severe drought – the prairie provinces, particularly Saskatchewan, were hardest hit.

One additional factor made this depression the most catastrophic in Canadian history: the virtual disappearance of the traditional avenues of escape for Canadians from the consequences of unemployment and business recession. In the depressions of the 1870s and 1880s, many of the victims of unemployment in Canadian towns could return to the family farm and await the return of better days. If this was not feasible, another escape route was emigration to the United States, a course of action taken by uncounted thousands. A third option was to move out west to Canada's last frontier and begin farming. By the 1930s, however, these methods of escaping the depression had all but disappeared.[2] Unemployment was as severe in the United States as in Canada; the western frontier had vanished; the family farm continued to be a haven (except in drought-stricken areas), but for a much smaller segment of the population. Furthermore, the highly restrictive 'residence' clauses of most municipal relief departments, which restricted assistance to those who could prove they had resided within the municipality from which they were seeking help for a stipulated period – commonly a year or more – made leaving one's home a hazardous endeavour. The callous treatment of transient young men, drifting in their thousands across Canada in search of employment, was not something to foster mobility in the mind of the average unemployed Canadian.[3] The result, according to the Royal Commission on Dominion-Provincial Relations, was that the 'livelihood of hundreds of thousands of citizens seemed to be entirely dependent upon public charity.'[4]

Unemployment Relief in the 1930s

Public charity in the early 1930s meant, in most areas of Canada, hastily improvised municipal relief supplemented by aid from private charitable organizations.[5] Public policy for dealing with the needs of the unemployed moved through three stages. Initially, an attempt was made to create jobs through public works projects, principally at the municipal and provincial levels, with some federal assistance. These job-creating programs were limited in scope, emphasizing hand labour, chiefly 'pick and shovel' jobs, but insufficient in number to meet the demand.[6] The disparity between the numbers of jobs and job seekers was such that the work had to be rationed in terms of time allowed on a job (in Toronto, for example, married men received approximately one week's work in eight during the winter of 1930-1), or by restricting jobs to municipal residents, men with families, or men without bank accounts.[7] The second policy stage, as the lines of unemployed continued to grow, involved an additional eligibility test for a job – that of financial need. At this point, the schemes became work-for-relief projects. However, governments discovered that such make-work programs were considerably more expensive than simple relief. In Ontario the government had to spend $2, in most municipalities, to provide a man with $1 in wages.[8] It was soon acknowledged that providing relief would be cheaper than trying to supply jobs. By the end of 1932 public works programs had been sharply curtailed, and governments turned their efforts to keeping people alive by providing what was termed 'direct relief.'[9]

The administration of direct relief, particularly in the early 1930s, reflected the deep distrust of dependent people that had pervaded both public and private charity administration up to this time. Help was dispensed in kind (food hampers, secondhand clothing, and orders for coal and wood)[10] or through the use of vouchers, initially for specified items of food, fuel, and clothing to ensure the recipient did not squander his voucher on luxuries. Later a wide-open voucher system was more commonly used, which permitted recipients to make their own selections up to the value of the voucher. There was a gradual drift toward cash relief, a trend supported by some social workers[11] but observed with considerable ambivalence by the Canadian Council of Child and Family Welfare, which was still wrestling with nineteenth-century phantoms. In January 1934 the council issued a statement on the topic of cash relief, because of the 'widespread discussion' of the subject, in which it outlined its support for a 'flexible system' of relief-giving. This system would permit the issuance of relief in kind as well as in cash, but the latter only in individual cases 'where investigation and supervision standards were sufficiently developed to justify such procedure.'[12] This position was becoming increasingly difficult to justify, particularly in view of the existence of three income security programs paying cash benefits – workers' compensation, mothers' allowances, and old age pensions. In only one of these programs, mothers' allowances, was social work supervision of any consequence, and most social workers in that program had the common sense to acknowledge that their clients, in the overwhelming majority of cases, could write the textbook on the careful management of money.

Undoubtedly, the movement for cash relief was supported by the organized agitation of the unemployed. This largely unrecorded history of attempts to introduce 'citizen participation' into policy-making and administration was a lively aspect of municipal politics in the 1930s. In Saskatoon, for example, there were no fewer than nine associations of the unemployed, which sprang up during the 1930s to press their demand for more adequate relief and to resist the controlling and arbitrary nature of the welfare system.[13] The Saskatoon City Council responded to the agitation for cash relief by holding a plebiscite in 1934 among relief recipients to determine their preference between cash and the voucher system. The cash system was overwhelmingly endorsed and subsequently adopted, although cash grants for clothing were not included until 1939. In 1935 the Ontario government outlined a new relief policy in which it recommended to the municipalities a cash relief system but qualified it by suggesting that it be associated with a full work program where feasible.[14] Surveying the administration of unemployment relief in Canada toward the end of the 1930s, Grauer reported that unemployment relief in Canada was dispensed in three ways: relief in kind, by the voucher system, or in cash. The first two methods were most common, with the use of vouchers predominating.[15]

The development of a more enlightened unemployment relief policy was hampered by the traditional stance of the two senior levels of government, last enunciated during the brief depressions of the 1920s, that poor relief was primarily a municipal responsibility. This position, supported by references to the BNA Act, meant that the federal government and, to a lesser extent, the provincial governments were reluctant to set policy and administrative guidelines even though they carried the major share of the cost (see Table 7.1). Thus, unemployment relief policy was largely developed at the municipal level, with the result that administrative procedures and policies differed from place to place with a consequent absence of standards for even minimum levels of aid.[16] Furthermore, as administrative costs were

Table 7.1

Relief disbursements through provincial and municipal agencies, all provinces, 1931-7 ($ millions)

Year ending March 31	1931	1932	1933	1934	1935	1936	1937	7-year total
Dominion share	3	33	34	28	43	41	52	234
Dominion loans to provinces	—	11	15	9	21	32	14	102
Provincial share	9	39	39	49	75	70	52	333
Provincial loans to municipalities	—	1	2	2	3	2	—	10
Municipal share	9	21	21	24	24	24	23	146
Total	21	93	94	101	142	135	127	713

Source: A.E. Grauer, *Public Assistance and Social Insurance,* A Study Prepared for the Royal Commission on Dominion-Provincial Relations, Table 3, 14.

not shared by the federal or provincial governments, municipalities attempted to economize in this critical area by the use of inadequate numbers of staff, with little or no training for their demanding jobs.[17]

The federal government's reluctance to come to grips with the unemployment relief problem[18] was not primarily a constitutional issue. The federal inertia was directly linked to the prevailing residual approach to social security. The essence of this approach is its 'emergency' character, and federal policy with regard to unemployment and unemployment relief was couched in these terms. It moved from year to year in the anticipation that each year's appropriations for unemployment relief and related measures would be the last. It was even customary for the federal minister of labour to announce in the spring of each year, like a Native shaman dispelling an evil spirit, the imminent end of all federal aid to unemployment relief. Despite these ritual incantations, the 'emergency' appropriations continued each year of the Depression, finally ending in 1941.

Canada's chickens had come home to roost. The country, having failed to define the problem of unemployment in the 1920s as a national issue requiring long-range planning, although advised to do so by a royal commission in 1919 and a parliamentary committee in 1928, had to face the gravest depression crisis in Canadian history with little more than the rudimentary form of public organization laid out by the Fathers of Confederation. As the Royal Commission on Dominion-Provincial Relations noted, 'The magnitude of relief costs hopelessly exceeded the financial capacities of the provinces and the municipalities. During the eight-year period their combined revenues fell short of total relief and current expenditures by over $750 million.' This was a staggering sum when one recalls that government expenditures on public welfare in 1926 amounted to only $99 million (see Table 7.2).

The federal government, with its wider powers of taxation and borrowing, came to the rescue of the provinces but continued to point out, as it had during the unemployment emergencies of the 1920s, that unemployment relief was an area of provincial jurisdiction and that federal intervention was a temporary measure to meet circumstances of extreme and unusual gravity. Supported by this rationale, the federal government assumed about 40 per cent of the total outlay on relief during the period from 1930 to 1937 and lent the four western provinces additional millions to enable them to meet their share of relief costs.

The scale of economic dependency created by the decade of depression shattered two 'received truths' that had impeded a comprehensive approach to social security: the idea that welfare services were properly the sole responsibility of the provinces and their municipalities, and the belief that the fluctuations of the business cycle were best remedied when left to the 'forces of the market place.'[19] A Conservative government contributed to the overturning of both of these pieces of conventional wisdom by introducing federal aid to the provinces for unemployment relief in 1930 on a year-to-year emergency basis, which was continued by the succeeding Liberal regime until 1941, and by R.B. Bennett's unsuccessful 'New Deal' legislation in 1935. In announcing his plan of reform in January 1935, Bennett provided Canada with the spectacle of a Conservative prime minister asserting that his New Deal 'means government intervention ... government control and regulation. It means the end of laissez-faire.'[20]

The genesis of Prime Minister Bennett's New Deal has been ascribed in the first instance to the report of the Select Committee on Price Spreads and Mass Buying, which had been established in 1934 to investigate charges that large business corporations had deliberately used their powers to depress wages and fix prices.[21] The commission's report found that the most severe effects of the Depression in Canada were being felt by the farmers, industrial workers, and small producers, while most of the larger corporations were sustaining good profits. This report, coming in advance of a general election slated for the fall of 1935, after nearly five years of Conservative government that coincided unhappily with the most severe aspects of the Depression, meant that the prime minister had to counteract the 'party of big business' label that his opponents were applying to the Conservatives. In January 1935, Bennett, taking a lead from Franklin Roosevelt's 'fireside chats' to the American public, announced in a series of radio addresses his proposed New Deal. He declared his intention to submit a series of bills to Parliament aimed at remedying a number of situations revealed by the Report of the Committee on Price Spreads, including artificially depressed wages, sweated labour conditions, and price-fixing.

Additionally, he proposed the establishment of a national contributory unemployment insurance scheme, a contributory old age pension scheme, and health, accident, and sickness insurance. His program of reform was subsequently introduced into Parliament and placed on the statute books in May and June of 1935.[22]

Employment and Social Insurance Act, 1935

Of particular interest to this study is the Employment and Social Insurance Act, passed by the House of Commons on 12 March 1935.[23] Prime Minister Bennett had promised a great deal in his celebrated radio talks of January 1935. He had announced his determination to do away with 'emergency relief measures' and introduce 'a sound and scientific insurance against unemployment.' He spoke of a system of insurance against old age, involving 'recognition of thrift on the part of those who provide for their old age,' and, he added, 'health, accident and sickness insurance must be developed in the same way.'[24] His 1935 legislation met his promise for an unemployment insurance system, but it made no mention of a contributory old age pension plan and merely provided for an investigation of health insurance, including sickness cash benefits, as well as a plan for unemployment relief for those not eligible to draw unemployment insurance benefits.

The core of the act was a system of unemployment insurance and employment exchanges modelled on (or, more precisely, copied from) the British legislation of 1935. The act required compulsory coverage of all employees over the age of sixteen and earning less than $2,000 per year. A sizeable number of occupations were excluded, such as agricultural workers, domestic servants, loggers, trappers, fishermen, and longshoremen. The list of excluded occupations amounted to an estimated one-third of the labour force.

A minimum contribution period of forty weeks within a two-year period was required before the worker could claim thirteen weeks of benefit. A longer contribution record could lengthen the period of benefit payments. A flat rate of benefit, graded according to sex and age, was provided for. Male workers over twenty-one could qualify for the highest weekly benefit of $6.00; for women in the same age bracket, the maximum benefit was $5.10; workers under twenty-one received less. For married workers, a supplement of $2.70 was to be paid, with 90 cents for each child under fourteen (or sixteen if in school or defective). The flat rate of benefit was defended on the basis of its administrative simplicity. The total amount of benefit could not exceed 80 per cent of the income normally earned when in work. In cases of a disputed claim, an appeal system was provided for. The system was financed by employers and employees each contributing five-twelfths of the required premium with the federal government contributing two-twelfths, as well as the entire cost of administration. Premiums, like bene-fits, were to be on a flat rate but varied according to the age and sex of the worker. The highest premium was 25 cents per week payable by a male worker over twenty-one; the lowest premium was 6 cents for a female worker aged sixteen to seventeen.[25]

The Employment and Social Insurance Act meant that a further and significant redefinition of one of the principal causes of poverty and dependency had occurred. By this act, Canadians had defined unemploy-ment as a socioeconomic problem of national dimension rather than a per-sonal problem and a local responsibility. The economic system was seen as culpable on two grounds: it not only produced recurring periods of unem-ployment for which insurance protection was required, but the wages paid during 'good times' were recognized as insufficient, in a majority of cases, to permit saving for anything other than the briefest interruptions of income. The act was also an acknowledgment that a reasonable degree of protection in times of unemployment was the worker's right and not a sub-ject for charity.

However, the act was in trouble on constitutional grounds. The Liberal opposition in Parliament, led by Mackenzie King, contended that in trying to implement a federal social insurance scheme without first seeking an amendment to the Constitution, Prime Minister Bennett was attempting to ride roughshod over the BNA Act and that he was fostering the vain hope in the minds of the public that the courts and Privy Council would sanction his legislation. The government argued, on the other hand, that its social insurance measures and labour statutes concerning maximum hours, minimum wages, and weekly rest in industry were constitutionally valid on a number of grounds, including the federal government's obliga-tion to enact legislation consonant with the draft conventions of the ILO, its residual power to legislate for the 'peace, order, and good government' of the country, and its authority to levy any form of taxation. However, the Privy Council thought otherwise and ruled the Employment and Social Insurance Act and much of the remaining reform legislation as ultra vires the Dominion, on the grounds that the legislation dealt with matters of 'property and civil rights' in the provinces and was therefore beyond the powers of the dominion government, and that the use of the general resid-ual powers of the Dominion was only justified in 'some abnormal circum-stances' or 'some extraordinary peril to the national life of Canada, as for example, epidemics and pestilence.' This not only indicated how lawyers could disagree but also reflected the detachment of high-ranking lawyers from the dire circumstances of the day.

A contemporary critic of the Privy Council decision noted that outside of the First World War there had only been one national crisis in Canada that was held by the Privy Council in London to justify the use of the

Dominion's residual powers – and that was the degree of drunkenness existing at the time the Canada Temperance Act was adopted in 1878: 'According to the noble lords of the Privy Council the evil of intemperance at that date presented a greater emergency than did the unemployment and sweated labour conditions in Canada which promoted the Employment and Social Insurance Act, since the Canada Temperance Act was considered as a valid exercise of residuary powers and the latter act was not.'[26]

The repudiation of the majority of Bennett's New Deal legislation by the courts was a blow against the unemployed, as well as against's hopes for health insurance; but it at least emphasized, dramatically, the need for a constitutional amendment before any type of nationally administered social insurance scheme could be implemented.

On the strength (or weakness) of his proposed New Deal, Bennett faced the electorate in the fall of 1935 and was badly defeated. One analyst of the situation argues that Bennett's defeat was not a repudiation of his New Deal but a consequence of five years of depression, a superior Liberal Party organization, and the rise of two new political parties of protest – the Co-operative Commonwealth Federation (CCF) in Saskatchewan and the Social Credit Party in Alberta. Both of the latter siphoned off voters who might otherwise have supported Bennett's plan of reform. There was also division within his own party: a splinter Conservative group called for more radical measures, while the more traditional Conservatives of Ontario and Quebec's business community were frightened by their leader's plan for government regulation of business.[27] The prospect of government intervention, particularly federal intervention, did not sit well with Quebec politicians sensitive about provincial rights, and as a result, Conservative representation in that province was almost wiped out. As Birch puts it, 'Bennett's legislation was radical enough to frighten his supporters among the business classes – the Liberals gained thirty-three seats in Ontario in consequence – but not radical enough to attract voters who favoured dissident parties.'

The Liberals assumed office with a resounding majority; but they inherited the problems of heavy unemployment and its attendant miseries, all still unsolved. Although opinion in the country was receptive to federal action to cure the country's malaise, Prime Minister King avoided any precipitous moves, not wishing to alienate his Quebec supporters by either tinkering with the Constitution or launching conditional-grant schemes. These were soon to be effectively employed against want and destitution in the United States under the terms of the new Social Security Act; but to King they smacked of federal interference in provincial affairs and violated his firmly held conviction that only the government responsible for raising revenue should spend it.

The government moved instead to test the validity of Bennett's New Deal legislation and appointed a National Employment Commission, which was given the task of supervising the administration of federal relief funds (about which so much bitter federal-provincial controversy had raged) and of recommending programs and projects to stimulate employment.

The Privy Council's decision, handed down on 28 January 1937, highlighted the need for constitutional amendment. All parties in the House of Commons were now agreed that amendment must precede needed social legislation. Attempts were made by federal and provincial officials to decide on an amending procedure, but these failed. Coming on top of this development was a report by the Bank of Canada on the desperate financial position of Manitoba and Saskatchewan, whose economies had been dealt a double blow by the combination of depression and drought. The bank's report, noting that revenues for both provinces were hopelessly dwarfed by their financial commitments despite quite orthodox fiscal policies, suggested that a comprehensive inquiry into the financial powers and responsibilities of all government bodies might be in order.

Royal Commission on Dominion-Provincial Relations, 1937-40
The prime minister, seeing a way out of the constitutional impasse, promptly announced a royal commission to inquire into all aspects of dominion-provincial relations, with particular reference to financial matters, and 'to make recommendations as to what should be done to secure a more equitable and practical division of the burden to enable all governments to function more effectively within the spheres of their respective jurisdictions.'[28]

The commission's report was a signal document. It took no less than three years in preparation (1937-40), and it was the first comprehensive look into the working of Canadian federalism since Confederation. The final report and recommendations were tabled in 1940; unfortunately the war intervened. But the recommendations represented a unanimous opinion of the commissioners and are of central interest to our discussion.

First, the commissioners considered the division of powers between the federal and provincial governments. While accepting that some federal powers would have to be widened, they held that provincial autonomy must be maintained and strengthened. To achieve this goal, the commissioners proposed that the federal government assume responsibility for certain functions of government that were best performed, from the standpoint of equity and efficiency, on a national rather than a provincial basis. In this category, the commissioners placed the responsibility for the unemployed employable.[29] They recommended a national system of unemployment insurance and a federally administered scheme of unemployment assistance for those able-bodied unemployed who, for a variety of reasons, could not qualify for insurance benefits. The commissioners also recommended that a contributory scheme of old age insurance should be made a federal responsibility, arguing that the provinces were unlikely to inaugurate such schemes since they would impair the competitive position of industry within the province and cause administrative difficulties arising from the mobility of labour.

Apart from these two major exceptions, the balance of the social services – provision for the unemployable, widows' pensions, mothers' allowances, child welfare, public health insurance (when and if it was introduced), workers' compensation, and education – should, the commissioners thought, remain provincial responsibilities. However, chiefly by a rearrangement of taxation powers, each province would be enabled to meet its responsibilities 'in accordance with average Canadian standards.'[30] This latter point involved a second major recommendation of the commission: the provision of a National Adjustment Grant to replace all other conditional or unconditional federal grants to the provinces, to be calculated on the basis of fiscal need.[31] In return for this grant, the provinces would vacate the fields of personal income tax, corporation, and inheritance tax in favour of the federal government.

An interesting feature of the commission's recommendations was that the National Adjustment Grant would be unconditional in nature. This recommendation was based upon the commission's belief that conditional grants in Canada had been the cause of much federal-provincial disharmony, and that contrary to the evidence offered by American experience, nothing could be done to improve the administrative headaches that were so prominent a feature of Canadian conditional grant programs, notably unemployment relief grants during the 1930s.[32]

In retrospect it is clear that the Royal Commission on Dominion-Provincial Relations advanced thinking on social security matters in three ways. First, the evidence marshalled by the commission left no doubt that provincial revenues were not equal to the new social welfare roles being assigned to them and that some realignment of responsibilities and revenues was imperative. Second, certain income-maintenance functions of government, such as social insurance for old age and unemployment, were a logical responsibility of the federal government. However, it was also the commission's view that provincial and municipal governments were to remain accountable for the majority of their social service responsibilities, although with increased financial aid from the federal purse. This view counteracted the argument that the answer to the fiscal and administrative difficulties facing the provinces was centralization of services at the federal level. Finally, the commission advanced the concept of a national minimum of social services for Canada to be achieved by gearing the federal adjustment grant to provincial fiscal need. The minimum was further reinforced by several references to the need for redressing regional inequalities.

The Depression as a Force for Change

The Depression of the 1930s was thus a significant force for change in the development of social security programs in Canada. The crucial points bear repeating. The Depression was so devastating in its effect that it brought home to the average Canadian the interdependence of citizens in an industrial society. Unemployment was seen less as a result of personal inadequacy and more as a common and insurable threat to the livelihood of the average citizen. Second, the concept of local responsibility for the relief of the unemployed was replaced first by the assumption of provincial and then of federal responsibility. From this point on, unemployment was seen as a national problem rather than a purely local or regional one. Related to this second point was the fact that although arguments were developed during the 1930s in favour of full federal responsibility for a wide range of social services, these were fully explored by the National Employment Commission and the Royal Commission on Dominion-Provincial Relations and rejected by both bodies. At the end of the depression decade, Canadian thinking tended to support the view that provincial governments and their municipalities would maintain their traditional interest in and control of social services (with certain newly defined exceptions – contributory insurance against unemployment and old age as well as unemployment relief), but that sufficient federal help should be extended to all provinces to assure a 'Canadian standard' of social services from coast to coast.

The Canadian Welfare Council reviewed the report in the light of its implications for social services and voiced some reservations.[33] It took issue with the report's rejection of conditional grants-in-aid, which had so strongly coloured the commission's recommendations. The council pointed out that where there had been a settled, permanent policy and well-qualified administrators at both levels of government, conditional grants worked well – the grants-in-aid for technical education and the control of venereal disease were offered as examples. The federal grants to unemployment relief costs, on the other hand, were characterized by 'emergency' legislation that changed from year to year (sometimes month to month), complicated by the absence of qualified staff to administer it.[34]

The council's major objection to the commission's recommendations on social services concerned the proposal that the federal government assume responsibility for all employable unemployed. While not questioning the advisability of federal responsibility for unemployment insurance, the council argued that employable people in need of financial assistance who were not covered by unemployment insurance or who had lost their entitlement to benefit should be the responsibility of provincial and municipal welfare departments. Citing experience in the United States and the United Kingdom, the council took the position that 'the ascertaining of such need and the provision of care differ so markedly from person to person and place to place ... that only a relief plan, administered by the neighbours of those in need, can judge and adjust relief budgets according to actual needs.'[35]

This approach to problems of financial need, redolent of the Elizabethan poor law, was evidence of the private charitable agency philosophy of relief-giving that was still part of social welfare thought in Canada in the late 1930s and early 1940s. Not everyone in the social welfare community shared this view. Some social workers argued that federal responsibility for all unemployed employables was desirable because of the limitations of the Unemployment Insurance Act in terms of its coverage and in terms of the time limitations on receipt of benefits. The council's proposals were seen as creating artificial distinctions between workers with identical problems and helping to perpetuate the uneven standards of provincial and municipal relief that were so evident in the 1930s. Furthermore, federal responsibility for both groups of unemployed would more likely 'pose the question of broadening the provisions of the Unemployment Insurance Act' as well as encouraging a national attack on the employment problem.[36]

The Depression also gave birth to parties of protest. The CCF and the Social Credit Party both emerged on the Prairies – an area most seriously affected by depression and drought – and the Union Nationale Party in Quebec.[37] The Social Credit Party of Alberta and the Union Nationale in Quebec remained essentially one-province movements; but the growth of the CCF during the early 1940s forced the Liberal Party to the left of centre and affected the course of social security planning.

There was a marked increase in social science research in Canada during the Depression. McGill University was a major centre of this activity. There Leonard Marsh spearheaded the work of a number of scholars to produce a series of carefully documented studies that added immeasurably to the country's limited supply of factual data on the Depression's impact on the health and welfare of Canadians. At the University of Toronto, Harry Cassidy carried out his studies of welfare services almost single-handedly.[38] A few studies also emanated from Dalhousie University, where the journal *Public Affairs* was initiated, and from the University of British Columbia, where the studies were supervised by Coral Topping.

Finally, it is important to note that while the seedbed for developments in social security planning in Canada was laid during the Depression, change itself did not occur. This is in marked contrast with other countries, such as the United States, where the Depression decade saw the beginning of that country's social security system. In Canada the developments in income security that did take place followed the traditional pattern of means-tested, residual types of programs.

While the ideas and proposals were germinating, the actual development of social security measures during the 1930s was all but submerged by the need to provide a subsistence living for thousands of unemployed Canadians. In addition to the unemployment relief program, two new categories of public assistance emerged: allowances for 'burned-out,' or psychologically disabled, veterans and pensions for the blind. There was considerable interest but little effective public action on the risk to income adequacy posed by the costs of medical care as well as the cost of housing. These latter two issues, at this stage, need only be dealt with in brief outline.

War Veterans' Allowances

In 1928 a House of Commons committee on pensions and ex-soldiers' problems reported that 'one of the most serious situations confronting ... the country generally is that relating to the employment and care of ex-members of the forces suffering from disability, broken down or burned out.'[39] The problem emerged as a public issue in the late 1920s, as veterans' associations petitioned Ottawa to provide assistance to elderly veterans who, it was claimed, had become 'pre-aged' by their war service. The typical burned-out veteran was a man in his fifties or sixties who was having trouble holding a place in the labour market. Undoubtedly these older workers were, in the main, unskilled people who had been left behind in the economic race as the pace of industrialization continued during the 1920s, bringing with it a demand for a more skilled labour force. The burned-out veteran was actually a segment of the larger problem of older, unskilled workers squeezed out of the labour market by increasing mechanization on the one hand and on the other by younger, more vigorous men competing for the diminishing number of labouring jobs.

The Liberal government, under Prime Minister Mackenzie King, waited until March of 1930 to introduce a measure into the House of Commons to pay allowances to veterans to 'provide assistance for certain veterans who are not in receipt of pensions; are only partially pensionable or who are unemployable.'[40] The opposition alleged that the timing of the legislation was a vote-getting device as a federal election was expected in the same year. This may also account for some of the vigorous criticism of the measure when it was introduced into the House of Commons, but the main objections to the bill are worth noting.

The opposition complained that the War Veterans' Allowances Act would result in two classes of war pensioners. The first class was granted a pension on proof of war-related disability, as a right and including maintenance for wives and children (as well as widows and orphans of deceased pensioners). The new legislation introduced a second category that did not confer any right to benefit but merely made the provisions of the Old Age Pensions Act applicable to ex-soldiers who were adjudged to be disabled, broken down, or burned out, or whose pensions were too small to maintain them. To further emphasize the disparity between the two pieces of legislation, one member of Parliament pointed out that a pensioner under the Pensions Act suffering from permanent disability was entitled, if married, to $125 per month. The burned-out veterans, under the proposed War Veterans' Allowances legislation, would receive, if married or a widower with children, a maximum of $40 per month subject to a strict means test.

Another significant difference in the two classes of legislation was the provision for an appeals procedure under the Pensions Act and the absence of such a provision under the War Veterans' Allowances Act.

The government made it clear that a payment made under the War Veterans' Allowances Act was not a pension but an allowance – thus emphasizing the discretionary nature of the assistance. It was also pointed out that ex-soldiers would normally become eligible for an allowance at age sixty-five (this age was reduced to sixty in committee deliberations of the House of Commons), rather than having to wait until age seventy to collect the old age pension. Further to this, provision was made for allowances to be granted at earlier ages, 'at any age, in fact,' if in the judgement of officials the veteran was in need and unemployable.

The allowances under this new legislation and the test of means were modelled on the Old Age Pensions Act, but the cost of the program was entirely a federal responsibility in keeping with the federal government's responsibility for veterans under the BNA Act.

By 1 April 1939, 20,010 veterans were in receipt of war veterans' allowances, the legislation having been amended in 1936 and 1938 to relax the eligibility criteria and the means test. Further amendments in 1943 and 1944 made it possible for widows of burned-out veterans to receive a compassionate allowance, and orphans, if in need and not otherwise provided for, became eligible for allowances.[41]

In 1930 this legislation, despite its public assistance character and its minimal allowances, must have been welcomed by many needy veterans. One has to keep in mind that at this time the state of public welfare in Canada was so rudimentary that apart from three special categories – old age pensions, mothers' allowances, and workers' compensation – the availability of a system of cash relief was relatively unknown. Indeed, 'relief departments' in most cities during the 1920s only operated in the winter, when unemployment was particularly high. Any assistance granted was of an emergency nature only and seldom paid in cash. The usual form of assistance was in grocery orders, orders for coal and wood or used clothing, and, if a recipient was faced with an eviction order, rent would sometimes be paid. Therefore, a widening of the public assistance program offering a regular and dependable source of cash relief was undoubtedly a boon to those fortunate enough to qualify.

Blind Pensions

In 1937 the Old Age Pensions Act was amended to make provisions for the payment of a pension to every blind person, as defined by the legislation, who was in financial need and over the age of forty. The amount of the pension was the same as under the Old Age Pensions Act – $20 per month – but the total allowable income including the pension was somewhat higher.[42] As in the case of old age pensions, each province was required to pass enabling legislation to take advantage of the amendment to the Old Age Pensions Act, which provided for the federal government to pay 75 per cent of the cost of blind pensions with the provinces responsible for the remainder. This additional measure of help with welfare costs was quickly accepted by the provinces; within the space of four months, eight provinces had passed enabling legislation, and the ninth followed suit shortly thereafter. There was little argument raised over this additional assumption of responsibility by the federal government of a welfare matter, as there had been in 1927 when the Old Age Pensions Act was passed. The inability of the provincial and municipal governments to carry the burden of welfare services and income-maintenance costs had been dramatically exposed by the Depression. By 1937 the provinces were only too ready to surrender their provincial rights in the welfare field in return for federal assistance.

The provision of pensions for the blind was the result of at least ten years of lobbying at the provincial and federal levels of government by various groups and organizations, notably the Canadian Federation of the Blind, formed in 1927 with a primary interest in the pension issue, and the Canadian National Institute for the Blind, formed in 1918.

The blind in Canada had hoped for a separate act to cover aid to the blind that would include not only income-maintenance features but treatment and training provisions. However, to hold out for a separate act would have involved further delay of the much-needed financial help, so inclusion under the Old Age Pensions Act was accepted. Beginning the pension at the age of forty was another compromise in the interests of keeping the costs of the program down, as well as a gesture to the incorrigible pessimists who expressed fears that pensions to the blind at twenty-one would weaken their resolve to become independent.[43]

The blind at age forty and over were thus bracketed with the elderly of seventy and over. The blind under the age of forty were ignored, as were a very large group of Canadians with loss of vision in one eye or with some type of progressive eye disease. Provision for treatment or prevention of blindness was not covered. Any amount received by pensioners over the permissible amounts resulted in a dollar-for-dollar decrease in their pension, thus providing them with little incentive to seek employment. This policy might have been defensible in 1937, in the midst of a depression when even sighted people had difficulty finding work, but in the war period of the 1940s, when the supply of labour was scarce, many blind people were offered small or part-time jobs but were inhibited by the prospect of reduction in pension, as well as the total loss of pension rights if their income in one year exceeded the maximum permissible amount. Slight increases in the basic pension of $5 per month in 1943 and in the maximum permissible other income in 1944 eased the situation only slightly. By 1945 a total of 6,882 blind persons in nine provinces were in receipt of pensions costing the federal government a total of $1,512,903.[44]

The Costs of Medical and Hospital Care

One of the most common threats to the adequacy of income is the cost of medical services. Quite apart from the fact that illness or accident may interrupt income through time lost from work, there is the additional burden of paying for the doctor's services, drugs, hospital care, and ancillary services.

With the scientific and technological advances in medicine in the twentieth century, rapid strides were made in the treatment and alleviation of many common ailments and diseases that in earlier times had often proved fatal or whose symptoms had to be endured with resignation. Medical care and particularly care in a hospital (now a centre of scientific healing rather than the charnel house it was in the mid-nineteenth century) became a highly valued commodity. Concurrently, the development of scientific and clinical medicine required scientifically sophisticated equipment as well as a range of professional skills, as a division of labour within the medical field rapidly expanded. These developments accelerated the cost of medical and hospital care at the same time as people became aware of their value.

The Depression of the 1930s aggravated the problem of paying for the costs of medical and hospital care. As per capita income fell following 1929, more and more families found their reduced incomes barely sufficient to meet food, clothing, and shelter costs. The fear of a large medical or hospital bill plagued uncounted thousands; the plight of neighbours, friends, and relatives struggling to meet such costs was a common topic of conversation in the 1930s.

In order to obtain medical care, people had to pay a market price for the doctor's services unless he or she was willing to take patients' financial circumstances into consideration when setting the fee. The situation in Canada vis-à-vis medical and hospital care was, with one or two exceptions, residual in character during the 1930s. The very poor had limited access to health care through appeals to charitable agencies, in charity wards of local hospitals, or as charity cases in an outpatient clinic. Those people 'on relief' would in some jurisdictions be entitled to receive medical care, although at the beginning of the Depression federal cost-sharing of aid to the unemployed was limited to food, shelter, and clothing. As late as

1937 there were many urban centres and still more rural districts without any systematic arrangements for providing doctors' services to relief recipients.[45] The medical care offered to the poorest section of the community was not without its cost. The contribution exacted from the recipients of this care was frequently their self-respect as they could not fail to escape the fact that they were charity cases.

For the bulk of the population, medical care was channelled through the private sector, with doctors, dentists, and nurses selling their services on a fee basis, while drugs and medicine were distributed by private wholesale and retail drug outlets. The only exceptions to this generally prevailing residual situation were the medical and hospital care provided by provincial Workmen's Compensation Acts and the 'municipal doctor' system in Saskatchewan and parts of Alberta and Manitoba.[46]

By the 1930s, hospitals, which were generally municipal institutions, were subsidized by provincial governments, but a per diem rate was still required from the patient. A long stay in hospital could therefore be a costly affair; only by proving poverty could an individual escape from the payment of hospital charges.

Agitation for Health Insurance

The economic insecurity engendered by unpredictable medical costs led to agitation for health insurance. The first initiative in Canada took place in British Columbia as early as 1919, when a royal commission recommended a provincial system of health insurance and outlined a plan for implementing it. In the years between the two world wars, nearly all Canadian provinces as well as the federal government investigated the subject of health insurance, although the interest was greatest in western Canada. There were far more words on the subject than deeds. British Columbia in 1936 passed a Health Insurance Act that was never brought into force because of opposition from the medical fraternity. Alberta passed a similar piece of legislation in 1937, but it, too, remained a dead letter. The movement for a social insurance system to protect people from the costs of medical care failed in Canada because too many influential politicians regarded compulsory social insurance as a 'foreign' idea, or not compatible with the tenets of a free enterprise economy. The medical profession, whose acceptance of government health insurance was contingent on its undisputed control of all vital aspects of the program, was even more critical. In 1934 the Canadian medical profession laid down certain 'principles' under which it would be prepared to accept government health insurance. These included (a) that the majority of members on health insurance commissions be representatives of organized medicine; (b) that the method of remunerating doctors for their services must be suitable to organized medicine; (c) that the fee schedule be under the complete control of organized medicine; and (d) that the system be restricted to those below a certain income level.[47]

While compulsory health insurance failed to make headway in the 1930s, voluntary group medical hospital plans began to develop, notably under the auspices of the medical profession. The Associated Medical Services of Ontario, which began in 1937, was one of the first and most successful.

Voluntary group medical and hospital care plans covered a growing minority of Canadians in the 1930s. These plans were best suited to the stable working-class and middle-income groups. The labourers, the unskilled, the itinerant workers, and their families, whose need for medical care was generally greater than any other group, were seldom able to afford coverage. Not infrequently the chronically ill and the elderly were also excluded.

Housing Legislation

Housing policy in Canada up to the 1930s depended entirely upon the operations of the private market. This laissez-faire approach was challenged by a few reputable studies, the most influential of which was a report on housing in the Toronto area published in 1934. This study, the Bruce Report, argued strongly that reliance on the private market meant that thousands of Toronto's low-income families lived in houses that were 'unsanitary, verminous and grossly overcrowded.'[48] It called attention to the relationships between poor housing, ill health, and social pathology, and pressed for community action to provide 'satisfactory dwellings for those who are too poor to afford them.'

The Toronto report and a similar study in Montreal the same year were local efforts and considerably dependent on volunteer groups. In 1935, however, the first official and nationwide challenge to the laissez-faire approach to housing was documented in the report of a Parliamentary Committee on Housing. The construction industry of Canada made the following concession in its brief to the committee: 'Our investigations of housing for low-income groups show that provision of this class of housing cannot ultimately be profitable to private enterprise. The responsibility of housing these groups is, in the final analysis, the responsibility of the state.'[49]

The response to these calls for government action was a 'timid part-way measure'[50] called the Dominion Housing Act (1935), the first legislation since 1921. It did little more than attempt to stimulate the private market by providing federal guarantees to private lending institutions for new house construction. Its effects were barely noticeable. Two years later, the federal government went a step further by passing the Home Improvement Loans Guarantee Act to aid in the rehabilitation of old houses and to assist in the conversion of larger homes into apartments. The sum of $50 million was set aside for these purposes and was expended in three years. By this time war had intervened, and the act was discontinued because of wartime rationing of materials.

The Dominion Housing Act of 1938 was a more substantial measure and reflected the growing acceptance of deficit financing as a means of bringing the country out of the Depression. It was organized in three parts. Part I of the act continued the loan procedure for new home construction as outlined under the 1935 legislation with some useful modifications. Part II outlined the first provisions in Canada for low-rental housing projects. Because the provision of housing was, by judicial interpretation, a responsibility of the provinces, the provisions of this section required that enabling legislation had to be passed by provincial legislatures. As only five provinces did so, while four, including Ontario, did not, the act was inoperative in almost half the country. Furthermore, little was accomplished under Part II as a result of the difficulty in getting the organizations started, delays in plan preparation, and, most of all, problems concerning the acquisition of sites. The onset of the war halted those projects that had managed to get under way, but of the $30 million appropriated for low-rental housing in 1938, not one dollar was spent.[51] Part III of the act was a tax-compensation measure intended to encourage the small owner-occupant. It, too, was little used and expired in 1940.

Despite these few federal initiatives in housing during the 1930s, house construction suffered a disastrous decline during the Depression. Housing policy, such as it was, appeared to be solely concerned with increasing the aggregate number of new homes; little or no consideration was given to examining the housing needs of various income groups and what impact, if any, federal policy was having on these needs.

It was not until the surging interest in postwar construction during the early 1940s that a more adequate analysis of housing needs and policies in Canada was made. This was the comprehensive report that was part of the work of the Advisory Committee on Post War Reconstruction, set up by the federal government in the second year of the war (the Curtis Report, 1944). Unfortunately, the progressive tone of the Curtis Report was not reflected in the federal government's housing policies that finally emerged after the war ended. But the report's review of the expedients proposed for the 1930s confirmed their complete inadequacy. It included, notably, the first overall computations of Canada's great housing 'backlog' of slum clearance, substandard housing, and overcrowding.

A Crack in the Residual Mould

By 1939 Canada was spending about $312 million for public welfare (defined here to mean health and income security programs). This represented about 27 per cent of all government expenditures and 5.6 per cent of the gross national product, down slightly from the 6.6 per cent of the GNP spent on public welfare in 1933, the depth of the depression. Table 7.2 illustrates how public welfare expenditures grew since the Fathers of Confederation assigned the responsibility for hospitals, asylums, charities, and eleemosynary institutions to the provinces and their municipalities.

Table 7.2

Government expenditures on public welfare, selected calendar years, 1866-1939

	Total public welfare expenditures ($ millions)	Public welfare as a percentage of total government expenditures	Public welfare expenditures as a percentage of GNP
1866	.5	3.2	.12
1874	.9	3.1	.18
1896	2.4	12.5	.23
1913	15.1	20.7	.44
1926	99.0	12.5	1.90
1933	230.5	24.7	6.60
1939	317.2	27.1	5.60

Source: Irving J. Goffman, *Some Fiscal Aspects of Public Welfare in Canada* (Toronto: Canadian Tax Foundation 1965), 30.

Does this growth in expenditure suggest that by 1939 Canada's social security system had broken free of its residual mould? The advent of the first provincial workers' compensation programs in 1914 produced what might be described as a hairline crack. Veterans' pensions, minimum wage legislation, old age pensions, and other federal and provincial initiatives suggest more cracking, but the mould remained intact. Even the convulsions of the greatest economic depression in Canadian history did not cause it to shatter. This would require the cataclysm of the Second World War.

8
The Second World War: Catalyst for Social Security Advances

The Second World War had a profound effect on Canada's economic and social structure. It ended the most severe unemployment crisis in the country's history and appreciably raised the standard of living for the large majority of Canadians; but more significantly, it speeded up the processes of industrialization and urbanization. Industry expanded its capacity for production, particularly secondary manufacturing, and there was a corresponding increase in the degree of sophistication and complexity of the industrial process. The technical mastery needed to turn out planes, ships, tanks, and armaments of all kinds required the creation of a skilled work force, and many Canadians received special training as a result of their work in war industry. In addition, the trades training offered to members of the armed forces enabled them to look forward to higher levels of earnings after the war.

The war industry's demand for labour brought about a shift of population to the larger urban centres; the growth in the proportion of wage earners in the labour force reached its highest point since 1918; the number of women in the labour force doubled; and there was a sharp rise in trade union membership, from 358,967 in 1939 to 724,188 in 1944.

The war also had a profound impact on the role of the federal government. One scholar has written that the War Measures Act 'converted Canada overnight from a confederation into a unitary state. The government over-rode or supplanted most of the normal procedures of peace; it became the largest and most important employer of labour; it used its fiscal and monetary power to effect maximum war production, borrowing billions, raising billions by taxation.'[1]

While the federal power increased greatly during the war, the provinces experienced a change in their situation as well. With the virtual disappearance of unemployment relief costs, coupled with an increase in personal income, provincial revenue soared at a time when there was little or no increase in provincial expenditures, as most capital expenditures were curtailed as a result of the wartime shortage of skilled men and materials. Agricultural surpluses were soon a thing of the past, even as farm output increased 30 per cent. One result of these changes was that the provinces ended the war in sound financial shape, while some, notably Ontario and Quebec, had increased their capacity for industrial output to a considerable degree. The latter two provinces, being the most populous and the most industrially advanced, were particularly conscious of their growth and status at the end of the war. Whereas in 1939 all provinces had been considerably reduced in stature by their heavy financial commitments arising from unemployment relief costs and their consequent dependence upon the federal government, they now, by virtue of their sound financial position and enhanced industrial capacity, adopted an independent stance that was to affect the course of social security developments in Canada.

Canada was slow to take up social security planning in the early years of the war, and, in fact, there was a noticeable movement to curtail existing social services on the grounds that all public funds should go into fighting the war.[2] This was also a reflection of a still-dominant residual concept of social welfare. With unemployment a thing of the past, with rising incomes from war industry, could people not afford to take care of themselves?

As if to illustrate this attitude, the federal government's expenditures on health and welfare fell from $154.1 million in 1939-40 to $102.7 million in 1942-3 (see as well Appendix Table A1). Many provinces and municipalities followed the federal lead and curtailed their public welfare programs. However, as the war progressed, manpower requirements and a concern for maintaining morale in the country and in the armed forces enlarged the federal government's activities in a variety of respects. In addition to administering the Dependants' Allowances programs for families of men and women in the armed forces, the federal government undertook the building of homes for war workers in areas where housing shortages existed, paid the moving expenses of war workers and their families from one centre to another, and provided grants to provinces to pay half the cost of provincial day care programs to enable more women to enter the labour force. Rationing, wage and price control, and rent control were introduced to prevent possible shortages in basic items from being exploited.

In these and other ways the federal and provincial governments came to understand that social services were not a luxury to be dispensed with in a time of more pressing need but were a vital element in the smooth functioning of the wartime economy – and, as British experience was proving, a valuable contribution to the war effort.[3] A number of significant developments in social security occurred during the Second World War: two new income maintenance programs – unemployment insurance and family allowances – were created; and the planning of a comprehensive social security system for Canada was initiated. The first of these developments was the enactment of the Unemployment Insurance Act of 1940.

Unemployment Insurance

As mentioned in the preceding chapter, the Conservative government under R.B. Bennett introduced the Employment and Social Insurance Act in 1935. When this legislation was declared unconstitutional by the Supreme Court of Canada and the Privy Council of Great Britain on the grounds that it involved intrusion by the federal government into areas reserved for provincial legislation, it became evident that constitutional amendment would have to precede any federally sponsored social insurance program.

By 1938 Prime Minister Mackenzie King, who had supplanted R.B. Bennett after the 1935 federal election, had obtained the permission of all provinces save three (Alberta, Quebec, and New Brunswick) to amend the Constitution to permit the federal government to initiate unemployment insurance. A Liberal victory in the 1939 Quebec provincial election helped to bring that province into the ranks of the six who were already willing to give their consent to a constitutional amendment. New Brunswick followed suit, leaving Alberta as the remaining holdout. Under pressure from Mackenzie King, Alberta joined the majority in the early months of 1940. On 10 July 1940 the British Parliament amended Section 91 of the BNA Act to give the federal government exclusive jurisdiction over legislation in the field of unemployment insurance, the first modification of the original distribution of social service responsibilities.

The Second World War hastened the beginning of unemployment insurance in Canada. The need for a nationwide selective service system to mobilize all technical and labouring skills for the war effort coincided with the need for a well-organized, nationwide system of employment bureaus for the effective operation of an unemployment insurance scheme. The result was that the hitherto provincially organized (but federally subsidized) employment bureaus were taken over and expanded for the dual purpose of mobilizing the labour force for the war effort and administering an unemployment insurance scheme.[4]

The prime minister had to face considerable opposition in his cabinet against the new measure. His finance minister was concerned about the cost of unemployment insurance, but Mackenzie King prevailed by taking what he described as a firm stand – 'it was a real fight.'[5] An Unemployment Insurance Bill was introduced and given its first reading in the House of Commons on 16 July 1940; it received royal assent on 7 August. A new and significant social minimum had been established.

The Unemployment Insurance Act of 1940, like its predecessor the Employment and Social Insurance Act of 1935, was modelled on British legislation. However, the 1940 act departed from the 1935 act and British precedent in at least one important aspect – benefits and contributions were wage related, as opposed to the flat-rate system. In this respect it adopted the North American view that 'differential benefits based on a work record are a reward for productive effort.'[6] Certain principles were evident in the framing of this act. It was definitely asserted that benefits under this scheme would be paid as a right established by contributions previously made. Thus, one of the more enduring myths of the welfare state was implanted in Canada – that benefits as of right are inseparably linked to contributions. Payments and benefits were to be actuarially related, except in the case of the low-paid worker who would receive a relatively higher percentage of his wages in benefits. It was also stated that one of the aims of the legislation was to protect the normal standard of living of the wage earner, although how this was to be accomplished by setting average benefits at 50 per cent of wage rates and a differential of only 15 per cent between the married and single rates, regardless of the number of dependants, was not explained.

The federal government, in 1940, did not make any provision for the unemployed not covered by insurance or for those whose benefits had been exhausted. Undoubtedly, with the federal cabinet having so much concern for the cost of the scheme (the federal government's contribution was to be one-fifth of the total aggregate employer-employee contribution, plus all administrative expenses), there was little likelihood of their agreeing to a federally financed unemployment relief program. Furthermore, with Canada's labour force rapidly approaching maximum utilization as a result of the war, the issue was easily shelved. This decision was to have serious implications for many unemployed Canadians in the 1950s.

Unemployment insurance began at a particularly favourable time in Canada – a period of rapid rise in employment opportunities and of minimal unemployment. The scheme thus had the necessary breathing space to work out the myriad administrative details involved in collecting and recording contributions and paying benefits. It also allowed for a buildup of the unemployment insurance fund from which benefits would be paid. Mackenzie King was particularly impressed with this argument for getting the insurance plan in operation without delay as he, like many others at the time, anticipated considerable unemployment after the war.[7] Long overdue though it was (the Liberal Party first embraced the idea in 1919), it was a considerable achievement to set up a nationwide system of exchanges, with regional divisions and statistical services.

An Evaluation of the Unemployment Insurance Act, 1940

The federally administered program aimed at covering 75 per cent of wage earners. This may not seem sufficiently inclusive; but it was the largest social security program in Canadian history up to that time, covering 4.6 million people, including dependants, in its first year of operation. However, those covered were mainly urban wage earners. Excluded from coverage were important segments of the labour force, including workers in agriculture, forestry, fishing, private domestic service, stevedoring, government, and police forces; nurses and teachers; workers in hospitals and charitable institutions; and most classes of workers earning $2,000 a year or more.

The program's adequacy was compromised from the beginning by an exaggerated concern for work incentive. It was generally held by those who formulated the plan that benefit schedules must be held well below the wage earner's normal take-home pay to maintain incentives to rejoin the labour force at the first opportunity. Thus, the benefit scales provided approximately one-half of the wage rate with a 15 per cent supplement for a married claimant.[8] The Marsh Report (see below, p. 109 ff.) noted that not one of the seven benefit scales provided a 'living wage' standard and that the 15 per cent supplement inadequately recognized the obligations of married men. These and other deficiencies of the program, including the fact that many workers with full-time attachment to the labour force had difficulty in establishing eligibility for benefits, did not become a public issue during the wartime employment boom and the similarly low unemployment rates of the early postwar years. It was not until the recessions of the 1950s that the inadequacies of the act were revealed.

The Unemployment Insurance Act was the first large-scale income maintenance program in Canada (apart from the First World War system of veterans' pensions) to set up administrative machinery to hear appeals from claimants who felt their case had not been fairly dealt with. The Marsh Report noted that 'hard cases' and doubtful cases under the insurance system had an opportunity for a fair hearing before panels composed of employers' and employees' representatives, with neutral chairmen: 'Such panels have been established in over thirty centres. If the decisions of the Courts of Referees thus contributed are appealed, an Umpire (a Judge of the Superior Court) takes the case under consideration and gives a final verdict' (Marsh Report, 103). Such machinery emphasized the claimant's right to his benefit – a marked advance on the discretionary public assistance method that had characterized social security programs up to this point, with the exception of workers' compensation.

Administratively, the unemployment insurance system was enhanced by its national and unified structure. Although federally administered, the system was decentralized regionally; a network of some 200 offices and branches ensured that service would reach all principal areas of Canada. By contrast, the only other social insurance scheme in Canada at this time was workers' compensation, which had not been adopted in all nine provinces and had significant variations in policy from one province to another.

Comprehensive Planning for Social Security

The first attempt at formulating an integrated system of social security for Canada developed out of the federal government's postwar plans, launched as early as December 1939.[9] Planning was initially concentrated upon the needs of servicemen and women on their return to civilian life. However, it was impossible to plan for 800,000 members of the armed forces as well as nearly 900,000 employees in direct war production in isolation from the rest of the population. Consequently, plans for the demobilization of the armed forces as well as for the workers in war industries became part of the larger question of postwar reconstruction for Canada and Canadians as a whole.

In early 1941 the government established a Committee on Post-War Reconstruction, composed of senior academicians and labour and business leaders, to examine the economic and social implications of the transition from war to peace.[10] The principal of McGill University, F. Cyril James, was named chairman, and Leonard Marsh, who had been the director of a co-ordinated social research program at McGill during the preceding ten years, was named the committee's research director.

The Beveridge Report, 1942

In November 1942 the Beveridge Report, Britain's plan for postwar reconstruction, giving form and substance to the goals expressed in the Atlantic Charter, was published in England and created a sensation in Canada and the United States. Writing lucidly, and using Bunyanesque imagery, Sir William Beveridge identified five giants that stood in the path of reconstruction and progress: Want, Disease, Ignorance, Squalor, and Idleness.[11] Beveridge devoted most of his attention to the abolition of want, which he defined as the lack of income to obtain the means of a healthy subsistence – adequate food, shelter, clothing, and fuel. In Beveridge's view, want was the easiest of the five problems to overcome. His plan was based on the careful surveys of poverty and living standards conducted in the 1930s, which indicated that from three-quarters to five-sixths of want resulted from the interruption or loss of earning power. The remaining 20 to 25 per cent was almost wholly attributable to society's failure to relate wages to family size. From these well-documented findings, Beveridge planned a redistribution of income through two methods: a comprehensive and universal social insurance plan to meet interruptions or loss of earning power arising from sickness, disability, unemployment, or old age; and a system of children's allowances to counter the failure of the wage system to take account of family size. In addition, maternity grants and funeral grants would be paid to help meet these common life situations that called for unusual expenditure.

The Beveridge plan was, in large measure, an administrative pulling-together, a rationalization and extension of the already considerable British network of social insurance and public assistance programs. What was new, and in a sense revolutionary, was the proposal for a universal health service that would 'ensure that for every citizen there is available whatever medical treatment he requires, in whatever form he requires it, domiciliary or institutional, general, specialist or consultant.'[12] Another innovation for the British public was the proposed system of children's allowances. Beveridge insisted that his plan for eliminating want assumed the existence of three essential elements: a national health service, a system of children's allowances, and an economy that would ensure the end of mass unemployment. These proposals, together with educational reform and a housing program, would clear the 'five giants' from the path of progress.

The social minimum that Beveridge was prepared to guarantee to all British citizens was by no means lavish – it was at a subsistence level, nothing more. It provided a base on which the citizen could build by his or her own efforts. But the assured base was the citizen's right, and it could be claimed without the taint of charity. England was on the threshold of wiping away the last vestiges of the Elizabethan poor law.

Mackenzie King recorded in his diary in December 1942 that he and Franklin Roosevelt 'had quite a talk about Beveridge's Report.' The president said that the report 'had made a real impression' in the United States. He told King (who hardly needed telling) that social security was politically popular, as well as 'being on the right lines in the way of reform.'[13] King replied that Canada 'had most of this program already between the federal government and the provinces' – an astonishing statement that reveals King's complete detachment from the lives of ordinary Canadians as well as his inadequate grasp of the Beveridge proposals.

Report on Social Security for Canada, 1943

Principal James and Ian Mackenzie, minister of pensions and health, discussed the Beveridge Report in December 1942, and the decision was taken to produce a Canadian social security plan for submission to Parliament in February 1943. The task of preparation was assigned to Leonard Marsh on 21 December 1942. Between that day and 17 January 1943, less than one month later, the first draft of the *Report on Social Security for Canada* was prepared. The contemporary press and some critics made too much of the speed with which the report was written. It was, in many respects, the distillation of the research, writing, thinking, and planning in social security and related fields that had been going on in Canada, the United States, Britain, and elsewhere during the preceding decade and longer.

It included the monumental Rowell-Sirois Report; the work of provincial royal commissions; the research conducted at McGill under Leonard Marsh into questions of health, unemployment, housing, and income; the research of Harry Cassidy at the University of Toronto; the reports of the Canadian Welfare Council, the Montreal Council of Social Agencies, and the Toronto Welfare Council; and the planning by the League for Social Reconstruction. Added to this was the stimulation provided by American and British studies and program developments in the field of social security, notably the New Deal legislation of President Roosevelt's era. Included in the group whom Marsh secured as consultants were five of the most accomplished Canadian specialists in private and public welfare and one of the principal experts in social insurance legislation from the International Labour Organization, whose headquarters, after the fall of France in 1940, had been moved from Geneva to Montreal. As Marsh states in his introduction to the republished *Report on Social Security for Canada* in 1975,

> Of course the report was prepared under pressure. But so was all the work of the Committee, its members, its tiny secretariat, and its widely ranging collaborators. That the Advisory Committee in two and a half years produced a substantial final report, six sub-committee reports, and nearly twenty contributory reports and memoranda was a tribute to the pace of wartime service that was evinced on other 'fronts' of the time in munitions, aircraft, tanks and shipbuilding production, to say nothing of training programs and administrative undertakings of all kinds. But to suggest that it was hasty, in conception or in the materials assembled, was to forget that the writer had been lecturing on these subjects for more than ten years previously at McGill University; that he had been employed on a series of related research topics, all concerned at one point or another with employment, housing, education, and social welfare services in Canada; that he had multiple contacts with administrators and welfare specialists in Canada and the United States.[14]

On 15 March 1943, the report was presented to the House of Commons Committee on Reconstruction and Rehabilitation. In his letter of transmittal, Marsh pointed out that his report was 'essentially a preliminary appraisal, not a blueprint with all the details filled in,' and that the report attempted to set out the following: the main features of existing social security provision in Canada; the methods by which these provisions could be improved and extended; and the principles governing the planning of a comprehensive social security system in the Canadian context (*Report on Social Security for Canada,* hereinafter referred to as the Marsh Report, 2).

The Marsh Report pinpointed for the first time in Canada, in clear and unequivocal fashion, the role that a social security system, buttressed by a comprehensive employment policy, could play in lifting people out of poverty and securing for them a defensible social minimum:

What this minimum should be is a matter of definition. Certainly, however, it means the direct elimination of poverty. It raises the level of those families whose incomes are inadequate at present levels or whose family needs are too great, to permit proper provision for health care or savings against the risk of disability or unemployment. It prevents penurious old age and the necessity of parents becoming dependent on their married children in later life and straining the resources of these younger families. (Marsh Report, 30)

Based on a careful study of living standard budgets, it was estimated that a *minimum subsistence budget* for a family of five required an annual income of $1,134 in 1940-1. This level of budget was 'conceded but not recommended,' and its limitations in terms of providing anything more than short-term emergency support were clearly spelled out. A preferable standard, the *desirable living minimum budget,* provided over a long period of time a better than subsistence living for a family of five. In 1940-1 this called for an income of $1,500. The 1941 census revealed that 33.4 per cent of urban male heads of families and a conservative estimate of 50 per cent of male heads of rural families earned less than $1,500 per year and were thus below the recommended desirable living minimum budget. While those families with fewer than three children would be marginally better off, larger families would be living at a correspondingly reduced level.

The report documented the failure of unemployment relief in the 1930s to approach a defensible level of assistance in most jurisdictions in Canada. It examined current programs such as mothers' allowances and old age and blind pensions and found them inadequate in terms of a desirable living minimum budget. Even the new Unemployment Insurance Act failed in five of its seven categories of benefit rates to approach a minimum subsistence budget. The only income-maintenance programs that paid adequate benefits were the dependants' allowances program for men in the armed forces and veterans' pensions (not including war veterans' allowances, a form of public assistance for veterans).

Having established a defensible standard-of-living floor below which no Canadian family should be allowed to fall, the Marsh Report offered proposals for meeting the principal types of contingencies that characterize industrial society, which would both protect Canadians from falling into poverty and raise the incomes of those individuals and families whose standard of living was less than the desirable minimum. It emphasized throughout that training and employment programs were essential supports.

Marsh's proposals were aimed at protecting Canadians from the principal contingencies that characterize industrial society, which he identified as those that interrupt earning capacity, either intermittently, as in cases of unemployment and sickness, or in a more prolonged way, as in cases of

disablement and, most common of all, old age. Additionally, there are contingencies that affect the adequacy of income, which Marsh subdivided
into two categories: those situations requiring special expenditures that
may strain a family's budget, such as births, deaths, accidents, and major illness; and the threat to income adequacy following from society's failure to
relate wages to the size of a worker's family. The threat to income adequacy
posed by low wages would have to be addressed by other types of programs,
primarily minimum wage laws and worker retraining and upgrading.

Marsh's proposals for a comprehensive social security system to meet
these common exigencies may be summarized as follows:

- A national employment and investment program to maintain full employment, coupled with an occupational training scheme to assist those who
  experience more than normal difficulty in finding a place in the workforce.
- A vastly expanded system of social insurance protection, operated by the
  federal government, to protect workers from the risks of income interruption that Marsh termed 'employment risks.' The sole exception would be
  workers' compensation, which would remain a provincial responsibility.
- A social insurance program to protect all gainfully employed persons,
  including the self-employed, from what Marsh termed the 'universal risks'
  of old age, permanent disability, or death (in effect, those risks now covered by the Canada and Quebec Pension Plans).
- A comprehensive system of health insurance, including all medical, dental, pharmaceutical, and optometrist's services, provincially administered but jointly financed by the federal and provincial governments
  with contributions from the insured population.
- A universal system of family allowances.

Implicit in the Marsh plan was an extension in the coverage of the existing Unemployment Insurance Act to decrease the number of unemployed
who had to apply for welfare when they failed to qualify for UI benefits.

The total expenditure of the Marsh plan for social security (excluding
the programs of public investment) was estimated to amount to between
10 and 12.5 per cent of the national income, at full implementation. Based
upon what Britain and the United States were preparing to spend for similar purposes, this was a 'reasonable commitment' (Marsh Report, 267).

Public Reaction to the Marsh Report

On 16 March 1943 the Marsh Report was released to the public together
with the *Health Insurance Report* (the Heagerty Report) and a draft of a Health
Insurance Bill. Canadians opening their newspapers on 16 March to read of
the Marsh Report's proposals for social security as well as the medical insurance plan might have been excused for thinking that they were witnessing

the arrival of the millennium. The Marsh Report captured the most attention. The reporting was balanced and informative. Useful summaries or
'highlights' of the report appeared on the front pages with more detailed
discussion inside. The words 'billion dollars' figured prominently in the
headlines, helping to promote one of the biggest news stories of an eventful
year. French Canadian papers gave the report equal treatment: 'Travail et
sécurité pour tous' was the headline of Montreal's *Le Jour* (20 March 1943).

The media quickly applied the tag of 'Canada's Beveridge Report' to the
Report on Social Security for Canada. However, there were significant differences. The Beveridge Report concerned itself almost exclusively with the
question of providing an assured minimum of income security. Questions
of health policy were left to another committee, and the matter of postwar
employment policy, which Beveridge considered crucial, became the subject of a second report that he issued in 1944 (*Full Employment in a Free
Society*). Therefore, the Marsh Report was much more all-encompassing in
its proposals, including as it did health policy, postwar employment and
training, as well as income security. There was another important distinction noted by one perceptive reviewer:

> Britain already has a well established and fairly comprehensive social secu-
> rity system, whose principles are familiar to the British public and reason-
> ably well understood. Sir William Beveridge could, therefore, take a good
> deal for granted. Canada, on the other hand, has only a few scattered poli-
> cies of social security, and the principles of the subject are by no means
> familiar to the Canadian public. Marsh therefore could take nothing for
> granted. He had to start from scratch, explain precisely what social security
> is, why we need it and what it can be expected to accomplish.[15]

Comment from the business community included the viewpoint that
the majority of Canadians were determined to have a job and a decent
standard of living after the war, even to the point of experimenting with
socialism or communism to get it. For this reason, 'those who presume to
speak for private enterprise must ... hesitate to offer any real objection to
the adoption of the basic principle of "social security" itself.'[16] Other business comment seemed blinded by ideology: 'When men become dependent upon the State for their welfare, and when the state encroaches
farther and farther upon the confines of private business, there develops a
power over the individual which may be seized and perpetuated by dangerous politicians. Thus the dangers of an ideological totalitarian conquest
lurk in the humanitarian concepts of any widespread compulsory scheme
of social security insurance.'[17]

Trade union reaction varied from indifference to positive acclaim. The
Canadian Congress Journal, the voice of the Trades and Labour Congress of

Canada, ignored the report's appearance. The Canadian Congress of Labour's journal, the *Canadian Unionist*, gave the report immediate coverage in its March 1943 issue and followed it up in the next issue with an incisive and laudatory review by the congress's new director of research, Eugene Forsey.[18] The president of the Canadian and Catholic Confederation of Labour, however, criticized the Marsh Report as an influence tending toward 'centralization.' 'Nothing,' he alleged, 'could be more contrary to national unity as we conceive it in Quebec.'[19]

The Canadian Welfare Council greeted the report with restrained approval, repeating the charge that the report had been 'prepared in haste.'[20] While noting the similarity in the thinking behind the Beveridge and Marsh Reports, the council's review conceded that the report's basic proposals were 'related to the Canadian setting.' It also drew attention to a feature of the report that went largely unremarked by other commentators – the fact that Marsh had devoted a special section to the social security needs of women – which was further evidence, in the council's view, of the report's comprehensive quality.[21]

The Progressive Conservative Party, having announced a 'New National Policy' in 1942 that included a commitment, in the abstract at least, to social security, full employment, collective bargaining, and medical insurance, fell back upon more traditional responses when faced with a set of concrete proposals for social security. John Bracken, the party's leader, saw in the Marsh Report the 'danger of a demoralized people being supported in idleness and rationed poverty.' Another critic had said that if implemented, it would 'make a Santa Claus of the State.'[22]

Obviously, the Conservative Party required a more informed critic. Bracken hit upon the idea of asking Charlotte Whitton, in March of 1943, to write an 'unprejudiced summary' of the main proposals of the three reports that had drawn so much attention in Canada – the Beveridge, Marsh, and Heagerty Reports. This was done to ensure that they were 'reliable as a basis for Canadian policy,' particularly in view of 'the hurried manner with which at least one of these Canadian reports has been conceived and published.'[23] Whitton was also invited to offer her own proposals for Canada's postwar social security plans. Toward the end of 1943 she published a slim volume of summary and comment on the three reports, together with her own proposals, under the title *The Dawn of Ampler Life*.

The Whitton Proposals
Charlotte Whitton's plans for postwar social security were predicated on a high national income and a 'living wage policy' guaranteeing every adult male a wage sufficient to support him, his wife, and two or three children.[24] Both of these goals would be a federal responsibility.

Building on this foundation, Whitton recommended:

- An expansion of 'social utilities' – that is, community services that protect and advance well-being, such as schools, hospitals, children's services, technical and vocational training, and, with the cooperation of the private sector, housing for low-income families – all under provincial and municipal jurisdiction but with financial assistance from the federal government.
- An expansion of provincial child welfare services, which, together with the 'living wage policy,' housing for low-income families, and the extension of income tax deductions for dependent children, would obviate the need for family allowances.
- A public system of medical care providing a 'general minimum standard' of health services for the whole population, financed entirely out of a combination of federal, provincial, and municipal taxes and administered by the provinces.
- A system of 'income insurance' administered by a federal board, independent of Parliament, covering all wage earners and self-employed whose earnings exceeded the income tax threshold.[25] In return for a compulsory contribution, this scheme would provide small, flat-rate benefits in cases of loss or impairment of income, either permanent or temporary. Whitton indicated that the benefit would require supplementation either from personal savings, private insurance, or social assistance.
- An expansion of provincial and municipal social assistance programs, with the financial support of the federal government. This was a priority for Whitton because she feared the widely predicted unemployment at war's end. Her 'income insurance' scheme would need time to build up a reserve before it could begin paying benefits, which was another reason for Whitton's insistence that social assistance be expanded.
- That the federal government take the lead in setting up the new social security system, but that the administrative responsibility be assumed by provincial and local governments, except in the case of 'income insurance.' Federal financing would be by means of grants-in-aid, distributed according to the needs of the provinces on the recommendations of a Dominion Social Assistance Board, an administrative device that Whitton hoped would overcome politically inspired wrangling between the federal and provincial governments, and that would also set certain minimum conditions.

The Cassidy Plan

Harry Cassidy, one of the most experienced observers of Canadian social services, offered his own proposals for social security in a book published in 1943.[26] Like Whitton, Cassidy offered merely an outline of a plan based on two major premises: that full employment and agricultural prosperity be achieved, and that sufficient money to finance the new measures be raised and distributed among the cooperating governments.

On these two premises, Cassidy called for:

- A comprehensive system of social insurance to protect wage earners and the self-employed against loss of earnings arising from unemployment, sickness, disability, industrial accident, pregnancy, retirement, or death. The plan would be financed by compulsory contributions from the insured, his or her employer, and the federal government; the latter would administer the program except for workers' compensation, which would remain a provincial responsibility.
- A system of family allowances administered and financed entirely by the federal government, providing benefits in cash, kind, or a combination of the two.
- At least four expanded categorical programs of social assistance: old age, disability, mothers' allowances, and general assistance. These programs would continue to operate under provincial and municipal authority but with financial aid and some supervision from the federal government.
- A complete rebuilding and extension of the existing system of provincial and municipal social services. The importance of national leadership through greatly increased financial assistance, technical and advisory services, and the setting of standards was stressed.

Comparing the Three Proposals

As Cassidy pointed out, there was in the three major plans agreement on 'the distribution of administrative and financial responsibility between the Dominion, on the one hand, and the provincial and local authorities on the other.'[27] All three favoured federal cost-shared agreements, referred to as 'conditional grants,' not only to assist provinces financially but to promote national standards in social welfare.

The Marsh plan emphasized establishing an assured minimum standard of living and protecting people from falling into poverty. Furthermore, and this sets the Marsh plan apart from the other two, the form of protection offered was, as far as possible, provided as a matter of right, linked to citizenship or to prior contributions to a social insurance plan. By contrast, both Whitton and Cassidy called for an expansion of the discretionary social assistance method as a means of meeting financial need.

Whitton's recommendations had a strong residual flavour: 'housing for low-income families,' which was a recipe for segregating people, and a national health care plan offering a 'general minimum standard' of health care, which would have resulted in a two-tier medical system, are examples. Similarly, Whitton's suggested 'income insurance' plan appeared to be a form of private compulsory insurance, whose coverage and benefits were predicted to be well below any notion of adequacy or comprehensiveness. Whitton's overall plan was influenced by her pessimistic projections for postwar national income. Marsh, who was somewhat more optimistic on the basis of his public investment program, could afford to plan more comprehensively.

Cassidy, while less conservative than Whitton, also visualized a prominent role for discretionary social assistance programs. He supported an expansion of social insurance against a range of risks, as well as a universal system of family allowances. His view of the latter program was muddied by his suggestion that the allowance might be a combination of cash or in-kind services, thereby weakening the program's horizontal equity and antipoverty goals.

Whitton's basic criticism of the Marsh proposals was that they represented an attempt to introduce ideas from a different (i.e., European) social background. Specifically, the emphasis on social insurance and on federal leadership and control were indicative of an overreliance on the Beveridge plan.[28] The Marsh Report did recommend that the federal government assume a dominant administrative, financial, and planning role in a comprehensive system of social security, but this has to be viewed in light of the vast increase in the federal government's role in the preceding decade. The Great Depression brought the federal government reluctantly into areas of provincial jurisdiction, and this trend accelerated a thousandfold with the outbreak of the Second World War. In view of this history, it is understandable why Marsh, when asked to plan a comprehensive nationwide social security system, should assign new and major responsibilities to the federal government. What Marsh may have failed to appreciate was Quebecois nationalism and its hostility to any expansion of federal powers in areas of provincial jurisdiction such as social insurance or health care.[29] In this respect, the Whitton proposals, and to a lesser extent those of Cassidy, were more in tune with Canadian political realities.

Government Reaction to the Marsh Report

All three reports were largely the work of individuals. The Marsh Report, having been prepared at the request of the Advisory Committee on Reconstruction and published by the King's Printer, was the closest to an official report. It is of interest to compare the official reception afforded the Marsh Report and the Beveridge Report by their respective governments. The Beveridge Report was presented to the British Parliament with acceptance of its principles and a pledge for implementation at least in part from the government. The Marsh Report, on the other hand, was not tabled in Parliament but merely presented by the Advisory Committee on Reconstruction to the Parliamentary Committee on Social Security for their information. The government ignored the report. This was confirmed by the fact that at the Conference on Reconstruction, held in Ottawa in 1945, the dominion proposals for a considerable enlargement of Canada's social security network were made without a single reference to the Marsh Report.

The Marsh plan was criticized for its recommendation that the federal government should assume responsibility for all unemployed employables, although the report countered many of the objections raised. The most serious objection to the Marsh plan was its centralizing tendency, which may have been administratively commendable, but politically it was anathema to Mackenzie King, who saw it as dangerous to federal Liberal Party support in Quebec, where provincial autonomy was jealously guarded.

The projected expenditures of the Marsh plan may have tempered government interest in a comprehensive plan. To ensure a minimum income to Canadians would cost an estimated $1 billion annually. The same amount would have to be expended, it was thought, in the years immediately following the war on public works projects as an antidote to expected unemployment. The Canadian cabinet, comparing these costs with the entire prewar budget of the federal government of $500 million, realized that the national income would have to remain at a wartime level to support a postwar budget in the range of $2.5 billion. To support such costs, full employment and restoration of international trade were imperatives. According to the *Economist*, 'these views lead to the proposition in Ottawa that if national income is maintained at war levels, social welfare follows from prosperity. But if income is not maintainable then social expenditures as per the Marsh report could not be undertaken. Result: more interest in proposals to ensure full employment than in social security.'[30]

Another obstacle to a government commitment to a program of comprehensive social security was the strong conservative element in the Mackenzie King cabinet and the lack of awareness of the potentialities of income-maintenance programs as a means of raising standards of living. This is clearly revealed in Mackenzie King's account of the cabinet discussion that took place on the question of family allowances in 1943, prior to the inauguration of that program. In arguing for family allowances, King told his cabinet: 'I said quite frankly that I thought the Creator intended that all persons born should have equal opportunities. Equal opportunity started in days of infancy and the first thing at least, was to see that the children got the essentials of life. I then spoke of modern society making impossible chances in life for multitudes of people.' One of Mackenzie King's cabinet colleagues interrupted to say 'that most men would come up who had this early struggle; to ease it for them was not to help eventually.' King replied 'that we all knew the individual cases of this kind ... what was not known was the multitude of persons who were crushed at the beginning of life and never had a chance to start at all.'[31]

Counteracting the conservative elements in the cabinet, and in the country generally, was the marked growth in the support for Canada's socialist party, the CCF, commencing in the closing months of 1942. The fear of an Axis victory had passed, and Canada's troops were not yet in battle. With this reduced sense of urgency a certain amount of labour unrest developed, largely centred upon the government's wage stabilization orders and the wartime restrictions generally. In the Ontario provincial election held in August 1943, the CCF Party, unrepresented in the legislature prior to the election, picked up thirty-four of ninety seats to become the official opposition. A few days later, it won two federal by-elections, and in 1944 it became the government of Saskatchewan, replacing a Liberal regime. The CCF was also the official opposition in the British Columbia legislature. By September 1943 a Gallup Poll reported that the CCF had overtaken the Liberal Party in popularity in Canada generally (CCF 29 per cent, Liberals 28 per cent), in Ontario (CCF 32 per cent, Liberals 26 per cent), and in the west (CCF 41 per cent, Liberals 23 per cent). Faced with this pressure from the left as well as apparent interest in social security on the part of the Progressive Conservatives, Mackenzie King fought back. His speech from the throne in January 1944 'bristled with promises – to industrialists, to exporters, to farmers, to men now in the armed services, and to the nation at large by way of housing, health and social security measures – a truly table d'hôte bill of fare.'[32] The social security measures promised a 'national minimum of social security and human welfare,' which included family allowances, contributory health insurance, and a contributory old age pension scheme. Also promised was a new federal department, the Department of National Health and Welfare, superseding the Department of Pensions and National Health.[33]

In the federal election of 11 June 1945, Prime Minister Mackenzie King's Liberal Party faced the electorate with the slogan 'A new social order for Canada,' and was returned but with a sharply reduced majority. The CCF representation in the House of Commons rose from eight to twenty-nine seats, a much smaller gain than had been expected. King's move to the left, as represented by his social security proposals and the family allowances system introduced in 1944, thwarted the CCF's bid for major party status.

In retrospect, the Second World War exerted a variety of influences on the development of social security in Canada. The wartime period witnessed the first countrywide discussions of a comprehensive social security system for Canada, a consequence of the fact that 'peace aims are war weapons.'[34] Furthermore, 'the war was ... responsible for lifting counter-cyclical policy from the classroom to the forum.'[35] Income maintenance proposals could now be supported for their stabilizing effect on the economy, as in the case of unemployment insurance and family allowances. This facilitated the planning of social security schemes that would have been considered financially irresponsible in prewar years. The sudden rise in strength of the CCF in Canada during the war, aided by the support of the Canadian Congress of Labour, strengthened the hand of liberal elements in the federal government and pushed Ottawa into a considerable amount of social security planning. A significant feature of this planning was the first comprehensive plan of attack on poverty in Canadian history, contained in the Marsh Report.

Concern with postwar problems was marked by other reports that came out of the wartime era and that represent landmarks in Canadian social security planning: the Curtis Report on Housing and Community Planning (1944), and the Report of the Advisory Committee on Health Insurance (1943) (the Heagerty Report), which presented detailed proposals on health insurance and public health. The Curtis Report, which was followed by the passage of the National Housing Act (1944), will be summarized below. The Heagerty Report, and its sequel, will be discussed later in this chapter.

The Curtis Report, 1944

The Curtis Report,[36] of which Marsh was editor and research coordinator, outlined Canada's housing and community planning needs in the postwar world and clearly identified the threat to the adequacy of income that low- and medium-income families and individuals experienced in their search for shelter. Allowing the free play of market forces in the housing field with a minimum of government intervention had resulted in a serious deficiency in housing, particularly for the low-income group, which in 1941 was identified as urban families of five with incomes of less than $1,200 per year – approximately one-third of the population. This deficiency in the housing stock was illustrated in the degree of overcrowding that markedly increased as family income declined, in the amount of substandard housing and slum-like conditions that threatened the health and general well-being of the occupants, and in the fact that 89 per cent of the lower third of urban tenant families were paying more than the desirable proportion (estimated at one-fifth) of their budget for rent. As this class of housing accommodation was likely to be substandard, the families concerned were in double jeopardy.

The Curtis Report recommended large-scale intervention by government with federal authorities providing the leadership in the housing market and in town planning. A particular target of priority was the provision of low-rental housing. The federal government responded with the National Housing Act (1944). This act was described as 'An Act to Promote the Construction of New Houses, the Repair and Modernization of Existing Houses, the Improvement of Housing and Living Conditions and the Expansion of Employment in the Postwar Period.' A Canadian housing authority writing in 1968 noted: 'The emphasis on "the expansion of employment in the postwar period" makes it clear that the fundamental intention of the legislation was more economic – in terms of avoidance of a post-war depression akin to that of 1919-21 – than social, that is, a concern with the well-being of all Canadians in terms of their housing requirements.'[37]

Between 1945 and 1950 the federal agency that had produced a total of 45,930 wartime houses in centres where war industries were located was taken over by a new federal agency, the Central Mortgage and Housing Corporation. CMHC initiated a home-building program entitled Veterans'

Rental Housing, which in the period 1947-9 aimed at building 10,000 homes per year. This limited program was the only sizeable attempt at providing low- and moderate-income housing, and this initiative must be viewed not as basic housing policy but as part of a larger program of veterans' benefits. It did not represent the main thrust of Canadian housing policy in the post-World War Two era. That policy (which must be inferred, as there was little in the way of explicit government goals for housing) was supposedly the attainment of home ownership by every Canadian family through the 'normal' channel of home provision: the private market. To assist the average Canadian, the federal government, through the CMHC, was to see that there were adequate supplies of mortgage money at rates lower than prevailing market rates. Periods of amortization were increased, down payments lowered, and the amount of loans increased. This policy made it possible for thousands of Canadians to become home-buyers rather than tenants, and it certainly added impetus to the phenomenal increase in suburban growth around Canadian cities that characterized the new Canada of the 1950s. Slum clearance, on the other hand, encountered continuous delays; the housing needs of the lower third of families in the income scale continued to be neglected.

The Family Allowance Act of 1944

As already noted in Chapter 6, the first indication of official interest in family allowances in Canada occurred when the subject was investigated by a parliamentary committee in 1929 and by a Quebec provincial commission in 1932. Apart from these brief flurries of interest in family allowances in the late 1920s and early 1930s, the subject was a dead issue in Canada until 1942. In that year the CCF convention expressed itself in favour of family allowances.[38] However, it was not until the publication of the Marsh Report in 1943, in which children's allowances were highlighted as the 'key to consistency' in any social security system if benefits in time of unemployment, sickness, or disability were not to exceed wages for some in full-time employment, that Canadians began to discuss the concept of family allowances. The issue soon became a point of heated discussion. Once again, Charlotte Whitton opposed the scheme. The core of her argument against family allowances was that rather than providing cash allowances for children in all Canadian families, well-to-do and poor alike (which she termed wasteful), the social services should be extended to benefit the most needy. Whitton urged an extension of 'social utilities' in the fields of health, education, and protection of children, as well as provision of low-cost housing and the maintenance of adequate wage levels. Children's allowances, she claimed, would not provide the health measures, better housing, improved educational facilities, and the school meals that were so urgently required in many parts of Canada.

Those who supported family allowances said that 'social utilities,' though needed, were not a substitute for cash allowances. The aim of the cash plan, it was argued, was to provide for the minimum requirements of the child – shoes, clothes, and three meals a day. Without these basics the child would hardly be in a position to take advantage of, for example, schooling. Furthermore, services in kind, it was said, would, under the Whitton plan, be geared to the lowest income groups and be subject to the taint of 'charity.' Marsh made the point that 'there must be a reasonable leeway for parents' decision in the expenditure of the budget for their children. It is an impossible situation to imagine that all guidance and all services should be provided by non-family agencies' (Marsh Report, 199). It should be pointed out that the Marsh Report fully supported the strengthening of social assistance programs (albeit for a more restricted role) as well as the expansion of housing and other social welfare services as essential auxiliaries to the social security plan.

Whitton's concern that cash grants would be wasted was not borne out by evidence of the Dependants' Allowances Board, which, during the Second World War, was responsible for issuing cash allowances to the wives and children of servicemen at the rate of 600,000 cheques per month. The misuse uncovered under this scheme ranged from 1 to 3 per cent of the cases.[39] In addition, allowances were taxed on a sliding scale, so that families with incomes over $3,000 per year did not gain from the scheme. The government estimated that only 100,000 families were in the latter category, so the vast majority of Canadian families derived some benefit from the allowances.

Some people saw the scheme for family allowances as an incentive for poor families to have more children; an unhappy side issue to this argument was the contention that family allowances would increase the birthrate among French Canadian Catholics and that the plan was a political manoeuvre to gain Liberal support in Quebec. The strength of feeling generated on this issue may be seen in the government decision, upon introducing the scheme of family allowances, to award them on a sliding scale decreasing in amount after the fourth child. This provision was criticized by French Canadians who charged that large families were being unfairly penalized, and Charlotte Whitton correctly pointed out that this policy conflicted with the government's expressed concern for all children.[40]

The strongest arguments in favour of family allowances were the income and nutritional studies that had been done during the late 1930s and early 1940s. Even in wartime, with all able-bodied men and women able to find employment, only 43.7 per cent of families of wage earners, outside of agriculture, had sufficient income to guarantee them a satisfactory nutritional diet. Furthermore, Canada had the highest infant mortality rate of any white country in the British Empire.[41] As infant mortality bears a close correlation to per capita income, putting more cash into each Canadian home, it was argued, would be one method of attacking this problem. It was also pointed out that since 1918, tax exemptions had been granted for children under income tax regulations. In 1944 these exemptions amounted to $108 per child, a provision that provided no help to those families below the income tax threshold.[42]

The attitude of labour toward family allowances had traditionally been a carbon copy of American trade union opinion. Labour tended to see family allowances as a substitute for adequate wages and a device to weaken their bargaining power for higher standards of pay. In 1929 the Canadian Trades and Labour Congress went on record as opposing family allowances. By 1944 the Canadian Congress of Labour had formally endorsed the idea, although when the suggestion was made by the National War Labour Board in 1943 that family allowances might be an alternative to raising the wage ceiling, labour objected strongly. It charged that the taxpayers were being asked to assume the obligation of industry to pay adequate wages.[43] By 1945 Canadian unions fully accepted the family allowance scheme and saw that, far from weakening their bargaining position, it gave labour extra resources with which to withstand the financial pressures of a strike or lockout.

The family allowance concept had obtained the support of a majority of professional social workers by 1944. In her submission to the 1929 parliamentary committee studying the question of family allowances, Charlotte Whitton was said to have represented the 'organized social services.' In 1943, when she returned to the attack on family allowances, Whitton represented a small minority of the social work profession. Other prominent social workers fully supported the concept of family allowances, as did the Canadian Association of Social Workers.[44] Furthermore, two social workers served as consultants on the final drafts of the Marsh Report.

In 1944 the Canadian government introduced a bill into Parliament to provide for family allowances to all children up to the age of sixteen, provided they were attending school or unable to do so on medical grounds, on a graduated scale depending upon the ages and numbers of children.[45] The proposed cost of the scheme was estimated to be $200 million a year, involving a gross distribution of $250 million in allowances with $50 million expected to be rebated through the income tax processes. This was a gigantic sum to propose for a welfare scheme – exceeding all welfare expenditures by all units of government in Canada, including public health and unemployment aid, in any typical year from 1936 to 1939.[46] But as the prime minister pointed out, this sum was the amount Canada was then spending on the war in a two-week period. Only a gifted prophet could have foreseen that by 1955 the Canadian national income, less than $12 billion in 1945, would be around $30 billion.

The House of Commons was told that the purpose of the Family Allowance

Act was to protect the rising generation, assuring children of their basic needs. Its second purpose was to maintain purchasing power in the postwar era. There was some halfhearted opposition from Conservatives during the first reading of the bill, but at the second reading the legislation was passed unanimously – a rare event for such a momentous piece of legislation.[47]

The Family Allowance Act was Canada's first universal welfare payment program.[48] It was, of course, an extension of the principle of allowances for children already granted under provincial mothers' allowances and workers' compensation programs as well as in unemployment and general relief, where payments were commonly based on the number in the family. The federal government's dependants' allowances scheme for the armed forces and the tax relief given for children under the Income Tax Act were similar in principle to the new act. But in view of the Canadian penchant for schemes of a limited public assistance nature, one wonders why the universal type of payment was selected.

Why Universal Family Allowances?

A universal type of program fitted the two stated objectives of the legislation: a concern for the well-being of all Canadian children[49] (a reflection of a common desire among all Canadians to leave the inequalities and misery of the 1930s behind them), and a desire to maintain purchasing power in what many feared would be an economic slump when the war ended. But there were other, unstated factors that contributed to the selection of a universal welfare payment program.

In 1944 the wage stabilization scheme of the federal government, introduced in 1942, was under increasingly heavy attack from labour leaders who claimed, with some justification, that unskilled labourers had had their wages frozen at less than a living wage and that the wage freeze must be relaxed for this group. The government, fearing a general rise in prices and wages if it granted this request, is said to have had family allowances recommended as a way around the impasse. This was strenuously denied by the government at the time of the bill's introduction. It claimed that the Family Allowance Act was completely divorced from its wage control policy. However, the fact that the National War Labour Board recommended family allowances as an alternative to the removal of the wage ceiling indicates that this was a significant element in the introduction of family allowances in Canada.

There were also political factors. Mackenzie King, it is said, hoped that the Conservatives would oppose the measure and thus provide him with an issue for the next federal election. In addition, the Liberal Party was being threatened from the left by the CCF Party in Saskatchewan and Ontario. In June 1944, a little more than a month prior to the passage of the bill on 1 August 1944, the CCF replaced the Liberal government in Saskatchewan.

Mackenzie King was also accused of trying to win more support in Quebec for Liberals there who were suffering by reason of the conscription issue.

Constitutional issues were also involved. Any scheme of family allowances had to be one that did not infringe upon provincial rights. The making of cash grants to citizens of Canada who were not required to accept them (and in fact had to apply for them) was well within the powers of the federal government, although Conservatives attempted to argue that the act would invade the legislative sphere of the provinces.

The government was probably encouraged in its plans to launch a universal, non-means-tested program of family allowances by the Child Endowment scheme introduced in Australia in 1941. This plan provided allowances at a flat rate of five shillings a week for each child after the first under sixteen years of age. The reasons for excluding the first child included the additional cost (to have included the first child under the Australian plan would have nearly doubled the cost), plus the fact that the basic wage in Australia was considered sufficient to provide for the needs of one child in the family.[50] The fact that Canadian wage rates of unskilled labourers were considered less than adequate probably ruled out the possibility of the Canadian plan not paying an allowance for the firstborn. The Australians rejected any suggestion of a means test for the allowances on the grounds that it would be unpopular and administratively expensive. Their method of financing the scheme included a payroll tax on employers, an acknowledgment that the allowances were a special supplement to wages. It was hoped the tax would cover two-thirds of the cost, with the remaining third coming out of general revenue, part of which would be recovered by the abolition of tax deductions for all children other than the first. Federal authorities, for constitutional reasons, were unable to make use of payroll taxes, and Canadian labour leaders were in any case utterly opposed to any suggestion that family allowances were to be seen as a wage supplement. However, the Canadian government did introduce an element of selectivity into the Family Allowance Act, in somewhat the same way as the Australian plan, by reducing the income tax relief for children for whom family allowances were drawn.

By May 1946, 92 per cent of all children under sixteen years of age, numbering 3,333,763, were in receipt of benefits. The average monthly payment per family was $14.18, and $5.94 per child. This was considerably below the average minimum payment recommended by Marsh of $7.50 per child (Marsh Report, 204; see n. 45).

It must be pointed out that the single greatest advantage of family allowances as presented in the Marsh Report was lost sight of. His system, with benefits related to a minimum but defensible standard of child care costs, would have replaced, with administrative simplicity, all other allowances for children under public assistance or social insurance programs. Income maintenance programs could then have concentrated on establishing income standards for single people or couples, leaving the family allowance system to pick up on the child allowances under such programs as mothers' allowances, workers' compensation, public assistance, war veterans' allowances, and others. The family allowance scheme, as devised by Marsh, would have provided a consistent range of benefits to all children, thus furnishing, in the report's phrase, 'the key to consistency' for the whole social security system.

The Family Allowance Act nevertheless introduced a new element into Canada's social security picture – the universal welfare grant, payable to all children born in Canada or with three years residence prior to application – marking a new level of federal government concern for the welfare of its citizens. It was an amalgam of hope and fear – hope for a better postwar world with increased life chances for all, and fear of a postwar depression.

The distance from the mainstream of social work thinking of Charlotte Whitton's objections to family allowances was confirmed in 1949 when the federal government decided to amend the Family Allowance Act to repeal the provision that reduced the amount of allowances for the fifth and subsequent children in a family. In addition, the government said it would reduce from three years to one the residence period required for immigrant children. Whitton exploded in anger: 'It is a disgrace for the Canadian government to plan to spend millions more on the baby bonus at a time when such expenditure was never needed less ... While the generous baby bonus payments are being made, Canada is leaving adequate and humane care of the aged without attention.' Her comment was quickly rebuffed by leading social workers. R.E.G. Davis, executive director of the Canadian Welfare Council, commented: 'It is disquieting to have the case put in this either-or fashion, pitting the undoubtedly real needs of our aged against the needs of our children.' F.N. Stapleford, executive secretary of the Neighbourhood Workers' Association, Toronto, and Nora Lea, executive secretary of the Protestant Children's Homes, Toronto, supported family allowances as 'one of the most progressive and worthwhile pieces of legislation ever enacted by the Canadian Government.'[51]

An Attempt to Expand Canada's Social Security Network at the End of the Second World War

On 6 August 1945 a Dominion-Provincial Conference on Reconstruction opened its deliberations in Ottawa. Another event on that same day added a sense of urgency to the meeting: the first atomic bomb was dropped on Japan, and capitulation was only a few days away. The time for demobilization of the armed forces and the reconversion of industry was at hand.[52] The last full-scale dominion-provincial conference had been held in January 1941 to discuss the recommendations of the Royal Commission on

Dominion-Provincial Relations. As has been pointed out earlier, one of the principal recommendations of that commission was that the provinces be enabled to meet their social service responsibilities at a 'national Canadian standard' through the payment of National Adjustment Grants from the federal treasury on a fiscal needs basis. As a result of its calculations, the federal government decided that three provinces would not be entitled to a grant in the initial period – Ontario, British Columbia, and Alberta. Not surprisingly, the premiers of these three provinces were opposed to proceeding with the 1941 conference on the basis of the commission's recommendations, claiming that the commission's proposals, involving a major revision of federal-provincial fiscal relations, were matters to be considered in peacetime, and hasty action, prompted by the war emergency, should be avoided.[53] The conference ended on its second day, but the demands of the war meant that the Canadian government had to have control of the major tax fields. The federal government proposed that the provinces withdraw from the fields of personal and corporation income tax and accept in return a grant from the federal treasury to replace the lost revenue.[54] This request for cooperation was made in 1941, perhaps the gloomiest year of the war for the allies, and immediately agreed upon. In this way one of the principal recommendations of the Royal Commission on Dominion-Provincial Relations – the centralizing of the major direct tax fields under the federal government – came into being, although only as a wartime measure.

Developments during the war, principally the federal government's commitment to a policy of full employment and a high level of national income, plus a number of social security proposals, made a return to the prewar division of taxing powers undesirable from the federal point of view. Therefore, the first task of the 1945 Conference on Reconstruction was to secure a continuation and broadening of the federal occupancy of direct tax fields so that the peacetime goals that had been discussed up and down the land during the war emergency could be put into effect. These goals were summarized in the federal government's brief to the conference as a high and stable level of employment and income and a greater sense of public responsibility for individual economic security and welfare.[55] The federal government's plans for meeting these goals were four in number and were set within the framework of a free enterprise economy. They included encouragement to private enterprise and industry, a carefully timed program of public works, the federal social security proposals, and fiscal proposals aimed at a redistribution of taxing powers and revenues between the two senior governments.

The federal fiscal offer consisted of unconditional subsidies in return for the provinces vacating the fields of personal income taxes, corporation taxes, and succession duties to the federal government for a trial period of three years. These subsidies would increase or decrease in relation to the value of the gross national production per capita as compared with that of 1941. The federal government described these grants as more generous than the payments made under the Wartime Tax Agreements of 1941.

The public investment program was aimed at 'providing productive employment ... when international and other conditions adversely affected employment.' The primary responsibility for full employment was to be left largely with the free enterprise economy, assisted by infusions of government capital timed to compensate for any approaching economic slump.

The aim of the social security proposals was, in terms of the Marsh Report, quite a modest one. The government promised 'to provide, on a basis of small regular payments against large and uncertain individual risks for such hazards and disabilities as unemployment, sickness and old age.' To effect these aims, the federal government offered to assume full responsibility for old age pensions for Canadians aged seventy years and over; to share in the cost of a public assistance scheme for the needy aged sixty-five to sixty-nine; to assume financial responsibility for a public assistance type of program to meet the income needs of unemployed employables (those who for a variety of reasons could not qualify for insurance benefits); and to share in the cost of a health insurance scheme. A brief review of the federal government's social security proposals to the provinces in 1945 follows.

Old Age Pensions

The most notable aspect of the social security plans was the application of the 'universal' concept to old age pensions. The federal government proposed a twofold expansion of programs for the elderly: a system of universal pensions for all Canadians with twenty years' residence in the country at the age of seventy, at the rate of $30 per month and without a means test, to be financed and administered by the federal government; and federal grants on a fifty-fifty basis for a provincially administered scheme paying pensions of up to $30 per month, on a means test, to persons sixty-five to sixty-nine years of age.

Unemployment Assistance

Following the recommendations of the National Employment Commission, the Royal Commission on Dominion-Provincial Relations, and the Marsh Report, the 1945 federal social security proposals included a 'practicable and comprehensive system of assistance for the able-bodied unemployed' – those who were without the protection of the unemployment insurance system. The plan was to be administered by the federal government through the existing unemployment insurance system, and benefits would be paid at uniform rates across the country for three categories of recipients. For persons who had exhausted their benefits, or who lacked the full qualification to receive a benefit, and for those who were not insured but could demonstrate a record of previous employment, the scale of assistance would be approximately 85 per cent of the benefit rate. For an individual who was not insured and who had no adequate record of previous employment, assistance would be provided 'at a flat rate which would not conflict with insurance benefits or wage rates for comparable employed persons' (*Proposals of the Government of Canada*, 44). There would be no thoroughgoing means test, but assistance would not be extended to 'those who are not dependent on their own employment for a livelihood or to those who have an adequate income independent of employment.' This policy had a sexist bias, since it eliminated claims from secondary earners in families, most of whom were women. This program was to last until the Unemployment Insurance Act was extended to cover the remainder of the workforce.

It seems clear that the social security proposals of the federal government were aimed at filling the gaps in the social security system, rather than at implementing a program that involved a rebuilding and extension of the existing framework into a comprehensive whole.[56]

What is remarkable about these two proposals is that, despite a wide interest and movement in English-speaking countries toward social insurance techniques, Canada at this point was offering the provinces a combination of public assistance and universal income maintenance plans. It is also noteworthy that a universal pension plan did not figure in any of the social security plans sketched out by the Canadian experts, Marsh, Whitton, and Cassidy. The idea may well have been borrowed from New Zealand, where a superannuation benefit plan was introduced in 1940.[57] The government stated in its brief to the provinces that, 'In developing its proposals with reference to old age pensions, the federal government has given careful attention to the experience of other countries (in particular the plans and proposals now in operation or under consideration in Great Britain, the United States, Australia and New Zealand)' (*Proposals of the Government of Canada*, 37). More cogent reasons for the offer of full federal assumption of the cost of pensions to the group aged seventy and over will be discussed below.

Turning to the modified public assistance scheme for unemployed employables, one's first concern is to question the adequacy of the proposed benefits. In two categories out of three, benefits were set at 85 per cent of regular unemployment insurance payments – payments described by the Marsh Report as substandard. The federal government obliquely acknowledged the question of adequacy of benefit rates by stating: 'If it should be deemed necessary by any municipality for it to supplement the rates of assistance available in any particular cases, the provision of such a supplement would remain a matter for the provincial government or the municipality concerned, and subject to whatever conditions they wish to apply for the purposes of the supplement' (*Proposals of the Government of Canada*, 44).

The question of differentiating between the 'employable' and the 'unemployable' was to be decided in this way: 'In the absence of more specific evidence of unemployability, a person who has remained on assistance for a period of two years, without being able to obtain or keep employment other than of a casual nature, would be declared ineligible and transferred to the responsibility of the provincial government and municipality.'

The question that immediately springs to mind as one considers the rather limited social security proposals of the dominion government is: What had happened to all the talk about a comprehensive social security system? The explanation may be the result of a number of factors.

The Canadian government never endorsed the idea of initiating a comprehensive social security system, apart from the rather vague generalities contained in the speeches from the throne in 1943 and 1944. It studiously ignored the Marsh Report. The government's intentions and priorities were made clear in April 1946, ten months after the federal election, when the two labour congresses presented their annual list of legislative demands to the federal cabinet. The Trades and Labour Congress, which had assisted the Liberals to victory by failing to endorse the CCF, was sharply rebuked by Finance Minister Ilsley for its 'costly' demands. (Labour had requested that the government carry out its social security promises.) Ilsley's reply was that the government's priorities were for reducing taxes, balancing the budget, and retrenchment. This prompted the Montreal *Star* to comment that 'this reckless expenditure over and above Canada's already colossal commitments for social security schemes should be set aside as outside the range of practical politics.'[58]

Furthermore, the government's social security proposals in 1945, according to James Maxwell, were used as bait to gain provincial agreement to the whole reconstruction plan, of which the most crucial section, from the federal standpoint, was the securing of the fields of personal and corporation taxes and succession duties.[59] For this reason decisions regarding social security measures were taken in the light of how they would most lighten the financial load on the provinces (so as to make them financially attractive), rather than from the standpoint of devising a comprehensive scheme. As the burden of old age pension payments was a steadily growing one for all provinces, the old age pension proposals that increased federal financial contributions were bound to look appealing. Similarly, as the provinces had expressed the fear that the Unemployment Insurance Act would not cover the large-scale unemployment expected at the end of hostilities, the federal government offered to provide unemployment assistance to all unemployed employables and promised a widening of the unemployment insurance system.

Another reason for the government's apparent lack of interest in a comprehensive plan was that it related its social security proposals to their effect on consumption. A primary goal for federal policy was the maintenance of full employment, and the income maintenance proposals were to be instrumental in attaining this end. Finally, by steering clear of social insurance schemes, the federal government was avoiding the issue of constitutional amendment, which in 1945 would have been considerably more difficult to achieve than in the dark war days of 1941.

The remaining federal proposals for social security concerned the provision of a program of health insurance plus an expanded health program. We need at this point to refer briefly to the Heagerty Report.

The Heagerty Report

The Heagerty Report on health insurance and public health, made public in 1943, resulted from a study begun in early 1942 at the request of the federal government as part of the plan for postwar reconstruction. The report's specific proposals called for a joint federal-provincial program of health insurance with the medical care and public health provisions being administered by the provinces and the federal government assisting with grants-in-aid and help in standard-setting and technical consultation. The report envisaged the whole population being covered for a full range of benefits in kind, including medical, dental, pharmaceutical, hospital, and nursing services. However, the way was left open for the provinces to limit benefits to those having less than a certain income, a serious impediment to universal coverage. The plan would be financed from three sources: contributions from the federal and provincial governments as well as from the insured. The annual insurance premium per person for all citizens sixteen years and older was to be $12. Indigents would have their fee paid by the provincial government. In addition to this 'registration fee,' all income tax payers would pay a health insurance tax of 3 per cent up to a maximum of $30 per year for a single person, or 5 per cent up to a maximum of $50 in the case of married persons. Federal grants to provinces to assist in the development of public health programs were also included.

Critics of the Heagerty Report pointed out that the regressive nature of the proposed financing formula was 'a flagrant violation of the principle of ability to pay.'[60] The administrative arrangements were termed 'heavily weighted in favour of the doctors and others providing the services.' Those who both consumed and paid for the services were, according to labour, inadequately represented. The bill made no provision for securing the additional medical manpower that it was anticipated would be required, nor did it mention anything in the way of federal help with provincial capital expenditures to build medical schools, hospitals, and clinics.

These criticisms aside, there was a widespread degree of support for the principle of health insurance, not only from the Canadian Congress of Labour, the Trades and Labour Congress, and the Canadian Federation of Agriculture, but from the Canadian Medical Association, the Canadian Dental Association, and the Canadian Life Insurance Officers' Association.[61] This remarkable unanimity was part of the revolution in thought and aspiration that Canadians entertained for the postwar world in reaction to the searing experience of the Depression and its effect on health standards and access to health care.

The Heagerty proposals, after a number of revisions, were referred to the Dominion-Provincial Conference on Reconstruction in 1945. By this time the health plans had undergone substantial alteration and the original plan for national legislation in the interests of promoting national uniformity and adequacy had been dropped. The plan now contained four specific proposals: a federal grant for planning and organization; a series of grants to the provinces for specific public health services; federal financial assistance for hospital construction; and proposals for health insurance involving a two-stage program. The first stage of the health insurance program would provide all insured citizens with basic medical services – a general practitioner service, hospital care, and visiting nurse service. The second stage would enrich the service by providing consultant, specialist, and surgical services, dental care, special nursing services, pharmaceutical, and laboratory services. The federal government offered to meet 60 per cent of the cost of the services provided that costs did not exceed the federal estimates.

These proposals were presented to the provinces as part of a larger package, the 'Green Book Proposals,' covering a wide range of health, welfare, and fiscal plans for the postwar years. As the two levels of government failed to agree on fiscal items, the entire package was jettisoned and the first significant plan for a comprehensive public medical care system in Canada was stillborn.

The Failure of the 1945 Conference on Reconstruction

Provincial attitudes toward the federal proposals at the preliminary meeting went as expected. The have-not provinces – the Maritimes and the Prairie provinces – were generally in favour, since they stood to gain financially from 'renting' their tax fields to Ottawa, although Premier Douglas of Saskatchewan voiced regret at the federal government's departure from the key recommendation of the Royal Commission on Dominion-Provincial Relations that the federal grants to provinces should be calculated on a fiscal needs basis instead of the proposed per capita grant. However, for Ontario and, to a lesser extent, Quebec, the proposed fiscal arrangements would have brought about a net transfer of current income from their residents. In addition, Quebec's concern for autonomy was voiced by Premier Duplessis, a political foe of Mackenzie King and an arch Quebec nationalist.

A round of meetings, lasting nine months, between the federal and provincial governments resulted in two concessions by Ottawa: an increase in the payments to the provinces; and a promise to limit its own utilization of certain taxes. Seven of the nine provinces were willing to sign an agreement with the federal government, but Ontario and Quebec refused, with Ontario arguing for a bigger federal payment and an enlarged social security program. Duplessis's stated objections concerned Quebec's fears that the proposals were damaging to Confederation and his reluctance to rent the field of succession duties to Ottawa. The conference, unable to reach agreement, broke up.

The result was that the federal government's social security and public investment proposals were shelved, although the Dominion promised that if its proposed tax agreements with the provinces could be negotiated, discussion on implementing the social security and public investment proposals could continue. But for the time being the door to further advance in Canada's social security system was closed.

National Health Grants, 1948

A small advance in the field of health care occurred in 1948, when a system of national health grants was established by Ottawa to enable the provinces to survey their health needs, assist in the costs of hospital construction, and expand the field of professional training and public health. But placed against the background of the government's wartime plans for a national health insurance scheme, as outlined in the Heagerty Report, this was a meagre initiative on what had clearly been identified as a major social security issue.

Furthermore, the decision to launch the national health grants program was prompted by a warning issued to Health and Welfare Minister Paul Martin by the eminent Canadian Dr. Wilder Penfield that he would be forced to close his famous Montreal Neurological Institute and move to the United States if the federal government did not involve itself in a more vigorous way with the health needs of the country. This information was quickly relayed to Mackenzie King, who, with his senior cabinet colleagues, quickly came to the decision to establish a fund to finance health research, hospital construction, disease control, and professional training. Although this program was later to be characterized by Liberal supporters as another example of that party's step-by-step planning for health care, it is clear that without the intervention of one of Canada's most distinguished medical men, there would have been no health grants program in 1948.[62]

9

The 1950s:
'Our Conservative Decade'[1]

The Second World War era appears in retrospect as a watershed in social security developments in Canada. For the first time, Canadians were introduced to the idea of a comprehensive social security system. This introduction did not imply either acceptance or understanding of the concept on the part of the majority. Indeed, it is probably true that most Canadians saw unemployment as the greatest single threat to their welfare – a view that tended to obscure consideration of other universal risks. This was a legacy of the Depression, when the blight of joblessness loomed so large that it became for most people the sum total of the many sources of social insecurity afflicting Canadian society at that time. Unemployment spelled poverty, the shame of being 'on relief,' the fear of unexpected medical bills, inadequate housing, a dependent old age, and a bleakness of prospect for the young. As a result, there was undoubtedly widespread support for the federal government's commitment to a policy of full employment announced in 1945. What was not as widely appreciated was that the notion of a comprehensive social security system, first broached during the war, had been displaced by an essentially residual approach that revealed itself, principally but not exclusively, at the federal level by the discarding of any notion of comprehensive planning. This was replaced by a return to narrowly defined policy initiatives on behalf of 'deserving' categories, generally those outside the labour force. For the remainder – those in the labour force and their dependants – a policy of full employment would have to suffice. If there was poverty and inequality in the country, full employment and a steady rate of economic growth would take care of it.

That this was the view of the postwar Liberal government in Ottawa seems undeniable. Its commitment to a comprehensive system of social security, despite the rhetoric of Mackenzie King during the Second World War, was shallow. The foot-dragging performance on urgent social security matters that characterized the 1950s is compelling testimony to this fact. It was not until the federal Liberal Party was dismissed from office in 1957 that its interest in social security revived.[2]

Countering this residual approach to social security were a number of new socioeconomic elements in Canadian life that emerged during the Second World War. At the war's end, Canadians had become aware of two large social security programs – unemployment insurance and family allowances – that did not stigmatize and that conferred a right to benefit, transforming the citizen from a supplicant to a claimant. Social security thus became imbued with positive, dignity-enhancing values, replacing the negative image of the typical income-security arrangement of the 1930s with its means test and discretionary payments. Thus, a pattern for future development was firmly established. From this point on, there would be a growing resistance to the type of social security program that diminished self-respect, had the flavour of emergency (and, therefore, of personal failure), and involved means-tested allowances. The public, having had a taste of legislation that conferred rights to benefits, would soon ask for more.

The interest in more and better social security coverage was enhanced by the fact that the average Canadian family prospered during the war. The spectre of unemployment had faded away with the outbreak of hostilities. Women were actively encouraged to join the labour force, which they did in the thousands. For many families this meant two or more incomes as wives and older children found employment opportunities at every turn. By the end of the war, the standard of life for most Canadians, compared with that endured during the Depression, had undergone a marked transformation. Many families had managed to build up their stock of possessions or had a nest egg of savings that would be spent in the immediate postwar years to acquire a house, a car, furniture, appliances, and other things being marketed for consumers. They were determined to hold on to them and to their newly acquired standard of living. There was a widespread conviction that in the postwar world government would be held responsible for protecting the citizen against the universal risks to livelihood.

The history of industrialized countries the world over testified to the point that the greater the degree of urbanization and industrialization, the greater the need for social security on a comprehensive scale. War pressures stepped up Canada's industrial capacity and the rate of urbanization. The unprecedented rise in the birth rate in the late 1940s and early 1950s and acceleration in the rate of social change acted as new and additional pressures for better social security arrangements. Much of the demand for increased social welfare services first fell upon the municipalities and the provinces, which, in turn, brought pressure to bear on the federal government to share in the costs of the burgeoning provincial health, education, and social welfare programs.

As a result of the interplay between these competing forces – those that would minimize the role of government in social security and those that would extend it – what developed following 1945 was a patchwork of programs, conditioned by both residual and institutional concepts. The system as a whole lacked any notion of integration or comprehensiveness. Developments since 1945 have been described either as 'piecemeal' by government critics or as 'step-by-step' policies by supporters. The 'piecemeal' label appears a more apt description. Lord Beveridge consistently warned that a 'step-by-step' development is only defensible if it is governed by some unity of design. This is precisely the element that was missing in Canadian social security policy following the Second World War.

The Marsh Report (260-2) had suggested a ranking of priorities if the government felt it could not undertake a comprehensive social security plan:

(1) the strengthening of unemployment insurance – extending its coverage and improving benefit scales

(2) health insurance, 'as the most important basic measure additional to unemployment insurance because it is applicable to the whole population and is more likely to produce rapid beneficial results'

(3) children's allowances, as 'a key measure for satisfactory establishment of all the income maintenance insurances'

(4) funeral benefits, 'as one of the easiest of social insurance measures to put into effect and as a small contribution to needs pending the advent of survivors' insurance'

(5) the disability/old age/survivors group of insurances

(6) sickness cash benefits and maternity benefits, 'comparatively simple insurances but delay in implementing them would be tempered to some degree if health insurance, providing universal medical care, were in existence.'

Marsh added a second listing of priorities if government planning was related to the 'special exigencies of the immediate post-war transition' – a reference to an expected sharp rise in unemployment rates. It was suggested that earlier consideration might be given to a contributory system of old age insurance, 'to lay the basis for more organized measures assisting the retirement of older persons from the labour market.' From this point of view, the priorities might be unemployment insurance, health insurance, the disability/old age/survivors group, children's allowances, sickness and maternity cash benefits, and funeral benefits.

By the war's end, Canada had children's allowances and unemployment insurance in place. The dominion government's 'Green Book Proposals' in 1945 reflected a reasonable ordering of priorities – extending the unemployment insurance system, instituting federal programs of unemployment assistance and health insurance, and improving old age pensions. These were shelved, and with them went any notion of an overall design. The vacuum has been filled, in the main, by ad hoc responses to political, social, and economic pressures.

Old Age Security

In 1951 the Old Age Pensions Act of 1927 was superseded by two pieces of legislation following intensive lobbying by pensioners' organizations and labour unions. The first of these, a response to public demand, was to replace the hated Old Age Pensions Act with a universal system. Thus, the Old Age Security Act, financed and administered by the federal government, which paid a pension of $40 per month to all Canadians at the age of seventy, came into existence. The only eligibility test was twenty years' residence in the country. The universal program was extended to Aboriginal Canadians, as the first old age pension legislation of 1927 had excluded them. A second and related piece of legislation was the Old Age Assistance Act, which provided a pension of up to $40 per month for those sixty-five to sixty-nine, but on a means-test basis. This program was administered by the provinces with pension costs split equally with Ottawa.

An amendment to the BNA Act was considered necessary prior to the introduction of the universal Old Age Security Act because the financing of the pension had a contributory element in that 'earmarked taxes' on personal and corporate income, as well as a sales tax, were levied to offset the cost of the universal pension.[3] The Liberal cabinet in Ottawa at the time was dominated by conservative-minded individuals who disliked the idea of a universal pension and insisted that an earmarked tax be imposed to remind Canadians of the consequences of pension demands. It was hoped that such a tax would dampen enthusiasm for any further increases.

Quebec agreed to the amendment, but only on the condition that provincial governments were free to enact their own pension legislation, which would be paramount over similar federal legislation, current or future. This amendment would have significant repercussions when the federal government decided to introduce the Canada Pension Plan.

The Old Age Security Act, a universal demogrant, removed once and for all the sense of personal failure that accompanied acceptance of an old age pension under the original act. However, the companion piece of legislation, providing pensions for those aged sixty-five to sixty-nine, remained firmly in the residual pattern, retaining the means test and certain administrative procedures that a parliamentary committee had deplored, such as the practice of attempting to recover the cost of pensions from the estates of pensioners.[4]

Allowances for the Blind and Disabled

The 1950s saw the passage of two additional pieces of limited, means-tested legislation: the Blind Persons Act (1951) and the Disabled Persons

Act (1954). These statutes empowered the federal government to enter into an agreement with each province and territory to share the costs of allowances paid to the blind and to the severely and totally disabled, aged eighteen to sixty-five, on a means-test basis.[5]

The tendency for residual programs to concentrate their energies on the outer margins of need is well illustrated by comparing the population at risk among the severely or totally disabled group with the number of persons drawing Disabled Persons' Allowances after the first two years of the program's operation. Estimates of the total of severely or wholly disabled Canadians in 1955 put the number at 236,000. Of this number, it was estimated that 51 per cent were dependent upon their families for their income, 26 per cent lived on savings, industrial and public pensions, and public assistance, while 23 per cent derived their principal income from employment. Therefore, approximately 100,000 people between eighteen and sixty-four, categorized as either severely or totally disabled, had no income or very little income of their own.[6] After two years of operation, the Disabled Persons Act, which was restricted to persons who were severely and permanently disabled, was paying allowances, on a means-test basis, to only 31,825 individuals – an indication of how a policy of 'helping those in greatest need,' the hallmark of the residual approach, may become a method of severely rationing help rather than extending assistance to meet genuine need.

The Unemployment Assistance Act

In 1956, as a result of high levels of unemployment, the federal government, in consultation with the provinces, passed the Unemployment Assistance Act, providing for federal sharing of general assistance costs for those in financial need not covered by the existing categorical programs of old age assistance, blind and disabled allowances, mothers' allowances, and war veterans' allowances. The group most directly affected were the unemployed who had exhausted their unemployment insurance benefits or who were not qualified to draw them.[7] Assistance under this act was granted on the basis of a needs test, rather than the customary means test. The change was designed to make public assistance more responsive to the needs of individuals and families. A means test generally placed a ceiling on the amount of help provided – in the case of old age assistance, for example, the ceiling in 1951 was $40 per month. In contrast, the needs test, in theory, involved an assessment of the applicant's budgetary requirements as well as assets and resources, and help under this formula attempted to fill the gap between resources and budgetary requirements. Consequently, the needs test introduced the possibility of higher and more appropriate rates of social assistance. Provincial treasuries were given partial protection against the increased cost by the federal government's offer to share 50 per cent of assistance costs with no ceiling specified. The expectation was that, with the provinces free to set the level of assistance granted on the basis of a careful assessment of need and with the federal government meeting half the cost of assistance payments, the level of social assistance rates would rise. However, given the bias against assisting people who were employable, the results were disappointing. A survey of unemployment assistance rates in 1961 by the Canadian Welfare Council revealed that they were still noticeably inadequate.[8]

The Failure of the Needs Test

The failure of the needs test to raise social assistance rates to a defensible social minimum revealed the strength of residual concepts of social security in the provinces, particularly with regard to the able-bodied unemployed. However, other dependent groups in the population, whose assistance was eligible for cost-sharing by the federal government under the Unemployment Assistance Act, fared no better. Even the sick and disabled who could not qualify under the terms of the Disabled Persons Act and the one-parent family suffered from the parsimonious allowances. More comprehensive planning might have helped, such as raising provincial minimum wage rates, thereby allowing social assistance rates to be more generous, or extending the provisions of the Unemployment Insurance Act, not to mention taking up the public investment policies recommended by the Marsh Report.

Moreover, programs with a strong residual cast commonly involve a degree of official intrusion into the lives of individuals and families by the administration of the means and needs tests, their periodic review, and the often obligatory 'home visit' by welfare department representatives. The needs test, in fact, increased the amount of official intervention into the lives of people because not only were the applicants' resources and assets reviewed, as under a means test, but their budgetary requirements were assessed as well. This required the applicant to review spending patterns with a welfare official and tailor these to the rates of social assistance offered, with the threat to personal autonomy that such a procedure entails.

New Housing Legislation

Amendments to the National Housing Act in 1954 provided federal government financing to the provinces and non-profit organizations for the construction or renovation of housing or hostels for low-income families, the elderly, the disabled, and students. The number of dwellings completed or renovated under this program remained insignificantly small compared to the need.

The Costs of Hospital Care

The 1950s closed with the enactment of a more comprehensive, institutional piece of legislation, the Hospital Insurance and Diagnostic Services Act (1957), which came into effect on 1 July 1958, and between 1958 and 1960 all provinces and territories signed cost-sharing agreements with the federal government. These arrangements enabled the federal government to provide approximately 50 per cent of the cost of provincial hospital insurance plans to cover a basic range of inpatient services in acute, convalescent, and chronic hospital care, with the significant exceptions of mental hospitals, tuberculosis sanatoria, and institutions offering custodial care, such as nursing homes and homes for the aged. The fundamental condition for federal cost-sharing, which illustrates the comprehensive nature of this legislation, was that benefits of the program were to be made available to all citizens within a province on uniform terms and conditions, regardless of age, sex, or physical condition. By 31 March 1963, 98.8 per cent of the population was covered by hospital insurance.

An important characteristic of a comprehensive, national coverage of social security is that it contributes to a sense of community solidarity by virtue of its universality, thus avoiding any unnecessary divisions within society – notably between the dependent and independent. The method by which provincial governments elect to finance their share of hospital insurance either contributes to, or detracts from, this feeling of community solidarity. If the feeling of solidarity is considered desirable, then a program financed out of general revenue or sales tax revenue is to be preferred over one that uses patient charges or premiums.[9] Where patient charges or premiums are employed, subsidies must be made available for low-income groups. Only those provinces with relatively high levels of per capita income can contemplate a premium system; otherwise, they face the administrative problems and expense of income testing a sizeable proportion of their population. It is significant that although many provincial programs began with a variety of premiums and patient charges, the trend has been to eliminate premiums in favour of general revenue, income tax surcharges, or sales taxes.

Thus, while all provinces relied on general revenues to finance their share of hospital insurance, some provinces augmented this with a system of premiums, as in Ontario and Manitoba; others, such as British Columbia, Alberta, and the Northwest Territories, authorized charges at the time of service. By eliminating premiums or patient charges, the possibility of invidious comparisons between one individual and another was reduced and any financial barrier to treatment removed. Such an approach was more in keeping with the universal concept, while those provinces that insisted on retaining patient charges or premiums indicated a predilection for the residual concept.

The inception of the Hospital Insurance and Diagnostic Services Act introduced a new component of the social minimum into Canadian social security policy. The social minimum in hospital care, prior to government hospital insurance, was care in a charity ward for those people without commercial or other types of insurance coverage and unable to pay the per diem cost of hospital care. If the actual treatment was not inferior to that received by other patients with similar complaints, the price extracted was in terms of the humiliation that sensitive people would feel at having to plead poverty in order to receive treatment. As the Hospital Insurance and Diagnostic Services Act required that benefits of the program be made available to all on equal terms, the new social minimum in hospital care became the most medically suitable treatment the provincial government and its various hospital boards were able to provide.[10]

10
The 1960s:
Filling the Gaps

While in opposition from 1957 to 1963, the federal Liberal Party developed a number of social policy proposals that it hoped would win back the favour of the Canadian electorate. However, when returned to power in 1963 as a minority government, and again in 1965 after the Liberals tried for a majority but failed, they were dependent upon the support of the New Democratic Party and the small Quebec wing of the Social Credit Party. The necessity to tilt slightly to the left in terms of social policy in order to stay in power also contributed to the flurry of social program developments in the 1960s.

Youth Allowances

In the 1960s a new demogrant program, youth allowances, was introduced – an idea pioneered by Quebec in 1961. This was an extension of the family allowances concept to include children up to the age of eighteen, provided they were in full-time attendance at school, unless physical or other disabilities prevented this. The Youth Allowances Act (1964) was recognition of the increasing years of dependency of the young as the requirements of Canada's technological society called for greater educational preparation. It was, in effect, the recognition of a new source of dependency in a technological society.

It is significant, however, that the effectiveness of the family allowances program was seriously compromised by the government's failure to keep the benefit structure in step with the rising cost of living. Two provinces, Newfoundland and Quebec, attempted to remedy this situation by establishing supplementary programs of family allowances within their own borders.

The Canada and Quebec Pension Plans, 1965

After nearly a decade of political agitation by pensioner groups, social organizations, and labour unions to improve living standards in retirement, there was general support in all three major political parties for a contributory pension plan. The private market in pensions, which developed most easily in large companies and in the public sector, left more than half of Canadian workers uncovered. An additional problem with private pensions was that most of them were not portable. What workers required was an occupational pension that would move with them from job to job or from one part of the country to another. Only a national, public system could meet this goal.

In 1963 the Liberal government announced its intention to introduce a contributory pension plan. As already noted, under the 1951 amendment of the BNA Act, provinces were free to develop their own pension legislation. Ontario toyed with the idea briefly, but Quebec, determined to emphasize its special status within Canada, developed its own plan. This proved to be a boon for all Canadians because in the negotiations to produce the greatest degree of uniformity between the two plans to ensure portability nationwide, both plans became more adequate and comprehensive than initially envisaged by Ottawa or Quebec City. An additional amendment to the BNA Act was required and quickly arranged.[1] The compromise meant higher contributions – Ottawa's original plan called for employees to pay 1 per cent of pensionable earnings, whereas the QPP originally set its at 2 per cent. They compromised at 1.8 per cent. Higher contributions were deliberately sought by Quebec, which was eager for investment capital. For at least a decade or more, the pension funds would take in considerably more than they paid out, as full pensions would not be paid during the ten-year transition period. Quebec and Ontario had wanted a twenty-year transition period, but Ottawa held out for ten. The excess funds would be available to the provinces at prevailing rates, and all provinces expressed interest in this idea. The original Ottawa plan was strictly pay as you go – that is, contributions would equal benefits paid out, with a small reserve to meet unforeseen claims.

In return for their contributions, Canadian workers would receive a retirement benefit equal to 25 per cent of pensionable earnings at age seventy, or at ages sixty-five to sixty-nine conditional upon a 'retirement test.' There would also be a pension for the surviving spouse and other survivors, in cases of premature death, and funeral and disability benefits. Most of these elements were improvements over the original Ottawa plan.[2]

The two plans covered 92 per cent of the labour force, including the armed forces. All employees between the ages of 18 and 70 who earned more than $600 per annum and the self-employed who earned at least $800 were required to contribute. Employees and employers each contributed 1.8 per cent of insurable earnings up to a ceiling of $5,000. The self-employed contributed the full 3.6 per cent. Excluded from coverage were employees and the self-employed who earned less than the set minimums, as well as casual employees, family workers, and some migratory workers (exchange teachers, for example). Housewives were not covered, and women's groups questioned this oversight.[3]

For the first time in Canada's history of social security, the decision was taken to provide for an automatic increase in C/QPP benefits to offset increases in the cost of living. Benefits were to rise with the cost of living but were limited to 2 per cent a year. This same formula was applied to the universal old age pension, but other equally critical programs – unemployment insurance, family allowances, and most provincial social assistance programs – were not afforded this protection. Toward the end of the 1960s, it was evident that the rate of inflation was exceeding the 2 per cent limit by a considerable margin. The result was that by the early 1970s, the risk to income adequacy posed by inflation had only been marginally offset. Furthermore, inflationary pressures in the latter 1960s had resulted in a rapid rise in wages, but the contributory earnings ceiling, which was also linked to the cost of living during the transition period, had failed to keep pace with the increase. By 1970, the government acknowledged that average industrial wages were $6,400 per annum, while the earnings ceiling on which contributions and benefit rates were calculated had only reached $5,300. This first attempt to deal systematically with the risk to income adequacy posed by inflation was not a conspicuous success, but it was an important first step, and improvements were to follow in 1974 (see Chapter 12).

Bryden identified a serious question of equity centred on the fact that the initial proportional rate (1.8 percent) for calculating the worker's contributions, combined with the maximum pensionable earnings ceiling, meant that the contribution as a percentage of total earnings was regressive, as Table 10.1 indicates. The regressive nature of the formula governing contributions, by which a worker who earned $20,000 per annum paid a smaller proportion of his or her income in contributions than one who earned $2,000, resulted in a shift of the tax burden for these new pensions from upper- and middle-income ranges to the lower middle and below. This nullified what many authorities saw as a central role of social security programs: a more equitable sharing of income.[4]

The Guaranteed Income Supplement (GIS), 1966

For those Canadians already retired and therefore ineligible for benefits under the Canada Pension Plan, or who would retire before they could build up sufficient contributions in the scheme to draw anything but the most minimal amount of pension, a transitionary measure, the Guaranteed Income Supplement Plan, was introduced in 1966 to provide a guaranteed minimum income for people drawing the old age security pension.[5] Eligibility for this guaranteed income was to be on the basis of an income test. The income test, as distinct from the needs test, is self-administered

Table 10.1

Canada Pension Plan, 1973: worker's contribution as a percentage of gross income

Contributor's gross annual income* ($)	Net percentage paid in tax
2,000	1.25
3,000	1.28
5,000	1.34
7,000	0.91
10,000	0.60
15,000	0.33
20,000	0.23

* Married taxpayer with two dependent children.
Source: Kenneth Bryden, *Old Age Pensions and Policy-Making in Canada* (Montreal: McGill-Queen's University Press 1979), 210.

and dispenses with an exhaustive examination of personal assets and resources. The application, which has to be renewed each year, has been compared to an income tax return. Pensioners with some income in addition to the old age security pension, but having less than the guaranteed income level, are eligible for partial benefits.[6]

Did the income test represent a shift away from the institutional concept of the demogrant toward the residual concept of demonstrated need? If client satisfaction was any criterion, it did to a degree. A federal white paper issued in 1970, *Income Security for Canadians*, noted: 'In terms of acceptability to the recipient it [the guaranteed income supplement] is better received than social assistance but less acceptable than the demogrant or social insurance' (22). However, because the GIS was available only to those who qualified for the universal old age security pension, the sense of stigma-free benefit embedded in OAS carried over, to a large extent, to the annual application for the supplement, and this seemed to neutralize any sense of discrimination.

The Canada Assistance Plan

The year 1966 also saw the introduction of a program whose intention was to improve and expand social assistance and social services in Canada. This was the Canada Assistance Plan (CAP), a scheme to consolidate all the categorical, cost-shared, social assistance programs into a single, comprehensive program of financial assistance, together with an expanded range of social services to help people retain or achieve independence. Additional federal funds would also be available to improve the administration of public welfare.

The plan's genesis lay in the recognition that the categorical approach to public assistance was administratively cumbersome and socially unsound in that a focus on the cause of financial need, rather than need itself, made it difficult for many to qualify for help. Under this new plan, each province was free to combine the federally assisted categorical programs – unemployment assistance, old age assistance, blind persons' allowances, and disabled persons' allowances – together with any provincial public assistance programs in a single administrative framework.[7] The federal government agreed to meet half the costs of all shareable items, with no upper limit on the federal contribution, provided the assistance was given on a needs-test basis, a concept first introduced in the Unemployment Assistance Act (1956). The exception to this arrangement was Quebec, which elected to receive instead an income tax abatement with cash adjustments.

With financial need being the sole test of eligibility, it became a general expectation that there would be neither a residence requirement nor a work requirement for the welfare received. In this way, those who framed the legislation hoped to emphasize the right to assistance when in need.

Included in the cost-sharing arrangements for the first time was a broad range of health services, counselling, assessment, and referral services, homemaker and day care services, costs of nursing home care and welfare institutions for children, prescribed items incidental to carrying on a trade or other employment, and other special needs of any kind. Also included as a cost-shared item for the first time was the cost of expanding and strengthening the administrative structure of public assistance services. The decisions about which services to supply and what levels of financial assistance to provide were left to the provinces.

The Canada Assistance Plan had the potential to assist the 'working poor,' as the legislation decreed that assistance could be granted to persons in need or likely to become so unless provided with the necessary funds and/or social services. Additionally, the Canada Assistance Plan broke new ground by requiring that provinces establish an appeal procedure for clients of the system.

The Canada Assistance Plan, hailed in 1965 as one part of a federal plan for the 'full utilization of human resources and the elimination of poverty,'[8] must be judged by its aspirations. In terms of its inclusiveness, the expected extension of assistance to the working poor failed to materialize to any appreciable extent. Alberta was the only province where this policy was openly adopted, although other provinces did in fact subsidize employed people through their social assistance programs, but were reluctant to publicize the fact to avoid escalation of program costs.[9]

Undoubtedly, moving away from the categorical approach to a generalized needs-test approach, coupled with the ability of the provinces and territories to supply a much wider range of critical services with half the cost paid by Ottawa, improved the overall inclusiveness of social assistance programs. But serious problems remained, the most important being the absence of standards relating to levels of financial aid to recipients.

The issue of inadequate rates of assistance was pinpointed in 1971 by the Special Senate Committee on Poverty, which noted that there were wide variations in basic rates from one province to another that could not be accounted for by reference to regional differences in living costs.

The first national analysis of social assistance programs, prepared by the National Council of Welfare in 1987, found that the basic needs package on which provinces calculated the amount of social assistance consisted 'of only the most rudimentary items.' This 'skeletal definition of what is considered to be essential results in meagre basic needs allowances.'[10] A second factor contributing to the abysmally low rates of assistance identified by the 1987 study was that people who were considered 'employable' by welfare authorities were more stringently treated than those who were 'unemployable.' A third factor was the failure of provinces to fully index these bare subsistence rates of social assistance to the cost of living.

The most dispiriting aspect of Canadian social assistance programs is the contempt directed at people on welfare by the general public and, most shamefully, by our political leaders from all major parties. The fact that at least 40 per cent of welfare recipients are children fails to diminish the level of verbal abuse aimed at welfare recipients. The National Council of Welfare study finds that the root of this attitudinal problem lies in the fact that public assistance has its roots in the Elizabethan poor law, and this dubious heritage 'still influences the way social assistance is delivered and affects the attitudes that many Canadians have toward welfare recipients' (9).

It is virtually an axiom of social security experience worldwide that where social welfare programs are designed exclusively for 'the poor,' they become second-rate services – invariably punitive, grudging in administration, meagre in benefit, and, above all, stigmatizing to the user. The Canada Assistance Plan attempted to reverse this by developing a program directed at the poor that would emphasize the right to benefit, raise the level of allowances to something akin to adequacy, and, in doing so, enhance the dignity of the recipient. The federal government's verdict after four years of operation was that 'considerable progress is evident when social assistance practices are compared with those of the past, but much remains to be done.' But later assessments were not so positive. The program's failures were underlined in the findings of the Senate Committee on Poverty, which was unreservedly critical of public assistance as a technique for fighting poverty, describing it as a 'record of failure and insufficiency, of bureaucratic rigidities that often result in the degradation, humiliation and alienation of recipients.'[11]

Citizen Participation

In the 1960s the concept of democratic involvement or citizen participation – the involvement of people directly affected by social welfare programs in the planning, implementation, and evaluation of policies and programs – began to find active sponsors. The appearance of welfare rights groups, consumer organizations, and tenant associations was a phenomenon of the late 1960s, and one to which administrators of social welfare agencies across the country began, albeit reluctantly, to accommodate themselves. The Canada Assistance Plan provided for federal sharing of the costs of activities and programs that fostered the participation of consumers of welfare services, although it must be admitted that most welfare rights groups have developed independently of any government assistance. The minister of national health and welfare recognized this new trend in social security by establishing a National Council of Welfare in 1970 to act as an advisory body to his department; included on this council are representatives from low-income, welfare-recipient, and other disadvantaged groups.

Risks to the Adequacy of Income: The Cost of Medical Care

The next gap to be filled in Canada's social security network in the 1960s, medical care insurance, witnessed the usual contest between the residual and institutional schools of thought. Hospital insurance having been realized for the great majority of Canadians by 1960, a program of medical care insurance, particularly for the lower-income groups or those without private insurance through their employers, was an obvious and growing need as the cost of medical care escalated sharply.

Royal Commission on Health Services, 1961

The struggle between the residual forces and those backing a comprehensive public program came to the surface in the hearings before the Royal Commission on Health Services, appointed in 1961 by Prime Minister Diefenbaker to study the existing facilities for health care in Canada and recommend those measures that would ensure the best possible health care for all Canadians. The resulting report, published in 1964, is a landmark in Canadian social security history.[12] There were many contentious issues debated before the commission, such as the type of payment plan best suited to assure equal access to medical care, the range of programs to be offered, the cost of programs and their impact on the economy, and, the most fundamental issue of all, the appropriate role of government in ensuring its citizens access to the best possible health care. Seldom have the arguments surrounding the residual and institutional concepts of social security been outlined with such clarity.

The advocates of the residual view, reiterating the arguments presented before the Heagerty Committee in 1942-3, wished to limit government action to subsidizing individuals and families who were unable to pay the 'full economic cost' of health insurance. The normal and preferred method of paying for health services, from this point of view, was for individuals to make their own arrangements either through their place of work or through a private insurance company. Great emphasis was laid on the preservation of the voluntary system of health insurance as opposed to the compulsory nature of a universal, government-administered system. The 'freedom of the individual' or 'free choice of doctor' was said to be at stake. It was claimed that private insurance and voluntary non-profit organizations were making rapid progress in meeting the health insurance needs of the vast majority of Canadians. This point of view was presented most forcefully by the insurance companies, the representatives of the medical profession, and the Canadian Chamber of Commerce.

The opposing view, voiced by the potential consumers of the health service – labour unions, farmers' organizations, and consumer groups – argued for a government-controlled comprehensive health service. Their grounds for holding this position included the concept that a comprehensive health service should do more than meet sickness and accident costs: it should be oriented not only toward the prevention of illness but also to the better distribution and organization of medical services. This latter argument is at the core of all modern arguments for comprehensive health care.

The proponents of comprehensive medical care contested the claim of insurance companies and others that the private market and the voluntary non-profit organizations in health care were capable of protecting even a substantial proportion of Canadians from the costs of medical care. They noted that the voluntary prepaid schemes were most effective in large industries where the employer frequently made a contribution toward the health insurance premium. They were not successful in offering coverage to the chronically ill, the elderly, the self-employed, low-income groups, workers in small establishments, and farmers. The consumer groups were particularly vehement in their objections to the means-test approach that was inherent in the proposals of the insurance companies. Adequate health care, they argued, was a right of citizenship, and access to such care could only be guaranteed by removing any financial burden through a tax-supported and publicly administered plan.

The commissioners' reactions to this fundamental division of opinion led them to state that, although they were initially in sympathy with the view that full-scale government action in health care was unnecessary, they found little in the proposals of the insurance industry and most medical profession briefs to indicate that anything less than a compulsory, government operated and financed scheme would assure universal coverage. The argument by the insurance companies and others that they could provide insurance coverage at a price within the reach of the vast majority of

Canadians, leaving only a small residue of medically indigent citizens who would require government subsidy, was rejected by the commission. The facts were surely convincing enough. As the commission's report put it, referring to the existing state of health insurance coverage in Canada in the early 1960s, 'After more than thirty-five years of endeavour on the part of the voluntary plans and commercial insurance companies, only slightly more than one-half of the population of Canada has any degree of voluntary insurance protection and this for medical services alone. Of these, the coverage held by nearly three million is wholly inadequate. Over 7.5 million Canadians had no medical care insurance whatever' (vol. 1, 743). Thus, the Royal Commission on Health Services came to the conclusion that a comprehensive, universal health service administered by government and financed by means of provincial general revenues, federal government grants, sales or other taxes, or by premiums was the only means of assuring access with dignity to adequate health care services for all Canadians. This was the same conclusion reached by the Heagerty Report in 1943.

However, the debate continued when representatives of the federal and provincial governments met to work out a cost-sharing agreement. The Alberta representatives repeatedly espoused the residual point of view by asking the federal government to approve a plan under which only low-income families would be subsidized for medical care insurance. The Ontario government, another advocate of the residual approach, won its fight to have private insurance companies accepted as non-profit carriers for the provincial medical care service.

Medical Care Act, 1966

Despite these and other objections from the provinces, the Medical Care Act, as passed by Parliament in 1966, emerged as a solidly comprehensive measure. The five criteria for federal sharing in provincial medical care programs reflected the tone of the Royal Commission on Health Services:

(1) provincial plans must be administered on a non-profit basis by a government agency or an agency designated by, and accountable to, government

(2) plans must provide comprehensive coverage for all medically necessary services rendered by a physician or surgeon[13]

(3) plans must be universally available to all provincial residents on equal terms and conditions; they must cover 90 per cent of the insurable population within the first year of operation and 95 per cent within three years

(4) all provincial plans must provide portability of benefits from one province to another or continued coverage when the insured resident is temporarily absent from his or her home province

(5) insured services must be delivered in a manner 'that does not pre-

clude, either directly or indirectly, whether by charges made to insured persons or otherwise, reasonable access.'[14]

It took three years following the implementation of the act on 1 July 1968 before all provinces and territories had signed cost-sharing agreements with the federal government. At that date, for the first time in Canada, virtually the entire population was provided with a substantial degree of protection against the costs of medical care – a significant advance in social security, but one that came exactly a quarter of a century after the publication of the Heagerty and Marsh Reports.

The Medical Care Act added another facet to the Canadian definition of a social minimum in health care. Access to a doctor's services prior to 1968, except in Saskatchewan, where a comprehensive medicare system had been introduced earlier in the decade, had been circumscribed by a variety of market considerations, such as the ability to pay either the doctor's fee or an insurance premium, plus a number of other impediments customarily found in the contracts of most insurance plans, both commercial and non-profit, such as utilization fees, waiting periods, exclusion of preexisting conditions, and so on. By requiring that all provincial plans provide a comprehensive range of medically necessary services by a physician or surgeon on equal terms and conditions to provincial residents, the Medical Care Act effectively removed these barriers; Canada's concept of a social minimum in health care now included, for the bulk of the population, the unfettered access to a doctor's services.

Even so, the refusal of the federal government to plan comprehensively in this field – in particular, the failure to encourage the development of alternatives to treatment in expensive, acute-care hospital beds – was to have repercussions on the total government health care bill.

Housing in the 1960s

Housing became a political issue at the close of the 1960s as interest rates, land and building costs, and property taxes soared, making it increasingly difficult for people in the lower third of the income strata to achieve home ownership. In 1969 a federal government Task Force on Housing and Urban Development, chaired by Paul Hellyer, made a number of recommendations designed to ease the housing situation.[15] In 1972 two researchers published the Dennis Report, the results of their study into the problem of low-income housing, which provided Canadians with the first full-scale review of housing policy in Canada since the Curtis Report (1944).[16]

The Dennis Report identified shelter costs as a critical threat to income adequacy for low-income individuals and families – a fact that, as the text acknowledged, had been amply established in earlier reports. It noted that in 1967 approximately 400,000 low-income households spent in excess of 40 per cent of their income for shelter alone and more than 50 per cent when the costs of household operation were added. In comparing shelter costs to income ratios, the report found that the bottom fifth of people in the income distribution table spent twice as great a proportion of their income for shelter, not infrequently of an inferior quality, as did families with average incomes. To these and other perennial housing problems of the poorest Canadians had to be added a new factor. Housing costs were beginning to affect the opportunities for people higher up on the income scale to buy their own house. It was this much larger and more vocal minority, better able to make their dissatisfaction known to the politicians, that created the political furore and the talk of a 'housing crisis' at the end of the 1960s.

In reviewing housing policy in general, the Dennis Report charged that Canada's policy reflected 'an almost religious belief in the private market' as a mechanism for deciding the distribution, price, and environmental quality of the housing stock. The principal role accepted by a succession of federal governments, according to the report, had been to assist the private market by providing large sums to help finance its operations. As a result, a perverse type of redistribution had occurred in that the bulk of housing funds had been used to house middle- and upper-income households.[17]

This residual approach to housing has produced the expected, classical residual results.[18] By and large, public housing in Canada – that is, subsidized low-rental housing designed to offset the risk to income adequacy of shelter costs – is reserved 'for those in greatest need.' As such housing comprises only about 2 per cent of the housing stock, it is in perpetual short supply. Low-rental housing in Canada, typically large-scale apartment complexes, quickly become identified as 'ghettoes for the poor' and are seldom tributes to good design or careful environmental planning. As with all programs aimed exclusively at the poor, the residents of these public housing projects feel stigmatized, not only because their place of residence clearly identifies them as both poor and dependent but because living in public housing underlines their failure to own their home, a goal that is widely equated, however unfairly, with the virtues of thrift, good citizenship, self-reliance, and stability.[19]

By the early 1970s the risk to income adequacy of shelter costs was firmly within the residual sector, and no institutional solutions with any major impact were in sight.

11
Stemming a Residual Tide

The early 1970s were highlighted by a thorough revision of the unemployment insurance system – the first complete revision since the program's inception in 1940. The changes, announced in a white paper published in June 1970, *Unemployment Insurance in the 70's,* resulted in legislation that came into effect on 27 June 1971. The Unemployment Insurance Act of 1971 extended the program's inclusiveness by easing the qualifying conditions for benefits and widening the program's compulsory coverage to include 96 per cent of the labour force, representing an additional 2.3 million workers. The adequacy of the program was enhanced by raising benefits to the point where they would equal approximately two-thirds of the contributor's wage.[1] Furthermore, two long-standing risks to income interruption were finally covered when insured workers became eligible for unemployment benefits for reasons of temporary sickness or disability (after a two-week waiting period) or pregnancy.

In contrast to this advance in social policy along *institutional* lines, the remainder of the decade saw a resurgence of *residual* concepts of social welfare, stimulated in part by what was termed the 'rediscovery of poverty.'

The Rediscovery of Poverty
In April 1965, the Liberal minority government, under Prime Minister Pearson, announced a number of measures to bring about 'the full utilization of human resources and the elimination of poverty.' These measures included action on health care, a contributory pension plan, and a renewed federal-provincial social assistance program.[2]

A spate of studies on poverty in Canada – its extent, causation, and possible remedies – began to appear.[3] Canada's 'official' examination of the poverty problem was the work of a special Senate committee, which was established in 1968 and reported in 1971. The committee's central finding was that Canadian welfare programs were spending $6 billion a year to meet financial need, and yet one in five Canadians was defined as 'poor.'

Furthermore, 60 per cent of the poor were employed most or all of the year and therefore largely ineligible for traditional welfare aid. The solution to this problem, according to the committee, was a form of guaranteed annual income (a negative income tax plan) financed and administered by the federal government and available to all Canadian citizens below a certain income level, *except* single, unattached individuals under forty years of age. The guaranteed income level would be set at 70 per cent of the Senate committee's 'poverty line' (a relative measure of poverty related to 'the average standard of living') and updated annually to changes in the cost of living for families of various sizes. For every dollar of other income, the guaranteed income would be reduced by 70 cents to encourage work incentives and contain the overall cost. The program would be financed by eliminating the universal programs of old age security and family and youth allowances, as well as the income-tested supplement of the universal pension. The social insurances and certain contractual programs for veterans and Native peoples would be retained.[4]

A sharp response to the Senate's report was *The Real Poverty Report*, also released in 1971, prepared by four disaffected staff members of the Senate committee. The authors said their report was a protest against the Senate committee's failure to meet its mandate, which was to report on *all* aspects of poverty in Canada. The dissidents argued that some fundamental causes of poverty were largely ignored by the Senate committee, such as the power of corporations, the inequitable tax system, the lack of collective bargaining power for a majority of the workforce, the failure to challenge the mythology of the 'free market,' and the tendency of the federal government to be unduly influenced by the rich and powerful. A solid demonstration of this last point had been the reception business and corporate interests had given to the release, in 1966, of the report of the Royal Commission on Taxation (Carter Commission) and a subsequent white paper entitled *Proposal for Tax Reform* (1969). The Carter Commission had recommended greater equity in the tax system by increasing its progressivity and eliminating the tax loopholes favouring business and corporations. The force and intensity of the business lobby, arguing that more equity would damage economic growth, resulted in a full retreat by the government, first in its white paper on tax reform and again when tax reform legislation finally appeared in 1972.[5]

The Real Poverty Report called for a policy of full employment, greater public control of corporations, centralized collective bargaining, reform of the welfare system, and a guaranteed annual income in the form of a demogrant. The demogrant plan, financed and administered by the federal government, would replace universal OAS/GIS and family and youth allowances. It would be available to all Canadians, and other income would reduce the demogrant at a rate of 60 cents for every dollar of additional family income until the demogrant was completely taxed back. The social insurances would be retained but improved.[6]

The Quebec government had commissioned its own review of income security and poverty among the working poor, which also reported in 1971. The Commission of Inquiry on Health and Social Welfare (the Castonguay-Nepveu Report) proposed a three-tier income security plan: a negative income tax scheme (NIT); a program of universal family allowances; and a social insurance strategy. The NIT plan would replace the conventional social assistance program and would be a two-stage plan, called General Social Allowance Payments (GSAP), that would provide all low-income persons with a variable allowance, the level of which would be determined by the degree of income inadequacy, regardless of cause. The plan offered the applicant a choice of two support levels. Stage one would be designed for the working poor who had small but regular earnings, and it would provide a basic allowance that was below a minimum income level but when combined with the recipient's earnings would bring that person's income to the minimum level or even above. Any other income would reduce the basic allowance by 33 cents for every dollar for the first $2,500 earned, and 60 cents for every additional dollar. The second stage was to be directed at those who were unable to work or who chose not to. They would be guaranteed a higher basic allowance, based on family size, but any additional earned income would be taxed back at a 100 per cent rate. The applicant would have the right to choose either stage and to move from one stage to the other if that would improve his or her standard of living.

For families with children, both levels of support would cover about 70 per cent of the costs of child rearing, and the family allowances, the second tier of the three-tier plan, would consist of flat-rate benefits, keyed to the age of the child, and would cover the remaining 30 per cent. These family allowances would be subject to a special income tax that would tax them back as income rose above a certain point. The universal OAS/GIS would remain, as would the social insurances, to form the third tier.[7]

The study of poverty in Canada in the late 1960s and early 1970s also revealed an indefensible degree of inequality[8] in the distribution of income (see Table 11.1). Further, it showed that the social security system was having a negligible effect in narrowing the gulf between the bottom fifth and top fifth of families on the income scale. In addition to pointing out the inequalities of Canadian family income, research into the extent of poverty in Canada served to emphasize once again the long-standing issue of regional inequalities between one province and another, between regions within provinces, and between rural and urban areas. Canadians became more aware of the regional disparities in average weekly earnings, in unemployment rates, in per capita spending on the services of health professionals, as well as in other indicators of general living standards (see Tables 11.2 to 11.4 and Figure 11.1).

Table 11.1

Distribution of family income in Canada (as a per cent of total family income), 1951-72

Year	Bottom fifth	Second fifth	Third fifth	Fourth fifth	Top fifth
1951	6.1	12.9	17.4	22.4	41.1
1957	6.3	13.1	18.1	23.4	39.1
1961	6.6	13.5	18.3	23.4	38.4
1967	6.4	13.1	18.0	23.6	38.9
1969	6.2	12.6	17.9	23.5	39.7
1971	5.6	12.6	18.0	23.7	40.0
1972	5.9	12.9	18.3	23.7	39.1

Source: David Ross, *Canadian Fact Book on Poverty* (Ottawa: The Canadian Council on Social Development 1975), Table 10, 24.

Table 11.2

Unemployment and average weekly earnings, June 1976

	Unemployment rate (seasonally adjusted) (%)	Weekly earnings* ($)
Newfoundland	12.4	224
Prince Edward Island	12.4	162
Nova Scotia	10.5	194
New Brunswick	11.5	202
Quebec	7.8	224
Ontario	6.3	231
Manitoba	4.5	207
Saskatchewan	5.0	215
Alberta	3.8	238
British Columbia	8.8	262
Yukon Territory	n.a.	316
Northwest Territories	n.a.	268
Canada	7.0	229

* Industrial composite = annual average of larger firms.
Source: Economic Council of Canada, *Living Together: A Study of Regional Disparities* (Ottawa: Minister of Supply and Services 1978), Table 4-6, 44.

A particularly disturbing element of Canadian poverty was its alleged relationship to racial and sexual discrimination. The Economic Council of Canada's *Fifth Annual Review* noted the 'continuing difficulties faced by Indian, Eskimo and Métis people in coping with, and adapting to, the

Table 11.3

Expenditure per person on dentists' services*

	1961	1966	1971
Canada	6.39	7.02	8.02
Newfoundland	1.98	2.20	2.79
Prince Edward Island	3.93	4.43	4.70
Nova Scotia	3.48	4.59	4.66
New Brunswick	3.43	3.69	4.21
Quebec	3.97	4.61	5.08
Ontario	8.55	9.36	10.70
Manitoba	6.65	6.26	7.58
Saskatchewan	5.27	5.49	5.36
Alberta	7.00	7.88	8.97
British Columbia	9.85	9.87	11.70

* Annual expenditure in constant 1961 dollars.
Source: Perspective Canada (Ottawa: Information Canada 1974), Table 3:36, 57.

Table 11.4

Social measures by selected provinces and selected years, 1966-76

	NF	PEI	NS	NB	PQ	ON	MB
Housing and telephones							
Crowding index, (persons per room) 1976	.74	.60	.59	.62	.62	.55	.60
Telephones, 1975 (number per 100 inhabitants)	36.1	41.0	47.5	46.9	55.0	61.4	55.9
Health							
Infant mortality rate, 1972-4 (number of deaths)*	19.3	17.7	15.6	15.9	16.5	14.2	17.0
Expenditures on physicians as a percentage of personal income, 1971	1.51	1.86	1.75	1.48	1.71	1.66	1.78

[continued on next page]

Table 11.4 [continued]

	NF	PEI	NS	NB	PQ	ON	MB
Education							
Percentage of population aged 16 attending elementary and secondary schools, 1974-5							
Male	74.9	62.1	76.9	75.9	81.5	88.7	84.4
Female	74.0	79.2	83.3	80.8	81.9	88.5	86.2

*   The infant mortality rate is the number of deaths of infants (under one year old) per 1,000 live births.
Source: Economic Council of Canada, *Living Together: A Study of Regional Disparities* (Ottawa: Minister of Supply and Services 1977), adapted from Table 4-11, 58.

Figure 11.1

Unemployment rates by region, 1953-75

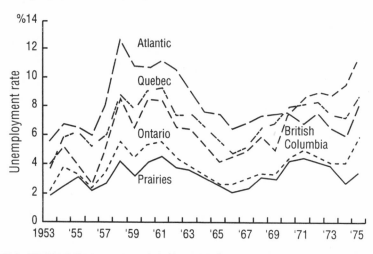

Source: Perspective Canada II (Ottawa: Minister of Supply and Services 1977), Chart 6.11, 118.

problems of the major society, both because of present attitudes within the white community and because of strong cultural differences.'[9] The Senate committee's report said that the plight of Native peoples was 'a blot on Canada's record and a cause for shame for all Canadians.' This situation was the result of a 'basic misunderstanding and/or lack of appreciation of native cultures' coupled with a record of government paternalism.[10] *The Real Poverty Report* spoke more bluntly of discrimination against Native people, women, and French Canadians. It referred to a century of systematic oppression of Native people and cited a study that claimed that in 1965 over 40 per cent of Native and Métis *families* earned $1,000 or less – the level of absolute deprivation for an *individual*. Seventy-five per cent of Native and Métis families lived on $2,000 or less, in 'conditions of absolute deprivation.'[11] The Economic Council of Canada drew particular attention to the fact that the average age at death for all Canadians in 1965 was a little over sixty-two years, while the average for Inuit was only about twenty years and for Natives approximately thirty-six years.[12] The council also cited the infant mortality rates among Natives and Inuit: in the Northwest Territories in 1966, there were 108.8 deaths per 1,000 live births for Inuit and 46.2 for Natives, compared with the national figure of 23.1. Equally unsettling were statistics that indicated the extremely high percentage of registered Natives in receipt of social assistance. When these were contrasted with the percentage for Canadians other than registered Natives drawing benefits under the Canada Assistance Plan, the social and economic position of Natives in Canada was starkly revealed (see Table 11.5).

Table 11.5

Registered Natives receiving social assistance, 1972-3 and 1973-4, and total population in receipt of benefits under the Canada Assistance Plan, 1972 and 1973

Region and province	Natives receiving social assistance (%)		Beneficiaries under the Canada Assistance Plan (% of total population)	
	1972-3	1973-4	1972	1973
Maritimes	84.5	84.6	48.8	38.2[a]
Quebec	44.9	39.6	8.6	7.4
Ontario	25.5	25.9	4.8	4.4
Manitoba	78.2	78.5	8.8	8.0
Saskatchewan	75.9	73.3	8.6	7.3
Alberta	72.9	70.4	6.0	5.6
British Columbia	47.1	42.8	6.6	5.2
Yukon	78.7	69.3	3.6	2.2
Canada[b]	56.9	54.8	7.0	6.2

[a] The breakdown for the Maritimes for 1973 is as follows: New Brunswick, 13.7%; Prince Edward Island, 7.5%; Nova Scotia, 7.2%; and New Brunswick, 9.7%. A similar breakdown for Natives in the Maritimes is not available.

[b] Does not include Natives in the Northwest Territories and Newfoundland.

Source: Statistics Canada, *Social Security National Programs, 1976*, Table 1, 690, and Table 2, 604.

The particular vulnerability to the risk of poverty experienced by one-parent families headed by women and the similar plight of single, elderly women received renewed recognition following the publication in 1970 of the *Report of the Royal Commission on the Status of Women in Canada*. The commission noted that in 1967 the average income for all women who were heads of families was $2,536, compared with the average income of male heads of families of $5,821.[13] Furthermore, while Canadian families generally became more prosperous over the period from 1951 to 1965, families headed by women did not keep pace. During this period, the proportion of families headed by women with incomes under $3,000 declined by only 24 per cent. This contrasted with a drop of 58 per cent in the case of families headed by men.[14] In addition to the problem of poverty, the unintended consequences, or sexist bias, of social security policies and programs that discriminated against women prompted a series of recommendations from the commission.[15]

Another cause of dissatisfaction with the social security system was the concern over the increase in costs in relation to the apparent ineffectiveness of the system as an antipoverty device. In the 1960s spending on social security by all three levels of government had increased from $3,898.5 millions in 1963 to an estimated $11,289.6 millions by 1972. To keep these costs in perspective, they were generally related to some measure of the country's ability to provide for them, such as the national income or the gross national product (see Table 11.6). Considered in this light, the growth of social security expenditures appeared less alarming. Furthermore, when Canada's expenditures for social security were related to similar expenditures by other Western industrialized nations, our spending was clearly not out of hand (see Table 11.7). However, the Senate committee was undoubtedly expressing a popular, if misguided, sentiment when it wrote: 'The whole welfare system, at all levels, costs Canadians more than six billion dollars a year, yet it has not significantly alleviated poverty let alone eliminated it. Welfare rolls have not diminished. The problems grow, costs go up and up and will in time, suffocate the taxpayer.'[16]

A federal white paper, *Income Security for Canadians* (1970), reflected some of the foregoing dissatisfaction with the existing income security system, principally the need to curb costs and to devise a method of funnelling the maximum number of welfare dollars to those in greatest need. What emerged from the rediscovery of poverty, then, was an attack on the principle of universality – in effect, a resurgence of the residual concept in social security policy.

The white paper recommended a substantial change of emphasis in Canadian social security by suggesting that the system of family allowances and youth allowances be scrapped and a system of family benefits related to income be substituted. It proposed to deal with the problem of poverty in

Table 11.6

Government expenditure on social security as a percentage of gross national product and national income, fiscal years 1963-4 to 1971-2

Fiscal year	Gross national product	National income	Government expenditure on social security	% of GNP	% of National income
	$ millions	$ millions	$ millions		
1963-4	44,358	33,458	4,069	9.2	12.2
1964-5	48,364	36,106	4,454	9.2	12.3
1965-6	53,636	40,015	4,727	8.8	11.8
1966-7	59,265	44,130	5,391	8.6	11.5
1967-8	66,799	50,088	6,445	9.6	12.9
1968-9	73,225	55,548	7,370	10.1	13.3
1969-70	81,285	61,653	8,548*	10.5	13.9
1970-1	86,871	65,141	10,193	11.7	15.6
1971-2	96,015	72,730	11,290	11.8	15.5

* Includes estimated data. See also Appendix Table A3.
Source: Department of National Health and Welfare, *Social Security in Canada* (Ottawa: Information Canada 1974), Table B, 71.

Table 11.7

Expenditure on public social security schemes as a percentage of gross national product, 1966

Austria	18.5
West Germany	17.4
Netherlands	16.7
Denmark	13.2
United Kingdom	12.6
New Zealand	11.8
Ireland	10.2
Canada	9.6
Australia	8.2
United States	7.2

Source: Andrew Armitage, *Social Welfare in Canada* (Toronto: McClelland and Stewart 1975), 6.

old age in much the same way. The importance of the universal old age security demogrant would be downgraded by being frozen at $80 per month. All further increases in old age pensions would be limited to the guaranteed income supplement, the income-tested segment of the old age security program, which would now become a permanent rather than a transitional measure. Less radical changes were recommended for other sections of the income security network to strengthen the Canada Pension Plan and to improve the social assistance programs.[17]

A Plan to Restructure Family and Youth Allowances

A major change, planned but not realized, involved the replacement of universal family and youth allowances with an income-tested or 'selective' system called the Family Income Security Plan (FISP). This program would have paid maximum benefits to the poorest 36 per cent of families; slightly higher but gradually diminishing benefits to 34 per cent of families; and no benefits at all when family income exceeded $10,000 per annum (about 30 per cent of all families). These allowances would also have become taxable for the first time. Thus, the stigma-free, administratively simple, universal system of family and youth allowances would have been replaced by a program that was potentially socially divisive and stigmatizing. In addition, the administration of this program would have been both costly and cumbersome. It is one thing, administratively speaking, to test the incomes of old age pensioners, whose level of income in the majority of cases is stable from month to month and year to year. It is quite another matter to consider testing the incomes of 2.2 million families when such income, in many cases, may vary from week to week, month to month, and year to year.

Moreover, was it necessary to sacrifice the sense of community solidarity inherent in a universal program and to expose the individual family to possible stigmatization in order to discriminate, in a positive way, in favour of the poorest Canadian families? The principle of 'selectivity within universality' could have been introduced by paying a higher allowance to families with four or more children, to combat the poverty associated with large families. One-parent families, another high-risk poverty group, might have been provided with additional allowances as well.[18] The Canadian Council on Social Development suggested higher allowances for all children, graded according to age, combined with a special tax schedule to recoup 100 per cent of the allowance at some given point on the income scale. In addition, the council recommended that the tax exemption for dependent children under eighteen be eliminated.[19]

The white paper ignored the implications of tax relief provisions for child dependants, which provide the greatest benefits to those with the highest taxable income. The Economic Council of Canada in 1969 offered an illustration of the inequities that result from what Richard Titmuss termed 'fiscal welfare'[20]: 'It is perhaps not widely appreciated that tax exemptions constitute, in effect, a form of transfer payment. For example, for families with two young children, who are in receipt of family allowances and have annual gross incomes of $2,700, $6,500, and $18,500, the exemptions in effect transfer to each $10, $114, and $270, respectively, in the form of tax savings. In other words, those whose incomes are too low to pay taxes gain nothing, and other families tend to gain in relation to their incomes.'[21]

The Significance for Social Security of the 'Rediscovery' of Poverty

The rediscovery of poverty in Canada resulted in a direct challenge to the principle of universality in program design; instead, selectivity was favoured, which was found in the recommendations of the Senate committee's report, *Poverty in Canada*, and in the federal government's white paper *Income Security for Canadians*. And to what end? As the National Council of Welfare pointed out, the white paper displayed a 'total lack of even pretensions to adequacy' in its proposed Family Income Security Plan, and the proposal amounted to little more than taking benefits away from the not-so-poor families and giving them to the poorest families.[22] There was no recognition of the need to redistribute more of the nation's wealth in order to deal adequately with poverty, even though the Royal Commission on Taxation, with impeccable logic, had provided the government with the rationale for introducing greater equity into the taxation system. Social security planning, as evidenced in the white paper, talked 'only of redistribution of existing income security payments.'[23] This was to become the pattern for future social security developments.

The 'rediscovery' of poverty also introduced the concept of a guaranteed annual income to a much wider public. The fact that this idea was also being talked and written about in the United States during this time only heightened the interest (President Johnson had declared a 'war on poverty' in 1964).[24] The GAI held out the promise of a right to a minimum income, free of means and needs tests. Canada had achieved guaranteed income for the elderly with the old age security pension and its income-tested supplement. But extending this same right to people of working age was quite another matter. The Senate committee on poverty dodged the issue by excluding single, unattached people under the age of forty, but in doing so starkly revealed its nineteenth-century attitudes toward the able-bodied unemployed. The Castonguay-Nepveu Commission made a better effort at including everyone, but even it framed its recommendations on the basis of those who were able to work and those who could not or were not expected to. One Quebec commissioner noted that the problem of work incentive had no basis in reality because of long-term changes in the demand for labour.[25]

The proposal to replace the family allowance system with the Family Income Security Plan met with prolonged and sharp opposition in the House of Commons. A revised bill that responded to some of the justified criticism of the original plan was reintroduced into the House in 1972. Despite the continuing criticism, an all-party agreement to pass the bill was obtained early in July 1972. Members were plainly ambivalent about the measure, regretting the loss of the universal principle but reluctant to deny the possibility of increased benefits to the poorest Canadian families. However, the measure died on the order paper on 7 July 1972, when debate on it ran out of time and the required unanimous consent of the House to continue government business was denied by one vote. Further action on the bill was forestalled by a federal election in October 1972, which resulted in the Liberal Party losing its massive majority to become, once again, a minority government, with the New Democratic Party holding the balance of power.

With the life of the government dependent upon the support of the NDP, a revision of the social security proposals was predictable. By April 1973 another set of proposals appeared, entitled *Working Paper on Social Security in Canada,* presented by the new minister of national health and welfare, Marc Lalonde. It jettisoned the attack on the principle of universality and reaffirmed the role of the demogrant by offering to triple family allowances and increase the old age security pension. In addition, a new plan to protect income security programs from inflation was announced. By the end of 1973, it was evident from the favourable reaction of the provinces to the new initiatives from Ottawa that the strong resurgence of the residual concept, evident in the 1970 white paper, had been turned back.

Constitutional Issues

Because of its overriding importance, the final development of the early 1970s remains to be discussed separately. In June 1971 Prime Minister Trudeau and some members of his cabinet met with provincial premiers in Victoria, British Columbia, for three days of discussion aimed at reaching agreement on a new Constitution for Canada. This was a remarkable chapter in a story that goes back to Confederation and that is inextricably linked to the development of social security in Canada. It relates to what Richard Simeon has called 'the tension between "nation-building and province-building."'[26] It concerns the locus of decision-making power in Canada and how it has tended, over the years, to alternate between Ottawa and the provincial capitals.

At Confederation a strong central government was established, but between 1867 and 1930, excluding the emergency created by the First World War, judicial interpretation of the BNA Act, combined with the social and economic consequences of industrialization, shifted power to the provincial level to the extent that the federal government was all but immobilized in the face of the crisis brought on by the Depression. As a result of the Depression, but more particularly because of the Second World War and the reconstruction period following it, the locus of power moved back to Ottawa. This shift, in contradistinction to the flight of power from Ottawa to the provinces prior to the 1930s, was accomplished not by judicial interpretation and socioeconomic change but by political and administrative arrangements. In the 1960s and early 1970s, the locus of power was reversed once more, moving back to the provinces as a result, again, of political and administrative arrangements between the two levels of government.[27]

We need to remind ourselves that the Rowell-Sirois Report of 1940 favoured a strongly centralizing policy in recommending that the provinces relinquish the major tax fields of personal income and corporation taxes and succession duties to the federal government in return for an unconditional grant based upon the fiscal needs and legislative responsibilities of the provinces. In another respect, however, policies having to do with social security matters were to be decentralized, with certain exceptions such as unemployment insurance. There was a strong assumption that the federal government was to eschew any notion of initiating programs, standard setting, or supervising national adjustment grants. The Rowell-Sirois recommendations did not secure agreement between the provinces and were shelved in 1941 for the duration of the war. However, in order to finance the war, Ottawa obtained full control of the three fields of taxation, with the provinces receiving compensating grants. At the war's end the federal government argued for the retention of exclusive control of the principal taxation sources if a policy of full employment and economic stability was to be realized. The tax-rental agreements proposed in 1945, as distinct from the Rowell-Sirois recommendations, represented a stronger centralization, with Ottawa playing the major role in mapping out social security developments.

The Debate over Conditional Grants

Although the tax-rental agreements of 1947 did not include Ontario and Quebec, decision-making in economic policy and in social security develop-ments had moved firmly back to Ottawa. However, the rapid development of provincial economies following the Second World War and of provincial government structures to meet the increasing demands for services set the scene for more devolution of decision-making power from the federal to the provincial governments. The beginning of this process is seen in the interac-tion between federal and provincial governments in the period from 1945 to 1960, which has been termed an era of 'cooperative federalism' character-ized by the 'sharing of decision-making powers and financial responsibility for particular programs or projects between the two levels of government.'[28] Its typical device was the conditional-grant program of which there were no fewer than fifty-six instituted between 1945 and 1962. In the late 1950s and early 1960s, provincial spokespersons became increasingly critical of the conditional-grant and shared-cost programs for their lack of flexibility, for the failure of cost-sharing formulae to consider differential fiscal needs, and for the impact of these programs upon provincial autonomy. This last argu-ment assumed greater significance from the 1960s on, notably in Quebec.

Viewing conditional grants as an invasion of provincial rights was pri-marily, but not solely, the Quebec point of view. Premier Manning of Alberta argued before the 1960 federal-provincial conference that shared-cost programs have four inherent weaknesses: they transfer policy decisions from the provincial legislatures to the Parliament of Canada; they may cre-ate serious financial problems for participating provinces; they force a mea-sure of uniformity that is beyond the dictates of desirability; and they increase the costs of social security programs by increasing the distance between the consumer and the administrator.[29] While Quebec's resistance to anything that could be construed as centralization sprang from unique historical and cultural reasons, other provinces gradually joined in the demand for some change in the shared-cost arrangements. In 1960 Premier Douglas of Saskatchewan suggested that all conditional grant programs should be examined with a view to converting some of them to grants that would be unconditional within specific areas of government activity.[30] The Quebec view was much less conciliatory: it demanded that in the case of well-established programs, the federal government should cease taking any part and that compensation should take the form of additional taxation rights and of corresponding equalization payments.[31]

Despite this flurry of criticism, it is important to remember that the value of the shared-cost and conditional-grant programs in launching needed services has been generally recognized, and relations between Ottawa and the provinces in the post-Second World War era have been cordial and constructive in comparison with the friction that developed around cost-sharing arrangements for unemployment relief in the 1930s. The pessimism of the Rowell-Sirois Commission about cost-sharing programs being a prime source of intergovernmental bickering was not borne out by postwar experience. The increase of professional personnel at the provincial level was an important factor in the postwar era. It meant that the people in charge of programs at the two levels of government shared a common professional training and common attitudes and values within their area of competence. Thus, there was a broad basis for agreement in the event that differences arose. This was particularly crucial for social security programs, which had been the source of so much friction in the 1930s. Although there were numerous political differences between Ottawa and various provincial governments, these differences did not disrupt the shared-cost arrangements. At the same time, it is important to realize that for the first time since the 1930s grants-in-aid were being challenged by influential Canadians outside Quebec.[32]

What were the reasons for the movement toward greater provincial autonomy? The most recent swing to centralization had occurred during the Second World War and the following period of reconstruction. The atmosphere of the Cold War years and the Korean War maintained the emergency to a degree. But in the 1960s international tensions seemed to have eased, and there was less reason for the concentration of power at the federal level.[33]

The fact that provincial and municipal governments were responsible for a steadily increasing proportion of public expenditure influenced the progress of decentralization in several ways.[34] In the 1950s and early 1960s, several provinces developed administratively to the point where they were engaged in long-range planning of their economies (Quebec being the paramount example), which gave rise to increasing dissatisfaction with the programs initiated by Ottawa. The marked development of provincial economies contributed to the growth of provincial elites in administration, politics, and industry. And just as the creation of an elite in the federal civil service during and immediately following the Second World War played its part in the centralizing process that took place then, the new provincial elites, men and women who identified their futures with the provinces, exerted their influence on the decentralizing process.[35]

The influence of Quebec and its 'Quiet Revolution,' usually associated with the death of Premier Duplessis in 1959, is important here. The inward-looking isolationism of the province, which had been developed in part to shield French Canada from the impact of the dominant Anglophone culture surrounding it, was shattered; it was replaced by a drive to join the mainstream of North American economic and social development, while at the same time promoting what Smiley has called 'Quebecois nationhood.'[36] For this new purpose Quebec required money for economic development, new educational expansion, and costly social services. It therefore exerted increasing pressure on Ottawa to permit it to have a larger share of tax revenue and an end to cost-sharing arrangements. Responding to this pressure, Prime Minister Pearson, in a 1962 speech, suggested that the federal government should withdraw from the field of permanent joint programs once they were well established across the country, and that social security measures were particularly well suited for this type of change. Cost-shared programs in this category, of relatively long standing, could be handed over to the provinces, with a corresponding increase in provincial leeway to levy taxes sufficient to pay the additional cost. Programs that were not sufficiently established to be handed to the provinces should be reviewed every five years when federal-provincial fiscal arrangements were negotiated. Such a policy, Pearson noted, would not deter the Liberal Party from bringing forward new cost-sharing programs, but it did mean that any new program would operate on a shared-cost basis for five years before being handed over to the provinces. In 1965 Parliament passed the Established Programs (Interim Arrangements) Act, which allowed the transfer to the provinces of the full responsibility for certain well-established shared-cost programs, such as hospital insurance, social assistance costs, and health grants, together with the appropriate amount of financial compensation. Quebec was the only province to take advantage of this legislation, achieving another validation of its claim to special status.

Criticism of shared-cost programs broke out again at the time of the Medical Care Act, passed in 1966 but not implemented until 1968. The Lesage government in Quebec (1960-6) had said it would never sign another cost-shared agreement. Health care was clearly a provincial responsibility, but it was a costly undertaking, and without federal financial help, probably seven of the nine provinces (Saskatchewan pioneered the plan in 1962) would have had difficulty launching a comprehensive program. Furthermore, those provinces with governments hostile to a plan that excluded the private insurance industry (Alberta, Ontario) would have claimed the scheme 'unaffordable' without federal help. The solution to this dilemma was to frame the federal legislation in such a way that did not require a province to sign a conditional grant agreement. The federal government simply offered to share the cost of any provincial medicare plan that met its five principles;[37] Lesage, who favoured medicare, accepted this face-saving formula, but his political successor, Daniel Johnson, did not, and the argument broke out all over again.

The rancour that developed between Ottawa and some of the provinces over the medicare issue resulted in the idea of a thorough review of the Canadian constitution, with the eventual aim of redrafting it in line with the changes that had taken place in Canada since 1867. Quebec's demands for autonomy were again vociferous, with the federal government being asked to withdraw from all social security programs within Quebec borders, including unemployment insurance and the demogrant programs.

A critical aspect of the constitutional review centred upon a restatement of the division of federal and provincial powers and responsibilities as they related to social security programs. The federal position was outlined in a working paper on the Constitution published in 1969.[38] In response to the view that Ottawa should restrict its role in the social policy area, particularly in social security, the federal government offered four reasons why it must continue to play a significant role in this field. The government argued that it must have the power to redistribute income between persons and between provinces in the interest of greater opportunity and equality. Furthermore, this transfer of income from one part of the country to another, from one family or individual to another, and from one generation to another through such mechanisms as equalization grants, unemployment insurance, family allowance, and old age security payments, would help to foster a sense of community. A third reason for a national presence in social security was the need to promote a standard of services across the country in view of the mobility of Canadians. Finally, social security expenditures had a recognized role as an economic stabilizer. It was important that the federal government retain the ability to exert the necessary fiscal leverage when the economy required it.

If the provinces were willing to concede these four arguments, it was suggested that in a revised Constitution the division of powers and responsibilities between the federal and provincial governments might be restated in the following manner: the Parliament of Canada and the provincial legislatures would have equal powers to make general income support payments to persons and concurrent powers in respect to social insurance measures. There were three provisos to this: that unemployment insurance would remain an exclusive federal matter; that workers' compensation would remain an exclusive provincial concern; and that Parliament's power would be considered paramount with respect to retirement insurance and associated benefits, such as survivors' and disability benefits. Under this arrangement, social services, defined by the federal government as 'services provided by the state to individuals or families, or paid for by the state on their behalf to ensure their health and welfare,' and which include the critical aspects of social security such as hospital and medical care insurance, would fall under the exclusive jurisdiction of the provinces. However, the federal government argued that there should be some mechanism for recognizing the national interest in certain critical services, such as hospital and medical services, to ensure a comparable standard of service in all parts of the country, as well as to contribute to research into Canadian health problems and to promote the development of the necessary technology or legislation to assist in overcoming them. The national interest in such social service programs would be expressed through the mechanism of the conditional grant, provided that a broad consensus existed between the provinces and the federal government on the value of the programs and that the people of any province refusing to participate should not suffer a fiscal penalty.[39]

Where income support programs are combined with a large component of social services – the social assistance programs being the most common example – a clear division of responsibility is difficult to achieve. This being the case, the problem of drawing boundary lines would be left to the courts.

The Victoria Conference, 1971
The foregoing positions on income security and the social services formed the basis of the federal position when provincial and federal leaders met at the Victoria Conference in 1971 not only to amend the Constitution in these and other key areas but to agree on a formula for repatriating the Constitution from Britain.

The Quebec position acknowledged that Parliament had the right to make laws in relation to the following areas of jurisdiction: family allowances; manpower training allowances; guaranteed old age income supplements; youth allowances and social allowances; unemployment insurance and old age pensions; and supplementary benefits to survivors and disabled persons irrespective of age. However, and this was the nub of the issue, Quebec insisted that provincial laws in these same areas must enjoy legislative primacy, and that whenever a federal statute was rendered inapplicable, in whole or in part, by a provincial statute, the provincial government must receive the fiscal equivalent of whatever monies the federal government would have spent in the province had its legislation applied.[40]

From a social policy perspective, one can appreciate Quebec's position in view of its record of comprehensiveness in social policy planning – the Quebec Pension Plan and the work of the Castonguay-Nepveu Commission were examples. In this respect, Quebec was well in advance of any other jurisdiction in Canada. The piecemeal initiatives in social policy emanating from Ottawa must, therefore, have been doubly objectionable to that province. They not only created resentment for all the long-standing political and cultural reasons among the French-speaking majority, but now, more than ever, Ottawa's limited initiatives were seen as unnecessarily complicating provincial planning.[41]

The federal government was prepared to concede that it would make greater efforts to dovetail federal and provincial social policy to ensure that the two levels of government were not working at cross purposes. Furthermore, some devolution of federal responsibility to the provinces was promised, which would provide the freedom of action required to meet the particular needs of people in the various regions of Canada. However, Quebec insisted upon a radically decentralized federalism that would give it effective control over the field of social policy, with compensating fiscal transfers from the federal government. This was denied, and the federal government's stand was supported by the other provinces. The Victoria constitutional conference ended with a double veto – the provinces with English-speaking majorities and the federal government refused the degree of devolution demanded by Quebec, and Quebec refused to accept the Victoria Charter,[42] and an opportunity to amend and repatriate the BNA Act was lost.

12
Unfinished Business:
The Social Security Review of 1973 to 1976

In January 1973, in the speech from the throne, the federal government called for a joint federal-provincial review of 'Canada's total social security system.' To initiate the study, a *Working Paper on Social Security in Canada* was issued by the minister of national health and welfare, Marc Lalonde, in April 1973. This document outlined the 'broad directions of policy that would, in the view of the Federal Government, lead to a more effective and better coordinated system of social security for Canadians.'[1]

Leading off the review was a new Family Allowance Act, passed in December 1973, which raised monthly benefits from an average of $7.21 per child to an average of $20 per child. This represented a complete reversal of the position argued in the 1970 white paper, although an element of selectivity was reintroduced in that family allowances would now be taxable.[2] Allowances were also to be increased each January in line with increases in the consumer price index. Furthermore, as evidence of a new federal flexibility toward the provinces, family allowances could be varied at the request of a province on the basis of age and/or number of children in the family.[3]

The review was conducted within a framework of five 'strategies': community employment, social insurance, income support and supplementation, social and employment services, and what the working paper nebulously termed a 'federal-provincial' strategy. More precisely, the last strategy involved jurisdictional concerns and reflected the federal government's intent to work toward a greater harmony between the jurisdictional aspirations, vis-à-vis social security, of both levels of government.

The formulation of five strategies to direct a review of Canada's total social security system had a larger than usual element of public relations flummery. At least three of the strategies – community employment, social insurance, and the federal-provincial jurisdictional strategy – were little more than window dressing, lending a spurious air of comprehensiveness to the review.[4] The principal task of the social security review was to attempt to come to grips with one of the most intractable problems in the social security system: the risk to income adequacy created by low or intermittent earnings, in effect a program to assist the working poor. A secondary goal, which emerged from the studies conducted by the working party on social services, was the effort to free personal social services from their residual straitjacket and move them toward a modern, institutional response to the human problems of urban-industrial society.

The Community Employment Strategy

Of the five strategies, the first, community employment, was soon relegated to a number of pilot projects across the country designed to improve both the job skills and the labour market for people with 'particular and continuing difficulty' in finding and holding employment. As discussed in the working paper, the community employment strategy held out the possibility of the government engaging in a substantial program of job creation by providing 'socially useful' employment for people who had suffered prolonged unemployment. This aspect of the program fell victim to government spending restraints in 1975, and the result was a much-reduced scale of program directed toward those who were severely disadvantaged in the labour market. This gave the program an even more pronounced residual character in a situation that called for such programs to be addressed to a much wider constituency, particularly in view of the concern for youth unemployment.[5] The failure of the federal government's proposals to promote employment underlined its reliance on the private market 'both to create jobs and to dispense economic and social justice.'[6]

The Social Insurance Strategy

The social insurance strategy, as outlined in the *Working Paper on Social Security*, was that the social insurances should be the first line of defence against unforeseen losses of income, supplemented by private pension arrangements. To improve social insurance as a first line of defence against loss of income owing to retirement, disability, or the death of a breadwinner, certain positive changes were made in the Canada and Quebec Pension Plans. The most significant was the raising of the year's maximum pensionable earnings (YMPE) on which contributions and benefits were calculated, year by year, until it equalled the average of industrial wages in Canada, at which level it would be maintained. This meant that by 1980, the maximum retirement pension would approximate $250 per month, compared with a maximum of $90 per month in 1973. A second amendment involved the removal of the ceiling on cost-of-living increases for the Canada and Quebec Pension Plan benefits. From January 1974, such benefits were to be adjusted annually for the full increase in the consumer price index.[7]

To improve the situation for people already retired, the basic universal old age security benefit was raised from $80, where it had been fixed in 1971, to $100 per month. The guaranteed income supplement was also increased, and both were indexed to the consumer price index on a quarterly basis. The raising of the universal pension as well as the indexing of it to the cost of living marked a reaffirmation of institutional values and a complete reversal of the residual policy put into effect in 1971.[8]

Critics of the Canada and Quebec Pension Plans argued that more fundamental changes were required to improve their adequacy and equity as income security measures. The Canadian Labour Congress, for example, recommended the following changes in 1975: pension benefits should be gradually increased to 75 per cent of earnings from the existing 25 per cent, and the retirement age should be lowered from sixty-five to sixty by 1981; the YMPE should be abolished so that pension benefits and contributions would be based on each person's full earnings; contributions to the plan should be shared one-third each by the employee, the employer, and the government; and the Canada Pension Plan fund should be administered by a pension council composed of a wider range of the general public, including farmers, employees, employers, and government.[9]

Criticism of the Canada and Quebec Pension Plans by the Royal Commission on the Status of Women in Canada resulted in some changes during the review period. Equality of status between men and women in relation to survivors' benefits was implemented. In answer to the request that some provision be made for spouses who work in the home, a small concession was made. The provinces and the federal government agreed that on the dissolution of a marriage, pension credits earned by spouses during the marriage should be divided equally. This did not answer a principal criticism of the Canada and Quebec Pension Plans: that spouses who remain at home do not have the opportunity to contribute to the plans and thereby qualify for a pension in their own right. This admittedly complex issue was promised further study. A proposal that would enable contributors who leave the labour force to raise children to drop those months of low or zero earnings from the calculation of their average lifetime earnings for benefit purposes was vetoed by Ontario but was eventually accepted in 1983.[10]

The reliance on the private pension field to supplement what many regarded as an inadequate public pension was a further manifestation of the residual philosophy in Canadian social security policy. Indeed, the Canadian Council on Social Development's 1975 report on retirement policies in Canada charged that the Canada and Quebec Pension Plan benefits had been held down deliberately to allow private pensions to flourish.[11] The apparent social insurance 'strategy' was to countenance the inadequate benefit levels of the two plans and to urge Canadians to arrange for supplementation of their social insurance and old age security benefits through savings and other private arrangements – the most common form being retirement, disability, or survivors' benefits obtained through company pension and benefit schemes. This recommendation was made with the full knowledge that, to quote the federal government's 1970 white paper *Income Security for Canadians,* 'there is a very uneven distribution of income protection for retirement, disability and survivors available through private industry.'[12] This was a serious understatement of the problem. The Canadian Council on Social Development reported that of the 2.8 million persons covered by private pension arrangements in 1970 (about 40 per cent of the working population), some 1.8 million were employed by government or crown corporations. This meant that nearly 70 per cent of those employed by private companies were not covered by occupational pensions. A report on private pensions in the *Labour Gazette* stated:

> Even for those covered, the projected benefits are often not paid because people quit their jobs long before they collect any service ... The Canadian Labour Congress quotes estimates that only 4 per cent to 10 per cent of benefits are ever collected. Company contributions to pension plans are based on the assumption that few of their employees will stay with them through to retirement and many people who change jobs do not even receive interest on their own contributions when they are refunded, let alone receive a fair share of the employer's liability arising from the years they worked there.[13]

Furthermore, it was widely acknowledged that, except for a minority, most private pension schemes were not indexed to the cost of living. The private pension industry had attempted to deflect criticism by attacking the idea of full indexing as financially unsound or by raising the flag of individualism with the argument that Canadians value independence and 'prefer to look after themselves over and above minimum levels provided by government.'[14] The Canadian Council on Social Development claimed that the Canada and Quebec Pension Plans were popular with Canadians because of such attributes as universality, portability, and the indexing to the consumer price index. The council argued that the two plans should be given a central role in the overall pension system.

One result of relying on the private pension industry to supplement an inadequate public pension would be the creation of two classes of Canadians in retirement: those who receive a generous private pension as well as the public pension, both enhanced by a working life free of periods of unemployment and with average or better wages; and a second group, if not a majority of Canadians then at least a sizeable minority, who must depend primarily on the public system because they are not in receipt of an occupational pension plan or are in receipt of one whose value has been diminished by periods of unemployment or low wages. This category of pensioner would be required to seek additional income from a provincial system based upon demonstrated need and subject to the exercise of considerable official discretion.

The Income Support and Supplementation Strategy

The raison d'être of the social security review was the income support and supplementation strategy. Its significance should not be underestimated. For the first time, a serious attempt was made to develop a plan on a national level to supplement the incomes of the working poor.[15] A comprehensive plan for improving the income security of the working poor would have included, as a first priority, a policy of full employment. However, this possibility was ruled out from the beginning by the federal government, which labelled full employment for Canada as a 'simplistic assumption' and argued that the nation's social security system should be constructed 'with this reality in mind.'[16] Higher rates of unemployment were inevitable, the working paper said, because industry could not be expected to grow at exactly the right rate to absorb increases in the labour force. The real issue here was not acknowledged. The government was not prepared to intervene in the economy to ensure a sufficient number of jobs to satisfy the number of job seekers. Commenting on the government's willingness to leave job creation largely in the hands of the private market, the Canadian Council on Social Development, hardly a fierce critic of government, said that it was 'not so sure that the economic system is capable of creating enough employment opportunities, nor can it be relied upon to correct the present economic and social injustice.'[17] Lord Beveridge's comments on the means of attaining full employment are pertinent: 'Full employment cannot be won and held without a great extension of the responsibilities and powers of the State exercised through organs of the central government. No power less than that of the State can ensure adequate total outlay at all times, or can control, in the general interest, the location of industry and the use of land. To ask for full employment while objecting to these extensions of State activity is to will the end and refuse the means.'[18]

Having dismissed the possibility of full employment, the federal and provincial governments moved to devise a plan for supplementing the incomes of the working poor without at the same time reducing the incentive to take temporary or low-paying jobs, which a condition of widespread unemployment helped to promote. What evolved from three years of proposal and counterproposal was a two-tier approach: an income support program for people who were not expected to work – the disabled, mothers with young children, or those for whom work could not be found – and an income supplement program for a segment of the working poor.[19]

The Income Support Program

It was proposed that people who were outside the labour force (the traditional clientele of the social assistance programs) be offered a form of guaranteed income based upon demonstrated need. What was new in this plan was that it would have a built-in incentive to encourage recipients to add to their income.[20] Benefit rates would be set by the provinces 'at levels appropriate to the different groups of people involved,' a policy that would invite the exercise of considerable official discretion. It was assumed that the most adequate benefits would go to those who were totally unsuited for the labour force, such as the seriously handicapped, or to those, like single mothers, who might be required to remain at home to care for young children. However, the decision as to who was 'employable' and 'unemployable' would be at the discretion of provincial officials. Considerable effort would be exerted to prepare those people deemed 'not currently employable' for a return to the labour force through training, rehabilitation, counselling, and the provision of social services such as day care for mothers with children (see the community employment strategy and the social and employment services strategy). Some national standards would be agreed to and Ottawa would share about 55 to 65 per cent of the costs.[21]

The Income Supplement Program

This proposed federal-provincial cost-shared scheme would have assisted the working poor on the basis of demonstrated need. Eligibility would be restricted to families with dependent children and to single individuals and childless couples aged thirty-five years and over, except those already in receipt of old age security and guaranteed income supplement benefits. The working poor would be eligible for an income supplement that, together with what they could earn, would bring their income up to an acceptable level. In point of fact, it was estimated that most families receiving the maximum supplement agreed upon ($960 per year for a family of four) would still not escape poverty.[22] The work incentive would be preserved by the fact that the supplement would be reduced by only $1 for every $3 earned. By contrast, people on the income support program would have their support payments reduced by $3 for every $4 of earnings. Again, certain national standards would have to be agreed to, and the federal government offered to share two-thirds of the cost with the provinces.

The income support and supplement strategy was a major effort to reform social assistance in Canada, last attempted in 1966 when the Canada Assistance Plan was brought into being. However, this initiative represented a continuation of the residual policy of designing programs for the poor and reemphasizing the *cause* of need. The Canada Assistance Plan, on the other hand, had attempted to move away from the categorical approach by concentrating on the *fact* of need.

The income supplementation strategy offered the possibility of three improvements over existing social assistance programs: it would be more inclusive as it would cover many, but not all, of the working poor; it would be less demeaning because of the possibility of simpler eligibility tests (something akin to the income test for the guaranteed income supplement); and it would encourage recipients to improve their situation by earning additional income.

The disadvantages of this particular strategy were that the income supplements and supports were not sufficient to lift the recipients out of poverty. Furthermore, one of the goals of the two-tier program was that the 'total financial rewards of those who work would always exceed benefits to those who do not work.' This was a refashioning of the 'less eligibility' principle of the 1834 English Poor Law, and did not square with the notion of 'social security.' A further shortcoming was the exclusion of single people and childless couples under the age of thirty-five from the income supplement program. Given the growing unemployment, particularly among youth, this was an illogical suggestion, but probably included to control costs. A third and most telling aspect of the working paper proposals was the complete silence on the question of income redistribution. Although the working paper had been prepared, the government said, in the belief that Canadians supported the values of 'independence, interdependence, and fairness in the distribution of the fruits of a growing country' (6), there was no mention of introducing a greater measure of fairness in the tax system as one means to this end.[23]

The Social and Employment Services Strategy

Until 1966 social services were the sole responsibility of the provinces.[24] In that year the federal government, through the cost-sharing arrangements of the Canada Assistance Plan, began to influence the development of social services in Canada by sharing the cost of services, having as their object 'the lessening, removal or prevention of the causes and effects of poverty, child neglect or dependence on public assistance.'[25] These services included rehabilitation, casework, counselling, assessment and referral, adoption, homemakers, day care, and community development. With the help of federal financing, provincial social services began to expand. But the cost-sharing provisions of the Canada Assistance Plan had two major impediments to the orderly development of social services: federal money was only available for services provided to people who had been assessed by a provincial needs test or to people who were likely to become 'persons in need' if the services were not provided; and the range of services that could be cost-shared did not reflect the growing needs for such services in Canadian communities.

The social and employment services strategy, as outlined in the working paper, would have restricted its focus to those services required to make the employment and income support and supplementation strategies fully effective. That is, people (principally social assistance recipients) who were having particular difficulty in finding and holding a job would be provided with training, counselling, rehabilitation, special work situations, and homemaker and child-care services to help them secure a foothold in the labour market. This narrow and residual view of the role of social services was rejected at the outset by the provinces that were looking for more money from the federal government for a wider range of social services applicable to all Canadians, not just the poor. The provinces insisted that the working paper's terms of reference be broadened to include an examination of the appropriate role of preventive, rehabilitative, protective, and developmental services in a revised social security system.[26] Following two years of study and negotiation, the federal and provincial ministers of welfare announced in February 1976 that agreement had been reached on a new approach to the financing and development of social services in Canada.[27] The significance of this agreement was that it acknowledged the importance of an enlarged role for personal social services in the lives of all Canadians: 'The legislative proposals recognized that social services are essential to ensure the opportunity for personal development for all Canadians and to prevent and alleviate the social and economic problems of individuals and communities. The future federal legislation is intended to assist the provinces in responding to the changing social and personal needs of Canadians in order to ensure that adequate services are available to all Canadians.'[28]

To meet this new objective, the federal government promised to introduce a Social Services Act to provide federal cost-sharing for a wider range of services to be made available to all Canadians: information and referral; crisis intervention; family planning; protective, preventive, and developmental services for children (such as foster homes, group homes, adoption, and head-start programs); day care for children and adults; rehabilitation and transportation services for the disabled; homemaker services and meals-on-wheels; social integration centres (such as halfway houses or friendship centres); counselling services; services related to employment; and community development and community-oriented preventive services.[29] Services that were primarily related to education, health, recreation, social assistance, or manpower, and that were covered by other financial arrangements, were excluded.

A Federal-Provincial Jurisdictional Strategy

This strategy was designed to address the perennial and growing problem of the tension created by provincial demands for greater autonomy in planning and administering social security programs. The federal government's working paper adopted a familiar stance: it expressed the hope that greater harmony would result from policies and programs designed to be sufficiently flexible to permit provincial governments to tailor them to the needs of their citizens. The federal government, for its part, hoped that the provinces would accept the logic of a national presence in the social security field in the interests of a Canadian social minimum in program standards and norms as well as the promotion of a fairer distribution of income.

The new Family Allowance Act, which took effect in January 1974, appeared, on the surface at least, to provide a successful demonstration of a new jurisdictional harmony between the federal and provincial governments. As mentioned earlier, the provinces could vary family allowance payments according to the age and/or number of children in the family, although these payments were subject to a national minimum and a national average per child. Alberta and Quebec took advantage of this option. A small but significant detail revealed in the House of Commons five years later indicated that while Alberta developed its program in consultation with Ottawa, Quebec created its quite different approach without consulting federal authorities.[30]

During the three-year period of the social security review, there was considerable debate over the problems stemming from the divided jurisdiction of cost-shared programs. The Canada Assistance Plan, for example, although born in harmony, had latterly been identified by the provinces as a cause of increasing intergovernmental wrangling due to the perceived rigidity of its cost-sharing regulations. The strategy of the provinces appeared to have been to limit as far as possible the federal government's role in income support, supplementation, and social services to that of cost-sharing. The federal government, on the other hand, called for a greater federal role in the administration of certain programs for the reasons already outlined. As an example, Ottawa argued for the right to share in the administration of the income supplement program, but this proposition was rejected by the provinces. Similarly, in the field of social services the provinces emphasized their undisputed constitutional responsibilities. The issue of national norms and standards appeared to be taking second place to provincial prerogatives.

The Denouement

The energy crisis of 1973, which developed after the publication of the *Working Paper on Social Security,* the rising levels of unemployment, and the serious inflationary pressures in 1974 and 1975 resulted in demands for more use of demonstrated need, a curtailment of universal programs, and a cutback in government spending generally. Toward the end of 1975, the government introduced wage and price controls and cut $1.5 billion from the projected 1976-7 expenditures. Numerous programs were reduced, frozen, or abolished. The indexing of family allowances was frozen for one year.

Opportunities for Youth, the Company of Young Canadians, and Information Canada were abolished. The Local Initiatives Program, which together with Opportunities for Youth had been aimed at reducing the high incidence of unemployment among young people, was drastically reduced. Changes in the Unemployment Insurance Act had the effect of tightening eligibility, denying coverage to workers over the age of sixty-five, and eliminating the differential for beneficiaries with dependants. This was not a congenial environment for advances in the social security system. In addition, the issue of constitutional powers and prerogatives was sharpened by the election of the Parti Québécois, an avowedly separatist party, in Quebec in 1976. These pressures threatened to wreck the plans for an income support and supplementation program. In an effort to save the scheme, Ottawa accepted 'virtually all of the conditions set out by the provinces.'[31] Federal authorities agreed to limit their participation to a cost-sharing role, to scale down the cost of the plan from an estimated $1.1 billion to less than $350 million, and to allow the provinces to establish either a one- or two-tier system under their own jurisdictions. This meant that rather than one plan of income supplementation with national standards and with federal participation in the administration, there would now be ten provincial plans, with national standards less certain. Despite these accommodations, Ontario opposed the plan, citing the cost that it felt Ottawa had underestimated. Some of the Maritime provinces also expressed the fear that they would not be able to meet their share of the income schemes, but the opposition of Ontario was probably decisive in shelving the proposals.

Lalonde now turned his attention to the proposed Social Services Act, hoping to salvage something out of the three years of work. But the federal-provincial jurisdictional strategy for combining flexibility with a national perspective failed here as well. During the summer of 1977, Quebec and at least two other provinces unexpectedly expressed objections to the new Social Services Act that was before Parliament as Bill C-57.[32] Quebec viewed the proposed act as an invasion of provincial jurisdiction, an old complaint but put forward with more determination by the Parti Québécois. Instead of the cost-sharing arrangement, Quebec asked for an equivalent amount of tax points to finance its own program of services. Ontario expressed an interest in the same arrangement.

In addition to jurisdictional issues, administrative complications were being forecast. The dividing lines between shareable social services under the Social Services Act and other services such as health, recreation, and education, which were being financed under other arrangements, were predicted to be extremely difficult to draw. Even detailed interpretations of federal cost-sharing regulations would not answer the problem.[33] Indeed, the regulations appeared to be so complex that federal scrutiny of provincial programs seemed inevitable.

Block Funding for Social Services

One solution to the jurisdictional and administrative dilemma posed by Bill C-57 was to finance social services in somewhat the same way that health services were financed – by block funding. When Bill C-57 was introduced for first reading in June 1977, Lalonde had defended a cost-sharing arrangement for social services by saying: 'Because social services in Canada are still in the developmental stages, the federal and provincial ministers concluded that shared-cost financing would be appropriate at this time.'[34] Three months later Lalonde announced that social services would be financed by block funding, and Bill C-57 was withdrawn.

Under the block-funding offer, each province would receive a per capita payment from the federal government based upon the national average federal contribution for social services under the Canada Assistance Plan and the Vocational Rehabilitation of Disabled Persons Act in the fiscal base year 1977-8, estimated at $22 per capita. To cover the cost of expanding the social services as visualized in Bill C-57, an extra $5 per capita would be paid for a period of five years beginning in 1979. Payments would be increased from year to year to compensate for inflation.[35]

Only three conditions were attached to the block-funding offer: eligibility for social services must not be tied to any minimum period of residence in the provinces; the federal contribution must be acknowledged in informational literature related to services; and the province must provide certain types of cost and program data on social services to the federal government.[36]

Political, administrative, and fiscal considerations dictated the change in policy. Quebec was unwilling to take part in any more cost-shared programs, and Ottawa was equally unwilling to be seen as interfering in an area of provincial jurisdiction, particularly with the Parti Québécois in power. The administration of the new act would have been very complex, but more importantly, Ottawa was concerned about costs, and cost-sharing had proven to be expensive in the past. From the federal point of view, block funding seemed an answer to a number of contentious issues.

Block funding also had certain advantages for the provinces. It provided them with complete autonomy in designing and administering their social service programs. Those who wished to see an expansion of social services were alarmed by the switch to block funding. The financing formula itself was a matter of concern. Federal contributions were to be based on payments made under two pieces of legislation that were primarily oriented to people in economic need. Critics of this formula argued that it was not an adequate base on which to build social services of a comprehensive nature.[37] Some commentators noted that there was no guarantee that the federal grants would be spent on social services, and that certain national standards contained in Bill C-57 might be lost, such as the establishment of appeal procedures and the designation of certain services as 'universal.'[38] The proposed change to block funding left many people with the feeling that the concept of a national minimum in social services, and of national leadership to attain it, had been lost. However, before these changes could be confirmed in a signed agreement or legislation, the federal government announced in November 1978 that, with the concurrence of at least eight of the ten provinces, the entire proposal (both the income support and supplementation strategy and the social services strategy) was being withdrawn as part of a general retrenchment in government expenditure.[39] The planned reforms of Canada's social security system collapsed with little public protest. Undoubtedly, the mind-numbing detail and the shifts and changes in strategy precluded intelligent public discussion.

Income Support and Supplementation, Mark II:
A Refundable Child Tax Credit

On 24 August 1978 the minister of finance, Jean Chrétien, announced a number of changes in social programs, including a major restructuring of benefits for children. These included deep cuts in the family allowance benefit from an average allowance of $25.68 per month (which would have climbed, with indexing, to about $28 per month on 1 January 1979) to an average of $20 per month. At the same time, tax exemptions for dependants aged sixteen and seventeen would be reduced from $780 to $460. An additional $50 per child exemption over and above the regular tax exemption was to be cancelled.[40] The money saved from these cuts and reductions would be transferred by means of a refundable child tax credit to low- and moderate-income families. Families with net incomes of $18,000 a year or less in 1978 would qualify, in 1979, for a tax credit of $200 for each child under the age of eighteen. As the family's income rose above $18,000, the tax credit would be reduced by five cents for each dollar of family income over $18,000. A family with two children would receive a full credit of $400 if its income was below $18,000, a credit of $300 if its income was $20,000 or less, and the credit would disappear if the family income was above $26,000 (see Table 12.1). As the median income of families with children in 1978 was about $19,500, a substantial majority of Canadian families would receive some tax credit and a large proportion would receive full credit.

The use of the tax system to redistribute income in favour of low- and moderate-income families has been called 'the most far-reaching restructuring of federal support for families with children since the introduction of Family Allowances in 1944.'[41] For the first time, the income tax mechanism was to be used to bring benefits to families below the income tax threshold. At the same time, a step had been taken to reduce the inequities that resulted from using tax reductions for child dependants in a form that provided the greatest benefits to those families with the highest taxable incomes. This

Table 12.1

Child credits payable, 1979

Family net income	Number of children			
	1	2	3	4
$18,000 or less	$200	$400	$600	$800
20,000	100	300	500	700
22,000	0	200	400	600
25,000	0	50	250	450
28,000	0	0	100	300
30,000	0	0	0	200

Source: Canada, Parliament, House of Commons, *Official Report of Debates,* 6 November 1978, Table 2, 858.

was a modest but significant innovation in social security planning and one that, barring administrative complications, could be built upon.

Following the changes announced by the minister of finance, the employment and immigration minister, Bud Cullen, told of the government's intention to bring in legislation to change, in significant ways, the unemployment insurance system.[42] If Parliament approved, the unemployment insurance program would become a 'selective' scheme that would require a refund from claimants whose gross income, including unemployment insurance benefits, exceeded $22,000 in any calendar year. Qualifying regulations for unemployment insurance would be considerably tightened by requiring higher entrance requirements for claimants who received benefits in the year before a current claim and by requiring that new entrants to the labour force or workers returning after a long absence have forty weeks of insurable employment in two years before qualifying for benefits. In addition, the unemployment insurance benefits were to be reduced from 67 per cent to 60 per cent of weekly insurable earnings. The purpose of this change, the minister said, 'is to make it more attractive for potential unemployed insurance claimants to accept jobs now paying close to the current level of benefits.'[43] The expected saving from these and other amendments, estimated at $710 million, was to be used for job-creating programs in 1979-80.

Officials of the unemployment insurance program estimated that the tightening up of regulations would disqualify about 263,000 claimants by 1980-1. The Canadian Labour Congress charged the government with attacking the unemployed rather than unemployment, and provincial public assistance officials predicted a rise in their welfare rolls if the cuts were approved by Parliament.[44] Members of Parliament from the Maritimes were particularly critical of the scheme. David MacDonald, a representative from PEI, said the revised qualifications could make it impossible for thousands in PEI to have an adequate income.[45] Whether an unemployment insurance system should be used as an income supplement program is debatable. Undoubtedly the program has filled this role for many Canadians. But should an income supplement program be financed by UI contributions, which are regressive taxes on the incomes of wage and salary earners?

13
Social Security in the 1980s

To set the stage for the events of the 1980s, it is necessary to comment briefly on the nine-month interregnum at the federal level when the Conservative Party held power.

The Clark Government and Social Security

In May 1979, the federal Liberal government under Prime Minister Pierre Trudeau was defeated at the polls, and a minority Conservative government with Joe Clark as prime minister assumed office. In December of the same year, the new government lost a vote of confidence, and Parliament was dissolved to clear the way for another federal election in February 1980. The Conservatives went down to defeat and the Liberals were back in power.

The Clark government had too little time to place its stamp on Canada's social security system. More to the point, the government's agenda for social security took second place to its primary goals – energy self-sufficiency for Canada, controlling government expenditure, and encouraging the growth of the private sector economy. Indicative, perhaps, of the government's priorities was the fact that the minister of health and welfare, David Crombie, was not a member of the prime minister's eleven-member inner cabinet. Furthermore, in 1978-9, the Trudeau government had already carried out a preemptive strike on two of the Conservative Party's favourite targets in social security – universal family allowances and the unemployment insurance system.

The small number of social security initiatives taken by the Clark government included a continuation of the previous government's review of social program costs as one means of containing a burgeoning federal deficit; incremental changes to existing policy; initiatives involving further attempts at the federal level to integrate the income transfer and tax expenditure systems; and a six-month study of the medical care system, the result of which, following a change in political fortunes, was presented to the succeeding Liberal government.

A Review of Social Programs

The minister of health and welfare announced a major review of social programs soon after taking office in 1979, giving rise to fears that cutbacks in health and social services were being planned. The minister of finance, Mr. Crosbie, signalled an attack on the principle of universality when he told the House of Commons that 'there will be a review to see whether funds can be better directed to those who need them the most.'[1] There were strong indications that universal family allowances were the central target, since the minister of health and welfare had publicly supported the notion of universality for medicare and old age security on the grounds of equity but questioned the use of universal family allowances and of tax deductions for child dependants as methods of delivering family benefits. By reconsidering the role of universal family allowances, Mr. Crombie pointed out, the government was merely continuing a review that had been going on for up to three years under the previous Liberal regime.

The cries of alarm raised by the opposition Liberals over the fate of social programs at the hands of the Tories had a hollow ring. The Liberal record in connection with family allowances was a case in point. In 1978 the universal family allowance had reached $25.68 per month and was expected to rise with the cost-of-living indexing to about $28.00 per month. Instead, as previously noted, the allowances were slashed to $20.00 per month to provide the bulk of the funds to finance the refundable child tax credit.

The Liberal record on unemployment insurance, according to some commentators, was even more lamentable.[2] In 1971 a new Unemployment Insurance Act considerably liberalized coverage (from 80 to 96 per cent of salaried and hourly paid employees), raised benefits to 66.67 per cent of average weekly insurable earnings, and widened eligibility conditions. In addition, there were benefits provided for the first time for the exigencies of pregnancy, temporary illness or disability, and retirement. Changing economic and labour market conditions led to higher unemployment, and program costs jumped almost fivefold between 1970 and 1975.

In a classic example of blaming the victim, the Liberal government interpreted the increase in unemployment insurance costs as a scarcity of willing workers rather than of good jobs. Beginning in 1973 and continuing throughout the decade, changes were introduced in the new program to enhance work incentives and control program costs.[3] The Clark government, had it been granted the time, would have been hard pressed to discover ways of cutting back on unemployment insurance benefits that its Liberal predecessors had not already implemented.

An Incremental Change: The Spouse's Allowance

In 1975 the Old Age Security Act was amended to provide for an income-tested pension for spouses (90 per cent of whom were women) in the age group sixty to sixty-four, married to recipients of the old age security pension and the guaranteed income supplement. When first introduced, recipients had their allowance cut off when the older spouse died. These people then had to wait until they were sixty-five before becoming eligible for federal pension benefits. In 1978 the Liberal government extended the benefits for six months, and in 1979 the Clark government, keeping an election promise, amended the Old Age Security Act again to permit recipients who became widowed to continue receiving an allowance until age sixty-five.[4] According to the National Council of Welfare,

> The flaw in the Spouse's Allowance is that it helps some near-aged Canadians but excludes others equally in need of financial assistance. Take the example of three poor single women aged between 60 and 65. One enjoys a Spouse's Allowance each month because her late husband had received OAS/GIS benefits and she had qualified for the Spouse's Allowance before he died. The second woman is also a widow struggling to get by on a low income, but she is not eligible for the program because her husband died when she was 50 or he was not yet 65 (in either case she could not qualify for federal assistance). The third woman is poor but was never married; she cannot receive a Spouse's Allowance because she was never a spouse.[5]

Stanley Knowles, the veteran New Democratic Party member of Parliament, made the most pertinent comment. He pointed out that the Spouse's Allowance Bill treated women as dependants rather than as persons: 'They get a pension on the basis of being able to answer the question: Have you got a man? Dead or alive, have you got a man?'[6]

Integrating the Income Transfer and Income Tax Systems

An expensive election promise by the Conservatives to allow a portion of mortgage interest and property taxes to be used as an income tax deduction emerged in the House of Commons as a proposal for a mortgage interest and property tax credit.[7] The popular interest in this tax measure reflected the fact that in the latter half of the 1970s, inflation had become a serious threat to the adequacy of individual and family incomes when shelter costs for many took up greater than expected proportions of disposable income. Interest rates edged up to 18 per cent and higher, which meant that having to renew a mortgage often became a financial nightmare for many families. Trying to get into the housing market for the first time was equally difficult; the sharp escalation in housing prices during the 1970s, coupled with record-high mortgage rates, pushed home ownership beyond the reach of many Canadians. For probably the first time in memory, middle-income Canadians were seriously impeded from achieving a goal that they had invariably achieved in the past – the ability to finance the purchase of a home.

The Conservatives' program, which was to be phased in over four years, would have assisted an estimated 3.8 million home owners with their shelter costs. Critics of the measure pointed out that it would do nothing for the 37 per cent of families who lived in rented accommodation and whose rents were rising under the impact of double-digit inflation. Furthermore, the program would be highly regressive even within the group who could qualify, that is, new home buyers and mortgage holders.[8] Opposition members pressed the government to introduce a shelter allowance that would help low-income families and individuals (elderly women living on their own and single-parent families in particular) who were paying more than 25 per cent of their income for shelter.[9]

The use of the tax system as a method of enhancing people's standard of living is as old as the federal system of personal income tax itself. In sharp contrast to income transfers through conventional social security or social welfare programs, whose cost and administration are the subject of regular public monitoring, comment, and study, the benefits provided through the tax system have been hidden from public scrutiny.

Richard Titmuss alerted social policy analysts to the size and significance of what he termed the 'fiscal welfare system' in the 1950s.[10] Since the Budget Control Act of 1974, the American federal government has published complete tax expenditure figures for both personal and corporate income tax. In Canada, the National Council of Welfare began to publicize effectively what it described as 'the hidden welfare system' in a series of reports beginning in 1976.[11]

From the first of these reports, Canadians learned how the so-called 'tax breaks' disproportionately benefited upper-income earners. In 1976, for example, the average tax saving from twenty tax exemptions totalled $2,068.40 for the 10 per cent of income tax filers with the highest incomes; median income tax filers saved an average of $400.00, while the 10 per cent of tax filers with the lowest incomes received no benefit whatsoever. The cost to the treasury of this foregone revenue was estimated at $7.1 billion, and 53 per cent of this amount went to the highest 20 per cent of tax filers.[12]

Following the collapse of the 1973-6 social security review, a federal task force was established to consider the feasibility of integrating transfer payments with the tax system. The task force reported in November 1978 at about the same time as the federal government introduced the refundable child tax credit.[13] The Conservative plan for a mortgage interest and property tax credit announced in the fall of 1979 (together with a refundable energy tax credit designed to protect low-income earners from the impact of a proposed 18 cent a gallon excise tax on petrol) was part of a move toward greater integration of the income transfer and income tax systems.

The Clark government, to its credit, was the first federal administration to give a public accounting of tax expenditures, thus facilitating a wider public appreciation of the size and significance of the tax expenditure system.[14] Information from the report indicated that in 1979, according to one estimate, tax spending came to 60 per cent of federal direct spending ($30.6 billion in tax spending versus $50.8 billion in direct expenditures).[15]

A New Study of the Medicare System

Before his brief tenure as minister of health and welfare ended, David Crombie, with the concurrence of provincial ministers of health, appointed a one-person commission to study Canada's health care system and report back within six months. The man selected was Justice Emmett M. Hall, who had headed the famous Royal Commission on Health Services (1961-4). The commissioner was asked to determine the extent to which the original principles of the medicare system were being maintained. It was widely believed and commented upon in the latter part of the 1970s that the system's universality and accessibility were in jeopardy because of the growing practice of extra-billing by some doctors and by the imposition of hospital user fees and health care premiums in some provinces. Mr. Justice Hall's review was put into a brief hiatus while the federal election of January-February 1980 was fought. His report was submitted in July 1980 to a Liberal government facing a new and difficult decade.

Social Security in the 1980s – The Liberals Resume Power

The Liberal Party, still led by Prime Minister Trudeau, resumed office in February 1980 with a majority government, but faced high and rising rates of unemployment and inflation coupled with slow economic growth, all of which would culminate in the economic recession of 1981-2, the deepest since the 1930s (see Table 13.1 and Figures 13.1 and 13.2).

The speech from the throne in April 1980 set out a sparse social policy agenda. Burdens would have to be shared equitably, the government said, and help would be directed to those who needed help the most. Among those so identified were the elderly, for whom inflation was a particular trial, and for those groups that faced special problems in finding jobs – young people, women, Natives, and the disabled.[16] People who had to face renegotiating a mortgage were also promised some relief,[17] but the most emphatic promise was that low-income pensioners would receive an increase in the guaranteed income supplement of $35 per month, per household, on 1 July 1980.

During the period from 1980 to 1984, the federal government's activities in the social policy field were dominated by its efforts to restrain public expenditure and by the growth of the federal deficit. Social policy became a matter of 'regulation and exhortation' (with little or no new expenditure of tax dollars), of the study, review, and realignment of existing programs, and,

Table 13.1

Unemployment, Canada and by region, 1966-83

Year	Unemployed (Thousands of persons)						Unemployment Rate (Per cent)					
	Canada	Atlantic region	Quebec	Ontario	Prairie region	British Columbia	Canada	Atlantic region	Quebec	Ontario	Prairie region	British Columbia
1966	251	33	86	72	30	33	3.4	5.4	4.1	2.6	2.4	4.6
1967	296	33	100	92	30	39	3.8	5.3	4.6	3.2	2.5	5.1
1968	358	38	124	107	43	47	4.5	6.0	5.6	3.6	3.2	5.9
1969	362	40	137	99	45	42	4.4	6.2	6.1	3.2	3.3	5.0
1970	476	40	160	139	70	67	5.7	6.2	7.0	4.4	4.9	7.7
1971	535	46	171	178	74	65	6.2	7.0	7.3	5.4	5.2	7.2
1972	553	54	178	171	78	73	6.2	7.7	7.5	5.0	5.3	7.8
1973	515	57	169	152	71	66	5.5	7.8	6.8	4.3	4.7	6.7
1974	514	65	169	164	53	64	5.3	8.4	6.6	4.4	3.4	6.2
1975	690	77	214	242	65	92	6.9	9.8	8.1	6.3	3.9	8.5
1976	727	88	233	240	71	96	7.1	10.9	8.7	6.2	4.1	8.6
1977	849	103	284	278	87	98	8.1	12.5	10.3	7.0	4.9	8.5
1978	909	105	308	298	97	99	8.3	12.4	10.9	7.2	5.2	8.2
1979	836	102	278	278	84	95	7.4	11.7	9.6	6.5	4.3	7.7

[continued on next page]

Table 13.1 [continued]

Year	Unemployed						Unemployment Rate					
	Canada	Atlantic region	Quebec	Ontario	Prairie region	British Columbia	Canada	Atlantic region	Quebec	Ontario	Prairie region	British Columbia
	(Thousands of persons)						(Per cent)					
1980	865	98	294	297	88	88	7.5	11.0	9.8	6.8	4.3	6.8
1981	898	104	314	293	96	91	7.5	11.5	10.3	6.6	4.5	6.7
1982	1,314	129	413	440	165	166	11.0	14.2	13.8	9.8	7.6	12.1
1983	1,448	139	427	474	217	192	11.9	15.0	13.9	10.4	9.7	13.8

Source: Statistics Canada, *The Labour Force*, and *Historical Labour Force Statistics*.

Figure 13.1

Annual average percentage change in the consumer price index, 1971-84

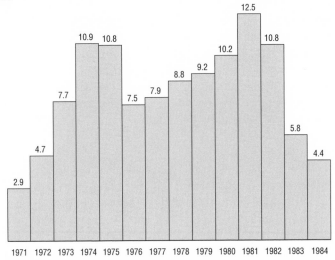

Source: Statistics Canada, *The Consumer Price Index*, December 1984, Table 2, 11.

Figure 13.2

Conventional one-year mortgage rates, 1980-4

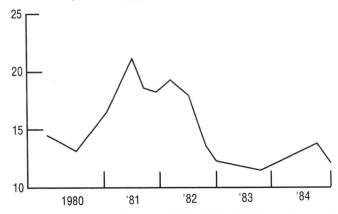

wherever possible, a preference for social programs that could contribute to a revival of Canada's sagging economy.[18] An example of the review of existing programs was the attempt to reform retirement income policy.

Pension Reform
Beginning in the late 1970s, a series of studies and reports was undertaken

on ways to improve the existing system of retirement benefits. These reports emanated from a variety of sources: governments (both provincial and federal) and interest groups representing the voluntary social welfare sector, women's groups, business groups, and the insurance industry. The reports spawned a series of regional and national conferences, and by 1983, when a parliamentary committee concluded its hearings on the subject, pension reform had been exhaustively examined.[19]

The reasons for this concentrated attention on retirement benefits were related to the demographics of an ageing society, the impact of double-digit inflation on pensions and savings, and the agitation on behalf of poor pensioners, particularly single, elderly women.

Demographic Factors

The 'baby boom' of the 1950s and 1960s had given way to a growing concern in the 1980s about the coming 'geriatric boom.' At the beginning of this century, the elderly comprised about 5 per cent of the population; by 1981, they made up 9.7 per cent. This percentage was predicted to rise slowly through the next three decades to 13.1 per cent, at which point the rate was forecast to move up strongly to a peak of 19.6 per cent by the year 2031 and thereafter begin a modest decline to just over 18 per cent by mid-century (see Table 13.2).

Table 13.2

Number of aged Canadians and their share of the population, trends and projections, 1901-2051

Year	Number of aged	Aged as a percentage of the population
1910	271,201	5.0
1911	335,317	4.7
1921	420,244	4.8
1931	576,076	5.6
1941	767,815	6.7
1951	1,086,273	7.8
1961	1,391,154	7.6
1971	1,744,405	8.1
1981	2,360,975	9.7
1991	2,985,900	11.1
2001	3,504,000	12.0
2011	4,074,100	13.1
2021	5,379,200	16.4
2031	6,644,400	19.6
2041	6,539,400	18.9
2051	6,388,200	18.2

Source: National Council of Welfare, *Sixty-Five and Older* (Ottawa 1984), 4.

Numerically, the 1981 population of people sixty-five and over was 2.3 million; it will increase to 3.5 million by 2001 and peak at 6.6 million in 2031. Providing pensions and other social services for this number will prove a formidable challenge, but it will not be the social disaster that some Jeremiahs predict.[20] While the number of dependent old people is increasing, the growth in the population of dependent young people (ages 0-17) is decreasing because of falling birthrates. Therefore, the total dependency ratio, which includes both the young and old as a proportion of the working-age population (18-64), will actually decline to an all-time low by the year 2011 (see Table 13.3). More importantly, comparing the numbers of dependent people with those who are actually in the labour force provides a more accurate projection of the economic burden to be faced. Because of the growing labour force participation of women, from 23 per cent in the early 1950s, to 52 per cent in the 1980s, and to a predicted 71 per cent by the year 2000, there will be more labour force members to share the burden. This projection holds true even with the trend to earlier retirement.[21] Furthermore, the cost of pensions and other services will be partially offset by lower child care and education costs.[22]

However, in the two decades following the year 2011, as the baby boom generation moves into retirement, the numbers of elderly will escalate swiftly, and the pressure on resources to provide for their needs will be considerable. This point is significant when we realize that the numbers of

Table 13.3

Dependency ratios, 1931-2031[*]

Year	Dependent group		Total
	0-17	65+	
1931	66.6	9.8	76.4
1941	56.5	11.2	67.7
1951	60.9	13.5	74.4
1961	72.8	14.3	87.1
1971	63.5	14.4	77.9
1976	53.5	14.6	68.1
1981	45.6	15.3	60.9
1986	41.9	16.1	58.0
1991	40.8	17.5	58.3
1996	39.5	18.3	57.8
2001	36.7	18.5	55.2
2011	32.5	19.9	52.4
2021	32.9	26.2	59.1
2031	33.3	33.7	67.0

* Defined as a percentage of the working-age population (i.e., 18-64).
Source: Canada, Health and Welfare, *Retirement Age* (April 1979), 17.

much older people – those seventy-five and over – will increase even more rapidly, requiring an expansion of services for the frail elderly, the majority of whom will be women. Nevertheless, given reasonable rates of economic growth and the avoidance of mass unemployment, the ageing of Canadian society should not be a cause for alarm. This viewpoint is supported by the fact that older industrialized countries are already coping with percentages of elderly in their population approaching those that Canada anticipates in the twenty-first century. For example, in 1981 Sweden's elderly comprised 16.3 per cent of its population; West Germany, 15.5 per cent; the United Kingdom, 15 per cent; Norway, 14.8 per cent; and Denmark, 14.4 per cent. The comparable Canadian percentage in 1981 was 9.7 per cent.

The Impact of Inflation
Between 1966 and 1977, inflation averaged 4.3 per cent a year, but between 1974 and 1982, the average rose to 9.8 per cent.[23] The majority of employer-sponsored pension plans lacked automatic indexing to the cost of living, and the impact of inflation on these largely unprotected private pensions was devastating. In sharp contrast, the basic public pension benefits (OAS/GIS) had been fully indexed to the consumer price index since 1973, and the C/QPP benefits since 1974. In addition, the federal government had provided increases to the income-tested portion of the old age security benefit, the guaranteed income supplement. However, the Canada and Quebec Pension Plans were not immune to the problems created by inflation. Maximum earnings on which benefits are calculated were originally equal to the average industrial wage (AIW). Under the impact of inflation, they have fallen to about 80 per cent of average wages (in 1984 the maximum pensionable earnings figure was $20,800 and the AIW $22,800). The 1984 federal budget recommended that the level of covered earnings equal the AIW by 1 January 1987, and be kept current from that point on.

Elderly and Poor
Despite the increasing amounts of money devoted to pensions by the federal government and to supplements and financial aid of various kinds by provincial authorities, an 'astonishing number' of elderly Canadians (about one in four) continued to live below the poverty line.[24] More than half of all old age pensioners (53 per cent) qualified for some or all of the income-tested guaranteed income supplement. Other nations did considerably better. In West Germany, for example, only 2 per cent of pensioners required any income-tested benefits added to their pensions.[25] Welfare organizations, trade unions, and the Canadian Advisory Council on the Status of Women campaigned vigorously for some additional resources for the needy elderly, and in particular for single, elderly women.

Women and Pensions

The struggle for adequate pensions for women became part of Canadian women's fight for equality. The beginning of the feminist movement in Canada was marked by the establishment of the Royal Commission on the Status of Women in 1967. The commission's report, published in 1970, and the creation of the Canadian Advisory Council on the Status of Women have provided women with an effective mechanism for monitoring and promoting equality, and the question of adequate pensions in old age was one such concern.

The chief problem for women is that pension schemes in both the public and private sectors were developed with men in mind. The model beneficiary of a retirement benefit scheme is a male who enters the workforce at eighteen and leaves at sixty-five. Women, for obvious reasons, have had difficulty fitting this pattern. Pension plans tend to view women as dependants of male workers. Most, if not all, public plans have provision for survivors' benefits, whereas private plans have a poor record of protection in this respect. The Council on the Status of Women has campaigned for an end to the concept of women as dependants of men in pension plans, advocating retirement benefits for all women in their own right. An additional problem for women arises from the fact that apart from the universal OAS benefits and the income-tested supplement, retirement benefits tend to be wage related, and thus the disparity between men's and women's wages is reflected in smaller pension payments for women. Furthermore, since women tend to take more part-time work than men, they are limited in their opportunities to qualify for an adequate public pension, and they are effectively disqualified from receiving an employer-sponsored pension since such plans usually exclude the part-time worker. In 1983 a council publication summed up the position of women in old age as follows: 'Whether a Canadian woman works in the labour force full-time or part-time, whether she leaves work to raise a family and subsequently returns, or whether she works as a homemaker, she can expect to be poor in her senior years. Pension reform in Canada is an absolute necessity if this injustice is to be remedied.'[26]

A Social Minimum in Old Age Redefined

The most persistent source of dissatisfaction with Canada's system of retirement benefits was its failure to maintain the twin goals of Canadian retirement income policy: an antipoverty objective involving the guarantee of an acceptable basic income to all pensioners, and an income replacement objective ensuring that the level of retirement benefits should be such as to prevent a serious drop in living standards.[27]

By the 1980s the Canadian system of retirement benefits consisted of *three tiers:* the first, a public system, the second consisting of employer-sponsored plans, and the third made up of private individual savings plans.[28] The first tier, the public sector, comprised the flat-rate universal old age security benefit and its two income-tested supplements, the guaranteed income supplement and the spouse's allowance (OAS/GIS/SA). These programs were seen as primarily responsible for fulfilling the antipoverty objective. The other major public programs in the first tier were the Canada and Quebec Pension Plans (C/QPP), both of which were compulsory social insurance programs covering almost the entire labour force and providing a wage-related retirement and survivors' benefit. These programs were seen as supplying a basic level of income replacement.

The second tier in the retirement pension system consisted of 14,586 employer-sponsored plans, covering 39.7 per cent of the labour force (1980 figures). Private pensions in Canada date from the nineteenth century.[29] The federal civil service pension was one of the first in 1870, and the Grand Trunk Railway had an employer-sponsored scheme by 1874. The federal government's annuity scheme of 1908 (see end of Chapter 3) was part of this continuing development of private pensions. The idea of employer-sponsored pensions appears to have spread from civil service groups and railways to public utilities, financial institutions, and then to large manufacturing firms. Further growth was encouraged by changes to the Income War Tax Act, beginning in 1919, which allowed the existing income tax deferment for employer contributions to be extended to cover employee contributions as well. The most significant increase in this form of retirement benefit occurred following the Second World War, partly as a reaction to the insecurity of the 1930s and partly as a result of the growth in the bargaining power of unions. The number of plans multiplied from 172 at the end of the First World War to about 600 by the mid-1930s, covering an estimated 10 to 15 per cent of the labour force. In 1947 there were some 3,400 plans in existence, and by 1970 the number had reached 16,137. This figure dropped to 14,586 by 1980, although the number of plan members had grown from 1.8 million in 1960 to 4.4 million in 1980, and to 5.1 million by 1993.[30] Moreover, the number of people covered by private plans says very little about the adequacy of such plans, since only a fraction of those covered (anywhere from 4 to 22 per cent) actually collect a pension because of the mobility of the labour force combined with the lack of portability typical of employer-sponsored schemes.

The third tier and the smallest (but rapidly growing) element in the retirement pension system was made up of those provisions within the Income Tax Act that encouraged individuals to save for their retirement. Changes in the Income Tax Act in 1957 and subsequently have provided significant income tax concessions to self-employed individuals such as doctors and other professionals who are allowed to deduct from their taxable incomes up to specified amounts a portion of monies contributed to a

Registered Retirement Savings Plan (RRSP). The income tax that would normally be paid is deferred until the money is withdrawn from the RRSP after retirement, when, for most people, the tax rate is significantly lower. Subsequent amendments to the Income Tax Act have widened the accessibility to this form of saving, but essentially only people with extra money to save and for whom the amount of tax deferred is significant take advantage of this scheme. This tier, although meant to improve the income replacement protection of people not covered by employer-sponsored plans, has not in fact filled this gap. Statistical evidence shows that 40 per cent of people with RRSPs also contribute to a job-related pension scheme. This third tier, then, is providing double coverage (and a tax subsidy) mainly to upper-income groups.[31] Some 2.2 million Canadians contributed to such plans in 1980.[32]

The Great Pension Debate

Beginning in 1978, public interest in improving the pension system accelerated, undoubtedly owing to the impact of inflation on the largely unprotected private pension sector. A spate of major studies appeared: *COFIRENTES+*, prepared by the government of Quebec (1978); *One in Three* by the Economic Council of Canada (1979); *Retirement without Tears* by a Special Senate Committee on Retirement Problems (1979); the Ontario *Royal Commission on the Status of Pensions in Ontario* (1980); and the federal task force on *The Retirement Income System in Canada* (1980). These and other reports set the stage for a national conference on pensions called by the federal government in the spring of 1981, when representatives of the pension industry, business, labour, provincial governments, pensioners' groups, women's groups, and members of Parliament and the Senate were invited to Ottawa for a three-day meeting to share their ideas on pension reform. There was general agreement that the pension system was in need of reform but much less agreement on what the fundamental problems were or in what direction change should occur. The conference was clearly designed to encourage a private market solution to the problems of the pension system, one consequence of the government's concern over the growing deficit.[33] More important, perhaps, was the philosophical bias in favour of a private market approach on the part of a majority of the federal cabinet and several of the provinces, notably Ontario. At the heart of the conference discussion was the now familiar debate between the residual and institutional approaches to social security reform.

The conference heard Senator David Croll condemn as a failure the policy established in 1965, at the time the C/QPP was brought into being, of deliberately holding down the level of public pension benefits, specifically limiting the C/QPP retirement benefits to a maximum of 25 per cent of the average industrial wage, in the belief that the private pension market would fill the remaining gap.[34] This had not happened for a number of reasons: private plans covered less than half the workforce, with a high proportion of lower-paid workers excluded; coverage was also restricted by lengthy and inflexible vesting provisions[35] and a lack of portability.[36] These conditions ensured that only a fraction of the covered workers would actually collect a pension. Protection against inflation was either limited or non-existent, survivors' benefits were inadequate where they existed at all, and in the case of marriage breakdown, a woman usually lost all rights to the pension credits of her husband. In addition, average pensions paid by employer-sponsored plans were, according to the Senate report, 'very low.'[37]

Pension industry spokespersons attempted to deflect criticism by downplaying the extent of poverty among the elderly,[38] citing 'unforeseen events that have transformed our society, our economy and our lifestyles'[39] – something that resembles a variation of the 'act of God' plea sometimes used by insurance companies to evade responsibility. The supporters of private pensions also decried the notion of indexed pensions, claiming it treated the symptom rather than the disease[40] and attacked positions that no one was defending.[41]

Institutional Approaches to Pension Reform

Labour unions, welfare organizations, women's groups, the Quebec and Saskatchewan governments, the Senate report, and one of four options proposed by the federal task force report, among others, supported an *institutional* response to the pension issue: namely, expanding the public system as the most direct means of improving the adequacy of pensions. Specifically, the Canadian Labour Congress advocated a doubling of C/QPP pensions by raising the level on which benefits were calculated from 25 to 50 per cent of average industrial wages (AIW).[42] The federal task force suggested raising the C/QPP benefit formula to 40 or 45 per cent of average industrial wages.[43] The Senate report recommended an approximate doubling of C/QPP benefits phased in over a five-year period,[44] while the Quebec report suggested that workers earning less than half the average industrial wage have their benefits increased by 50 per cent while continuing to provide 25 per cent of the AIW to the remaining half.[45] The Status of Women Council called for improved C/QPP pensions, including coverage for homemakers.[46]

The support for an institutional response came from those who maintained that retirement pensions, like education and health care, were primarily a social rather than an individual responsibility. But the most commonly advanced argument was the comparative administrative simplicity in changing essentially one pension plan, the C/QPP, which had solved the problems of coverage, vesting, portability, indexing, survivors' benefits, pension credit splitting on marriage breakdown (and was close to including dropout provisions for child care), against attempting to improve approximately 15,000 plans with unsolved (and some would say unsolvable) problems in all of the above categories. As the federal task force report noted,

> an enlarged C/QPP would unquestionably be easier and cheaper to administer than a myriad of employer plans. Since portability would be built in, and vesting would, in effect, be full and immediate, two major shortcomings of the present (private) system would automatically be avoided. Expanded pension benefits would also be available to those who now do not have the opportunity to become members of employer-sponsored plans and to qualify for the supplementary retirement income they provide. On the assumption that the enlarged public plans would disburse indexed benefits, inflation would not arbitrarily shift resources away from pensioners to others. The present gap between the treatment of public and private sector pensioners would also be reduced significantly.[47]

The Position of Trade Unions on Pension Reform

The union position at the 1981 pension conference in Ottawa was somewhat ambiguous. Through collective bargaining, many of the larger unions had been instrumental in developing occupational welfare retirement plans. Unionized workers, as a result, were twice as likely to be covered by private pension plans than non-union workers, and such plans were on average considerably richer in benefits. One consequence of the expansion of 'private' solutions to social issues is that the pressure to develop an adequate and universally available public plan is thereby reduced. A union spokesperson made the following revealing comment to a regional pension conference in 1982 (italics added):

> Because of the effective work of parts of organized labour in obtaining relatively good private pension arrangements in specific firms or industries, there is *certainly potential for resistance by sectors of the trade union movement to expansion of the public plans* based ... on the fear that those with better-than-average plans will be worse off [because] they have wasted their bargaining strength [and part of their settlements] in previous negotiations for something everyone else would be getting 'for nothing.' In industries with union-run multi-employer plans, these have provided a source of organizing and bargaining strength *which could be undermined by the expansion of public plans*.[48]

This statement illustrates the conflict between the values of community solidarity, which have nourished the development of social security systems, and those of the private market, which appeal to individual self-interest and have impeded their growth. Social security programs are an acknowledgment that people must act in concert against certain risks of modern society (not unlike the principle that fosters unionism) to ensure a form of protection that is both comprehensive and socially integrating. The values of the private market, when applied to social programs, invariably lead to undesirable forms of segregation. This is amply demonstrated in the health care field in the United States, with its crowded, overburdened municipal hospitals for the poor and its well-financed, state-of-the-art, profit-oriented institutions catering to the well-to-do, or in the primary and secondary education field in the United Kingdom, with its system of fee-charging schools attended by the children of middle- and upper-income groups, which both reflects and reinforces the sharp class divisions in that country.

Because of the conflict of interest on the issue of employer-sponsored pension plans, the Canadian Labour Congress joined in the charade that the goal of an adequate retirement income for all Canadians, and in particular for low-income and part-time workers, was a 'complex matter' but one, nevertheless, that would yield to more study and review.[49] In taking this position, the union movement blunted its attack on the private pension sector and the financial interests behind it. This also played into the hands of conservative elements within the federal government who favoured the private sector. A more predictable position for unions to have taken is suggested by the following comment: 'It is time to publicly acknowledge that the private pension industry has failed miserably. The time is past for ameliorative reforms. As a matter of public policy it is unconscionable that the private pension industry be allowed to continue to live off working Canadians and deny them the retirement security that they need and deserve. The private pension industry does not warrant another chance.'[50]

During the pension debate, the union movement was noticeably reluctant to raise the issue of private control of the vast accumulation of pension fund capital. The British social policy analyst R.M. Titmuss wrote in 1963: 'as the power of insurance interests (in combination with other financial and commercial interests) continues to grow they will, whether they consciously welcome it or no, increasingly become the arbiters of welfare and amenity for larger sections of the community ... Social policies will be imposed without democratic discussion; in this sense they will be irresponsible decisions.'[51]

Since the end of the Second World War, there has been a steady growth and concentration of pension fund capital under the control of four private financial intermediaries: chartered banks, trusted pension funds, life insurance companies, and trust companies. Together, they accounted for nearly 77 per cent of the assets of private pension plans in 1977 (which totalled approximately $260 billion). In contrast to this concentration of economic power, there is a lack of comanagement of pension plans and pension funds (as is common in European countries); union bargaining agents have difficulty in obtaining information about pension plans and often lack power to negotiate pensions on behalf of their members.[52] By failing to raise these issues, the union movement has lost an excellent opportunity to strengthen the democratic fibre of the nation.

Residual Approaches to Pension Reform

Representatives of business groups, the Economic Council of Canada, the pension industry, the provinces of Ontario and British Columbia, and three of the four options offered by the federal task force on pensions supported a private market solution and generally opposed any expansion of the C/QPP. The forces favouring a private market approach espoused the value of individual initiative and responsibility by placing the onus on the individual for any retirement income above the basic minimum available through the public plans.

At a conference of the Association of Canadian Pension Management in June 1982, a pension industry spokesperson, in discussing the need for an adequate pension, said: 'I believe ... that this need should be satisfied not as a matter of right but as a matter of affordability. The individual should have prime responsibility for the satisfaction of this need and government intervention should be minimal.'[53] The proposals for reform of retirement pensions by placing primary reliance on the private market system fell into two categories: those favouring a *regulatory* and those supporting a *mandatory* approach.[54]

The regulatory approach argued that all that was required was that higher standards be imposed on existing private plans with respect to vesting, inflation protection, and survivors' benefits. In addition, if workers were prevented from opting out of plans provided for them, coverage would increase over time, and no further action would be necessary. This position was supported by the business community, the federal Department of Finance, and most provincial governments.

Improved standards for vesting, such as providing locked-in vesting after five years of service and age thirty or after one year of service provided age and service totalled forty-five years, were agreed to by a coalition of thirteen major Canadian business and professional associations. Portability among the 14,586 plans proved to be more difficult. A federal green paper (a discussion document rather than a statement of public policy) attempted to break this impasse by suggesting a new form of individual registered retirement savings plan, which it called the Registered Pension Account (RPA). This would be similar to an RRSP but would provide for contributions by the employer as well, and all credits would be locked in until retirement.

The private market supporters were much less unanimous on how protection against inflation could be assured. Any reform in this area, it was feared, would cost too much. During periods of high interest rates, such as were experienced in the late 1970s and early 1980s, many pension funds received an interest windfall, and some pension experts suggested that a portion of these earnings be used to compensate private pensions for inflation. Another approach was that of the Parliamentary Task Force on Pension Reform, which suggested that private pensions be indexed to the consumer price index less 2.5 per cent (the idea being that it was quite reasonable to expect pensioners to bear the effects of the first 2.5 percentage points of inflation in any year). But such increases would be conditional on the financial performance of pension funds and the current productivity of the economy. Most private sector representatives opposed the idea of compulsory inflation protection for private plans. They tended to argue that fully indexed public plans would provide sufficient protection.

There was general support among those favouring regulatory reform of private pensions for improvements in both private and public pensions for the protection of spouses of pension plan members. There was a consensus on three areas of needed reform in private plans: the splitting of pension credits when marriages break down; providing survivors' benefits (at least 60 per cent of the initial pension paid was a suggested standard); and prohibiting the termination of survivors' benefits when a recipient remarries (something only the Quebec Pension Plan has done away with).

The flaw in this regulatory approach was that the suggested changes did not address the major defect of private plans: they did not cover a majority of the labour force. The National Council of Welfare suggested that regulatory reform might even reduce coverage by raising the cost of pensions and discouraging some employers from setting up a plan or leading to the phasing out of existing plans for cost reasons.

The second major category of residual approaches to pension reform – mandatory reform – attempted to solve the vexing problem of incomplete coverage by requiring all employers to provide a pension plan of minimum or better standards. This idea had the support of the pension industry and the associations of pension managers and actuaries, people who are closest to the day-to-day operations of private plans. This approach was also a major element of the reform plan put forward by the Ontario Royal Commission.[55] The mandatory position received little support from business organizations. They viewed it as too costly, particularly for small, struggling businesses, and the compulsory aspect was offensive to their individualistic values.

Pension Reform Delayed

Following the national pension conference in the spring of 1981, the federal government promised to outline its policies with regard to reform by July of that year. By that time, however, the economy had fallen into the deepest recession in nearly fifty years, and all hope for quick action on pension reform was set aside. The government position on pensions, promised for July 1981, finally appeared in December 1982 as a green paper. After reviewing a number of options for both the public and private sectors, the paper argued that although there was a large measure of agreement in the country on the nature of the problems facing the retirement income system, 'there was still a lack of consensus on appropriate solutions.' The government called for another year of study and referred the matter to a Commons committee composed of five Liberals, three Conservatives, and one New Democrat.

When the Parliamentary Task Force on Pension Reform finally reported in December 1983, a majority recommended that the focus of reform be on the private pension sector.[56] The sole New Democrat MP issued a dissenting report calling for the focus to be on enlarging the C/QPP and the old age security program. However, the committee's most contentious proposal was a pension for homemakers.

Pensions for Homemakers

A part of the process of developing social security programs involved a redefinition of the causes of poverty. In the nineteenth century, personal failure and character flaws were seen as prime causes. In the twentieth century, certain common risks that accompany life in an urban-industrial society have been identified, and for a majority of these risks Canadians have developed social security arrangements to protect themselves. In the 1960s, a major redefinition of the causes of poverty occurred when Canada acknowledged low wages and the resulting population of 'working poor' as a significant cause and category of poverty. This risk remains society's greatest challenge. In the 1970s, a further redefinition took place when the plight of single, elderly women began to be voiced in many arenas. One of the results of the extensive inquiries into pension reform in Canada during the late 1970s and early 1980s was to highlight the poverty of this group of women, many of whom have spent most or all of their adult lives doing unpaid housework.

The Parliamentary Task Force on Pension Reform proposed that the C/QPP should provide a pension for all homemakers, defined as a person 'who in any year, works only or mainly in the home to care for a spouse, a child under 18 or a dependent and infirm adult relative living in the home.' Such persons would be entitled to receive a C/QPP pension based upon the value of a spouse's labour in the home, set arbitrarily at one-half the average industrial wage ($11,400 in 1984). Homemakers who work in the paid labour force but who earn less than half the average wage would have their pension earnings 'topped up' to the homemaker pension level. Contributions to the C/QPP would rise to pay for this new benefit.

The Canadian Advisory Council on the Status of Women strongly supported the homemaker pension concept, although a number of regional women's organizations in British Columbia, Saskatchewan, and Manitoba did not. Several major national social welfare organizations, such as the National Anti-Poverty Organization and the Social Planning Councils of Winnipeg and Metropolitan Toronto, also opposed the idea.[57]

According to the Canadian Advisory Council on the Status of Women, in the late 1970s 75 per cent of widows and single women age seventy-five and over lived in poverty. It implied that this high risk of poverty would continue to be a common occurrence because of pay differentials between the sexes (most occupational pensions are wage related); because of inadequate coverage of women workers by employer-sponsored plans (only about one-third of women with paid employment participate in such plans); and because of the inadequate benefit structure of the C/QPP. Furthermore, survivors' benefits under employer-sponsored plans were minimal or non-existent, while the inadequate C/QPP benefits were reduced for the widow, although this was not the case for a husband, who, in the event of his wife's death, continued to receive the same pension. In the event of divorce, the C/QPP provided for equal splitting of the spouses' pension credits earned while the couple were married, although only a very small proportion (about 4 per cent) of former wives had applied for this credit. Only two provinces clearly recognized employer-sponsored pension plan credits as family assets to be divided between the couple on divorce. In other provinces, divorcing wives could not count on receiving a share of their husband's private pension credits. For all of these reasons, and because three out of five women aged sixty-five and four out of five over seventy-five were single, widowed, or divorced, the risk of poverty would remain high for this population group.

The National Council of Welfare's report on this issue opposed homemakers' pensions and demonstrated that it was riddled with inequities. The definition of 'homemaker' was particularly troublesome. A majority of married women and single mothers worked during the day and performed homemaking duties in the evenings and on weekends. Yet under the proposed homemaker pension scheme, if they earned more than half the average industrial wage (and most of them did), they would not be eligible for a homemaker pension. Another such inequity was that a wealthy widow could elect to remain at home to raise her children and eventually receive a fully subsidized homemaker pension. A low-income widow with children, who was forced to work but who only earned half the average wage, would receive the same homemaker pension as the wealthy widow but would have had to pay the full amount of the pension contributions.

Perhaps the most trenchant criticism of the homemaker pension is that the concept of homemaker is passé and becoming increasingly so as the role of women continues to change. A more direct way to help all pensioners in the future would be to improve the C/QPP by raising pensions to 37.5 per cent or even 50 per cent of the AIW, from the existing 25 per cent. For the present generation of homemakers, raising the OAS/GIS benefits would be the most direct route for the relief of poverty.

More Proposals

The Liberal government's February 1984 budget contained a set of proposals for improving pensions based upon a regulatory approach with a focus on private pensions.[58] Its most positive feature was a commitment to raise the guaranteed income supplement by $50 per month for single pensioners and one-pensioner couples.[59] Other changes would have to wait for the agreement of the provinces, but they included some minor but welcome amendments to the Canada Pension Plan.[60] The question of homemaker pensions was deferred until it could be discussed with provincial leaders, but most attention was placed on proposals for improving the private pension sector. The federal government's strategy was to propose amendments to the federal Pension Benefits Standards Act to raise the standards of private plans under federal jurisdiction relative to indexing, vesting, portability, survivors' benefits, part-time workers, and disclosure, and to express the hope that provincial governments would take similar action with respect to private plans within their jurisdictions.[61] But overall there seemed to be considerably less urgency to the pension issue. Perhaps the sharp drop in the rate of inflation to less than 5 per cent in 1984 was a factor.

The Medicare Crisis

In the fall of 1980, Mr. Justice Emmett Hall presented his report on the state of Canada's health insurance system to Parliament.[62] The commissioner had been asked by the Clark government in 1979 to review the extent to which the basic principles of Canada's national health care system – that is, the principles of universal coverage, reasonable access, portability, comprehensive coverage, and public administration – were being maintained. Hearings were held throughout the country, 450 submissions were received, and the commissioner noted: 'In my review I found a nation-wide demand for the continuation of what has now come to be known as Medicare. Canadians believe with justification that they possess one of the very best health services in the world and they want any difficulties or inequities remedied.'[63] The commissioner was presented with conflicting opinions about the nature of the perceived problems within the health care system as well as the means of overcoming them. Once again, the forces reflecting a *residual* concept of social security contested for public opinion with those of the *institutional* concept. Unlike the case of retirement benefits, the institutional concept appeared to gain a modest victory.

Is Medicare Threatened by User-Pay Policies?

A central concern for many Canadians in the late 1970s, and the principal focus of Mr. Justice Hall's review of Canada's national health insurance program, was the practice of extra-billing by doctors.[64] This development, which began to accelerate in the late 1970s, was viewed as a serious challenge to the health system's principles of universality and reasonable access by consumers' groups, labour unions, social welfare organizations, and others.

The medical profession and some provincial governments took an opposing view, arguing that medicare was underfinanced and that the existing 'priceless system' created excessive and unnecessary demands on the doctor's time. Extra-billing was seen as a solution to these problems by cutting down on frivolous demands on the system, introducing a greater sense of personal responsibility for health care, and reducing the overall cost. In addition, doctors claimed that extra-billing rewarded the better physicians for their superior quality of care. Furthermore, as independent professionals, doctors claimed the right to set the price for their services.[65] These positions were strongly contested.

Is Medicare Underfinanced?

The blame for the alleged shortfall in financing of the health care system was laid at the door of the federal government by some provincial administrations and by the Canadian Medical Association.[66] It was said that a change in the cost-sharing arrangements in 1977 had the effect of reducing the federal contribution to provincial health care costs. This, according to the Canadian Medical Association, led the provinces to cut back on hospital services and to introduce more and higher authorized hospital charges as one means of deterring overuse. Provincial governments also bargained more vigorously with their doctors over increases in medical fee schedules, which exerted a downward pressure on physicians' incomes. This in turn provided the rationale for an expansion in extra-billing by doctors.[67]

The 1977 change in funding resulted from the introduction of the Federal-Provincial Fiscal Arrangements and Established Programs Financing Act (EPF), which replaced three conditional grant programs for health, hospital, and postsecondary education costs with one block-funding arrangement covering Ottawa's contribution to the three sectors. The federal share now shifted from roughly 50 per cent of provincial expenditures in these three areas to a larger share of the yield from the personal and corporate income tax plus a per capita cash payment, which was also linked to the growth rate of the economy. Because federal funds for health care under EPF were now sensitive to the business cycle, as the economy went into a steep recession in 1981, federal contributions through EPF declined correspondingly.[68] Provincial ministers of health reacted angrily, claiming that Ottawa was cutting back on its commitment to medicare. Ottawa responded with the charge that it was the provincial share of health funds that was being cut. In the period from 1980 to 1984, there was an atmosphere of almost continuous acrimony between the Liberal minister of health and welfare in Ottawa, Monique Begin, and her provincial counterparts.

The purpose of EPF from the federal standpoint was to restrain social spending generally and the costs of medicare in particular, the latter having exceeded the rates of increase in the consumer price index.[69] The advantage of EPF for the provinces was that they no longer had to match federal grants with provincial dollars but could allocate both federal money and their own for any program purpose within the general area of health. It was hoped that this increased autonomy and flexibility in managing the health care system would result in greater economies.

The allegation that some provincial governments had used the block funding for purposes other than those intended by the legislation was the subject of a special investigation by Mr. Justice Hall, who concluded that such a charge could not be substantiated.[70] But the changes introduced by EPF did encourage the growth of free market concepts in the health care system, as shown by the increase in authorized charges for hospital services and the explosive increase in the use of extra-billing by physicians. Under the former conditional grant program for hospital costs, for example, the amounts collected provincially through authorized hospital charges were deducted from the federal contribution. However, under the new act this provision disappeared and with it the disincentive to apply authorized charges.[71]

A noted Canadian health care economist has argued that the restraint of health care costs in Canada has been accomplished by 'blunt instruments' such as budget controls, attempts to limit fee increases, and limitations on capital spending, rather than by 'resource management.'[72] Resource management would entail experimenting with alternate methods of health care delivery, such as community clinics, placing more reliance on non-physician services, slowing the graduation of new doctors, and experimenting with alternate methods of paying them.

The Impact of Extra-Billing

The great achievement of medicare in Canada is that it has reversed 'the traditional upside-down pattern of health consumption – where poor people used the health system least,' which is found in medical care systems where the rules of the marketplace dominate.[73] Extra-billing threatened to undermine this major social advance by inhibiting the low-income person or family from seeking medical care.[74] People with good incomes would not be discouraged from taking their complaints to a doctor, frivolous or not. In any case, as one researcher pointed out, 'the evidence of abuse by patients is anecdotal and formal attempts to examine its quantitative significance have concluded that the abuse is quite insignificant.'[75]

The notion of patient abuse of the system was countered by charges of physician abuse through such practices as unnecessary surgery, overutilization of laboratory tests, too many return visits being required, inefficient use of health manpower, and a widespread concern about the efficacy of a large and growing number of medical technologies and procedures.[76] These latter forms of abuse were extremely costly to the system and, unlike 'patient abuse,' had been verified by research.

Although medical associations contended that extra-billing could be seen as a reward for quality of care, others considered that the same goal might be reached by a peer-determined merit award system that could be reflected in the provincial fee scale.[77] One fundamental question raised before Mr. Justice Hall was who should ultimately determine the adequacy of physician incomes? The commissioner concluded that physicians had a right to be adequately compensated for their services, but that extra-billing, if allowed to continue, would eventually undermine medicare by establishing a two-class type of system.

Do physicians have the right to set their own fees? Mr. Justice Hall recalled that the Royal Commission on Health Services had dealt with this question when it said that such a point of view was a reflection of nine-teenth-century laissez-faire philosophy that had no validity when applied to the activities of any organized group in the twentieth century: 'When the state grants a monopoly to an exclusive group to render an indispensable service it automatically becomes involved in whether those services are available and on what terms and conditions.'[78] The strongest recommendation, therefore, of Mr. Justice Hall's review of the medicare system was that extra-billing by physicians should be made illegal. He also recommended abolition of authorized hospital charges and the phasing out of medical care premiums, both practices hostile to the principle of accessibility.[79] With regard to the remuneration of doctors, the commissioner recommended that when provincial governments and their respective medical associations could not agree on a fee schedule, the matter should go to an arbitration board for binding agreement.

The Role of the Federal Government in Medicare

The role of the federal government in the development of a system of health insurance in Canada has been an enabling and standard-setting one. The responsibility for providing health services rests with the provinces, but in an area as critical as health, there is considerable support for the notion of an 'over-riding national interest in the operation of health insurance plans and in the effectiveness of health care delivery.'[80]

In a discussion paper released in 1983-4, the federal government, acting on its mandate to uphold the principle of reasonable access to a comprehensive range of health services for all Canadians, declared that user charges and extra-billing were eroding the health insurance system and must be stopped.[81] It cited the support it received for this position from the review of the medicare system by Mr. Justice Hall in 1980 as well as the report of the parliamentary task force, *Fiscal Federalism in Canada,* in 1981. After failing to reach agreement with the provincial health ministers on ways of stemming the erosion of medicare, the federal government decided to bring in legislation that would restore the universality and accessibility of the plan.

The Canada Health Act

I have already suggested that Canadian social policy in the period from 1980 to 1984 was primarily a matter of study, review, exhortation, and regulation. After two or more years of study and at least three years of exhorting the provinces to take action on eliminating extra-billing by doctors and authorized hospital charges by provincial governments (with the only discernible effect being an increase in both practices), the minister of health and welfare finally moved to regulate the policies of provincial health ministries. On 12 December 1983, Bill C-3, the Canada Health Act, was introduced. The purpose of this legislation was to reassert the principles of medicare, particularly universality and accessibility, and to set forth the conditions to be met by the provinces for full payment of federal money for health care, including the financial penalties that would be incurred if the act were contravened.

The Liberal government, facing an election in 1984, may have hoped that the Conservative opposition would oppose the legislation, as a majority of provincial ministers of health had done. But the Conservatives denied the Liberals this political advantage by promptly announcing their support for the legislation, which was passed by Parliament on 17 April 1984. The Conservatives were undoubtedly influenced by opinion polls indicating that a solid majority of Canadians (77 to 80 per cent) opposed extra-billing and user fees.[82]

The Canada Health Act, which consolidated the Hospital Insurance and Diagnostic Services Act of 1957 and the Medical Care Act of 1966, declared that the primary objective of Canadian health care policy was to 'protect, promote and restore the physical and mental well-being of residents of Canada and to facilitate reasonable access to health services without financial or other barriers.'[83] The act outlined the five program criteria that provincial governments needed to meet in order to qualify for full federal funding: public administration, comprehensiveness, universality, portability, and accessibility. Provinces were also required to provide Ottawa with certain types of information on the operation of their health care systems and to give recognition to the government of Canada for its contribution to the health care service in any advertising or promotional material.

The act focused on the criteria of universality and accessibility. Under the act, universality was defined as meaning that a provincial health care plan must entitle 100 per cent of the insured population (it was 95 per cent under the old legislation) to the insured health services provided by the plan on uniform terms and conditions. Section 15 of the act outlined the penalty for failing to meet the five criteria and the informational requirements. They provided a judicious blend of carrot and stick. The act allowed the federal government to reduce provincial payments by an amount considered appropriate if a province permitted extra-billing or user charges. User charges in long-stay hospitals or institutions were exempted. The penalties took effect after 30 June 1984.

The amounts that were held back were recorded separately for each province, and there was to be a yearly report to Parliament on the operation of the act, which opened up the possibility for the federal government to spotlight the defaulting provinces publicly. If a province eliminated its user fees and extra-billing any time in the three years following the introduction of the act, the money deducted would be returned. With reference to universality, the act stated that Canadians should not be denied health services because they have not paid their premiums (only BC, Alberta, Ontario, and the Yukon required them).[84] As the minister said outside the House, 'How revenues for health insurance are raised is a provincial responsibility, but it should not be linked to receiving services.'[85]

Only three provinces, Newfoundland, Prince Edward Island, and Nova Scotia, had eliminated extra-billing and hospital user charges by 30 June 1984. The remaining seven began incurring penalties estimated at $9.5 million a month in July 1984, but before the three years had elapsed, all provinces and territories had ended extra-billing.

Although a new health act at the federal level offered an opportunity to expand the range of insured services, a goal which was raised repeatedly by various interest groups appearing before Mr. Justice Hall and the parliamentary task force on federal-provincial fiscal arrangements, the Canada Health Act was developed in a time of stringent economic restraint, and therefore it was a relatively cost-free piece of legislation from the federal point of view. The act was concerned exclusively with equality of access to health care, but as the minister of health and welfare pointed out, ensuring equality of access did not ensure either equality in the distribution of health services or equality of health status.

A Wider View

Health *care* is one but not necessarily the most important factor influencing health. A more balanced approach to the nation's health would also involve health *promotion,* which requires much more effort at lifting families out of poverty and providing for the unemployed. Too many Canadian governments see health promotion as limited to providing information on food, nutrition, and exercise. A third element is health *protection*, entailing the identification of health and safety hazards in the environment and developing regulatory measures to eliminate them. Of these three factors, Canada has, since the Medical Care Act (1968), made enormous strides in health care, which is concerned with primary prevention, immunization, early detection, diagnosis, treatment, and rehabilitation. Yet even here much remained to be done, while health promotion and protection shrivelled under the neoconservative sun.[86]

A New Conservative Administration in Ottawa

With the exception of the increases granted to recipients of the guaranteed income supplement, Ottawa's proposals for reforming the private and public pension sectors contained in the 1984 Liberal budget were placed on hold with the announcement of a federal election for September 1984. The election resulted in a majority Conservative government under the leadership of Prime Minister Brian Mulroney.

In the throne speech of November 1984, the new government announced its intention to enter into discussions with the provinces on a comprehensive overhaul of the pension system. The finance minister, Michael Wilson, in an economic statement to the country, expanded on the government's plans for improving the economy and reducing the federal deficit by questioning the wisdom of paying universal benefits, both family allowances and old age security.[87] The minister's statement caused some confusion in government ranks, if not in the country, as Prime Minister Mulroney had referred to Canada's universal programs, prior to the election, as a 'sacred trust.' By the end of January 1985, the government had backed away from tampering with the universal aspect of old age security payments.[88] How-ever, no similar commitment was made to protect family allowances.

The period of public discussion of pension reform appeared to be coming to an end. A closed meeting of federal and provincial officials in mid-January 1985 produced the announcement that Canada Pension Plan premiums would have to rise, but no decision was given on the amount and timing of the increase. The absence of any mention of improvements to the plan along with increases in contributions was notable. The Mulroney government, carrying out an election promise, introduced a bill in the House of Commons in January 1985 to extend the provisions of the Spouse's Allowance program to all widows and widowers aged sixty to sixty-five.

A Consultation Paper on Child and Elderly Benefits

In January 1985, Jake Epp, the minister of national health and welfare, issued a consultation paper[89] that was notable for a number of reasons, not all of them praiseworthy. For the first time, a federal document, prepared for wide public circulation, on a review of Canada's system of child benefits included both tax expenditures and direct program spending.[90] The paper also reviewed benefits for the elderly, but the same perspective was not accorded them. Not a word was written about the cost to the government of the RRSP and private pension programs, although the cost of two tax exemptions available only to the elderly and retired was noted along with the cost of old age security and its income-tested supplement. When RRSP and other private pension arrangements were mentioned, it was in relation to the importance the government placed on encouraging Canadians to save for their retirement. Furthermore, there were no options for change proposed for the system of elderly benefits as there were for the child benefit system. In fact, the paper said that no changes were needed.

The document did give a ringing endorsement of the concept of universality: 'The concept of universality is a keystone to our social safety net. Its integrity must not be called into question' (5). The paper also ruled out any 'special surtax' on old age security payments to recover more of the benefits paid to upper-income pensioners, as this would 'seriously disrupt our retirement income system and would unduly penalize those most affected by reason of retirement income from private savings in earlier years' (9). The same protection was not offered to higher-income families in receipt of family allowances.

The paper presented two options for changes in the child benefit system. One would eliminate the regressive child tax deduction and use the savings to increase the refundable child tax credit (RCTC) from $367 per child, per annum to $595 a child. The maximum credit could be focused on lower-income families by reducing the tax-back point (above which the tax credit is gradually withdrawn) from $26,330 to $20,500. A second option would involve reducing, but not eliminating, the child tax deduction, reducing the universal family allowance benefit by about one-third, and using the combined savings to increase the RCTC to $610 a child, while the tax-back point could be marginally reduced from $26,330 to $25,000, thus providing more child benefits for families in the $20,000 to 40,000 income range.[91]

The consultation paper's emphasis on using the RCTC as the major vehicle for providing child benefits ignored the drawbacks to that particular approach. The major difficulty was that the RCTC was calculated on the previous year's income. Given the economic uncertainty that prevailed in the 1980s, such a system did not respond to sudden cuts in income occasioned by spells of unemployment or the increase in part-time work. Nor did it consider the high rate of marriage breakdowns. At this time (1985), the RCTC was applied for at tax-filing time and paid in a lump sum, which attracted the attention of tax-discounting services. Some have argued, however, that a lump sum is useful for low-income families as it may permit them to purchase a major item without the expense of carrying charges.

These problems are avoided by the universal approach. The economist J.R. Kesselman suggested that a better formula for an enhanced child benefit would be to eliminate the child tax exemption and the RCTC and roll the savings of both into family allowances, which would continue to be taxable.[92] The unrivalled administrative benefit of a demogrant is that one application brings the allowances monthly for eighteen years. Arriving as they did in regular, predictable amounts, family allowances helped to even out swings in family income. They were uniquely free from stigma or any suggestion of fraud or fiddling. Needless to say, the administrative costs, estimated at half a percentage point of total benefits, made family allowances Canada's most administratively efficient program.[93] With appropriate restructuring of the tax system, family allowances could be as progressive in terms of income distribution as the RCTC is, without the negative aspects of tax discounters, lump-sum payments, and the yearly application for benefits. But the most powerful argument for the universal benefit system is that it avoids an obvious division of the community into 'haves' and 'have nots,' serving instead as a force for social integration.

The consultation paper is a bit of a historical curiosity in the light of its endorsement of universality and its pledge that any savings from the realignment of benefits would not be used to reduce the deficit but to help those in need – both merely echoes of the postwar welfare state consensus. The minister of finance and his department officials had quite another set of values: reducing the size of government and the cost of social programs while encouraging Canadians to look after number one. The whole purpose of the consultation paper may have been a last-ditch effort by the minister of national health and welfare to assert his authority over his department's programs and budget. If such is the case it did not succeed. From this point on, all significant changes in social programs were developed by the minister of finance.

14

A Sombre Anniversary

1 December 1992 marked the fiftieth anniversary of the publication of the celebrated Beveridge Report, which the *Globe and Mail* described as an 'outline of the most sweeping plan for government-sponsored social security ever set forth.' In March 1993, Canada observed the fiftieth anniversary of the release of the Marsh Report, *Social Security for Canada,* characterized by Leonard Marsh as a 'blueprint' for a comprehensive system of social security. As these two reports were written at a time of supreme collective effort to defeat Germany and Japan, it should come as no surprise that both emphasized a collective approach to social security in the postwar world. Viewing social security as a public responsibility as opposed to a private one was generally regarded as progressive, and the public consensus on this issue was reflected in the development of Canada's welfare state during the 1940s, 1950s, and 1960s. However, now, in the 1990s, support for the welfare state has fragmented. Nevertheless, the human problems of earning a living (typically requiring two wage earners), raising a family, and warding off or dealing with the largely *socially created* exigencies of life remain, and the greatest obstacles are low wages, unemployment, and underemployment. Even if we solve these latter problems, we must still deal with the more *natural* risks to human welfare: old age, illness, accident, disability, and family breakdown.

This chapter discusses the Mulroney government's policies on social spending during the period 1984-92 and the impact of these policies on the social security network designed to meet the common risks to income security. Although it will be argued here that the federal Conservatives' policies have been detrimental to the social security system and living standards, it seems only fair to point out that the erosion of social programs did not begin with the advent of Brian Mulroney's government. During the 1970s, the Trudeau Liberals also adopted neoconservative solutions for combating slow economic growth, rising unemployment, and inflation. In fact, it can be argued that the Liberal retrenchment in social spending in the 1970s set the stage for even greater cuts by the Conservatives in the 1980s and 1990s.

Briefly summarizing these Liberal forays into residual programming, we recall the attempt to eliminate universal family allowances in favour of a 'selective' plan in 1970, and the three-year 'social security review' (1973-6), which was principally concerned with developing an income supplement scheme for the working poor. Although this attempt failed, A.W. Johnson indicates that the planning undertaken for the review was the genesis of three provincial income supplement plans that were initiated between 1974 and 1980: Saskatchewan's Family Income Plan (1974), Manitoba's Child-Related Income Support Plan (1980), and Quebec's Work Income Supplement Program (1979).[1] Each of these programs confirmed the view that designing a program for 'the poor' inevitably results in a poor program. These provincial plans were administratively cumbersome, meagre in benefit, a prop to the low-wage sector, and socially divisive (the focus was on helping the 'worthy' segment of the poor – the working poor). In other words, quintessential residual social policy.

The Liberal finance minister's restructuring of family benefits in 1978 and the development of the refundable child tax credit (RCTC) were useful innovations to assist low-income families, but they were carried out at the expense of the family allowances program. By raising the profile of a refundable tax credit, Jean Chrétien, the finance minister, downgraded the significance of universality and made it that much easier for the Conservatives in 1992 to eliminate the concept from family benefits altogether.[2]

The blatant attack on the unemployment insurance (UI) system in 1976 and again in 1979 was more evidence of the Liberal shift toward neoconservative thought, as was the 'six and five' wage restraint program announced in 1982.[3] We recall as well the Liberal government's penchant for residual solutions to the demand for some much-needed improvements to the old age pension system. Therefore, when Mulroney headed a Conservative government in 1984, the institutional concept of social security and the idea of full employment as a government responsibility, the latter a keystone of social security, had been under attack by his Liberal predecessors for more than a decade.[4]

The Mulroney Government and Social Policy

Upon taking office in 1984, Mulroney's Conservative social policies contributed to the decline of living standards of low- and moderate-income individuals and families and to the erosion of the Canadian social security system in four principal ways: by ceding responsibility for economic growth and job creation to the private market; by cuts and changes to federal social programs; by regressive tax increases; and by paring federal transfer payments to the provinces that helped to finance provincially administered social programs.

'Jobs, Jobs, Jobs'

Neoconservative economic theory holds that unfettered free enterprise is the shortest route to economic recovery and job creation. Governments in Ottawa, over the period 1945-65, to a greater or lesser degree, tended to favour Lord Beveridge's belief that the question of maintaining full employment was too important to be left to the private market.[5] Some countries still held to this apparently outdated notion, Sweden being one of several examples, where the unemployment rate during the 1980s never exceeded 3.5 per cent.[6] Lars Osberg noted that in 1986, 'when Canada's unemployment averaged 9.5 per cent, Norway's unemployment rate was 1.9 per cent, Sweden's was 2.7 per cent and Austria had an unemployment rate of 3.1 per cent.'[7] But the economic doctrine of neoconservative regimes in London, Washington, and Ottawa maintained that the private sector, unhindered as much as possible by government regulation (but royally supported by tax revenues and tax concessions[8]), was the most reliable engine of economic growth.

Both the Beveridge and Marsh Reports regarded full employment as the indispensable foundation of a viable social security system (see Chapter 8). Canada made a tentative commitment to the goal of full employment in a 1945 white paper. Owing to the demand for Canadian resources and manufactured goods from a war-ravaged Europe, plus a buoyant domestic market, this commitment was seldom tested until the late 1960s and early 1970s. From that point on, unemployment rates never fell below 5 per cent and climbed to reach nearly 13 per cent in the recession of 1981-3. Since the early 1970s, however, the goal of full employment has been openly derided by the federal government as 'simplistic,' reflecting the growing influence of neoconservative thought, and replaced by the objectives of containing inflation and reducing the federal deficit. The foundation of the Canadian social security system was in this way seriously compromised.

The economic priorities of the Mulroney government were from the outset concentrated on reducing government spending, the deficit, the size of government, and the rate of inflation – a reprise of the former Liberal policy in some respects, but carried out with more ideological certainty. The pressing question of unemployment would be solved, the government contended, as obstacles to growth in the private sector were removed. This approach to the economy was given added impetus by the recommendations of the Royal Commission on the Economic Union and the Development Prospects for Canada (the Macdonald Commission, 1985).

Established by the Trudeau government in 1982, during Canada's worst recession since the 1930s, the commission spent three years and $20 million in an effort to chart a new course for the Canadian economy. Despite many submissions from labour, church, social welfare, and other community groups urging greater government involvement in the economy to stimulate growth and jobs,[9] the commission pushed a specific business agenda: 'In general governments should endeavour to facilitate the operation of the market mechanisms of our economy, rather than seek occasion for further intervention' (vol. II, 379). The commission's central recommendation was a free trade agreement with the United States for the long-term good of the Canadian economy; the report was highly critical of the UI system for its alleged interference with the 'flexibility' of the labour market and recommended further 'tightening' of the system. Perhaps to prepare Canadians for an economic future of low wages and underemployment, the commission suggested a form of minimal guaranteed income that would be financed by amalgamating a major portion of the social security network with certain personal tax exemptions and credits. One dissenting commissioner, Gérard Docquier, accused the commission of 'having endorsed market-based fantasies as a solution to Canada's nearly two million unemployed.'[10] Fantasy or not, from the Conservative government's standpoint, its neoconservative approach to social and economic policy, spelled out in the budget statement of 1984, had been impressively buttressed.

What were the results of these economic policies? When Mulroney assumed office in 1984 (after campaigning on the slogan 'jobs, jobs, jobs'), the national unemployment rate was 11.3 per cent and falling. It continued to decline to a national rate of 7.5 per cent in 1990 but rose again to 11.6 per cent by mid-1992, and was predicted to stay in the double-digit range until the mid-1990s or later.[11] Labour leaders and others charged that the Free Trade Agreement with the United States, which was concluded in 1987 and took effect 1 January 1989, was in part responsible for the high unemployment of the 1990s.[12]

The jobs that were created in the period 1984-9, according to the Economic Council of Canada, gave evidence of a disturbing trend toward what was termed 'non-standard employment' – jobs that were either part-time (less than thirty hours a week) or temporary (less than six months duration). These were typically low-skilled, poorly paid jobs with few fringe benefits, which contrasted sharply with so-called 'good jobs,' which required skills and training and were adequately paid and compensated with the usual range of benefits.[13] According to the council, this development had 'implications for living standards, social security protections, social mobility and income distribution.'[14] With a little more candour, one might have said that the prospect of a Canadian underclass was at hand.

There was also evidence of what was termed 'jobless growth' in the Canadian economy. Ternowetsky pointed out that in the period 1981-5, the five major chartered banks made profits of $8.5 billion but cut their workforce by 11,119 jobs. A similar pattern was found in the oil industry, where four of the largest corporations between 1981 and 1984 made combined profits of $5.6 billion and reduced their workforce by 6,987 jobs. Both banks and oil companies received substantial government financial assistance during this time, on the premise that such help would contribute to economic growth and jobs![15]

From the standpoint of future employment prospects in Canada, the Free Trade Agreement (FTA) between Canada and the United States was seen by some as almost wholly negative. Economist Marjorie Cohen pointed out that the service sector, the fastest growing source of jobs in Canada, was now wide open to American competition as a result of FTA: 'For the first time in any trade agreement in the world, services were included in the Free Trade Agreement in a comprehensive and extensive way.'[16] Canadian businesses in the service sector are no match for the American service sector, which is regarded as among the largest and most powerful in the world. Under FTA, the Americans can compete for a wide range of service jobs, including social services,[17] and the American businesses must be treated the same as their Canadian counterparts insofar as public subsidies or grants are concerned. This formidable competition will erode Canadian job opportunities as well as wages and working conditions. Some argue that FTA threatens the very autonomy of the country.[18]

What did Mulroney deliver? Certainly not jobs, jobs, jobs! After eight years at the helm, Canadians were faced with double-digit unemployment and the proliferation of non-standard employment, foodbanks, and homelessness.

A New (Conservative) Direction for Canada

In 1984, the new Conservative government in Ottawa identified four weaknesses in Canada's social security system: the level of social spending was too high; programs were not sufficiently targeted to those in greatest need; public assistance had become a substitute for earned income; and income security programs had weakened work incentives and self-reliance.[19]

The government's plans for dealing with these perceived weaknesses, for which little evidence could be found, had two overriding objectives: to cut social spending and thereby reduce the federal deficit, thus, implicitly, reducing the role of government in everyday life; and to require Canadians to adjust to the new competitive labour market using a combination of programmatic sticks and fiscal carrots. To accomplish these goals, three principal strategies were employed: partial indexing of social security benefits; the 'clawback' of universal benefits; and an emphasis on benefits that required a merging of the income tax and income transfer systems.

In his first full-scale budget in May 1985, Finance Minister Michael Wilson demonstrated his eagerness to deal with the high level of social spending and to act on his government's view regarding the ineffective distribution of social benefits. He announced that old age security (OAS) pensions and family allowances (FA), which heretofore had been fully indexed to the cost of living, would only be partially indexed (inflation less 3 per cent) beginning in 1986. This was despite the fact that in a consultation paper released in January 1985, Jake Epp, the minister of health and welfare, had said that OAS pensions would not be subject to change. Pensioners' organizations reacted with anger, and when the prime minister was personally challenged at a demonstration on Parliament Hill by Solange Denis, an Ottawa pensioner, for his failure to protect OAS as he had promised during the election, Mulroney looked suitably chastened.[20] To repair the political damage, the government reversed its decision with regard to OAS but kept the partial indexing applied to FA, over which there was no similar outpouring of anger.[21] The fact that OAS pensions are a much more significant item of monthly income helps to account for the difference in the degree of public reaction. But it was also the case that Canadians were less understanding of the values inherent in the universal family allowances system. They have been influenced by a barrage of unthinking criticism of universal programs as examples of government extravagance in the face of the 'alarming mountain of debt,' itself a distortion of reality.[22]

To compensate for what would be a reduction in the value of family allowance payments of at least 3 per cent a year, and to further the goal of 'target efficiency,' Wilson announced a substantial increase in the refundable child tax credit, directed at low- and moderate-income families and to be phased in over three years. At the same time, he restricted the benefits to fewer families by reducing the net family income ceiling to $23,500, above which benefits were to be phased out.

The finance minister then turned his attention to the *tax exemption* for child dependants, which, like all tax exemptions, yields the largest tax savings to people in the top income brackets. While he did not abolish the exemption, as community groups had urged him to do,[23] Wilson did announce a reduction in its value to be phased in over three years.

As a result of the 1985 budget, all three components of the family benefits system – family allowances, the refundable child tax credit, and the child tax exemption – were significantly altered. Family allowances would lose value each year to inflation. In 1992, for example, the FA benefit was $419 annually for each child (except in Quebec and Alberta, where family allowances varied with the age and/or number of children), but if it had been fully indexed to inflation since 1986, the amount would have been $504.[24] The RCTC would deliver higher benefits (but only on a yearly basis), phased in over a three-year period, to low- and middle-income families. The payment of the benefit once a year, after tax returns were processed, was a serious drawback for poor families faced with cash emergencies. The child tax exemption (CTE) was reduced in value from $710 in 1985 to an estimated $384 in 1989, but would still provide the largest tax break to higher-income families. Both the RCTC and the CTE would also be partially indexed when fully phased in.[25]

While there were some modest gains in child benefits for low-income families, the overall impact of the budget as a consequence of tax increases was decidedly regressive. The National Council of Welfare's analysis revealed that over the period 1986-90, in the case of two-earner couples with two children, the largest tax increase ($3,452) would be experienced by the middle-income ($35,000) family; the second largest ($1,879) by the low-income ($15,000) family; and the smallest increase ($1,125) by the representative high-income ($80,000) family. The same pattern held true for single-earner couples and single-parent families.[26]

Partial Indexing to Inflation

The impact of partial indexing on the social security and income tax systems has been so momentous and so little understood that it deserves more discussion. Inflationary pressures in the early 1970s led to full indexing of many social security benefits and components of the tax system.[27] Why did the federal government decide in 1985 to partially index child benefits and the personal income tax system? Because, critics said, partial indexing was a politically invisible means of cutting social program expenditures and raising taxes and thus helping to lower the deficit. Partial indexing has been described as a 'hidden, built-in tax grabber which automatically raises taxes without taxpayers' knowledge.'[28] As such, it proved to be enormously successful. Over the period 1986-91, it is estimated that program savings and increases in taxes from the partial indexing of family allowances and the personal income tax schedule, combined with the two percentage points cut in the GNP escalator, which determined the level of federal payments to the provinces under the Established Programs Financial arrangements (1977) to support medical care and higher education, totalled $27.5 billion, *almost the size of the federal deficit in 1989.*[29] The impact of partial indexing on the child benefit system deserves special note. Reviewing events in 1992 before a parliamentary committee, Ken Battle said that partial indexing was 'a most destructive change' because 'it pulled the rug out from under child benefits.' He estimated that between 1986 and 1991, $3.5 billion had been siphoned from the child benefit system to the disadvantage of low- and moderate-income families.[30] Partial confirmation of this can be seen by the steady rise in the consumer price index (see Appendix Table A2). The federal government could, of course, point to a sharp decline in the budget deficit from $47 billion in 1984 to $27 billion in 1989, but the National Council of Welfare's analysis of the federal budgets from 1985 to 1989 indicated that both the working poor and middle-income groups carried the heaviest load to effect this reduction, while upper-income taxpayers, with the strongest backs, carried the lightest (see Table 14.1).

Table 14.1

Income taxes (federal and provincial) for two-earner couples with two children, constant (1989) dollars, 1984-91***

	Working poor	Middle income	Upper income
1984	$175	$7,903	$34,775
1987	839	9,224	36,618
1988	765	8,375	34,516
1991	822	9,099	34,076
Percentage change	369.7	17.4	-6.4

* Taxes are less the refundable child tax credit. One child is under age seven, one child is over seven. Working-poor family earns $20,000; middle-income family $49,000; upper-income family $123,000.
Source: National Council of Welfare, *Help Wanted: Tax Relief for Canada's Poor,* Revised Version, November 1989.

Tax Reform: Merging the Income Tax and Income Transfer Systems

During the 1984 election, the Liberal government was criticized for the growing inequity in the tax system that permitted some high-income individuals and profitable corporations to escape their tax obligations. All three major parties promised tax reform. In his first statement to the country (*A New Direction for Canada,* 1984), Michael Wilson indicated that tax reform would receive high priority. For the government, tax reform was needed to promote efficient investment decisions and to simplify the tax system as well as its administration; in other words, to remove any obstacles to well-grounded prosperity and economic growth. The fact that the American government was also planning a reform of its tax system provided Canada with 'both an incentive and an example,' according to the Economic Council of Canada.[31] On 17 July 1987 the government issued its *White Paper on Tax Reform,* which emphasized the elements of fairness, competitiveness, simplicity, consistency, and reliability. It was recognized that trade-offs and choices were unavoidable, but fairness and the need to create a consistently progressive tax system were stressed. To this end, the white paper recommended converting the personal income tax exemptions and some tax deductions to tax credits.[32] These suggestions were welcomed by advocates of a more progressive tax system, but other recommendations contradicted this principle, such as a $100,000 lifetime capital gains exemption and a sizeable increase in tax deductible contributions to private pension plans and RRSPs.[33] It was pointed out that such tax concessions contributed substantially to the deficit – in 1987, for example, the cost of RRSP deductions in foregone tax revenue was over $2 billion.[34] The government claimed it was simplifying the tax system when it recommended reducing the number of tax brackets from ten to three, but the reduction in the top marginal tax rate from 34 to 29 per cent could only be attributed to a dubious neoconservative notion that economic growth and success in accumulating wealth needed to be encouraged and rewarded in this manner. Adding to these assaults on the principle of progressivity, the government made much greater use of sales and excise taxes, beginning in 1985. Although it introduced a refundable sales tax credit in 1986, which provided some protection for individuals and families with incomes under $15,000, it did not eliminate its regressive element.[35] However, the most significant change recommended by the white paper was the partial indexing of personal exemptions and tax brackets. This effectively raised taxes, without fanfare or notice of any kind, as long as inflation continued. The white paper's tax reforms emerged with only minor changes as proposed legislation in December 1987, and took effect in the 1988 taxation year.

The 1988 Budget: Phase I of Tax Reform
In the 1988 budget, which the government termed 'phase I' of tax reform, a small number of changes in the child benefits system were announced as part of the government's strategy for child care.

The National Strategy for Child Care, announced in December 1987 (with one eye on the forthcoming federal election), tried to placate both philosophical poles of the child care movement. The liberal pole sought a commitment to a universal, public day care system, while the conservative pole favoured some subsidy to private market or voluntary day care services and, for the ultraconservative, some financial compensation for those parents who stayed at home with their children. The attempt to meet these conflicting expectations resulted in an illogical mishmash of increased tax breaks for parents, promises of subsidies for child care services, as well as for a Canada Child Care Act, which was to replace the day care provisions of the Canada Assistance Plan (with its 'welfare' connotations) and provide the provinces and territories with both operating and capital grants for child care spaces.[36]

The changes in the child benefits system began with the elimination of the CTE, a form of which had been in place almost since the inception of income tax in 1918, and the substitution of a non-refundable tax credit.[37] Families with no taxable income would be unable to qualify for this additional help, a majority of whom would be among the poorest Canadian families, such as those on welfare. Here the government was displaying a prejudice against the poor and those on welfare. Despite overwhelming evidence to the contrary, the view persisted in some quarters that the poor lacked motivation and that the welfare system was an appealing alternative to employment. A non-refundable tax credit had the double advantage for this mind-set of encouraging employable people on welfare to find a job as well as helping those working at poverty-level wages to stay employed.

In addition, the child care expense deduction for children under the age of seven was doubled to $4,000, while the deduction for children seven to fourteen remained at $2,000, although the $8,000 a year per family limit, formerly imposed, was dropped to assist large families. There was considerable criticism of this form of help with child care costs because it was a regressive tax deduction that, the critics said, flew in the face of the government's own tax reform philosophy, which had been moving away from the use of tax deductions in favour of tax credits.

A further measure was a supplement to the RCTC of up to $100 per child for children under the age of six for 1988, and up to $200 for 1989 and subsequent years. Ostensibly this was to assist with child care costs, although children were eligible for the credit even if they did not attend a day care facility. The amount of the credit was derisory in the face of actual day care costs.[38]

'Clawback' and the End of Universality

Having won reelection by a sound majority in 1988, the Conservatives felt confident in moving against two pillars of the income security system – family allowances and old age security. Taking a leaf from the Liberal Party's notebook of 1978, when the Trudeau government required unemployment insurance claimants to repay a portion of their benefit if their net income exceeded a certain amount, the finance minister announced in his April 1989 budget that because of the ever-threatening deficit, the government would require higher-income parents and OAS pensioners to repay their benefits at a rate of 15 per cent of individual net incomes above $50,000. This provision would affect 2.9 per cent of all FA benefits and 0.9 per cent of all OAS payments. However, for a few it would mean a 100 per cent clawback of their benefits at tax-filing time and, more significantly, an end to the universal nature of the programs.

Although the reformed tax system was supposed to promote, among other values, fairness and consistency, both of these principles were violated by the clawback provision. The National Council of Welfare noted that in the case of a one-earner, $56,000-a-year family with two children, all of the FA benefit would be paid back. A second family with two children and both parents working, one earning $45,000 and the second $35,000, would not be subject to the clawback because the formula only considered the highest-income parent's net income. This family would pay the normal rate of tax on all its income, including FA, which would mean it would still keep about 55 per cent of the benefit.[39] The same objection was raised in connection with the OAS clawback by a Senate committee but without success. Hardly a model of fairness or consistency.

As a result of the Phase I of Tax Reform changes, the system of child benefits was a confusing mix of allowances, credits, and deductions:

- family allowances were now subject to a clawback
- the refundable child tax credit (RCTC) was received once a year (except for a minority of very low-income families, under $15,000 a year, who since 1986 received theirs in two instalments); the RCTC also provided a supplement for children under the age of six
- a non-refundable child tax credit
- a child care expense deduction of up to $4,000 for children under seven and $2,000 for children seven to fourteen could be claimed by families where both parents were employed, or where a single parent worked or took job training
- a refundable federal sales tax credit.

All these benefits, except family allowances, had to be applied for each year through the income tax return. Was the take-up rate of these benefits as complete as desirable – that is, did those for whom the programs were designed successfully apply for them? Given the surprising number of Canadians who are functionally illiterate[40] and given the complexity of the income tax return, an unsatisfactory rate of take-up would have seemed unavoidable. Some indication of the difficulty people experienced in claiming child-related tax credits may be gleaned from federal statistics, which report that for the 1985 taxation year the number of tax filers seeking child tax credits was just over 2.4 million, but only a little more than 1.4 million claims were allowed.[41] This welter of child benefits invited some restructuring.

New Child Tax Credit

As pointed out, over the period 1985-92, the Conservative government reduced the child benefit system to a confusing patchwork of credits, allowances, and deductions with some benefits paid monthly, some yearly, and some twice a year, on varying definitions of income. Some credits were refundable, some were not. In its 1992 budget, as part of the government's continuing 'child care strategy,' the government decided to amalgamate the various programs of child benefit with a view to assisting 'children in low and middle-income families.'[42] At the same time, and without any public discussion, it achieved a long-sought Conservative goal of eliminating the universal family allowance program entirely. In dismissing the program, the government white paper labelled family allowances as 'cumbersome,' an egregious description of the most administratively inexpensive and simple form of income maintenance in the whole system.

According to the white paper *The Child Benefit*, the key features of the new program would be a basic benefit resulting from the consolidation of the FA, the RCTC, and the non-refundable CTC. This would amount to $1,020 per year for each child under eighteen for families with two or more children with a net income of less than $25,921, with monthly benefits to begin in January 1993. Families not claiming the child care expense deduction, which was left in place, would receive an additional $213 per annum for each child under seven, plus an additional supplement of $75 per annum for the third and each subsequent child. For families claiming child care expenses for income tax purposes, their CTB supplement for children under age seven was reduced by 25 per cent of the expenses claimed.

The only new money added to the package was $400 million to pay for an earned-income supplement of up to $500 per family, to be directed at the working poor. Designed to reinforce the work incentive, families without a working member would not qualify.[43] The inadequacies of this particular supplement were detailed by the Canadian Council on Social Development: approximately one-half of Canada's poor children lived in families that would not be eligible for the credit, and only 30 per cent of families with earned income would receive the full supplement; only 16 per cent of poor, single-parent families would receive the full $500 credit.[44]

The new child benefit lacked a clear statement of a right-enhancing principle to justify its existence. Family allowances were based on the principle of universality – all Canadian children, by birthright or by immigration, were entitled to receive benefits. Social insurance has a contractual basis to support the notion of a right to benefit, but programs such as the new child benefit exist on the sufferance of government, which can vary the amounts at will and even withdraw them altogether. The fact that the new benefit is not taxable reflects a weakness that pervades the entire tax system: it should not be particular *types* of income that are tax exempt but particular *levels* of income.

The advantages of the new child benefit plan were its monthly delivery and the fact that all calculations for it were to be done by Revenue Canada, based upon tax returns. However, in its first year of operation, thousands of families had to repay some or all of their benefit owing to errors in the calculations. It had a modestly higher benefit for a majority of families (an average of $250 per annum higher for families with incomes under $50,000); and for families with earned incomes between $10,000 and $20,521, an additional supplement of $500 per annum, per family.

Community Criticism of the New Child Benefit

Concerns were expressed about the responsiveness of this system to changes in family size or status, but these were brushed aside with the assurance that the new system would be 'more responsive to family needs'

(*Child Benefit,* 9). There was considerable criticism of the limited amount of new money added to the benefits, particularly as it was directed at poor families. The amount of $400 million allotted for the 'working poor' was contrasted unfavourably with the government's announced intention to purchase fifty military helicopters (to hunt Soviet submarines) at a cost of $4.5 billion – over 1,000 times the amount the government was devoting to a long-standing and well-identified problem in Canada: poverty in families with children.[45]

In his testimony before the legislative committee considering Bill C-80 (the new child benefit), Ken Battle argued that the work-related child tax credit was not the best way to help the working poor. The special work-related credit simply added another categorical distinction to the system, inviting invidious comparisons between poor families with an employed member and those without. It would be preferable, Battle said, to pay a larger benefit to all poor families, whatever the basis of their poverty. Many middle-income families, he pointed out, would come out 'almost as much ahead as the poor,' and even the very well-off families were going to be better off if they could take advantage of the 1992 budget announcement of an increase in the child care expense deduction from $4,000 to $5,000 per annum for children under seven and from $2,000 to $3,000 for children seven to fourteen. Battle's overall opinion of the new child benefit was that it represented a 'modest but soon shrinking increase in benefit' (due to partial indexing) for some poor families and 'a very negligible improvement in the antipoverty power of the child benefit system.' His recommendations for improving the benefit were fully index the benefits and income ceilings, and change the whole system to either 'a fully income-tested option' (doing away with the child care tax deduction) or return 'to a universal option.' Either one, Battle contended, would substantially boost benefits to low-income families, especially the working poor.[46]

Unemployment Insurance:
An Impediment to Labour Flexibility

In 1984, the year the Conservatives became the government of Canada, the cost of unemployment compensation was $11.2 billion, with the federal government responsible for $2.9 billion of that amount. There was also an accumulated deficit in the UI account of $4.4 billion, largely created during the recession of 1981-3. The cost of UI placed it second only to elderly benefits in federal government transfers to individuals, making it a tempting target for deficit reduction initiatives. Having just had to reverse its decision to partially index OAS in June 1985, the government moved cautiously in approaching the UI program by appointing a Commission of Inquiry on Unemployment Insurance (Forget Commission) in July 1985.[47]

Three months later, in October, the Macdonald Commission on Canada's

Economic Prospects, appointed by the Liberal government in 1982, released its final report. Among a great many other suggestions, it outlined a new role for UI in the global, competitive economy. UI benefits were viewed as an impediment to labour flexibility and a contributing factor to the rate and duration of unemployment because of their alleged ease of access and generosity. They were also seen as subsidizing unstable patterns of employment by permitting employers to lay off their employees in a slack period rather than arranging part-time employment. The report recommended cutting back on the availability and the amount of benefit and, for employers, instituting a premium rate tied to their record of maintaining stability in their workforce.[48] Why did the Mulroney government require a second study of UI, having already received such impeccably conservative recommendations from the Macdonald Commission? Perhaps because unemployment was still above 10 per cent in 1985 and therefore a politically sensitive issue, particularly among Conservative backbenchers from the Atlantic provinces and parts of Quebec. Commissioning another report was an acceptable means of delaying a difficult political decision until, perhaps, the economy improved, which would ease the political complexities of cutting back on UI.

The Forget Report was released in December 1986 in a hail of controversy. The main recommendations of the report were leaked to the press prior to its publication, as were the central criticisms of a minority report prepared by the two labour representatives on the commission, which proved to be a scathing commentary on the majority's recommendations.[49]

For the government, the problem with the Forget Report was that it recommended not one but two major changes in Canada's income security system: first, a radical restructuring of UI, including tighter eligibility requirements, sharp cuts in benefits for all save those whose chances of requiring UI were minimal (an 'economic disaster' for parts of eastern Canada, the minority report claimed), and changes in financing, notably the ending of the federal government's contribution to UI; and second, a form of income supplementation (not spelled out) for those who would not qualify for UI under the recommended regime. Faced with these two complex recommendations, the Tory-dominated Commons Committee on Labour, Employment and Immigration recommended the report be shelved, and after some hesitation the government accepted this advice.

The essential failing of the Forget Report from the viewpoint of those who support the concept of social insurance as a form of collective provision against common risks to livelihood was that the majority of commissioners attempted to bend what is *social* insurance into a form of *private* insurance – a classic example of residual policy-making. Because the Conservative majority framed the recommendations for change, their views of social insurance were heavily interlaced with private insurance principles and concerns. For example, the report recommended that the federal government's contribution to UI be terminated: 'If UI is fundamentally a program of insurance against the loss of wage income, the benefits are not a "public good" but the right only of those who are insured. It also follows that the cost of benefits to individuals and the related administration costs should not be borne by the public purse but entirely by those who are eligible to receive benefits' (*Forget Report,* 275).

Commenting on what they had heard from submissions, the majority report said: 'Many provisions of the program are considered unfair – the different treatments of workers whose circumstances are similar' (presumably, the commissioners were thinking of the Variable Entrance Requirement, which permits easier access to benefits for workers in areas of high unemployment). Another provision labelled 'unfair' was 'The weak relationship between the amount of time spent in insurable employment and the amount of benefit received' (293). This refers to extended benefits to seasonal workers and benefits for self-employed fishermen. These elements of the UI program that violate equity were of great concern to the majority of commissioners. Indeed, to restore equity to the UI program was a principal motive behind many of their proposals. Here the confusion of private insurance with social insurance principles was revealed. An American scholar made this distinction between the two:

> Because of its voluntary nature ... private insurance must be built on principles which assure the greatest practicable degree of equity between the various classes insured ... Social insurance, on the other hand, is molded to society's need for a minimum of protection against one or more of the limited number of recognized social hazards ... Hence, just as considerations of equity of benefits form a natural and vital part of operating private insurance, so should considerations of adequacy of benefit control the pattern of social insurance ... The foregoing need not necessarily imply that all considerations of equity should be discarded from a social insurance plan; rather the point is that, of the two principles, adequacy is the more essential and less dispensable.[50]

The two labour commissioners issued a minority report that argued that the structure of UI, as established by the 1971 revision of the act, was still sound and should not be tampered with, except to restore some of the cutbacks to the program introduced from the mid-1970s on. The minority report emphasized the need for full employment and regional development and that high unemployment was the most significant problem to be faced. The majority report, on the other hand, devoted much of its attention to the various categories of claimants and to the administrative problems of the UI system itself.[51]

More Cutbacks to UI

Despite the government's decision to shelve the Forget Report, its interest in cutting the cost of the program remained. Proceeding more gradually, it made changes in the program that generally adhered to the advice it had received from both the Macdonald and Forget Reports. In June 1989 a bill was introduced into the House of Commons described as a 'sweeping overhaul' of the UI program. Its aim was to reduce the availability of UI by raising minimum entrance requirements and by imposing harsher penalties for quitting a job (up to three months' disqualification) or for being fired. The Canadian Congress of Labour charged that this would reduce the number of claimants by 155,000 across the country. The legislation reallocated about $800 million from the UI account to pay for job-training programs. Labour argued that the fundamental purpose of UI was to promote the social security of Canadians by supporting workers between jobs and that this basic purpose was distorted by burdening the UI fund with job-training costs. In addition to cutting back on benefits, premiums were raised in January 1990, again in July 1991, and once more in January 1992. Between 1989 and 1992, UI premiums rose by more than 50 per cent.

The most controversial change in the 1989 amendments was the decision to withdraw federal funding from UI. The federal government's contribution to UI had two purposes: it assisted in keeping premiums as low as possible; and, more importantly, it was an acknowledgment that unemployment was a national as well as an individual problem and that government had a responsibility to deal with it. To emphasize this point, the 1971 revision of the UI Act had tied the federal contribution to the unemployment rate. When the rate went above 4 per cent (the level below which 'full employment' was said to exist in those halcyon days), the government contribution automatically commenced, to underscore its responsibility to maintain full employment. By withdrawing the government's contribution effective January 1990, except in 'difficult economic times,' the Mulroney government was simply reiterating its economic credo: that job creation was the responsibility of the private market. However, in 1991 the UI account paid out nearly $19 billion in benefits but collected only $14.5 billion in premiums, resulting in a deficit the federal government had to finance because 1991, with over 10 per cent unemployment, qualified as a 'difficult economic time.'

Further cutbacks to UI took effect 18 November 1990 and served to reduce the program's coverage. Employment qualifications for benefits were increased from 14 to 20 weeks in some parts of the country, and the duration of benefit payments dropped down to 35 to 50 weeks from the previous range of 46 to 50 weeks. Among those who opposed the Canada-US Free Trade Agreement (FTA), some argued that competitive forces unleashed by the agreement would exert pressure to harmonize Canadian and American social policy. Unemployment insurance in Canada has been more generous and available than its American counterpart. In 1987, for example, the Economic Council of Canada's *Annual Review* reported that only about 25 per cent of unemployed Americans received UI benefits; in Canada, the figure was 85 per cent.[52] Critics of FTA charged that the federal government's cutbacks to UI were part of a strategy to harmonize the two economies. Much of the pressure for this type of change came from within Canada, as the president of the Canadian Manufacturers' Association made clear: 'It's simply a fact that as we ask our industries to compete toe to toe with American industries ... we in Canada are obviously forced to create the same conditions in Canada that exist in the US, whether it is Unemployment Insurance, Workmen's Compensation, the cost of government, the level of taxation, or whatever.'[53]

(Social) 'Expenditure Control Plan'

Another inviting target in what the newspapers referred to as a 'seemingly endless war against the federal deficit' were Ottawa's transfer payments to the provinces to support provincial programs of health, postsecondary education, welfare, and social services. The rationale for further cuts to social programs, announced in the February 1990 budget, was supplied by the Business Council on National Issues, an organization that represents the view of many of Canada's leading business executives. In addition to noting the size of the federal government's annual deficit ($30 billion) and the need to slow the growth of the country's debt, the council went on to say that 'since transfers to the provinces account for almost one quarter of all federal program spending, it is not surprising the Government has chosen to impose tougher limits on expenditure growth in this area.'[54] The council, as well as the finance minister, failed to consider the possibility of alternative methods of deficit cutting.

The principal targets of the expenditure control plan were CAP and EPF payments. CAP payments to the provinces to support provincial welfare and social services had, over the period 1985-90, increased at an average annual rate of 6.5 per cent. The new plan would place a 'cap' on CAP of 5 per cent annually for two years beginning in 1990-1, which was subsequently extended to 1994-5. However, this restraint was only applied to the 'have' provinces – Ontario, Alberta, and British Columbia. The Social Planning Council of Ottawa-Carleton predicted that the cap on CAP would cut $596 million from the social welfare system in its first two years. The affected provinces predictably raised objections. British Columbia said it wanted the courts to decide if the federal government had the right to make changes in the CAP unilaterally.[55] In this action, British Columbia was supported by Ontario, Alberta, and, on a matter of principle, Manitoba. The provinces argued that at the inauguration of CAP in 1967, it was agreed that this federal-provincial agreement could be terminated on one year's notice by either side, but that it could only be altered by mutual consent. The British Columbia Court of Appeal ruled in favour of the province, but this was subsequently overturned by the Supreme Court of Canada, which held that Parliament is supreme, subject to the limits imposed by the Constitution.

A coalition of community groups,[56] women's organizations, student, Native, antipoverty, and social planning groups argued that Canada's poor would bear the brunt of this particular deficit-reduction exercise because CAP paid for approximately half the cost of provincial social assistance plus a range of social services delivered to people in need. As provincial social assistance programs are the last resort for people with few, if any, resources to support themselves, social assistance becomes a mandatory responsibility of provincial governments, and therefore such costs can only be trimmed from the provincial side by impairing the adequacy of social assistance incomes. As such allowances are already well below any definition of adequacy, there is little room for savings here. Where small savings might be effected is the 15 per cent of the CAP budget devoted to a range of social services designed to assist in the 'lessening, removal or prevention of the causes and effects of poverty.' Taking this course would be 'penny wise and pound foolish.' It should be remembered that a Ministerial Task Force on Program Review (the Neilsen Task Force), which was established by the Mulroney government upon taking office in 1984 and which reported in 1986, described CAP as an 'effective federal-provincial partnership for the alleviation of the effects of poverty throughout Canada.'[57]

It will be recalled that under EPF, the federal government provides equal per capita financial assistance to all provinces for their medicare and post-secondary education costs. These EPF entitlements, set up in 1977, were calculated to keep abreast of the growth in the population and of the economy. The federal government argued that such a rate of growth could not be sustained because of its serious debt situation, and therefore, beginning in 1986-7, the annual rate of growth in EPF payments as a percentage of the GNP was reduced by 2 percentage points, and in 1989 by an additional one percentage point, to take effect in 1990-1. In 1990 a freeze on EPF entitlements for two years was announced, and this was subsequently extended through 1994-5, after which EPF payments would still be held to a formula of GNP minus three percentage points.

The National Council of Welfare estimated that with these spending restraints in place, the federal cash payments for medicare and postsecondary education to the provinces would run out in the fiscal year 2008-9.[58] Federal cash payments to Quebec would disappear even more quickly because of the fiscal arrangements between Ottawa and Quebec that were more heavily weighted in favour of tax transfers (EPF payments are a mix of cash and tax transfers).

While arguing that federal expenditures on programs such as CAP and EPF had to be curbed, there was little recognition on the part of Ottawa that other federal policies were raising the costs of provincial welfare programs – the reduction and cutbacks to UI, for example, and the generally poor economy and high unemployment rates, which many critics of government policy blamed on the effects of the Free Trade Agreement and the reliance on market forces for job creation. Concern was also expressed that if federal contributions to medicare ceased, Ottawa would no longer have the ability to enforce the standards of the Canada Health Act. To allay this concern, the minister of finance announced in February 1991 that the government would amend the Fiscal Arrangements Act 'so that, if necessary, other cash transfers to provinces would be withheld for purposes of enforcement [of medicare's national standards].'[59] The National Council of Welfare challenged the validity of this plan by arguing that it could not imagine the provinces letting this proposal go uncontested. The delivery of health care is within provincial jurisdiction, and 'it is difficult to imagine how Ottawa could continue to maintain its presence once the money for medicare dries up.'[60] (See Chapter 13 and the discussion under the Canada Health Act.)

Welfare Reform[61]

The impetus for welfare reform during the 1980s was the rising costs of provincial social assistance programs and their federal counterpart, the Canada Assistance Plan payments, which rose steadily from $2.08 billion in 1982-3 to $3.57 billion in 1989-90. Added to this was the increase in employable people on the provincial welfare rolls. In Quebec, for example, 36 per cent of social aid recipients were classified as employable in 1971; by 1987 this category had risen to 73 per cent.[62] Moreover, a larger percentage of these recipients were young, single people (with single women invariably being single mothers), and the length of stay of all employable people on social assistance was more prolonged.

Official attempts to explain the marked change in welfare clientele seemed rooted in age-old prejudices about the poor and dependent. Ignored to the point of denial were the continuing high levels of unemployment. During the 1980s, the 'official' rate of unemployment, which badly understated the true figure, never fell below 7.5 per cent; ignored as well were the vanishing full-time jobs, the plant closings, and the polarization of the labour market into 'good jobs and bad jobs.' Raised to prominence were the issues of welfare fraud, the decline of the work ethic (or moral standards), and the welfare system's contribution to the growth of 'dependency' (a modern version of 'pauperism').

Two provinces, Saskatchewan and Quebec, provided examples of attempts at welfare reform with this mind-set. Both jurisdictions saw it as an important first step to differentiate clearly between the unemployables and the employables (the deserving and the undeserving poor) on their welfare rolls and to subject the latter group to a reform program designed to move them back into the labour market. Both provinces offered various programs of job training, work experience, and forms of subsidized employment, and each promised far more than it was able to deliver in terms of educational upgrading and job training. Refusal to take part in the program resulted in a reduction in benefit in Quebec and a denial of benefit in Saskatchewan.[63] Both actions contradicted the informal terms of the Canada Assistance Plan, which promoted the policy that *need* was the sole criterion for judging eligibility.

In evaluating Saskatchewan's program, Graham Riches provides a convincing argument that its prime goal of reducing welfare dependency was not accomplished to any significant degree: 'In 1982, when the new government came to power there were 48,396 men, women and children receiving social assistance in the province. By 1984, when welfare reform was introduced, the welfare rolls had increased by 32 per cent to include 63,703 recipients. After three years of welfare reform, the numbers had declined by only 2.5 per cent.'[64]

Quebec's reform, introduced in 1988, classified its employable group into single people and families with dependent children. Single people were offered a program of intensive job searching, followed, if unsuccessful, by either training or work experience in community service, with both programs encouraged by small increases in benefits. The program for families was more comprehensive. The Parental Wage Assistance Program offered direct grants and tax assistance to encourage family heads to move into the labour force, the theory being that low-wage jobs would appear more acceptable. The same program was also open to families on UI or working at wages that placed them on a par, economically, with social assistance recipients. They were eligible for the same tax and grant incentives to encourage them to remain in the labour force.[65]

Why do governments persist in mounting programs that push people into the labour force, ill prepared for the most part for anything other than low-wage, unstable employment, when the labour market is already flooded with unemployed? Riches saw the Conservative government of Saskatchewan as 'ideologically driven,' and both he and Shragge (who has written critically of the Quebec program) argued that by developing a pool of cheap labour, a brake is applied on the aspirations of other Canadians, who are struggling to improve their pay and working conditions. One effect of the increased competition for jobs in the 1980s was the 'trend by employers (including governments) to take back concessions made to workers in the headier days of the 1970s.'[66]

Much of what passes for job training, job readiness, preemployment, entry-level skills, work habits, and work attitudes courses, which are typical components of these provincial 'welfare reform' initiatives, reflects the confusion between 'personal troubles' and 'public issues,' the brilliant conceptualization of C. Wright Mills.[67] *Troubles,* Mills says, 'occur within the character of the individual and within the range of his immediate relations with others ... *Issues* transcend ... local environments of the individual and the range of his inner life.' Mills elaborates using his famous illustration: 'When, in a city of 100,000, one man is unemployed, that is his personal trouble and for its relief we properly look to the character of the man, his skills, and his immediate opportunities. But when in a nation of 50 million employees, 15 million men are unemployed, that is an issue and we may not hope to find its solution within the range of opportunities open to any one individual. The very structure of opportunities has collapsed.'[68]

Not only has the structure of opportunities collapsed in Canada, compared to what it was in the 1950s and 1960s, but governments at both the provincial and federal levels have been hobbled by outmoded ideas concerning the unemployed (all they required was a change of attitude and/or more training and they would find employment), and by neoconservative economic theory that has insisted that the private market is capable of producing the required number of jobs.[69]

It might be useful to recall the experience Canada went through at the outbreak of the Second World War. People who had been 'on relief' (welfare) for up to a decade moved into the labour force or the armed services without so much as a single course in 'job readiness.' Women moved from the home to the aircraft factory or the munitions plant, and replaced men in a hundred different jobs (at a time when married women were typically found in the home) without a special course to help them make this transition. Incentives, financial or otherwise, were not required because people were offered jobs at the going rate. The experience of 1939-45 suggests that the problem Canada faces in the 1990s is large-scale unemployment, and Lord Beveridge's words, written in 1944, on solving this issue are worthy of repetition: 'We cure unemployment for the sake of waging war. We ought to decide to cure unemployment without war. We cure unemployment in war because war gives us a common objective so vital that it must be attained without regard to cost, in life, leisure, privileges or material resources. The cure of unemployment in peace depends on finding a common objective for peace that will be equally compelling on our efforts.'[70]

Unresolved Issues

Two issues of social policy that attracted public attention in the mid-1970s and 1980s and that were not resolved by the former Liberal government were the need for improved old age pensions and for a renewed concern for the care of Canada's children.

Old Age Pensions

In his 1986 budget address, finance minister Michael Wilson listed the improvements to the old age pensions system his government had already carried out and those it was prepared to bring into effect 1 January 1987:

- in 1985 the government had expanded the provisions of the Spouse's Allowance program to include all widows and widowers in need, age 60 to 64[71]
- amendments to the CPP that included provision for earlier retirement at age 60,[72] improvements in the flat-rate portion of the disability pension, and increases in benefits to the children of disabled pensioners and to orphans of former pensioners; the payment of survivor benefits even if the survivor remarries; and providing for a division of CPP pension credits on marriage breakdown[73]
- CPP contribution rates were raised to maintain the plan's financial equilibrium.[74]

Wilson also announced improvements in occupational pension plans in federally regulated industries such as banking and telecommunications, as well as business and industry in the two northern territories. These included the possibility of pension coverage for steady, but part-time, employees, better portability of benefits, and improved survivor benefits. Provincial governments were encouraged to pass similar legislation covering pension plans under their jurisdiction, and most complied.[75]

These changes were welcome but marginal; the essential problem identified during the 'great pension debate' of the late 1970s and early 1980s (see Chapter 13) remained. Two classes of Canadians in retirement were being created. One class is a fortunate but diminishing majority who spend their working lives in full-time, steady employment paying average wages or better, and who therefore receive on retirement the maximum C/QPP pension and, probably, a reasonable occupational pension. When combined with the old age security benefit and some personal savings, a financially secure retirement is possible. For the second class, a rapidly increasing minority, including the 22 per cent of the workforce who in 1989 lacked 'the stability of full-time, year-long employment'[76] and who therefore will have difficulty qualifying for the maximum C/QPP, and the approximately 54 per cent of workers who are not covered by an occupational pension plan – these people face the prospect of living in straitened financial circumstances. The addition of OAS/GIS improves the situation for some, but others fall into poverty.

Like the Liberals before them, the Conservatives continued to promote a *residual* solution to the pension problem. While allowing only minimal changes and improvements to the public pension system, which in the case of C/QPP covers virtually the entire workforce, they held out the hope for improvements in the private market's provision for pensions, which in 1986 only covered 46 per cent of the workforce, *down* from 48 per cent in 1980. The 46 per cent figure included public sector employees, 98 per cent of whom had an occupational pension. But of workers in the private sector, only one in three was as fortunate. Furthermore, the increase in private pension plans was minute. In 1970, for example, coverage of employees in the private sector was 30 per cent; by 1986 it was 32 per cent despite all the discussion about improving coverage and standards.[77] The government's preference was for Canadians to make provision for their own retirement through the private market and the RRSP program and its related tax deductions, which the Conservatives planned to increase fivefold over the period 1985-96. But this idea would be of most help to middle- and upper-income Canadians.[78]

Reforming the Pension System

As labour unions and community groups believed that improvement of the public pension system was the surest way to eliminate poverty from retirement, they continued to promote this type of change. In *Pension Reform 1990*, the National Council of Welfare offered some suggestions for improvements in both the public and private pension systems. For those already retired and living in poverty, their only hope was a substantial increase in the guaranteed income supplement. The council recommended an increase of $100 a month for single pensioners and $50 each for couples. In a move to make this increase more palatable to the government (one assumes), it took the unusual step of recommending that this benefit be subject to a higher reduction rate, thereby directing the benefits at a narrower band of low-income seniors – the poorest of the poor in the elderly group. This is an unfortunate, but not unforeseen, consequence of income-tested pensions: the tendency to focus benefits on an increasingly narrow range of beneficiaries.[79] The end of this road is the humiliating means test and its review of income and assets.

For future pensioners, improvements to the C/QPP were seen as the 'single most important task government could undertake to ... wipe out poverty among the elderly' (*Pension Reform,* 22). After reviewing a number of proposals with this objective, the National Council of Welfare recommended a Quebec government plan, developed in 1977 under the title *COFIRENTES+*. Using a two-stage formula, this plan would have the C/QPP replace 50 per cent of earnings up to half the average wage and 25 per cent thereafter up to the average wage. The effect would be to replace 37.5 per cent of earnings at the average wage level in place of the current 25 per cent. Thus, all C/QPP retirees would receive larger pensions, but the biggest increase would go to workers whose earnings were at half the average wage or below. For example, a worker who retired in 1989 and whose wages were half the average wage would receive a pension of $556.23 a month under the *COFIRENTES+* plan rather than $278.13 under the existing plan. The council believed that such a plan would remove most future beneficiaries of C/QPP retirement benefits from poverty.[80]

In relation to the RRSP program, the council suggested that there should be no tax assistance for retirement savings on earnings in excess of one and one-half times the average wage, which in 1992 would have been about $48,000. In addition, the council recommended the substitution of tax credits for tax deductions for the RRSP program (*Pension Reform*, 48-50).

One cannot leave the topic of poverty in old age without especially emphasizing the high risk of poverty for elderly, single women. Fifty per cent of unattached women, aged seventy-five and over, lived in poverty in 1986. Many of these women devoted their lives to caring for family members and were not in the labour force and could not qualify for a C/QPP benefit. In 1989 only 57 per cent of women in that age group were receiving C/QPP benefits in their own right compared to 96 per cent of men.[81] In addition, women's lower earnings resulted in lower pensions, which again put them at greater risk. Of those who retired in June 1992, the average pension paid to females aged sixty-five was $274.75; for males the corresponding figure was $488.39.[82]

Renewed Concern for the Care of Canada's Children

At the World Summit for Children in 1990, Prime Minister Mulroney took a leading role.[83] Canada produced a glossy brochure for the New York meeting that assured delegates that a majority of Canadian children were economically secure. While this was true, it was also the case that about 16 per cent, or 1,329,000 Canadian children, lived in poverty in 1988, and 700,000 received help through food banks in 1991.[84]

At a three-day national symposium on children held in Ottawa in 1991, in connection with the United Nations Convention on the Rights of the Child, the government was urged 'to put children where they belong – in the forefront of the nation's social, economic and political agenda.'[85] The symposium learned that

- one in six Canadian children lived in poverty
- poor children experienced a 50 per cent higher death rate from all causes and were twice as likely to suffer long-term disability and other health problems
- the average life expectancy of Aboriginal children was eight years lower than the national average
- suicide was the second leading cause of death among Canadian adolescents

- the high school drop-out rate was more than 90 per cent in some parts of the country.

Delegates at the symposium called for government action in a number of areas: the introduction of universal child care, an issue that had been advocated through most of the 1980s, and earlier; a substantial tax credit for the poor to remove them from federal and provincial tax liability; increases in the minimum wage (see Table 14.2); control by Aboriginal people over education and other programs affecting their children; and a call from the Child Poverty Action Group and the Social Planning Council of Metropolitan Toronto for protection against child poverty in Canada's Constitution.

Table 14.2

Minimum wages by jurisdiction, 1973-91

Jurisdiction	1973	1979	1991	As % of poverty line*		
	(in 1991 $)			1973	1979	1991
Federal	6.70	6.04	4.00	127	93	56
AB	6.70	6.25	4.50	127	96	63
BC	7.94	6.25	5.00	150	96	70
MB	6.70	6.35	5.00	127	98	70
NB	5.29	5.83	4.81	107	94	77
NF	4.94	5.83	4.75	100	94	76
NS	5.82	5.73	4.50	118	93	72
ON	6.35	6.25	5.40	120	96	75
PEI	4.94	5.73	4.75	112	107	85
PQ	6.53	7.22	5.30	123	111	74
SK	7.06	6.77	5.00	143	110	80

* Single person in the largest urban area in the applicable province, based on a forty-hour week, fifty-two weeks per year.
Source: Unequal Futures: The Legacies of Child Poverty in Canada, Child Poverty Action Group and the Social Planning Council of Metropolitan Toronto, 1991, 35.

Government actions in all of these areas had not impressed child welfare advocates.[86] It was estimated in 1990 that only 13 per cent of children requiring day care were in licensed child care facilities. The government announced a program to develop a further 200,000 spaces in 1987, but this would only meet an estimated 25 per cent of the demand.[87] Health care and social services for poor children would be jeopardized by the limitations imposed on federal funding for provincial health care through EPF programs and by the limits placed on Canada Assistance Plan contributions to British Columbia, Alberta, and Ontario, where nearly half of all poor children in Canada lived.

Child Poverty

The issue of child poverty in Canada has been broached many times over the past decade by community groups such as the Child Poverty Action Group, the National Council of Welfare, and the Canadian Council on Social Development. These groups have charged that the Mulroney government's tax increases, particularly the use of regressive sales taxes[88] and the partial indexing of benefits and personal exemptions in the tax return, have had a detrimental effect on the living standards of modest- and low-income families, the segment of the population the government stated it wanted to help. Mulroney claimed that more would have to be done for Canadian children in poverty and that more would be done.[89]

It was something of an anticlimax when, in May 1992, the 'more' the government promised was a $500 million, five-year program to help children 'at risk because of poverty.' The program was termed 'band-aid' by community groups as it appeared to focus on the results of poverty – child neglect, child abuse, and 'street kids' – rather than the roots of the problem.[90]

The Canadian Council on Social Development said that vital improvements in child poverty could only come with major policy changes in Ottawa. The government must

- stop fighting inflation and start fighting unemployment
- realize that the best way to help poor children is to give their parents a steady job at decent wages
- develop a national day care program
- increase transfer payments to the provinces for child welfare and social assistance since 37 per cent of recipients are children.

A federal government serious about eliminating child poverty could have begun by substantially increasing the new child benefit. If Ottawa was determined to keep the Goods and Services Tax (GST), then the refundable sales tax credit, which did not fully shield low-income families, should have been increased, as the National Council of Welfare had suggested, from $275 per adult and $100 per child to $400 and $200 respectively.[91] An even better suggestion, however, in line with making the tax system more progressive, would be to eliminate the GST altogether.

Of course, improvements to the living standards of low-income families must be paid for. If the federal government would follow J.K. Galbraith's advice, given at the 1992 Couchiching Conference, and put people back to work building roads and affordable homes,[92] then government revenues would increase and expenditures for UI and social assistance would decline. Government revenues, as one tax expert has suggested, would also increase if the income tax was made more steeply progressive. Neil Brooks, tax specialist and law professor, recommended raising the tax rates on the top two of the three existing tax brackets to 29 and 35 per cent respectively, from the existing 26 and 29 per cent. He would then introduce two more tax brackets for incomes of $70,000 and over and $150,000 and over, with tax rates of 40 and 45 per cent. Brooks estimated that even with provincial taxes added, the top marginal rate would be about 60 per cent, which was no higher than it was in the 1960s and 1970s, and would approximate the top marginal rate in many European countries. These measures would raise an estimated $4.9 billion. To complete the progressivity of the tax system, Brooks suggested that Canada should institute a wealth tax. Apparently, Australia and Canada are the only two countries in the industrialized world that do not tax wealth when it changes hands as a result of death or by gift. This measure would raise an estimated $1 billion.[93] With these and other tax-saving measures, it should be possible to take up the suggestion of the Child Poverty Action Group and others that the new Canadian Constitution include some specific protections for children. For example, a national income security program for families with children would help to ensure that all Canadian children have the opportunity to maximize their potential as citizens of Canada and the world.[94]

Constitutional Change and Social Policy

There was a time when an amendment to the BNA Act produced a significant improvement in ordinary people's lives.[95] In 1940, 1951, and again in 1964, the British Parliament, at the request of the Canadian Parliament, amended the act to enable the federal government to institute unemployment insurance, old age security pensions, and the Canada Pension Plan. Each of these amendments produced a measure of social justice that not only touched the lives of most Canadians but improved the lot of many. Efforts to amend the Constitution in the 1980s and 1990s with less clearly defined (if not conflicting) purposes have produced more problems than solutions and have raised the spectre of the breakup of the Canadian federation.

The situation of small-scale amendments leading to much-needed measures of social policy ended with the 'Quiet Revolution' in Quebec, and more particularly with the election of an avowedly pro-independence government in Quebec in 1976 under the charismatic leadership of René Lévesque. Prime Minister Trudeau, a staunch federalist, helped to defeat Lévesque's 1980 referendum on sovereignty-association for Quebec by promising major constitutional reform to meet that province's demands for greater autonomy. This promise was not kept, according to Desmond Morton,[96] and when the BNA Act was finally brought home in 1982 with the addition of an amending formula and a Charter of Rights and Freedoms, it was done without the concurrence of Quebec.[97] Mulroney attempted to heal this rupture by offering to meet Quebec's 'five minimum demands' for constitutional change with the Meech Lake Accord (1987). However, he could only obtain the agreement of the other provinces by offering them the same jurisdictional concessions demanded by Quebec. Trudeau denounced this agreement as a complete sellout of federal powers to the provinces, and over the three years it took to ratify the agreement, opposition to the deal increased to the point where unanimous approval was denied. Students of social policy were alarmed that had the Meech Lake Accord been approved, one of the five conditions would have given the provinces the right to opt out of federal programs in areas of provincial jurisdiction with full compensation. This measure might not have threatened existing programs such as medicare, but it would certainly have prevented the development of new national programs.[98] The demise of the Meech Lake Accord raised the level of invective between Quebec and the rest of Canada to new heights. Talk of Quebec withdrawing from Confederation became so commonplace that experts in various fields began to calculate the costs and benefits of such a separation.[99]

The failure of the Meech Lake Accord in 1990 led to another attempt at constitutional reform that culminated in the Charlottetown Accord of 28 August 1992, which, to the surprise of many, produced a compromise agreement between federal, provincial, territorial, and Aboriginal leaders.

The key elements of the Charlottetown Accord were Quebec was to have a veto over changes to national institutions;[100] the distinctiveness of Quebec was to be recognized; provinces would have the right to opt out of new national cost-shared programs with financial compensation; Ottawa agreed to remove itself from six 'key powers' that were within provincial jurisdiction – forestry, mining, tourism, recreation, housing, and municipal and urban affairs; new power-sharing deals were to be worked out for matters such as immigration; responsibility for culture and job training were to become areas of exclusive provincial power, although Ottawa was to retain some influence over national programs such as UI, the Canadian Broadcasting Corporation, and the National Film Board. In addition, the Canadian Senate would be replaced by an elected body with equal numbers of senators from each province, and in the House of Commons Quebec would be guaranteed 25 per cent of the seats in perpetuity. The right of self-government for Aboriginal peoples was to be recognized.

Students of social policy noted with interest the attempt made by Audrey McLaughlan, federal leader of the New Democratic Party (NDP), and Bob Rae, the NDP premier of Ontario, to entrench *social rights* in the Constitution, which would cover such programs as medical care, minimum levels of housing, food, and other necessities, high-quality primary and secondary education, and the protection of the environment.[101] The Conservatives argued that social rights should be an expression of goals, not legally enforceable rights. Legal scholars, on the other hand, argued that failing to

provide a justifiable right meant little more than entrenching good intentions in the Constitution.[102] This was, in fact, how they emerged in the
final draft of the Charlottetown Accord.

Another point of interest for students of social policy was the reappear-
ance of the opting-out provision with full compensation, which had been
part of the Meech Lake Accord. This provision raised the ire of the National
Action Committee on the Status of Women, which argued that a national
day care program would never develop if the opting-out arrangement was
allowed to stand. All debate over the merits and demerits of the Charlottetown Accord became academic on 26 October 1992 when it was decisively
defeated.[103]

The rejection of the Charlottetown Accord, despite the endorsement by
the three major political parties, the Aboriginal leadership, the labour movement, and the business community, will be the subject of academic specula-
tion for years to come. Preliminary opinion, however, suggested that outside
of Quebec, Canadians voted against the proposed weakening of the federal
government.[104] In Quebec, the meaning of the 'no' vote simply meant that
'for the majority of the population [the deal] was not good enough.'[105] Mel
Watkins maintained that a simple question lay at the heart of the referendum: 'How do we Canadians define ourselves?' The accord 'failed to answer
that question in a way that satisfied most of us and we gave it thumbs
down.'[106]

Several commentators argued that the only way to hold Canada together
(when we eventually return to constitutional matters) is to try for some
form of asymmetrical model of federalism.[107] Failing that, a type of sovereignty-association with Quebec seems inevitable.

The positive aspects of the referendum were that it was a large-scale exercise in participatory citizenship[108] and that its rejection did not exacerbate
French-English relations as did the failure of the Meech Lake Accord.
Because the Charlottetown Accord was voted down, both in Quebec and
five western provinces and the Yukon, Quebec nationalists and anti-French
elements in the rest of Canada could not exploit the outcome to arouse
French-English antagonism. Following the vote, the country, weary of the
whole constitutional issue, turned with relief to more mundane concerns.

Taking Unpopular Decisions

While the country was embroiled in the referendum campaign, the
Mulroney government pushed (some said rammed) a bill through the
House of Commons and the Senate to abolish family allowances and clear
the way for the new child benefit package. Senators charged that only nine
of forty witnesses had an opportunity to present their reactions to the bill
before the Conservative majority curtailed debate on the measure.[109] The
elimination of universal family allowances in 1992, and the substitution of

an income-tested benefit effective January 1993, provided support for the fears reported earlier in this chapter that the FTA with the United States would lead to the eventual harmonization of Canadian and American social and economic policy. Family allowance was a distinguishing feature of Canadian social policy, much admired by many Americans. That distinction was eliminated in 1992.[110]

In a similar vein, the decision taken in December 1992 to reduce the percentage of insurable earnings replaced by the UI benefit from 60 to 57 per cent, and to stiffen eligibility conditions, moved the Canadian UI system closer to the meagre benefit and restricted availability of the American UI program.[111]

The reason given for the UI cutback and other cost-saving measures announced by Don Mazankowski, the new finance minister, was the prospect of yet another record federal deficit. The incongruity of claiming the same emergency for eight years as a basis for policy changes and government cutbacks never seemed to register with the Tory leadership. While wringing its hands over the deficit, the federal government effectively raised medicare costs at the end of 1992 by introducing Bill C-91, which gave brand-name drug makers extended patent protection for an additional three years to a total of twenty. It was estimated that this would increase health care costs by $850 million a year by the end of the decade. This legislation added weight to the harmonization thesis.[112]

Mulroney made much of the fact that the unpopularity of his government (only a 17 per cent approval rating in 1992) reflected his government's willingness to take unpopular decisions for the long-term good of the country – a sign, Mulroney maintained, of responsible leadership. But surely it was disingenuous of the prime minister to suggest that his government's policies were universally unpopular. The large drug manufacturers were delighted with his government's decision in 1987 and again in 1992 to offer them increased patent protection from cheaper generic drugs at a substantial cost to Canadian taxpayers. His cutbacks on UI benefits were certainly greeted with approval by the Bank of Montreal, whose chief economist, Lloyd Atkinson, said Canada's high unemployment rate 'has become a stubborn, long-term problem because of too much pogey, too little training. If we are ever going to deal with this unemployment it will take a huge change in thinking about Canada's unemployment insurance, welfare and regional development programs.'[113] The federal government's consistent attack on Canada's social safety net has been urged on by large corporations and their lobbyists. Since 1984, despite Mulroney's assertions, his government's policies were undeniably popular in the boardrooms of Canadian and multinational corporations.

This chapter began by recalling that half a century ago, plans were laid for a more just and secure world at war's end. The Beveridge and Marsh

Reports, released in 1942 and 1943 respectively, were based on the common-sense idea that an ounce of prevention is worth a pound of cure. The notion that government should play an active role in marshalling a nation's resources to prevent poverty and maintain the well-being of all its citizens was a revolutionary idea for Canadians. The older, nineteenth-century notion was that government only extended help in dire emergencies (and it was poorly organized to carry out even this limited task). But more significantly, recipients of this older form of help had to endure humiliating tests of need before qualifying for help. One could not claim assistance as a right; it was necessary to go cap-in-hand to the helping agency.

The Marsh Report proposed to sweep away the old system and old attitudes and replace them with three things: full employment, a comprehensive range of social insurance protections against the common risks to social security, and universal programs providing benefits to citizens on the basis of right. The Canadian medical care system is a shining example of a universal approach to meeting human need and has proven to be more cost-efficient and effective in terms of improving and maintaining the health of Canadians than the American private market model, which that country was, and is, struggling to reform.[114] Old age, which fifty years ago was commonly a time of penury, is for a large majority of Canadians no longer so because of old age security, the guaranteed income supplement, and the Canada and Quebec Pension Plans. But the vision of the Marsh Report was only met by half-measures, with the result that serious gaps have remained and new challenges have not been addressed. For example, according to a 1989 report, 61.8 per cent of Canadian children of single mothers were living in poverty – the comparable figure for Sweden was 9.8 per cent.[115] The need for a national system of day care, one of the new social policy issues of our time, has been all but ignored. One authority has compared the Canadian day care situation to the state of public education in Canada in the 1850s: 'profoundly immature and underfunded.'[116] The pressing need for affordable housing and town planning and the shameful living conditions on Native reserves are only two priority items on a long list arising from government's laissez-faire approach to social and economic issues. That list is headed by the need of the country's unemployed for (to borrow a phrase) jobs, jobs, jobs!

But the Conservative government's plans for 1993 (apart from a federal election) included pushing through the North American Free Trade Agreement (NAFTA) with the United States and Mexico. This had labour and other community groups understandably alarmed as they recalled the economic damage done by the earlier FTA with the United States. A 'major review of social policy' in 1993 was promised, its goal to 'modernize' social programs.[117] These plans illustrated the government's continuing commitment to more privatization, more deregulation, and more reductions in the public sector – to the applause from large corporations and their acolytes. The Conservatives resolutely attempted to refashion Canada's social and economic policy in a nineteenth-century mode. Unless checked, this would have resulted in a narrowing of opportunity and equality in Canada. The unavoidable comparison with the spirit of generosity and hope that animated both the Beveridge and Marsh Reports added a sombre note to the fiftieth anniversary of those landmark reports.

15
Debating the Future of Social Security

1993 Federal Election

Prime Minister Kim Campbell[1] promised a major review of social programs after the election but would not be more specific other than to say that unemployment insurance and social assistance would be 'modernized.' But social security reform had been under consideration by the government for some time. In 1992 it was reported that a white paper on social security was being prepared jointly by the Departments of Health and Welfare and Employment and Immigration. Although the white paper was never released, the direction of the government's thinking was indicated in a speech given in 1992 by the minister of health and welfare, Benoit Bouchard, to a meeting of OECD representatives in London.

Three broad areas of social policy reform were being considered: 'breaking the spiral of dependence' of the unemployed; making training and job-readiness programs more flexible and tailored to individual needs; and maintaining and strengthening income support for those not able to work.[2] Cuts in social spending were forecast by the minister's emphasis on 'fiscal sustainability' of social programs. This was not the kind of information to release prior to an election by a government already trailing in the polls. However, the prime minister did say that she would throw herself on the railway tracks to protect medicare (a welcome variation on the shopworn 'sacred trust' theme her predecessor had so frequently and, according to his critics, so cynically employed).

The Conservative election platform, as it emerged, was centred upon the debt and deficit situation (even while insisting on the need to spend $4.8 billion on state-of-the-art antisubmarine helicopters for the military).

The Liberal Party platform stressed the importance of economic growth and job creation as a means of reducing the deficit, as well as cuts in defence spending (including the helicopters) and grants to business and other programs. A thin social policy platform included additional day care spaces, a prenatal nutrition program for low-income mothers, and pilot projects for an Aboriginal 'head start' program. Also promised was a national forum on health care to find new ways to control costs without abandoning medicare's five principles.

The NDP, traditionally a strong proponent of welfare state measures, offered a limited and politically uninspiring range of ideas: a job-creation program including a national day care plan; more money for social housing and assured amounts of federal money to the provinces for welfare costs and health care; action would also be taken to reduce the cost of prescription drugs. Money to pay for these proposals would be taken from the military budget as a peace dividend and from higher taxes on corporations and wealthy individuals. The NDP appeared to be, as they have been called, 'Liberals in a hurry.'

The Reform Party of Canada (with only one member in Parliament at the time of dissolution) called for what would amount to a *residual* approach to social policy, arguing that universal programs were unsustainable. Instead, they would encourage families, communities, non-governmental organizations, and the private sector 'to resume their duties and responsibilities in the social service areas.' Federal transfer payments to the provinces would be made without conditions, thus eliminating national standards for health care and social assistance. Unemployment insurance would be operated along the lines of private insurance (poor risks would have to meet higher qualifying conditions), and old age security benefits would be subject to a household income test. The country's debt and deficit, which was the Reform Party's central issue, would be eliminated in three years by draconian cuts in government spending, and social programs were not excluded.

The Bloc Québécois Party, which only nominated candidates in Quebec, centred its platform on the issue of independence for Quebec. The party supported social programs and opposed cuts to social assistance as a means of reducing the deficit. In line with its push for independence, the Bloc urged that federal transfer funds to the provinces should be unconditional.

All parties had proposals for reducing, if not eliminating, the debt and deficit, but the Conservatives and the Reform Party, emphasized this issue above all others. The other three parties took a more moderate stance, emphasizing job creation and economic growth as well as prudent fiscal management and retrenchment.

Canadians went to the polls in October 1993, and after nine years of Conservative government in Ottawa the Liberals won a comfortable majority of 179 seats. The Conservatives were reduced from 169 seats to 2 – an unprecedented defeat. Another singular outcome of this election was that the official opposition was formed by the new federal Quebec independence party, the Bloc Québécois, with 54 seats. The next largest group, and another regional party, was the right-of-centre Reform Party, with 52 members elected, 46 of whom came from British Columbia and Alberta. The only left-of-centre party, the NDP, was decimated, falling from 43 to 9 members.

The Significance of the 1993 Federal Election

The significance of the 1993 federal election for social policy was that the political composition of the Canadian Parliament was set for a shift to the political right, even as the right-wing Conservatives were replaced by the more centrist Liberals. The Liberals had little to fear from the weakened, left-of-centre NDP, but would feel the necessity to move to the right politically to undercut the influence of the Reform Party, whose electoral gains had been impressive (in addition to winning fifty-two seats, it had come second in over fifty other ridings). The Bloc Québécois, the official opposition, although more liberal on social policy matters, had one issue: independence for Quebec. The party could be counted upon to push for greater devolution of power from Ottawa to the provinces and an end to national standards in social programs, as they were indicative of federal interference in provincial affairs. These policies of decentralization were also part of the right-wing agenda. With both Prime Minister Jean Chrétien and his finance minister, Paul Martin, on the right wing of the Liberal Party, the stage was set for a paring back of the Canadian welfare state.

The Liberal Government's Program of Social Security Reform

On 31 January 1994, Lloyd Axworthy, minister of human resources development,[3] rose in the House of Commons to issue an invitation to Canadians to join in 'rebuilding the social security, labour market and learning framework of our country.'[4] The rebuilding of social security, he said, was part of the government's preelection commitment (which wasn't made public prior to the election) to put people back to work. Social security renewal would involve a 'radical review and redesign' of programs overtaken by the pace of change. Of principal concern to the government were unemployment insurance (a federal responsibility); federal aid to provincial social assistance and social service programs, with an emphasis on moving employable recipients back into the labour force; federal aid to provincially run, postsecondary education; and federal support of provincial child care and child development services. Not included in the review were the federal universal old age security program and its supplement for low-income seniors, the guaranteed income supplement; the C/QPP; and federal aid to provincially operated health insurance programs. These, in the government's view, did not relate to its central concern of 'helping people to get and keep jobs' – a complete denial of the interrelatedness of social security systems.[5] This rationale was demolished less than a month later when the budget statement of February 1994 indicated that the government had plans for reforming these programs as well.

The 1994 Budget and the Social Security Review

Lloyd Axworthy had given every indication up to this point of leading the social security reform process. However, this proved to be an illusion when the minister of finance introduced his first budget on 22 February 1994. In it, Paul Martin, the finance minister, announced significant cuts and changes to unemployment insurance[6] as well as proposed cost-saving changes in federal support payments to provincial social assistance programs under the Canada Assistance Plan, and to federal support for health and higher education through the Established Programs Financing arrangements. These, of course, were among the programs to be studied and subjected to a 'radical review and redesign.' Critics suggested that the finance minister had preempted the reform process in the interest of reducing the federal deficit. There was substance to this charge because Martin claimed in his budget message that the changes he announced to UI would save $725 million in 1994-5 and $2.5 billion per year thereafter. The proposed changes to the Canada Assistance Plan and Established Programs Financing would save 'at least $1.5 billion in 1996-97.' Martin's budget also forecast possible cuts to Canada's public pension system, although any changes, he said, would have to await the release of a government paper that would examine 'what the ageing society will need in terms of services and what, if any, changes are required to the public pension system to make it financially sustainable.' The Liberal government's social policy plans, at this point, were beginning to look and sound decidedly Conservative.

In 1991 the National Council of Welfare had criticized the Conservative government for announcing major changes in social policy in budget speeches. The council made the point that 'parliamentary traditions surrounding budgets are incompatible with the open consultations that are essential to developing good public policy.'[7] The council noted that budget measures are prepared with the strictest secrecy by a small circle of advisors and officials and without public consultation. Once the measures are announced, governments are reluctant to change them as this is seen as losing face. Furthermore, the council also argued that officials at the Department of Finance lack the sensitivity and knowledge required to institute changes to social programs. This advice had obviously fallen on deaf ears.

Lloyd Axworthy Resumes the Reform Process

Despite the preempting of the reform process by the finance minister, Axworthy proceeded to establish a Parliamentary Standing Committee on Human Resources Development to begin examination of proposed reforms and to hear submissions from the public on the subject. He also promised ongoing consultation between the federal, provincial, and territorial governments.

As an aid to public discussion, a group of fourteen experts was assembled by Axworthy to prepare a discussion paper indicating possible directions for change.[8] All of this work, including the public consultations, was to be completed by the fall of 1994, and new legislation introduced before the end of the year. This timetable unravelled with the announcement of a Quebec provincial election slated for 12 September 1994. Although the federal government denied it, most commentators agreed that Ottawa was anxious to avoid debating contentious social policy issues prior to the Quebec election as these could be used as ammunition by the pro-independence Parti Québécois in its bid to unseat the provincial Liberal government in Quebec. Thus, the green paper *Improving Social Security in Canada*, handed to the minister in midsummer 1994 by his expert committee, was not released to the public until 5 October 1994, well after the Quebec election and a Parti Québécois victory.

Following the release of the government's discussion paper, the Parliamentary Standing Committee toured Canada for five weeks in November and December 1994, listening to the public's reaction to the government's proposals for social security reform. It then prepared its own report and recommendations (together with minority reports from the Bloc Québécois and the Reform Party), which were submitted to Axworthy and released to the public on 6 February 1995.[9] This was something of an anticlimax, however, as six days earlier Axworthy had the humiliating task of announcing that his social security review had been shelved. This was necessary, he said, because both he and the finance minister agreed that reducing the deficit and preserving national unity were the first priorities and that the reform of the social security system could not be implemented without prejudicing these goals.[10] Clearly, the Quebec independence issue was the most significant reason for delaying social security reform. The new pro-independence provincial government in Quebec had put added pressure on the federal government by announcing its intention to hold a referendum on independence on 30 October 1995. For Ottawa to introduce a bundle of controversial changes in sensitive areas such as unemployment insurance, social assistance, postsecondary education, and medicare (with changes to old age pensions not far behind) would undermine the federal argument that the people of Quebec would be better off within the Canadian confederation than without. In shelving the social security reforms, the government was simply slowing the pace of change. Reform would continue and, if necessary, the most controversial elements dropped or amended. But the outline for profound modification in Canadian social security had been drafted and widely discussed. We now turn to an examination of the reform proposals.

The Government Offers Its Reasons for Reforming Social Security

The discussion paper *Improving Social Security in Canada* contended that the existing social security system was out of step with the times. The system was developed, to a large extent, in the 1950s and 1960s, a time of relatively full and stable employment. But in the decades since, Canada's social and economic situation had altered dramatically, and according to the discussion paper, social security programs must also change to conform to the government's larger agenda: 'helping people to get and keep jobs' (*Improving Social Security*, 9). To accomplish this would require meeting three objectives: improving the business climate for entrepreneurs; getting the government's finances in order; and (the centrepiece of improving employment prospects) 'helping people to gain and sharpen the up-to-date skills needed to succeed in today's market' (10). This was an impeccably neoconservative prescription for restoring the country's economic health, emphasizing a reliance on the private market for job creation and economic growth; the cutting of government spending and, in the process, changing the role of government (in his 1994 budget address, Martin spoke of the need for a 'new architecture for government'); and the placing of blame for high unemployment squarely on the unemployed (they lack the necessary skills). One is left wondering why, after nine years of a Conservative government that pursued the same goals utilizing the same methods, the economic situation and particularly the employment situation showed little sign of improvement. In fact, the discussion paper and its supplementary papers[11] indicated that the economic situation in Canada was deteriorating:

- Average unemployment had risen, decade after decade, since the Second World War, but most significantly since the mid-1970s (see Figure 15.1).
- The average duration of unemployment had increased from fourteen weeks in 1976 to twenty-five weeks in 1993, an indication, the discussion paper argues, that 'much of the increase in unemployment over the past two decades is structural' as opposed to cyclical – that is, 'related to changes within the labour market' rather than to the 'ups and downs of the business cycle' (17).
- Long-term unemployment in 1993 was three times the level it was in 1976.
- The economy was producing fewer 'standard jobs' – permanent, full-time, good wages and benefits – while the number of 'non-standard' jobs – temporary, part-time, self-employed – was increasing. In 1993 more than 60 per cent of all jobs created in Canada were part-time.
- Education levels demanded by employers continued to rise. Forty-five per cent of new jobs created in the 1990s were expected to require more than sixteen years of education and training (see Figure 15.2).
- There continued to be an unacceptably high drop-out rate from school, and there were disturbing levels of functional illiteracy (19). At the same time, 'over the 1971-91 period, the proportion of the population age 20 to 24 attending school full-time rose from 18 to 32 per cent.'[12]
- Female labour force participation has risen dramatically, as illustrated by the fact that in 1991 two-earner families comprised 60 per cent of all families, compared to 40 per cent in 1971.[13]

Figure 15.1

Unemployment rate in Canada, 1946-93

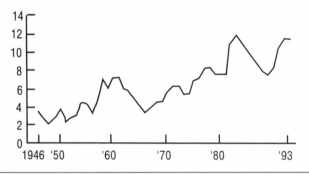

Source: Government of Canada, *The Context of Reform: A Supplementary Paper* (Hull: Minister of Supply and Services 1994), 13.

Figure 15.2

Education and training requirements for new jobs, 1990-2000

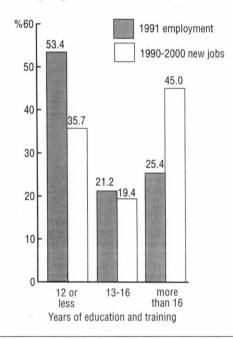

Source: Government of Canada, *The Context of Reform*, 11.

These developments related to the labour market have had some deleterious effects: from 1981 to 1993, the number of people on social assistance doubled from 1.4 million to 3 million, nearly 40 per cent of whom were

Figure 15.3

Poverty among children in selected countries, mid-1980s

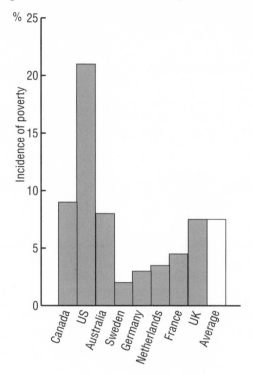

Source: Government of Canada, *Income Security for Children: A Supplementary Paper* (Hull: Minister of Supply and Services 1994), 2.

children; Canada has a higher than average rate of children growing up in poverty when compared to other advanced industrialized countries (see Figure 15.3).

Because of these and other marked changes, two stark choices were offered to Canadians: 'Either taxes, or earnings or total hours spent working must increase, or social spending directed to those not working must fall or become more effective.'[14]

The choices came down to this: the unemployed must either find a job or train or retrain to increase their job prospects. The discussion paper maintained that jobs were available or that they would become available, attracted by a well-trained labour force. Failing this, either taxes would have to rise (something the government had pledged not to allow) to pay for out-of-work benefits, or benefits would be cut. However, 'reforming' UI and social assistance programs might be of greater assistance in moving the unemployed back into the labour force.

Social Security Reform Proposals and Public Reaction

As laid out in the discussion paper, the reform proposals were grouped under three broad areas: *Working, Learning,* and *Security*. The main proposals of each area, briefly summarized, looked like this:

Working

(1) expansion of employment development services (for example, job counselling, job training, and related services)
(2) suggested reforms of the UI program
(3) meeting the needs of working parents by expanding child care services and promoting flexible work arrangements.

Learning

(1) proposed changes to federal funding of provincial and territorial programs of postsecondary education.

Security

(1) reforming or replacing the Canada Assistance Plan
(2) reducing child poverty.

Expansion of Employment Development Services

The proposed expansion of what the discussion paper called employment development services would include a range of measures designed 'to help people having difficulty finding and keeping a job' (*Improving Social Security,* 29). Programs to be expanded would include counselling, job search strategies, labour market information, classroom and on-the-job training, work experience projects, and earnings supplementation programs.

Critics of this proposal agreed that job-training/job-readiness programs are an essential part of a modern industrial economy, but that they only work satisfactorily when there is a supply of jobs awaiting those who have been counselled or trained. Otherwise, as economist Lars Osberg has said, 'when jobs are not available, policies to increase the supply of trained labour are pointless.'[15] One might also add that such policies are heartless.

This was a road that Canada had travelled down before. In 1981, a time of record high unemployment, two federal studies called for initiatives to increase the supply of trained workers, as well as to facilitate the transition from school to work and to bring certain disadvantaged groups into the workforce. Two major pieces of federal legislation were enacted: the National Training Program (1982) by the then Liberal government, and the Canadian Jobs Strategy (1985) by its Conservative successor. Both, according to Patricia Daenzer, 'predictably focused on the supply of labour' rather than addressing the demand for it. Furthermore, Daenzer points out, a concentration on the jobless meant that 'the liberal ideal of "individual fault" prevailed over the structuralist notion of state-induced market deficiencies.'[16]

However, the renewed faith in employment development services (to give job-training/job-readiness programs their latest designation) stemmed from 'new' economic theories based upon the importance of human capital. The central tenet of these new theories, according to economist Judith Maxwell, is that the 'cumulative knowledge of a person, a firm, an industry or a nation has an important bearing on the rate of growth in income and on success in the marketplace.'[17] But did this theory square with 26,000 Canadians, many with community college and university training, lined up in the winter cold for hours outside a Pickering, Ontario, plant to apply for one of 700 assembly-line jobs that required only high school graduation?[18] How do we account for Bell Canada announcing the layoff of 10,000 employees in the spring of 1995? Was it because they lacked skills?[19]

Canadian labour leaders rejected the 'skills-shortage' explanation of unemployment. The Canadian Labour Congress told the Parliamentary Standing Committee that the level of unemployment due to lack of skills was quite minimal.[20] Even the Canadian Chamber of Commerce was sceptical: a spokesperson for the Chamber said 'There's a hell of a lot of trained people who are unemployed. It's ridiculous to do this blanket training thing.'[21] The government, on the other hand, gave the impression that the problem of 'skills mismatch' was something of a Canadian pandemic. Axworthy was quoted as stating that three-quarters of those who were unemployed did not have the necessary skills to perform a job.[22] The members of the Bloc Québécois on the Parliamentary Standing Committee of Human Resources Development, in their minority report, contended that large-scale unemployment in Canada was not a result of a lack of skilled workers but of the lack of jobs. They charged the government with being 'totally divorced from reality' (*Improving Social Security*, 263).

The Canadian Labour Congress objected to money being taken from the UI fund to pay for job training. It said this was subverting the primary purpose of UI as an earnings insurance program that, 'in return for premiums paid, unemployed workers have a portion of their wages replaced ... It is the federal government's responsibility to fund training and other projects out of general revenue.'[23]

The government could take some small comfort in the fact that all advanced industrialized nations were experiencing serious and in some cases unprecedented levels of unemployment in the 1990s. The European Community has directed particular attention to youth unemployment and long-term unemployment. Countries of the EC were exhorted by their leadership to reduce overtime working, expand vocational training for both young and older adults, and make training available throughout an individual's working life (a concept picked up by the discussion paper). In addition to exhortation, the EC has established a special fund, the European Social Fund, to promote regional development and employment promotion and training measures.[24]

It is instructive to note that the Parliamentary Standing Committee was 'constantly told that job creation should have received greater attention' by the government (*Report,* 28). It is not surprising that the public would raise this issue given the fact that in the period 1989-94, living standards had declined in Canada, as had the proportion of people in the labour force (43.4 per cent in 1994 compared to 45.6 per cent in 1989).[25] Added to this were the all too frequent stories in the media of plant closings, business layoffs, and cutbacks in public services, all of which had produced a level of anxiety in those who were currently employed concerning their own job security.

The government admitted that its employment development policies had been directed primarily to the 'supply side' of the labour market – that is, 'helping workers to prepare for jobs through such programs as counselling and training.' Three reasons were given for this approach: a more skilled and flexible workforce would move efficiently between jobs, thus reducing dependence on UI and other support programs; improving the employability of groups who face barriers to employment – the disabled, for example – combined with employment equity policies would lessen their dependence upon income support programs; and (theoretically) a skilled workforce may help to create its own demand by attracting employers requiring well-trained workers.[26] For government to be 'active' on the supply side of the labour market, yet relatively 'passive' on the demand side, meant that many people would be hurt by prolonged unemployment; others, through the exercise of greater self-reliance and independent action, would prosper. Therefore, a reformed social security system must be designed with the casualties of the market forces in mind – the discussion paper referred to them as 'the vulnerable.' There was little thought of limiting the extent of vulnerability in the government's scenario. As the discussion paper says in one of its closing paragraphs, 'The best social security system is like a good health clinic – it fixes what's wrong, counsels on prevention [one can visualize the finger wagging], and sends you on your way' (81).

Reforming Unemployment Insurance

The second major reform proposal under the heading of *Working* involved two suggestions for redesigning the UI system. The first plan, most fully elaborated and apparently the government's first choice, would see UI transformed into a two-tier system, euphemistically called *Employment Insurance.* The first tier, termed Basic Insurance, would be for the occasional UI claimant – that is, for the best insurance risks. It would operate very much as the current UI system did, providing regular UI benefits as well as sickness, maternity, and parental benefits.

The second tier, termed Adjustment Insurance, would be for 'frequent claimants' – those who submit a regular UI claim three or more times in five years. In 1991 such claimants represented 38 per cent of regular UI claims or some 935,000 individuals, over half of whom were from Quebec and the Maritime provinces. Benefits for this second tier, the discussion paper suggested, 'might be lower, possibly income tested' (either on an individual or family income basis), and they might be contingent on the claimant's willingness to take part in community work projects or employment training programs. As compensation for reduced benefits, frequent claimants would receive 'more active assistance' in finding a job, and because of this additional investment on the unemployed worker's behalf, lower benefits could be justified (44-6).

The second proposal for revising UI would not change the existing program but would simply tighten eligibility requirements and reduce benefits for all regular UI claimants. As the discussion paper pointed out, this would be a continuation of the incremental changes that had occurred since the program's major revision and expansion in 1971. What the government did *not* mention was that the overwhelming majority of these changes introduced restrictions and cutbacks in coverage and benefits.

Reaction to the UI Reform Proposals

The report of the Parliamentary Standing Committee observed that 'Few issues aroused as much concern and concentrated passion in our hearings as the questions surrounding the reforms of unemployment insurance' (*Report*, 88). Indeed, hearings of the Standing Committee were disrupted in Montreal and Vancouver by angry protesters, and in one instance the meeting room was trashed. The angry reaction was ascribed to the suggested benefit reductions and other limitations recommended in the discussion paper, which also reported that non-standard employment, part-time and temporary, was on the increase. Many saw this as penalizing people who were taking advantage of the only work available.[27]

The Canadian Labour Congress, appearing before the Standing Committee, objected to the proposed changes to UI, most particularly because they were made without any prior consultation with management or labour, the two groups who are entirely responsible for financing the scheme. Quebec unions charged the Liberal government with being more dishonest than its Conservative predecessor. Gerald Larose, president of the Confederation of National Trade Unions, said that 'where the Tories talked directly of changing social programs to save money, the Liberals are pretending that they are offering reforms when their real motive is to cut spending.'[28]

Business reaction to the discussion paper triggered demands for sharp cuts in government spending, and as the Investment Dealers Association of Canada said, even before the release of the discussion paper, 'the government must start a long overdue attack on the "welfare state" ... to stave off a financial crisis.'[29] Business leaders called for cuts in payroll taxes, even though government officials claimed that such taxes in Canada were low by international standards (*Report,* 90). They warned against any increases in employment costs, such as 'experience rating' charges or extending the usual range of job benefits to part-time workers, and making flexible working time arrangements for workers with parental responsibilities. All of these initiatives would inhibit job creation, business claimed.

The Standing Committee's report rejected the two-tier system in favour of social solidarity, arguing that UI must remain an inclusive program based upon the concept of a pooled risk rather than a program that excludes people or places them in a separate program. The Standing Committee's report also said that the two-tier proposal would be unduly harsh and possibly stigmatizing to seasonal workers, as well as being economically destabilizing for some regions of the country where seasonal work was the norm. The fact that the chair of the Standing Committee represented a constituency in Nova Scotia where seasonal work was all too common was probably instrumental in the firm rejection of the discussion paper's two-tier concept.

The Standing Committee came up with its own proposal for restructuring UI, a variation of the Forget Commission's 'annualization' concept (see Chapter 14). The committee said that it was 'imperative that income coverage for seasonal workers be adequate to see them through the year' (without the ignominy of having to apply for welfare). At the same time, the Standing Committee argued, seasonal workers who applied for UI year after year should make an effort to improve their employability. These two goals could be accomplished by a general lowering of all UI benefit rates to provide the funds for extending benefits to seasonal workers from one season's work to the next, and this in turn would help finance employment development services in the off-season so that the unemployed could undertake training for more permanent employment (*Report,* 88-9).

The possibility of Adjustment Insurance benefits being subjected to a 'family income test' raised the ire of women's organizations and was acknowledged in the report of the Standing Committee: 'The Committee is opposed to making unemployment insurance benefits conditional on family income. We are concerned about the implications of such a measure for women's independence. Because men typically have higher incomes, women would be more likely to lose eligibility for UI. This would increase women's financial dependence on their husbands, with negative implications for their equity position within the home.'

Women also pointed out that discriminating against 'frequent claimants' of UI would affect more women than men because women tend to be concentrated in non-standard jobs where the risk of unemployment is more common. A general criticism of the discussion paper by women's organizations was its lack of gender analysis – a surprising lapse given the makeup of the expert committee (see endnote 8).

Does UI 'Generosity' Affect Work Incentive?

In a federal finance department report of January 1994, released just prior to the Liberal government's first budget in February 1994 when benefits were reduced for a majority of claimants, benefit periods were shortened, and qualifying conditions were tightened (see endnote 6), it was claimed that the Canadian UI system contained 'important disincentives to work,' that it was 'more generous than those of the US and the G-7 average,' and that this could 'create serious disincentives to find work.'[30]

This comparison was highly misleading as indicated by information released in one of the supplementary papers,[31] in which the Canadian UI system was compared to those of ten industrialized nations, including the G-7. Of the ten, Canada was

- the *least* generous in relation to the waiting period (the time between the filing of a claim and the start of benefit payments)
- *less* generous in the maximum duration of benefits than six of ten countries
- *less* generous than five of the ten countries with regard to periods of disqualification for quitting or being fired for misconduct (information on this point was unavailable for three countries)
- *considerably less* generous in the earnings replacement rate in six of the ten countries surveyed.

In relation to the earnings replacement rate, a significant index of 'generosity,' the supplementary paper noted:

> Canada's earnings replacement rate is on the low side when compared to France (80 per cent), Germany (63 per cent), Spain (80 per cent), the Netherlands (74 per cent), Belgium (79 per cent), or Denmark (73 per cent). On the other hand, countries such as the United Kingdom (23 per cent) and Italy (26 per cent) provide much less. At 55 per cent, the Canadian replacement rate is slightly higher than rates in the United States (50 per cent) or Japan (48 per cent). (*From Unemployment Insurance to Employment Insurance: A Supplementary Paper,* 62)

In the case of Japan, where unemployment rates average between 2 and 3 per cent, a 48 per cent replacement rate may not be a hardship on the unemployed as their chances of obtaining another job should be good. However, with Canadian unemployment rates in the 1990s exceeding 10 per cent, and in some areas by a considerable margin (see Figure 15.4), a replacement rate of 55 per cent was punitive.[32]

Figure 15.4

Unemployment rates by province, 1993

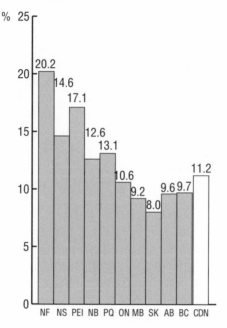

Source: Government of Canada, *The Context of Reform*, 15.

In a European study of disincentive effects of social security benefits, the authors indicated that, 'while there are undoubtedly ways in which the welfare state, and the taxes necessary to finance it, cause people to work less than they would otherwise have done ... the extent of such disincentives should not be exaggerated ... Our review of the evidence suggests that the number of effects that have been identified are small in size ... Perhaps more importantly, there are relatively few situations in which a disincentive effect has been clearly established.'[33]

Canadian research on the same topic came to a similar conclusion: 'that the assumed link between unemployment rates and the generosity of UI benefits is ambiguous at best.'[34]

What Responsibility Does Business Bear?

While there was passing mention of firm-initiated temporary layoffs that result in UI claims (but which also help to subsidize the firm's operations), and of the 'downsizing mentality' of management that rendered so many Canadians jobless, there were no corresponding proposals for changes in corporate or business behaviour in the discussion paper pertaining to their use of UI as there was for the employee's use.[35]

The discussion paper noted that 'The UI program allows some employers and industries to organize their work schedules around the weeks required to qualify for UI. A recent study by Statistics Canada reports that some businesses have structured their basic hiring and compensation practices around the UI program – for example, planning layoffs to coincide with UI qualification periods, and recalls with the end of benefits' (42).

Miles Corak, a researcher with Statistics Canada, in a report to government, strongly recommended that companies that regularly lay-off workers should pay higher UI premiums than those with a more stable employment history (this is known as experience rating). 'In this way, the UI premium would change from being a tax on jobs to a tax on unemployment.' The study also reported that companies that lay-off workers and 'leave them clinging to the false hope of being recalled are costing the unemployment insurance system millions as claimants expecting to be rehired have less of a tendency to search for a new job.'[36]

However, the government seemed more concerned about higher UI premiums being an inhibitor of job creation. In taking this position it was paying attention to business representatives who complained at any suggestion of increases in payroll taxes. In a background paper to the 1994 budget, the government maintained that by rolling back UI premiums by 7 cents for every $100 of insurable earnings (a measure announced in the 1994 budget), there would be 40,000 more jobs in the economy by 1996.[37] The Canadian Labour Congress called this statement 'absurd': 'If seven cents off premiums will create 40,000 jobs, then reducing premiums by $2.80 would create 1.6 million jobs and we will have arrived at full employment.'[38]

The government argued in a supplementary paper that the absence of experience rating in UI was consistent with some of the *secondary* objectives of unemployment insurance, such as redistribution of income, economic stabilization, and prevention of poverty.[39] Many authorities consider these to be among the *primary* objectives of social insurance programs such as UI. However, the government's reform proposals suggested that the primary objectives of UI were to strengthen the performance of the Canadian economy by encouraging investment, innovation, and trade. These goals would be achieved by requiring labour to be more flexible and adaptable to changing economic conditions. This view of the role of social security legislation has been described by R.M. Titmuss as the 'handmaiden model' of social policy: seeing social programs as primarily an adjunct to the economy. From this perspective, Titmuss says, social needs are to be met on the basis of 'merit, work performance and productivity' rather than on the basis of human need.[40]

The government's first reform proposal for UI follows this model precisely. UI benefits would be guaranteed for those who have demonstrated 'merit and work performance' by only claiming UI infrequently, while other workers in non-standard or seasonal work are punished by a highly discretionary system of benefits for their failure to demonstrate 'work performance and productivity.'

Experience rating is a feature of provincial workers' compensation programs and is defended on the basis that it promotes safety in the workplace. On the other hand, it has never been part of the Canadian UI system, although it was recommended by the Macdonald Commission (1985) but not supported by the Forget Commission (1986).

A third but minor reform proposal under the heading of *Working* was that any changes to the UI system should consider ways to cover people in non-standard employment. This proposal was important for women as they predominate in this growing sector of the job market.[41]

Meeting the Needs of Working Parents: Child Care

The government said that it was committed to supporting the provinces in expanding the availability of their child care services. But other than reiterating its 1993 campaign promises regarding federal support for child care (which were modest indeed), there was little to raise the hopes of harried parents looking for reasonably priced and good-quality child care (see Figure 15.5). The Standing Committee noted in its report that many witnesses expressed concern that the government's reform proposals fell short of advocating and endorsing a national child care program (27, 29). Child care in Canada, the committee was told, was a 'patchwork of services, programs and facilities that varies markedly among the provinces and territories' (27). The government looked at this same situation and remarked: 'Canada does not have a child care system as such. Rather it has a set of systems, each reflecting a unique history of local needs, preferences and opportunities.'[42]

When child care arrangements for European countries are examined, it is evident that the authorities there have removed their rose-coloured glasses and got on with the job of providing child care services for the children of working parents. In France, by the age of three, all children of working mothers are in state-supported child care, and parental costs are tax deductible. In Italy, more than 87 per cent of three to five year olds are in publicly funded primary schools, open eight to ten hours a day. In Denmark, 55 per cent of all Danish children from six months to two years are in crèches or municipally supported 'child-minding' homes. From three to six years, most Danish children are in publicly run kindergartens. And in Sweden, centres are operated by each municipality with funds from the state and

Figure 15.5

Licensed child care spaces versus potential demand, 1985-93*

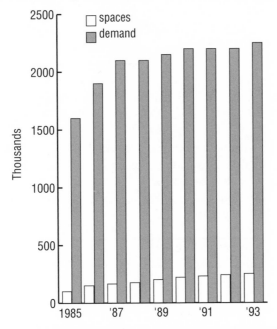

* The potential demand is estimated by the number of children under thirteen whose
  parents are working or studying more than twenty hours per week.
Source: Government of Canada, *The Context of Reform*, 28.

are open from 6:30 am to 6:30 pm for all children from two and a half years
on.[43]

The most commendable possibility of the government's approach to
child care was the linking of day care with the wider issue of child development for all children. But even this idea was given a residual cast when
one realized that the children the government was referring to were all the
children *at risk of poverty*.[44] Once again, the government seemed to be following the path laid out by its Tory predecessor: developing programs for
the poorest Canadians, a recipe for failure.

Meeting the Needs of Working Parents: More Flexible
Working Arrangements

Axworthy established a special advisory group in February 1994 specifically to assess and make recommendations on how shorter working time
and/or a redistribution of work could contribute to job creation and to
improved options for balancing family and work responsibilities.[45]

In relation to balancing family and work responsibilities, the advisory group recommended the right to an *unpaid* leave of absence from work following the birth or the adoption of a child, for a period of time equal to that allowed for maternity and parental leave (twenty-five weeks) under the maternity and parental leave provisions of the Unemployment Insurance Act. The report also noted that Quebec allows up to thirty-four weeks of leave and that consideration should be given to adopting this standard. However, how many two-earner families can afford this amount of unpaid leave? The advisory group also recommended that Canadian workers be entitled to five days of unpaid leave to care for immediate family members (this was also current practice in Quebec).

When contrasted with some European legislation, the Canadian recommendations look totally inadequate. For example, all working mothers in Sweden receive up to sixty days a year, paid leave, to care for a sick child, the right to work a six-hour day until her youngest child is eight years old, and a generous one-year paid leave following childbirth. This latter policy is strongly supported by child psychologists, who argue that infants require an extended period of close bonding to a parent figure, for the first year or eighteen months, for optimal development.[46]

Learning

The proposals under the heading of *Learning* were tied to the concept of life-long or continuous learning. The Canadian educational and training system must change to meet the challenges of rapid technological advance and its offspring, global competition. The need for upgrading skills or learning new skills and knowledge must be accepted as a continual, lifelong process for those in the labour force. A number of points were raised for discussion, but the central one was this: how should federal aid to provincial programs of postsecondary education be handled in the future, given that the existing block-funding arrangement was financially untenable (once again, the discussion paper's leitmotiv), and at the same time improve the access for all Canadians to educational and training institutions?

Under the Established Programs Financing and Fiscal Arrangements Act of 1977, the federal government contributed to provincial postsecondary education programs, through a block-funding arrangement, a combination of cash grants and tax points that in 1994 totalled about $8 billion annually (EPF-PSE). The monetary value of the tax points increases with economic growth, but because the 1994 budget decreed that federal transfers for postsecondary education would remain frozen at their 1993-4 levels (continuing a Tory policy instituted in 1989 and 1990), the cash portion would decline in amounts corresponding to any increase from the tax points. This meant that the cash grants under the existing system would disappear entirely within a decade. In 1994 the federal cash contributions comprised $2.6 billion of the $8 billion transferred to the provinces (*Improving Social Security,* 61).

To compensate, the federal government proposed directing a new contribution at students through an enhanced system of income-conditioned loans. 'In effect, this approach would replace declining cash transfers with a secure and stable source of student assistance that, in conjunction with the growing endowment of EPF-PSE tax points, would ensure that the total resources available continue to grow over time' (*Improving Social Security,* 62). The federal government defended this proposal on the basis that it would spread access to postsecondary education to a wider group of people. There would be no requirement to prove 'need,' and repayment of the student loan would be made contingent on the individual's ability to pay.

Reaction to this proposal was decidedly hostile from members of the university community. The Standing Committee noted that most student groups told them that the idea had no merit. Students predicted that under such a system, tuition fees would double or triple and that they would be saddled with substantial debt upon graduating. The government countered that tuition fees rose over the past decade and would continue to rise in any case, and that an expanded student loan scheme with repayments scaled to meet the student's income would ensure greater accessibility to higher education (*Improving Social Security,* 63). The students, on the other hand, saw the federal government 'shifting their debt load from its own shoulders to the students' (*Report,* 38).[47]

University administrators and faculty associations were equally negative. 'Cuts to university funding can only damage the nation's research infrastructure' (*Report,* 38). Other witnesses said that reducing operating grants to universities 'could lead to restrictions on the number of education spaces ... which in itself limits access.' Outdated equipment, reduced library facilities, and other services were also predicted if the proposed changes in funding were introduced.

There were some members of the university community who felt that a little competition for the student dollar, which would have been one result of the government's student loan proposal, could improve the quality of teaching and the general responsiveness to student concerns by universities. But these advocates for the discipline of the marketplace were a small minority.

Notwithstanding the criticisms from student and faculty associations, the Standing Committee report endorsed the income contingent repayment proposal, arguing that it would make it 'easier for individuals to return to school later in life and would make lifelong learning a reality' (85). The Reform Party members of the Standing Committee also supported the proposal, but concern over student debt load led the Bloc Québécois members to reject it.

Security

Reforming or Replacing the Canada Assistance Plan and Reducing Child Poverty

The discussion paper began its review of the issues under the heading of *Security* with a residual definition of social security as 'society's commitment to take care of its most vulnerable citizens – people without work, lone parents with limited means struggling to raise a family, children in poverty, and people who face barriers to employment due to disability or chronic illness' (69). These are the categories of people who make up the bulk of provincial and territorial social assistance caseloads. In other words, social security programs by this definition are programs for 'the poor' – not, as the term is generally accepted, as an organized system of public programs to promote and protect the health and welfare of all citizens.[48] The discussion paper was actually defining a *residual* segment – social assistance – of a largely *institutional* Canadian social security system. It may be that the federal government was attempting to blur the distinction between the two. This would square with the general tenor of the government's social security reform proposals: that Canadians should exercise more self-reliance and adopt a greater sense of personal responsibility for their well-being and leave the 'most vulnerable' to the social security system.

The need to reform the Canada Assistance Plan was based upon the government's conversion to 'active' as opposed to 'passive' income support programs. The implication was that social assistance programs robbed Canadians of their will to work and that reforms must aim at changing this. Doleful statistics concerning the rise in social assistance caseloads were detailed but devoid of any context. Increases in the number of people depending upon social assistance were not related to economic recessions followed by jobless recoveries, the high rates of marriage breakdown, and the increased restrictions placed on claiming unemployment insurance benefits. In fact, the discussion paper placed much of the blame on the lack of flexibility in CAP regulations. The discussion paper summed up its case in this way: 'Many people spend years on social assistance – even though with the right kind of employment and training support, they could find work. One problem is, CAP rules prevent the use of federal funding to provide the support they need. As a result the system doesn't help people prepare for work. In many cases, it does just the opposite' (20).

In 1993 the National Council of Welfare issued the results of a study it conducted into incentives and disincentives to work and came to a number of conclusions, a number of which deserve emphasis:[49]

- full employment is the best way to reduce dependence on welfare or unemployment insurance

- the trend toward part-time and short-term jobs must be halted
- minimum wage rates have suffered a serious drop in purchasing power since the mid-1970s, and thus jobs at these rates do not offer sufficient incentive for people with family responsibilities to move back into the labour force
- provincial and territorial governments need to look again at ways of providing subsidized prescription drugs, dental care, eye glasses, and other supports to low-wage workers
- allowances made by provincial welfare systems may not be sufficient to cover reasonable back-to-work expenses
- the tax-back rates on earnings by welfare recipients remain excessively high
- it is not uncommon for unattached individuals with earned incomes far below the poverty line to pay up to 12 per cent of their gross incomes in taxes (the council recommended a tax credit that would reduce federal and provincial income taxes to zero for the working poor)
- the lack of adequate and affordable child care remains a barrier to employment for many single mothers.

The policy implications of these findings were clear. The government, however, remained committed to its Employment Development Services strategy, arguing that it alone would eventually create good-quality job opportunities. But the long lines of unemployed, who were already trained, cast doubt on this optimistic forecast.

To begin correcting the 'passivity' of social assistance, the discussion paper suggested that this program should return to one of its most important original purposes: offering short-term, emergency assistance. Many policy people and community groups have been urging such action for years. It has been repeatedly pointed out to government that too many people are clients of the social assistance system when they should be handled by other, more suitable and less demeaning systems (one of the principal aims of the Marsh Report). The disabled, for example, who comprised about 20 per cent of welfare caseloads in 1993, could be covered by a comprehensive disability insurance scheme;[50] the unemployed, who comprised about 45 per cent, should be protected first of all by public and private market initiatives to raise the demand for labour, second by training and upgrading programs, and last by unemployment insurance; and one-parent families, who comprised about 28 per cent, should be covered by a range of universalist family policies, supplemented if necessary by income-tested supports, as is common in many western European countries (see page 272). This would leave social assistance programs to deal with situations not easily classifiable, but many would be short-term emergencies.

But such ideas, suggesting as they do an expansion of social security, a more 'active' role for government in terms of labour market demand, and changes to the tax system to raise additional revenue, are out of step with a government imbued with market-oriented strategies that compel people to compete for low-wage jobs in preference to accepting even more meagre and stigmatizing benefits.[51]

The Discussion Paper Builds Its Case against the Canada Assistance Plan

From the tone of the discussion paper and the supplementary paper *Reforming the Canada Assistance Plan,* it appeared obvious that the government was considering phasing out the Canada Assistance Plan. Therefore, it was necessary to detail the program's shortcomings and minimize its achievements.

The discussion paper reported that 45 per cent of all social assistance households in March 1993 were headed by an employable person. Given the calamitous rates of unemployment, the cutbacks in the availability of UI, and the increase in the numbers of single parent families, the 45 per cent figure could be anticipated. The discussion paper, however, fails to acknowledge these factors and places the blame on the fact that 'Today's social security system doesn't adequately bolster self-sufficiency' (72). Thus the government's thesis that programs such as UI or social assistance were too 'passive' and encouraged dependency.

A further difficulty with CAP involved its 'restrictive provisions,' which prevented federal funds from being used to support 'innovative provincial measures' designed to move social assistance recipients back into the labour force. Wage subsidy programs to make even minimum wage jobs look more appealing had been launched in Quebec (1988), British Columbia (1992), and New Brunswick (1992). None of these was cost-shared by CAP as it did not share in wage subsidy programs, although the scheme in British Columbia and New Brunswick, being a controlled experiment in helping single mothers move off welfare, had obtained federal support outside of the CAP program.[52] Although the possibility of the two levels of government getting together to amend the restrictive CAP regulations was raised, it was done so in the context of a 'possible first step' toward reform, but with the implication that a more permanent and better solution could be found (*Improving Social Security,* 74).

Another problem with CAP, according to the government, was the fact that it did not deal with all provinces and territories on an equal footing. The Conservative government's decision in 1990 to place a 5 per cent limit on growth in CAP transfers to the three 'have' provinces (those that did not receive equalization grants) as a deficit-reducing measure meant that the federal share of CAP-eligible expenditures for 1993-4 was estimated to be 29 per cent in Ontario, 34 per cent in British Columbia, and 50 per cent in

Alberta (up from a low of 45 per cent in 1992-3), while all other provinces and territories received 50 per cent funding (*Reforming the Canada Assistance Plan,* 24). Any change in program design would be an opportunity to promote greater fairness.

A further reason for rethinking the CAP program, according to the government, was the incidence of child poverty in Canada. Social assistance programs had been identified as a leading cause of child poverty because of the inadequacy of assistance granted. This should not have been laid at the feet of CAP, however, because the setting of social assistance rates was a provincial responsibility; the federal government merely picked up 50 per cent of the CAP-eligible, provincial social assistance costs (except for the three provinces already referred to).

These reasons for reforming CAP were designed to appeal to the provinces, but the federal government had fiscal and political reasons of its own for desiring change. Fiscally, getting rid of the cost-sharing formula would limit its financial exposure because the existing formula for federal cost-sharing meant that Ottawa was held hostage to the cost of whatever a provincial or territorial government spent on social assistance and related social services. Politically, getting rid of CAP would also eliminate the national standards that some provinces, particularly Quebec, considered as federal interference in areas of provincial jurisdiction. An end to national standards, sanctioned by Ottawa, would please Quebec federalists and discomfort the pro-independence faction. It would also please those who argued for more conditions to be applied to the receipt of welfare, such as 'workfare.'

The discussion paper identified two principal goals under the heading of *Security:* to remove the disincentives from social assistance that discouraged a return to work, including disabled recipients who wished to live more independently (89); and to set as a target the reduction of child poverty, recognizing that progress on this goal is directly linked to employment for the parents.

As already noted, it appeared from the weight of argument that the government wanted an end to the Canada Assistance Plan and its 'restrictive regulations.' Block funding with few strings attached (the Quebec card) appeared the preferred option and would address the first goal. Options for achieving a reduction in child poverty were more complex. The idea of a guaranteed annual income was raised and quickly dropped because of the additional cost; a block-funded federal contribution to provincial social assistance costs would permit provinces to use their social assistance budgets to the greater advantage of children, but with fewer dollars coming from Ottawa (a result of the 1994 budget) a reduction of child poverty from this idea appeared unlikely; a third option was an enhanced child tax benefit (the successor to the universal family allowance) that would target low-income families with additional benefits while removing them from middle- and higher-income families; another option involved 'combining the Child Tax Benefit and social assistance budgets for children to be paid to all low-income families, regardless of the family's source of income' (77). This would have the effect of removing children from the welfare rolls, an idea proposed by Ontario's Social Assistance Review Committee in 1988.

Consideration might also be given to increasing the working income supplement for low-income families – perhaps doubling it to a maximum of $1,000 per family, per year. The money for this program could be 'reallocated' from the child tax benefit. Other options included more subsidized child care spaces and additional income support for one-parent families.

In light of the success western European countries have had in reducing child poverty, it is regrettable that the government paid so little attention to their experience.

Family Policy in Europe

The Europeans have had considerably more success in dealing with poverty in families and particularly in single-parent families, accomplishing this without an exclusive reliance on targeting benefits on the 'most needy.' Norway's family policy provides an example of social policy that pays special attention to single-parent families in a positive way. Income support is described as 'generous,' and in response to conservative views of the role of women, single mothers are entitled to remain at home until their children are ten years old. However, Norwegian women have the option of choosing to work and are given various forms of support if they do so. In addition to universal family allowances, there are tax allowances and child care tax credits available to all working parents, plus additional cash benefits to single parents to offset the costs of child care. Furthermore, if a single mother requires job training in order to become employable, there are educational benefits. But the single mother's most important source of income is the 'transitional benefit,' which is designed to support a single parent and her children when she is temporarily unable to support herself. It is available on an income test for at least a year or until her youngest child is ten. It is available even if the woman is cohabiting, as long as her partner is not the father of her child or children. The transitional benefit is phased out if/when the woman begins to earn her own income. In 1985 the rate at which the transitional benefit was paid was about 35 per cent of an average full-time female wage. If the child's father fails to meet his maintenance payments, the state will step in and guarantee these. In Canada, by contrast, thousands of single mothers continue to be forced to chase after child-support payments from delinquent ex-husbands. Finally, there are also housing supplements for single-parent families. Kamerman and Kahn estimate that transfer payments to single-parent families in Norway together constitute 70 per cent of what the average single mother could earn and are tax free (while her salary would be taxable). *The result is that poverty is not an issue for these Norwegian families.*[53]

Another approach to protecting families with children from poverty is illustrated by French family policy. Here the direction of family policy is to support all children and especially the very young. Thus, French family policy includes universal family allowances beginning with the second child (largely financed by an employers' payroll tax); a single-parent allowance and an orphan allowance paid out of general revenue; an income-tested family allowance supplement; a universal young child allowance for nine months beginning in the fifth month of pregnancy; an income-tested, long-term benefit lasting until the child is age three that covers about 80 per cent of French families with children under the age of three; paid maternity leave at full wages for sixteen weeks; a universal but modest 'parenting' leave of up to two years for working parents, with three or more children, who reduce their working hours by half or more; and an income-tested housing allowance.

Sweden's family policy provides a further example of how to limit the risk of child poverty, and it should be a model to the Canadian government because it integrates work and family life. This policy is based upon the principle of gender equity, both in parenting and participation in the labour force. In Sweden, single-parent families receive supplementary income support, in addition to the universal family allowances that all Swedish children receive. These supplements may include income-tested housing allowances; child-support allowances at a modest level in cases where the father is unable to make or tardy in making support payments;[54] and priority status for high-quality child care services. All working mothers are entitled to an annual paid leave of up to sixty days to care for a sick child; the right to work a six-hour day until the youngest child is eight years old; and a generous one-year paid leave following childbirth.[55] Thus, Swedish policy supports the right (and the expectation) of both men and women to join the labour force but takes special care to ensure that women who are raising children on their own are given additional support to meet both responsibilities.

Even with these supports, single-parent families are considered socially and economically disadvantaged by Swedish authorities, but they are not considered 'poor.' They are seen as facing some social and cultural exclusion from the opportunities afforded two-income families, which in Sweden is the norm.

This view of low-income status as being not just a matter of minimum income but of social and cultural exclusion is common to countries of western Europe. It contrasts sharply with the Conservative government's attempt, in the dying days of the Tory regime (June 1993), to question the incidence of poverty in Canada by claiming that anyone who could afford the necessities for physical survival was not poor.[56]

As a result of their research on the success many European nations have had in keeping one-parent families out of poverty, Kamerman and Kahn have come to the following conclusion: 'A primary lesson from all the data, research, and reports of experiences that we have examined is that of universalism – not limiting most public programs to the means-tested poor. It proves very difficult to do special things for the very poor mother-only families without creating or seeming to create perverse incentives or inequities.'[57]

Canada, as we have seen, is moving away from universalism and toward programs that target the poor, despite the dismal experience with this approach in the United States. While targeting the poor may appear eminently sensible, in practice it fails to achieve the desired goal and promotes social disharmony. Witness the Republican Speaker of the House of Representatives, Newt Gingrich, in 1995, proposing to cut off all aid to single mothers under twenty-one and consign their children to orphanages. This was followed in 1996 by Democratic President Clinton signing a bill passed by the Republican-controlled Congress that catered to the most mean-spirited prejudices about poor and dependent people. The new welfare measure ended a sixty-one-year-old federal cost-shared program, Aid to Families with Dependent Children, replacing it with a block grant to the states with few strings attached. The new grant will save the federal treasury $55 billion over six years, but only by denying aid to needy people. Senator Moynihan of New York said the legislation will result in children sleeping on the grates of the streets in his city.

These policies are the product of years of 'targeting' income security and other forms of help on the poorest segments of the community. Low-income families who are only slightly above the 'welfare' level react negatively to the inequity inherent in such programs. Middle-class families complain about the cost to the taxpayer. The latter group tend to see themselves solely as taxpayers, being blind to the tax-supported occupational and fiscal welfare benefits they enjoy. Stories of welfare fraud abound in this type of situation, with little or no differentiation between administrative error, client error, or deliberate fraud. Aspiring politicians (and those a little desperate for approval) promise crackdowns on welfare fraud and stricter eligibility requirements.

Despite a long history of targeting and crackdowns, the United States has the largest proportion of poor children of any wealthy developed nation. Canada, now moving to adopt the same type of discredited policies and woefully lacking in progressive family policies, comes second in this shameful and wholly avoidable table. In 1992, of eleven OECD countries, Canada came last in the annual value of basic child benefits for a median income family with two children (see Figure 15.6). The ILO has said that the indisputable lesson from history is that 'the poor gain more from universal than from income-tested benefits.'[58] The discussion paper, in formulating the proposals for 'children in poverty,' appeared to have forgotten or ignored both history and research.

Figure 15.6

Child benefits for 1992

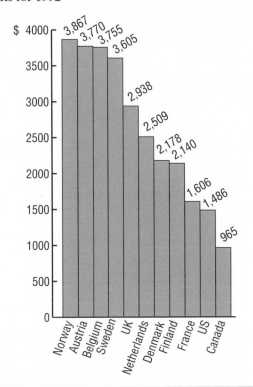

Source: Statistics Canada, *Vancouver Sun*, 27 June 1994.

Plans to Target 'Child Poverty' Put on Hold

In the supplementary paper *Income Security for Children*, the narrow goal of targeting low-income families with enhanced benefits through the child tax benefit (CTB) and/or the working income supplement (WIS) was discussed. Three main proposals were offered. The first was an enhanced and retargeted CTB combined with the WIS, which would provide additional income support for all low-income families but reduced support for those in the middle-income range.[59] The second approach was an 'integrated federal-provincial benefit.' This plan would merge provincial social assistance benefits for children with the federal CTB to create a single benefit system that would be available to all low-income families, on the basis of an income test, irrespective of their other sources of income.[60] The third approach would increase the WIS on the assumption that work would become more appealing than welfare. It would, of course, maintain and even emphasize the invidious distinction between the 'worthy' and 'unworthy' poor.

The denouement of the child poverty issue came with the postponement of the social security reform process for fiscal and political reasons. But an additional irony presented itself when the prime minister was expected to attend a UN conference on world poverty in Copenhagen in March 1995, along with other world leaders. He withdrew at the last minute 'to sidestep international criticism of his Liberals' historic retreat on social policy issues.'[61]

Was the Cupboard Really Bare?

The discussion paper made the following points repeatedly: the present social program budget was not sustainable and would have to be reduced; any improvements that required additional resources must obtain them by reallocation from other social programs; and raising taxes to secure additional funds for any needed improvements (even to reduce child poverty) was not an option.

The idea that tax revenues had been mined to exhaustion was repeatedly challenged before the parliamentary Standing Committee on Human Resources Development: 'A substantial majority of witnesses strongly expressed their concerns about a lack of fairness in the Canadian tax system. Some pointed to tax inequities as one cause of the growing income gap between the rich and poor in Canada. Many Canadians objected to profitable corporations having paid no taxes in recent years. They urged the government to explore these sources of revenue in the pursuit of deficit reduction and to apply them to areas of pressing social need' (*Report*, 47).

Witnesses also argued that the government should be examining tax expenditures as carefully as direct expenditures, and the Standing Committee's *Report* recommended that 'social tax expenditures be evaluated using guidelines similar to those being applied to direct program spending under the federal government's program review' (99; see Appendix Table A4).

Neil Brooks, a tax specialist at Osgood Hall Law School, argued that 'the government should not be permitted to touch one spending program that generally benefits the poor and middle-class, until it has repealed the inequitable and inefficient spending programs in the tax system that almost exclusively benefits the rich and large corporations.'[62]

The Ontario Federation of Labour published a report in 1994 on the tax concessions to corporations that, given the country's reported fiscal and debt situation, were difficult if not impossible to justify (see Appendix Table A5).

Catherine Swift, of the Canadian Federation of Independent Business, told the Standing Committee that companies receive more than $5 billion a year in federal subsidies that they did not require. 'A lot of these are political pork-barrel grants and subsidies. They're not motivated by sensible economic or business considerations.'[63]

Richard Shillington, a taxation specialist, in a critique of the Liberal government's deficit reduction strategy as it pertained to social programs, pointed out that Finance Minister Martin had a choice between cutting direct social spending or indirect social spending (i.e., social tax expenditures). Shillington said that Martin cut programs of direct social spending such as UI and federal transfers to provinces that support critical programs such as social assistance and 'virtually ignored' the social tax expenditure side. This was not a trifling amount of tax revenue to ignore, as social tax expenditures cost federal and provincial treasuries over $53 billion in 1992 (see Appendix Table A4). The result of this type of policy, according to Shillington, will be to 'maintain tax expenditures for well-off Canadians' and to 'reduce family security through spending cuts and changes to federal/provincial cost sharing.'[64]

Other suggestions for raising more revenue rather than cutting social programs included a 1 per cent tax on the more than $1 trillion of money market transactions, daily, worldwide.[65] There was also the perennial question asked by peace activists: did the Canadian military need to spend an estimated $11.9 billion on weapons, soldiers, and military bases in 1994?

The 1995 Federal Budget and the Canada Health and Social Transfer

Despite the announcement in January 1995 that the reform of social security programs had been shelved pending action to reduce the federal deficit as well as to outmanoeuvre the independence movement in Quebec, it was inevitable given the government's priorities that the budget would have an impact on social programs. The impact was undeniable – the budget called for a cut in federal transfers to the provinces of $7 billion by 1997-8.[66] But in addition, the budget went further, impinging upon the nature of Canadian federalism itself by carrying decentralization to the point of balkanization.

The 1995 budget announced the elimination of two long-standing federal transfer programs – Established Programs Financing (EPF) and the Canada Assistance Plan (CAP) – and their replacement by a new, block-funded program called the Canada Health and Social Transfer (CHST) beginning on 1 April 1996. The CHST, made up of both cash payments and tax points, will deliver federal contributions to provincial programs of medicare, postsecondary education, and social assistance and related social services. The issue of the inequitable treatment afforded the three 'have' provinces – Ontario, Alberta, and British Columbia – was immediately raised by them. Under the former Canada Assistance Plan, all but these three provinces received 50 per cent funding for all shareable programs from Ottawa. In his March 1996 budget, Finance Minister Martin promised to gradually reduce these inequities by half over the five-year period beginning 1998-9. He also said the government would guarantee that the cash component of the CHST would never be lower than $11 billion at any time during the 1998-2003 period. In this way, the federal government was signalling its intention to uphold the five standards of the Canada Health Act and the one standard remaining from the old Canada Assistance Plan that prohibited provinces from requiring a residence qualification from social assistance applicants (*Budget Speech*, 6 March 1996, 10-11; see endnote 67).

With one eye on Quebec and the independence referendum set for October 1995, the federal government praised the Canada Health and Social Transfer for ending 'the intrusions of previous cost-shared arrangements.'[67] The minister of human resources development was delegated to negotiate with the provinces 'a set of shared principles or objectives that would underlie the new transfer.' One knowledgeable observer 'doubted that the provinces will adhere to undertakings not backed by federal sanctions.' In the 1970s, he noted, 'provinces failed to honour the principles of medicare until forced into compliance by the Canada Health Act.'[68]

The C.D. Howe Institute claimed that critics of the CHST have 'wildly over-estimated' the damage being done to social programs. In a study commissioned by the institute, Thomas Courchene correctly pointed out that the somewhat loose standards, under the Canada Assistance Plan, relating to provincial social assistance programs did not prevent wide provincial variations in the adequacy of social assistance rates and related social services. Thus, the federal government's decision to drop standards altogether for welfare and social services (except for the residency requirement) should not have much impact. But Courchene skips past the fact that $7 billion over two years was being cut from federal funding to the provinces, and in the competition for needed funds the welfare area was widely predicted to lose out to health and postsecondary education. These deep cuts have already resulted in reductions in welfare rates in Manitoba, British Columbia, and Quebec, and they were used to justify politically inspired cutbacks in Alberta and Ontario. Social service agencies also reported reductions in critical services for low-income Canadians. Fourteen Canadian municipalities issued a joint statement stating, in part: 'Without provision to ensure adequacy of social programs, there is a danger of a downward spiral of reduced services, urban core decay, unemployment, poverty and associated social ills causing increased costs for policing and emergency response, poorer health and the costs associated with that, and decreased economic productivity.'[69]

The National Council of Welfare, in a sharply critical report on the CHST, argued that if the federal government insisted on a block-funded approach, it should have at least established a separate fund for the social assistance and social services programs. This would serve to protect the funds for the critical services provided to Canada's poorest citizens. It also recommended a number of principles and standards that should be part of any new funding arrangement. These included the concept of adequacy, defined as 'Income assistance sufficient to cover basic living expenses and measured by the cost of a "market basket" of goods and services available in the community'; the right of appeal; respect for the individual – in essence a prohibition of 'workfare'; accountability – provincial and territorial governments should provide the federal government with a full accounting of their spending on welfare services; and full disclosure – the general public should be provided with complete and up-to-date information on welfare services and policies, written in simple, everyday language.[70]

The Employment Insurance Act, 1996

In May 1995, Lloyd Axworthy told a House of Commons committee that there would be new legislation to replace the Unemployment Insurance Act not later than 1 July 1996. However, when first made public in the fall of 1995 (following the Quebec referendum), the legislation drew so much public criticism that, in a cabinet shuffle early in 1996, Axworthy was replaced by Doug Young, an MP from a New Brunswick riding described as a fiscal conservative. Prime Minister Chrétien obviously hoped that Young, who represented an area of the country dogged by seasonal unemployment, would be able to ease some of the restrictive Axworthy proposals, particularly those aimed at frequent users of UI. In doing so, he might also diffuse some of the mounting public criticism of the Liberal government, especially from the Atlantic provinces. A number of changes were made, but labour critics described them as 'marginal.'

The bill introducing the new legislation reached the House of Commons in December 1995. As it worked its way through the House, there was surprisingly little discussion of its contents in the media. Some commentators attributed this to the bill's complexity – 'few M.P.'s understood it.'[71] More importantly, public hearings on the bill were limited to about two weeks, and the government 'imposed a time limit on the committee's detailed analysis of the bill's many clauses.'[72]

The Employment Insurance Act (EI) was passed by the House on 13 May 1996 by a vote of 123 to 80 (the Reform Party and Bloc Québécois opposed it), and was put into effect in two stages, the first beginning 1 July 1996 and the second 1 January 1997. The principal elements of the plan are as follows:

- Contributors, both employees and employers, will pay slightly less in premiums, and claimants for benefits will receive less and for a shorter period.[73]

- Qualifying conditions for regular benefits remain the same as under the old legislation, except for new entrants to the labour force or for those who are reentering after an absence of two years or more, and for those new entrants who have less than fourteen weeks of insured employment behind them. These latter three categories face stiffer qualifying conditions.[74]
- Beginning 1 January 1997, a new 'intensity rule' will reduce benefits even further for frequent users of EI, such as seasonal workers. In partial mitigation, all claimants with dependants and with a family income under $25,921 will be exempt from the intensity rule and entitled to a family income supplement increasing their benefit up to 65 per cent of their insured earnings, rising to 80 per cent by the year 2000.[75]
- Beginning 1 January 1997, *hours* rather than *weeks* of work will be counted for insurance purposes. The government estimated that this change will enable 500,000 part-time workers to be covered by EI for the first time. This was important for women, many of whom seek part-time work, and in view of the increasing proportion of part-time work in the economy. However, its positive effects were vitiated by the fact that new entrants to the labour force will require 900 hours of insured work to qualify for benefits. Other workers will need 420 to 700 hours depending upon the rate of unemployment in their region.[76]
- After 1 January 1997, claimants receiving benefits of less than $200 per week will be able to earn up to $50 per week without affecting their benefit.
- At the other end of the income scale, the clawback of benefits from high-income earners, which formerly began at $63,570, will instead begin when the claimant's total yearly income exceeds $48,750.[77]
- EI will offer the unemployed 'Re-employment Benefits' to help them get back to work. These include wage subsidies, self-employment assistance, job creation partnerships, and other strategies.[78]

Of What Value Is Unemployment Insurance?

So much time was spent discussing the 'passivity' and other shortcomings of unemployment insurance in the discussion paper *Improving Social Security in Canada* that the value to the nation of such a program was obscured, if not lost, in the discussion paper's mantra: 'The system doesn't work any more. It needs to be fixed' (Summary, 5).

Quite apart from providing the right to a benefit and the dignity that accompanies it, unemployment insurance's chief virtue is its role as an economic stabilizer. By maintaining a portion of the spending power lost to a community when layoffs occur, UI protects other jobs and businesses. One federal government study estimated that in the 1991 recession, the presence of UI saved 25,000 jobs. In another study on the impact of UI on the 1981-2 recession, the deepest since the 1930s, it was estimated that without UI the economy would have dropped a further 15 to 20 per cent and the number of job losses would have increased by a similar percentage.[79] Unemployment insurance, according to Nancy Riche of the CLC, helps to promote more efficient job searches: 'Rather than being forced to take the first job that comes along, the UI recipient can search more widely for a job that matches her skills and needs. UI also serves employers' interests. If not for UI, employers would be unable to rehire many skilled and experienced workers after a forced layoff, thus requiring new investments in training and lost productivity.'[80]

Despite the unrivalled social and economic advantages of social insurance protection against the risk of unemployment, Canada has, over the period 1990-6, revised its unemployment insurance system to reduce benefits and make them more difficult to qualify for, thereby limiting the system's function as an economic stabilizer. The social consequences of withdrawing this form of protection from a majority of workers are seldom considered by the economists who not only defend the cutbacks but advocate them – 'moral hazard' is to be avoided at all costs; plunging individuals and families into deeper poverty is given scant consideration.

The new EI legislation arrived at a time when the national rate of unemployment was 10 per cent. Furthermore, even before the introduction of this new and more restrictive program, Statistics Canada had reported that in September 1995, only 37 per cent of the unemployed were able to qualify for UI, down from 66 per cent in 1990 and 75 per cent prior to the 1990 recession.[81] The decline is not only the result of the restrictions on qualifying for benefits but is also due to the increase in long-term unemployment, which means people lose their benefits before they can find another job. The result is somewhat perverse. The UI fund, which was about $6 billion in the red in 1992, was close to a surplus of $1 billion in 1995, an estimated $5 billion at the end of 1996, and, according to the Canadian Chamber of Commerce, the surplus would reach $9 billion by the end of 1997.[82]

What Did the Axworthy Attempt
to Reform Social Security Actually Accomplish?

Begun in early 1994 by former Minister of Human Resources Development Lloyd Axworthy, who promised legislation by the year's end, the process was quickly ratcheted down to avoid colliding with a Quebec provincial election and with the deficit-reducing plans of his more powerful cabinet colleague, the minister of finance. From a possible white paper outlining the government's legislative intentions, Axworthy's reform process produced a green paper (a discussion paper) offering a range of options for consideration. A parliamentary committee toured the country for five weeks to receive public reaction to the green paper, but coincidental with the release of the committee's report, the whole process was put on hold with the government pleading that national unity and deficit reduction must have priority.

At the beginning of this chapter, it was speculated that the Liberals may have borrowed their ideas for social security reform from their Conservative predecessors. What appeared to be the legacy of the Axworthy reform efforts adds weight to this thesis. We recall that prior to the 1993 federal election, Prime Minister Kim Campbell, when pressed to explain what her social policy plans were, would only say that 'unemployment insurance and social assistance would be modernized.' The work of the Liberal social security reform team fit quite comfortably within that job description. The discussion paper spent most of its time and effort on changes to the Unemployment Insurance Act and on replacing the Canada Assistance Plan. The balance of the paper was largely window dressing – child care, child poverty, flexible work arrangements, more help for the disabled, and improving access to higher education. These issues were treated in an insubstantial manner and lacked the argumentation in support of one course of action over another. This was in marked contrast to the treatment of unemployment insurance and the Canada Assistance Plan, which were linked by the pressing need, as the green paper saw it, to substitute 'active' for 'passive' kinds of help. There was no comparable energy or commitment behind the need to do something about child poverty or the disabled.

A surprising omission in the social security review was the failure to discuss, or even mention, the role of government in the provision of affordable housing. This gap was particularly puzzling given the amount of rhetoric devoted to the needs of the disabled and of families struggling in poverty.

To return to our question of what the Axworthy initiative accomplished, its legacy was a new Employment Insurance Act and the replacement of a valuable cost-shared program with a 'no-strings' block-funded approach, which slashed federal support of social programs by $7 billion over two years. Apart from contributing to federal deficit reduction, cutting unemployment insurance benefits and making them more difficult to qualify for, and endangering critical provincial services – apart from all this, perhaps we could say, as some policy analysts have said, that unemployment insurance and social assistance were 'modernized.'

The 'Reform' of Public Pensions

In his 1995 budget speech, Martin said his government was 'absolutely committed to providing a fair and *sustainable* system of protection for Canadian seniors' (*Budget Speech,* 20). As Canadians were now well aware, the word 'sustainable' (particularly when italicized) was a codeword for cutbacks. The minister followed this commitment with his view of the public pension system. It consisted, he said, of *two* pillars on which the public could build a retirement savings plan: a social insurance system covering the workforce (the C/QPP), and the universal old age security pension with its income-tested supplement, the guaranteed income supplement (OAS/GIS). In fact, the public pension system has a *third* and substantial pillar: the tax expenditure support for the provision of private pension plans and RRSPs.

It is characteristic of individuals, organizations, or governments who wish to see the role of the private sector enlarged at the expense of the public sector to decry the cost of social security measures, which in Canada are increasingly needs or income tested, while turning a blind eye to the cost of social tax expenditures, which have few such restrictions. It is particularly disconcerting to have a finance minister ignore this third and enormous pillar of tax-supported pensions, which in the case of RRSPs was established in 1957 as a matter of public policy to encourage those Canadians with no company pension plan or who were self-employed to set up their own savings plan or tax shelter for retirement. It is well recognized that tax deductions allowed for RRSP contributions confer the greatest benefit on, and are most utilized by, upper-income earners.[83]

The finance minister in his 1995 budget cut back on the tax expenditure contained in the tax deduction granted RRSP contributors but only *temporarily*. The deduction was to be restored and enhanced by 1997-8. This plan was altered in the 1996 budget, which acknowledged the third pillar of public pensions by freezing contribution levels to RRSPs at $13,500 per year until 2005, when (barring further changes) they will increase to $15,500 per year.

According to Monica Townson, the cost of foregone government revenue from providing tax exemptions for private pension plans and RRSPs amounts to about $12 billion a year in the 1990s, almost as much as the total cost of OAS. 'Given that OAS benefits are taxed and surtaxed through the clawback, the magnitude of tax expenditure on private retirement savings arrangements becomes starkly obvious.' Townson estimated that tax expenditures on private pension arrangements were about 40 per cent of the total cost of public pension programs such as OAS/GIS and the CPP.[84]

The Conference Board of Canada, a privately funded think tank, warned the finance minister not to consider taxing the $500 billion in Canadian tax-supported private pension arrangements, as is the case in Australia, where government also encourages its citizens to make private provision for their retirement. However, the Australian government taxes such plans when contributions are made, when contributions earn income within the plan, and when money is withdrawn as income. While admitting that even a 1 per cent tax on monies in private pension plans would go a long way to solving Canada's deficit, the Conference Board warned that such a policy 'would dampen over-all economic growth.'[85] However, when it comes to direct government spending, the Conference Board urged even deeper cuts and, while admitting that these too will slow economic growth, argued that cutting now would save having to take more drastic measures later on.[86]

Critics of public pension systems also raised the issue of the ageing of Canadian society bankrupting the nation with the cost of pensions and health care. They pointed to the projected increase of people over the age of sixty-five from 12 per cent of the population in 1995 to about 23 per cent in the year 2030. However, as pointed out earlier (Chapter 13), the dependency ratio is the critical factor. Townson reports that in Canada 'the total dependency ratio, which reflects the ratio of working age population to those aged 19 and under and 65 and over, is expected to decline steadily until 2011. Although slight increases are expected from that year until 2036, the ratio in 2036 will still be below the total dependency ratio of the Canadian population in the 1950s and 1960s.' Thus, Townson argues, the issue is primarily political and not economic.[87]

Reforming Public Pensions

Old Age Security and the Guaranteed Income Supplement

In his 1996 budget speech, Paul Martin, the minister of finance, proposed a new, tax-free, income-tested seniors benefit to replace the universal old age security pension and its income-tested supplement beginning in the year 2001. In effect, the once universal program, already clawed back through the tax system for higher-income seniors, will be supplanted by an income-tested plan that sharply restricts its maximum benefits to a much smaller segment of Canadian pensioners, defined as low- and modest-income Canadians.[88]

What spawned this change was the government's concern that, with the ageing of Canadian society, the cost of pensions would become 'unsustainable.' By targeting the seniors benefit more precisely on low-income seniors, and taxing back the benefit more rapidly as other income rises, the growth rate in the cost of public pensions will be reduced, making them more affordable to future generations and leaving sufficient resources for other programs and services (*Budget Speech*, 1996, 13).[89] The government also cited the fact that the number of Canadians age sixty-five and older will double by 2030, and that Canadians are living longer in retirement. On these projections, the government proceeded to construct the most pessimistic scenario by predicting that, whereas in the decade 1996-2006 there will be five workers for each pensioner, by 2030 there will be only three. There was no mention of events that might alter this dire forecast, such as the implementation of a national day care program that could release more women into the full-time workforce; a policy of full employment to provide jobs for the thousands of unemployed and underemployed; the possibility that immigration policy could introduce younger workers into the economy; or even changes in the birthrate.

The government emphasized that those currently drawing old age security would have the option of remaining with that program or switching to the new plan.[90] This choice would also be open to those who were sixty by 31 December 1995 and their spouses of any age, the government contending that people sixty and over would not have the time to adjust their savings program to take account of the change occurring in 2001 (*Seniors Benefit*, 7).

The main features of the seniors benefit are

- The maximum benefit will be $120 per year, per household, higher than the existing OAS/GIS. This means that singles will receive $120 but couples will share that amount. The new benefit will be fully indexed to the cost of living.
- In the case of couples, the monthly benefit will be divided equally and sent in two separate cheques. However, the amount of benefit will be based on family income, not individual income as under the OAS.
- The spouse's allowance program, for low-income people aged sixty to sixty-five who are married to recipients of the OAS/GIS program and low-income widows and widowers, will remain in place.
- The government will save $200 million in the new plan's first year of operation in 2001, and this will grow to $2.1 billion a year by 2011 and $8.2 billion a year in 2030.[91]

The National Council of Welfare criticized the government's decision to include all sixty year olds and their spouses with the existing OAS/GIS recipients. According to the council's analysis, seniors with other income of $30,000 or more will benefit by choosing the current system, and therefore the cost of OAS will be increased and extended in time, and most of this additional expense will be going to relatively well-off seniors (*Guide to the Proposed Seniors Benefit*, 22).

The National Council of Welfare would also like to see some of the savings devoted to improving the seniors benefit. It was critical of the $120 a year increase and suggested that $500 a year per household would be more appropriate. However, these 'reforms' have little to do with fighting poverty; they are essentially deficit-reducing schemes, and their intention is to shift the responsibility for pensions from the public to the private sphere, and to make retirement provision an individual rather than a collective responsibility.

Public pensions for the elderly, until quite recently, were considered almost untouchable by politicians. Obviously, this is no longer the case as

Ottawa moves resolutely toward the eventual elimination of the universal old age security program. The public appears to have accepted the fiction that social spending is a prime cause, if not *the* cause, of the debt and deficit. Linda McQuaig has ably demonstrated in her book *Shooting the Hippo*, however, that unemployment, economic recessions, and the disastrous interest rate policy of John Crow, the former head of the Bank of Canada, were the real culprits.[92] Taking advantage of the public mood that Canadians have indeed been 'living beyond their means' and 'demanding too much from government,' the disciples of a smaller role for the public sector and a greatly enlarged role for the private market were working hard to reduce Canada's largely *institutional* system of old age pensions to a *residual* remnant for 'the vulnerable.'

The Canada and Quebec Pension Plans

Unlike the OAS/GIS program, which is solely financed and administered by the federal government, the CPP is jointly managed by both the provincial and federal governments, and therefore any major changes to the CPP require the consent of two-thirds of the provinces containing two-thirds of Canada's population. However, in his budget speeches of 1994 and 1995, the finance minister signalled his concern for the sustainability of the public pension system, and in 1994 promised a paper on the 'changes required to the public pension system to ensure it is affordable' (*Budget Speech*, 10). The Quebec situation – a provincial election in 1994, won by the PQ, and a provincial referendum on independence in 1995, won by the federalists with the narrowest of margins – postponed the release of a potentially politically sensitive document. But following the referendum, in February 1996, the federal government, in concert with nine provinces and two territories, released *An Information Paper for Consultations on the Canada Pension Plan*.[93] The federal minister of finance and his provincial counterparts also agreed to consult with the public on the future of the plan, and a panel of federal-provincial representatives travelled to all major centres of the country for six weeks in the spring of 1996.

Prior to the release of the *Information Paper*, and beginning in the late fall of 1995, alarms were raised as to the future of the CPP. The doom and gloom forecasts, which the chief actuary of the CPP termed as 'silly,' emanated principally from neoconservative think tanks and others.[94] The former chair of the Economic Council of Canada, David Slater, warned that 'Canada's retirement income system was rapidly approaching a "crisis"' and that higher contributions and lower benefits were required to meet it.[95] A C.D. Howe Institute spokesperson strained credulity by comparing the CPP to a 'Ponzi scheme,' and he recommended that it be phased out in favour of a privately managed plan based on 'individual responsibility and control.' Not content with creating financial anxiety about the CPP, the same person envisioned an intergenerational conflict breaking out as younger workers rebel at the prospect of paying much higher contributions for fewer benefits.[96]

This hyperbole was sparked by the release of the *Annual Report* for 1995 by the chief actuary of the Canada Pension Plan, which stated: 'the financial projections shown in this report indicate that the existing 25-year schedule of contribution rates requires some revision to prevent the account from becoming exhausted by the end of 2015.' All this meant, according to the left-leaning Canadian Centre for Policy Alternatives, was that 'to maintain a fund equivalent to two years' worth of benefits, as the federal and provincial Governments had agreed to do, an upward revision would be required in the 25-year contribution rate schedule.'[97]

The *Information Paper*: One Perspective on the CPP's Problems and Possible Solutions

The reasons given for the government's concern for the financial stability of the CPP were essentially the same as those identified as necessitating the 'reform' of the OAS/GIS – demographics and a changed economic environment. In the case of the CPP, these two elements were compounded by what was termed 'enrichments' of the CPP since its inception in 1966 and an unexpected surge in disability claims over the preceding decade.

'Enrichments' since 1966

Although some would call the 'enrichments' badly needed improvements, by using the term 'enrichments' the government seemed to suggest that, in lean times, people could easily do without them. The 'enrichments' the *Information Paper* identify include:

- full indexing of benefits instead of a 2 per cent ceiling (1975)
- payment of survivor benefits to widowers as well as widows (1975); initially only disabled or dependent widowers received this benefit
- ending the retirement and earnings test (1975); originally, pensioners aged sixty-five to sixty-nine had to pass a retirement test to collect a benefit, and their subsequent benefit to age seventy was reduced if they earned more than a set amount
- the introduction of child-rearing drop-out provisions (1983, but made retroactive to 1 January 1978)
- an increase in disability benefit guidelines and a relaxation in the minimum contributory requirements for such a benefit (1987)
- widows and widowers in receipt of survivor benefits were allowed to keep them upon remarriage (1987). (23-4)

The Government's Suggested Options for Change

The government's proposed solution to the financial situation of the CPP over the next two or three decades was twofold: cut back on benefits to reduce outlay; and raise the contribution rate beyond what was already planned, and do it more quickly – within six or seven years – to reach what it described as a state of 'fuller funding' and a 'steady-state' of contribution rate at about 10 per cent, a figure satisfactory to business interests. Under existing projections, a contribution rate of 10 per cent (meaning that employers and employees would each be liable for 5 per cent of insurable earnings) would not be reached until the year 2016. The idea of 'fuller funding' would see the CPP fund grow from its current two years' worth of benefits, about $40 billion, to six years' worth, an estimated $120 billion. A portion of this money would be invested in the stock market rather than lending it to the provinces. This, it was suggested, would increase the plan's revenue and further stabilize contribution rates.

The *Information Paper*'s ideas for reducing costs were

- a 10 per cent reduction in the retirement pension, from 25 per cent to 22.5 per cent of pensionable earnings
- reduce the 'drop-out' provision from 15 per cent of non-working or low-income years to 10 per cent
- gradually raise the retirement age from sixty-five to sixty-seven
- tighten up the qualifying regulations for a disability benefit
- cut out the death benefit
- limit surviving spousal benefits to take account of the changing role of women
- provide partial pensions for those who wish to gradually withdraw from the workforce before age sixty-five but who wish to continue to work and earn further pension credits
- trim the year's basic exemption
- increase the years required to draw a full pension
- provide only partial indexing of benefits to the consumer price index
- improve on administrative efficiencies. (33-43)

Public Reaction to the *Information Paper*

During the spring of 1996, a panel of federal-provincial representatives toured the country, spending little more than a day in each of seventeen cities.[98] The first day of hearings, in Toronto, indicated that most Canadians would resist cuts to CPP benefits. Both labour and business representatives objected to suggestions that retirement benefits be reduced because this would disrupt company pension plans that had been developed over the past thirty years in the expectation that the OAS and CPP would be in place. However, the Canadian Chamber of Commerce favoured cuts in benefits over a higher contribution rate, citing the latter as a 'job-killing payroll tax.' Progressive Conservative provincial governments in Ontario and Alberta were expected to take this same position, but Quebec had already expressed its opposition to cutting benefits, and left-leaning provincial governments were seen as reluctant to accept cuts. Social groups, such as the Canadian Council on Social Development, said that no cuts were warranted.[99] Conspicuous by their absence was any mention of CPP improvements, such as the Canadian Labour Congress (CLC) advanced in the 1980s.

The CLC said that because the *Information Paper* lacked supporting analytical material and raised so many complex issues, 'the only thing that can be safely implemented by January 1st, 1997, is an adjustment to the contribution rates within the framework of the existing legislation.'[100] The Congress pinpointed one of the most serious shortcomings of the *Information Paper*: 'What are described as costs in the "*Information Paper*" are also people's incomes. To present a recipe for cuts with no discussion of their impact on incomes is nothing short of irresponsible.' The CLC also contested the government's assertion that there was a 'sustainability crisis,' and said it could 'see no reason to believe that Canada's public pensions cannot be afforded in the future.' Concerns about program costs, the CLC said, have to be balanced 'by equal concerns about the adequacy of retirement incomes.'

The Adequacy of Retirement Incomes in Canada

The question of the adequacy of Canada's public pension system failed to rate a mention in the *Information Paper*. The National Council of Welfare filled this gap by presenting statistical evidence to support its claim that the public pension system rated a failing grade when it came to keeping low-income pensioners out of poverty.[101] Its report indicated that in 1995, 39 per cent of old age security pensioners received some or all of the guaranteed income supplement, showing that they had little other income. Even those seniors drawing the maximum C/QPP pensions coupled with the OAS, and for some a portion of the GIS, were still below the poverty line if they lived in large urban areas (see Table 15.1).

But more significantly, many Canadians received much less than the maximum CPP benefit of $717.08 per month (1996) because they had spent their working lives at jobs that paid less than the average wage. These pensioners, even with OAS/GIS, ended up even further below the poverty line (see Table 15.2).

When average monthly CPP retirement pensions for women are compared with those for men, the situation is even worse. Figure 15.7 reveals this striking gap, which is the product of the disparity in wages and the concentration of women in lower-paid positions and in part-time work – a depressing comment on the state of economic inequality between the

Table 15.1

Retirement incomes of seniors with maximum C/QPP pensions, 1995

	Single person with maximum C/QPP pension ($)	Couple with one spouse with maximum C/QPP pension ($)
Old age security	4,690*	9,381
C/QPP pension	8,558	8,558
Guaranteed income supplement	1,410	3,109
Total income	14,658	21,049
Poverty line for a large city	15,819	21,442

* Figures are rounded to the nearest dollar.
Source: National Council of Welfare, *A Pension Primer: A Report by the National Council of Welfare* (Ottawa: Minister of Supply and Services 1996), 24.

Table 15.2

Retirement incomes of seniors with half the maximum C/QPP pension, 1995

	Single person with half the maximum C/QPP pension ($)	Couple with one spouse with half the maximum C/QPP pension ($)
Old age security	4,690*	9,381
C/QPP pension	4,279	4,279
Guaranteed income supplement	3,498	5,197
Total income	12,467	18,857
Poverty line for a large city	15,819	21,442

* Figures are rounded to the nearest dollar.
Source: National Council of Welfare, *A Pension Primer: A Report by the National Council of Welfare* (Ottawa: Minister of Supply and Services 1996), 25.

sexes in Canada. The basic problem is this: both the CPP and the QPP were designed to replace only 25 per cent of earnings up to the average wage. Thus, even when combined with old age security, this, as the National Council of Welfare has said, 'is not high enough to keep most people out of poverty' (*Pension Primer*, 24). There was not a hint of this situation in the *Information Paper*. All that was offered was a plan for cutting pension benefits, survivors' benefits, drop-out provisions, disability benefits, indexing, and so on, without any analysis of the impact of such cuts on people.

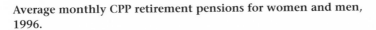

Figure 15.7

Average monthly CPP retirement pensions for women and men, 1996.

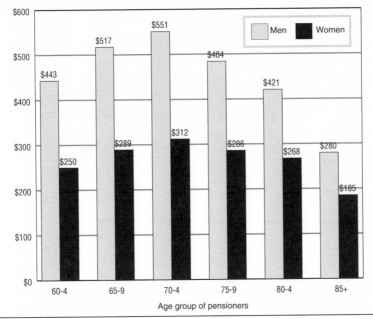

Age group of pensioners

Source: The National Council of Welfare, *A Pension Primer, A Report by the National Council of Welfare, Summer 1996* (Ottawa: Minister of Supply and Services 1996), 27.

The *Information Paper's* suggestion that the retirement age for claiming a pension be raised to sixty-seven from sixty-five is, like so many of its 'choices' for cost-cutting, offered without any context, apart from noting that both the United States and Sweden are moving in this direction. The National Council of Welfare reported a high rate of unemployment among older workers (*Pension Primer*, 30), but recent research into retirement patterns in Canada reveals a new and disturbing trend.[102] Studies have indicated that a majority of Canadians retire before sixty-five, and a growing proportion of those before sixty. These early retirees are sometimes victims of long-term unemployment as retirement is often disguised joblessness; they may be caught by downsizing or plant closings and, for most, have been offered only a minimum of compensation. Some are more fortunate and are offered retirement incentives, but these are a minority.

This situation also helped to account for the surge in disability claims on the CPP over the past decade. The older man or woman who is unemployed may face age discrimination in the search for a new position, and may end up on welfare after unemployment insurance benefits run out. When qualifying conditions for disability benefits were eased in 1987, provincial welfare authorities actively encouraged any older clients with some disabling condition to apply for CPP disability benefits. Private insurance companies did the same shifting of their responsibility on to the public system.[103] The result was that the cost of disability claims rose from less than $1 billion in 1987 to $2.5 billion in 1994. However, in 1995 the rate increase declined for the first time in a decade, due, it was said, to 'toughened eligibility guidelines for new applicants, a tightened appeals process and a systematic approach to reassessing beneficiaries whose medical condition may have improved.'[104] This reversal in the decade-long trend did not stop Ottawa from suggesting a number of cutbacks to disability benefits.[105]

The Disproportionate Effect on Women of the *Information Paper*'s Proposals for Cuts to Benefits

In an unpublished report for the National Action Committee on the Status of Women, Monica Townson[106] cautions that any changes to the CPP must be carefully weighed for their impact on women:

- Women will be hurt more than men by a reduction in retirement benefits. This is because fewer women than men receive company pension benefits and thus rely solely on the public pension system.
- Women would be hurt disproportionately by a move away from full indexing of benefits. Even a small amount of inflation each year means a steady erosion of benefits that are not fully indexed to the cost of living. As women tend to live longer than men and generally have lower pensions, they can ill afford any reduction in the purchasing power of their pensions.
- Women would be hurt by raising the qualifying age for a retirement pension – 'a move in the opposite direction from the preferences of workers,' Townson wrote. If older women lose their jobs, age discrimination will make it difficult for them to find another. For married women, a later retirement age has additional consequences as they tend to withdraw from the labour force at the same time as their spouses, sometimes to care for them as they are generally older.
- Reducing the number of drop-out years would also have disproportionate consequences for women because, in addition to child-rearing, many women now find themselves responsible for the care of elderly relatives as cuts to health and welfare budgets decrease these community services.

The Government's Plan: More Individual Responsibility, Less Collective Responsibility for Old Age Pensions

The government claimed that it was on a rescue mission for the CPP to prevent a 'sustainability crisis.' But others saw the so-called crisis as largely manufactured by fiscal conservatives, within and outside the government, anxious to establish a larger role for the private market in pensions and to reemphasize individual as opposed to collective responsibility for pensions. No doubt there will be those who will categorize such a development as 'modernization' of the social security system. The wringing of hands by the federal finance department over the projected 14.2 per cent combined rate of contribution slated for the year 2030, meaning that the worker and the employer would each contribute 7.1 per cent of insured earnings (a point that the *Information Paper* consistently failed to clarify, leading to the suspicion that this was just one more attempt to panic the public over the amount workers would have to pay), overlooks the fact that the US social insurance program had a 1995 combined contribution rate of 15.3 per cent. Furthermore, in 1991 combined payroll taxes were 26.2 per cent in Italy, 22.9 per cent in Austria, 21.0 per cent in Sweden, 18.8 per cent in the United Kingdom, and 17.8 per cent in Germany, while in Canada the combined rate was 4.6 per cent.[107] Monica Townson argues that the plan to sharply and quickly increase contribution rates is an ideological rather than a fiscal decision. If such a plan is accepted by the provinces, it will move Canada's public pension system closer to the residual private market model.[108]

The Quebec Pension Plan

The QPP underwent a similar reassessment but with less of a sense of 'crisis' and urgency. Quebec officials say that a jump in contribution rates is preferred to other options, such as raising the retirement age, reducing benefits, partial indexing, or abolishing the funeral benefit. As Quebec did not experience the same surge of disability claims (presumably it retained the original qualifying condition for a disability claim – five years of contributions), there is not the same urgency to cut those or other benefits. This interest in preserving benefits is also a testament to the strength of union support for the Parti Québécois.

Quebec Minister of State for Employment and Solidarity Louise Harel said Quebec would have 'no qualms about dealing with the Quebec Pension Plan's projected shortfall [for essentially the same reasons as those given by the *Information Paper* – demographics and a changing economy] in a different manner' from that proposed in the *Information Paper*.[109] However, Quebec strives to maintain compatibility with the CPP in the interests of labour mobility, and up to this point major changes have been accomplished with unanimity.

The Quebec government decided to raise its contribution rate on 1 January 1997 to 6 or 6.1 per cent. It will then hold public consultations during 1997 to have a reformed QPP ready for 1998. One change already suggested is an increase in contribution rates to 10.2 per cent by the year 2004, which is very similar to what Ottawa has in mind. But any new changes, according to Quebec officials, must meet three objectives: they must avoid penalizing current pensioners, aim to establish greater equity between generations, and guarantee that future generations will receive their full benefits.

A Quebec policy paper noted that a number of ideas were being discussed that would increase revenues without cutting benefits, including freezing the year's basic exemption (YBE) at $3,500. Those who earn less than this amount are not required to contribute to the QPP. Freezing the YBE while incomes gradually rise will enrol more workers in the plan, thus increasing the number of contributors. Quebec is also considering gradually eliminating the YBE for higher-income earners. Anyone making more than the average wage ($35,400 in 1996) would pay the contribution rate on the entire year's earnings, rather than the present $35,400 minus the YBE of $3,500.

For workers making less than the average wage, the YBE would be geared to income, an advantage to younger workers. It would be graduated so that lower-income earners would have a larger exemption than higher-wage earners. Thus, for example, someone making only $5,000 a year would have a YBE of $3,335 on eligible earnings; someone making $30,000 would only be allowed a $592 YBE.

Another income-producing measure being considered would be to require anyone receiving a QPP pension while still working to continue paying contributions. Heretofore, contributions stopped at age sixty-five, even if the person was still employed. The QPP is also aiming for 'fuller funding' – that is, a fund equal to six years of benefit payments. The QPP, unlike the CPP, is already more flexible in its investment policy for QPP funds.

Quebec's approach to pension reform reflects a greater concern for protecting current QPP benefits than Ottawa's approach. If the two plans are to remain parallel in terms of benefits, then the pressure will be on Ottawa to moderate its demands for benefit cuts.

A Temporary Halt to Ottawa's Residual Plans for Retirement Pensions

The federal finance minister's proposal to raise significantly the CPP contribution rate, effective 1 January 1997 (to be followed, the federal government hoped, by federal-provincial agreement on a number of reductions in CPP benefits, as well as permitting money from an enlarged pension fund to be invested in the stock market), was short-circuited by Andrew Petter, BC's finance minister, who offered an alternative, *institutional* solution to maintain the CPP's financial integrity. Petter suggested increasing the maximum amount of insured earnings on which contributions are paid. American workers, for example, pay contributions for their equivalent of the CPP on earned income up to $62,700 (as at May 1996). Why should

Canadian maximum insurable earnings be pegged at $35,800? Even employment insurance contributions were collected on earned incomes up to $39,000 (1996). The rationale for setting the CPP's insurable earnings ceiling at $35,800 has been to keep it in line with the 'average industrial wage,' but there is nothing sacrosanct about this formula. Raising the CPP insured earnings ceiling to $50,000 or higher, Petter argued, would contribute financial stability to the pension fund and would permit higher pensions to be paid in the future. As the present federal government, in particular its finance department, has a strong neoconservative bent, there is more interest in promoting *residual*, private market solutions to retirement pensions, and possible *institutional* solutions such as Petter's were never canvassed in the government's *Information Paper*.

As changes to the CPP require only the consent of two-thirds of the provinces containing two-thirds of the population, why did Martin shelve his plan to introduce a steep increase in CPP contributions beginning 1 January 1997? Even though British Columbia had only one potential supporter – Saskatchewan – for its proposal, Ontario wanted to see a large reduction in employment insurance payroll taxes to compensate for the steep increase in CPP contributions. There was also the position of Quebec to be considered. Although Quebec has its own equivalent of the CPP, it also has a vote on any changes to the CPP. The resistance to Martin's plans from British Columbia and Ontario would be tailor-made for the separatist government in Quebec to wring further concessions from the federal government in return for provincial cooperation. This circumstance was altogether out of line with the new spirit of federal-provincial cooperation that Ottawa was attempting to create. Thus, Martin announced that he would not push his plan on the provinces and would work to seek a consensus, but, undoubtedly, with the same end in view.[110]

Dissension over Employment Insurance Contributions

Offsetting the CPP increase to a limited degree was the announced decrease in employment insurance (EI) contributions, effective 1 January 1997, of 5 cents for every $100 in insurable earnings, up to a maximum of $39,000. The savings will amount to about $20 per year for each employee and $27 for employers.

Labour, business, and provincial governments were critical of this reduction. Business groups argued that, in view of the huge surplus in the EI fund (roughly $10 billion by the end of 1996), the deduction in premium rate should have been much more substantial, thus encouraging business to hire more employees. Labour groups were particularly bitter because they claimed that the huge surplus had been taken from the pockets of working Canadians and that some of the fund should be used to raise EI benefits, which have been cut repeatedly over the past decade. The governments of Ontario, Manitoba, Saskatchewan, and British Columbia complained that the cut in EI premiums should have been more substantial to offset further increases expected in CPP contributions. The federal government's position was that the EI surplus (expected to reach $15 billion in 1997) will help to reduce the federal deficit and will act as a buffer 'to mitigate unemployment insurance premium rate increases during periods of slowing economic growth.'[111] As a concession to business, the government offered a two-year premium holiday for small businesses wishing to hire new personnel.

Will Canada's Medicare System Survive?

In August 1995 and again in 1996, the future of medicare was debated at the annual convention of the Canadian Medical Association. A narrow majority of delegates defeated a motion advocating that people be allowed to purchase private insurance to cover all medical services. However, the 1995 meeting did approve the idea of a national debate on the place of private insurance in Canada's system of health care. For many Canadians this was a particularly inane idea, given the fact that we live next door to the United States, the world's leading exponent of private health insurance coverage for its population, and this proximity affords Canadians some knowledge of its costly and inequitable outcomes.[112]

Those in favour of introducing private insurance into medicare (which in Canada would result in what is termed a two-tier system) argue that medicare is financially unsustainable due to the need for more funding (a claim that is hotly disputed) combined with government cuts to health care. These proponents of a *residual* approach to medical care advocate user fees to cut back on frivolous demands on the service, although experience has shown that the principal effect of user fees is to reduce the use of the system by low-income individuals and families. Some hold the extreme view that people should be allowed to buy private insurance for all medical care; but the mainstream, right-wing view appears to be that people should be required to buy insurance for all medical services save those deemed 'core' services, which would be covered by public funding.

Precisely what constitutes a 'core' service has not been identified beyond pointing out that 'non-essential' services – such as the removal of tattoos, cosmetic surgery, or circumcision – should be a private responsibility. What savings would be effected by such a policy? According to health care economist Robert Evans, perhaps one-tenth of 1 per cent of the existing bill.[113] Preston Manning, the federal leader of the Reform Party, who believes that the costs of medicare must be sharply reduced, has said that his party would assure Canadian health services through public funding 'up to some minimal national standard.'[114] Note the word 'minimal.' One can visualize medicare under this approach – amputation of a limb covered by public funds, but not the more expensive option of reconstruction.

Those who support medicare agree that the system is expensive and not as efficient as it could be. A study released in January 1995, which was the first system-wide attempt to evaluate the relationship between health services and outcomes, maintained that savings of up to 15 per cent could be realized without jeopardizing the five basic principles of medicare: universal coverage, accessibility, portability between provinces and territories, comprehensive coverage of services, and a non-profit, public administration. This could be accomplished through such proven strategies as replacing expensive services (such as acute care beds) for less costly services (such as home care) and by a more judicious use of new technology.[115]

British Columbia provides another example of this type of cost-savings by requiring doctors to prescribe only the cheapest product in a given drug category. If doctors wish to prescribe a more expensive drug, they have to justify their choice on medical grounds. The government's rationale for this policy is that there are many versions of the same drug on the market but 'with wildly differing prices.' The BC government will only pay for the cheapest version that is medically effective. Patients who insist on a more expensive brand will have to pay the difference. The government hopes to save $30 million a year.[116]

The drug industry spent $90,000 on advertising to criticize the policy and claimed that it created one standard of medication for the rich and another for the poor. However, all patients face the same stricture. The cheapest medically effective drug will be supplied (in British Columbia senior citizens and low-income people pay only prescription-filling charges). The doctors in each case will have the option of requesting and defending a more expensive substitute.

Perhaps the most significant reductions in health care costs will come with more attention being paid to prevention. In their book *Strong Medicine*, Michael Rachlis and Carol Kushner decry the incidence of child poverty in Canada and note the well-established link between poverty and ill health. Social workers, they point out, should be in the forefront of those calling for preventive measures.[117]

The Liberal government in Ottawa, tilting to the political right, appears to favour a debate on what constitutes a 'core' service. In opening this debate it is preparing the ground for a two-tier system.

The Threat of Two-Tier Medicare

Canadians should be clear as to what two-tier medical care involves. Professor Bob Evans, a health economist, says that the only way a two-tier system could operate without harming the public system and the people who use it would be to have a completely separate but parallel private system, with its own hospitals, doctors, nurses, clinics, etc. No mainstream advocates of a two-tier system, such as the various provincial medical associations and the Canadian Medical Association, propose this because the cost would be prohibitive. Rather, they wish to poach on the public system when it is convenient to do so and use the addition of a relatively small amount of private money to enable their patients, who can afford the extra fee, to jump to the head of whatever line forms in the public system.

As Evans has said, 'When you say "why can't I buy it?" what you are really saying is, "I'll put in a bit of my money and then I'll use a bit of public money, to get ahead of everyone else." You are essentially saying to the doctor, "Great, charge the folks with a bit of extra money and make sure that the people who don't pay extra just don't get as good service..." So when a person says, "Well why shouldn't I pay a little for myself," the answer is because you are going to create a lot of trouble for me and for everybody else by doing it.'[118]

What Is Happening to Jobs?

A number of American analysts have, in this last decade of the twentieth century, raised a troubling view of the world to come.[119] One such analyst, Richard J. Barnet, claims that a worldwide job crisis threatens not only global economic growth but the capitalist system itself: 'Across the planet, the shrinking of opportunities to work for decent pay is a crisis yet to be faced. The problem is starkly simple: an astonishingly large and increasing number of human beings are not needed or wanted to make the goods to provide the services that the paying customers of the world can afford.'[120]

Some economists believe that this economic and social problem will be remedied by what Barnet describes as a technological fix, in line with economist Joseph Schumpeter's theory that capitalism develops by a series of 'gales of creative destruction' in which 'ageing markets, obsolete factories, and unneeded jobs are swept away and replaced by new plants with greater numbers of higher paying jobs producing for bigger markets.' The common example, often cited, is that of the people who once made buggy whips and harnesses becoming auto mechanics and car assembly-line workers, providing steady employment at better rates of pay. These types of standard jobs 'are poignant memories or just dreams for more and more people,' according to Barnet. 'This is true not only in factories but in banks, stores, insurance companies, brokerage houses, law firms, hospitals, and all sorts of other places where services are rendered ... Between 1979 and 1992, the Fortune 500 companies presented 4.4 million of their employees with pink slips, a rate of around 340,000 a year.'

The proposals in *Improving Social Security in Canada* for 'employment development services' and 'lifelong learning' and moving people off welfare and into the workforce reflected the idea that a highly trained and adaptable Canadian workforce will be well situated to take advantage of the next technological wave. But Barnet argues that because automation is increasingly displacing workers, even in new industries, the job prospects are dismal. 'Biotechnology, on which great hopes are pinned, is anything but labor intensive. Amgen, the largest biotechnology company, employs a mere 2,639 people.' Countering the idea that a trained workforce is a solution, Barnet argues that countries all over the globe are turning out highly skilled workers who will be just as capable (as Canadians) of filling technological niches.

Furthermore, a 1995 report by the ILO on world unemployment reports that 820 million people are unemployed and underemployed, creating 'the worst situation since the Great Depression.' Prospects for job growth are gloomy worldwide, including Canada. Based upon the Liberal government's fiscal and economic policies, the ILO predicts an unemployment rate of 11.5 per cent in Canada by the year 2000. The solutions, the ILO says, will not be found through nations competing with each other but through global cooperation.

Barnet agrees with this position and cites other American analysts who suggest that the application of Keynesian full-employment policies on a global level needs to be considered. In any case, he says, 'there are no national solutions to the job crisis. Coordinated strategies at the global level are needed to promote the sort of world economic growth that avoids flooding the planet with goods and services far in excess of what people want or the planet can afford.'

The increasing shortage of conventional employment can be offset by doing the things that are necessary and worthwhile. We would all have our own lists, but Barnet's ideas are a start: 'Building decent places to live, exploring the universe, making cities less dangerous, teaching one another, raising our children, visiting, comforting, healing, feeding one another, dancing, making music, telling stories, inventing things, and governing ourselves.'

The challenge, Barnet points out, is to package these essential and life-affirming activities as 'jobs.' And if we did live in communities where we visited, comforted, and healed one another, what would be the shape of social security then?

Some Long- and Short-Term Predictions
In the long term, if the job market erodes to the extent that Barnet, Rifkin, and others predict, the social insurances will have had their day, because they will have lost their supporting framework of long-term jobs and payroll taxes. What then? One possibility is a return to a *residual* form of social security where people, by and large, will be expected to provide for themselves, with a high probability that the wretchedness and misery of early industrial society will be repeated. On the other hand, society might opt for an *institutional* approach and fashion some type of universal income

guarantee that, unlike social insurance, would not be based on the individual's demonstrated contribution to the GNP but would be provided as a right of citizenship to ensure that all are included in society and enabled to play their part in its further development.

In addition, we might meet the challenge posed by Barnet and find a way to package essential, life-affirming activities as 'jobs.' A Quebec policy analyst has already written about the employment potential in the 'third sector' – work being carried out by voluntary enterprises, as distinct from public or private enterprise.[121]

The only remaining long-range prediction that it seems prudent to make, in the face of such dramatic social and economic predictions, is that in moving into a world of massive joblessness, we will need to emphasize the values of cooperation and solidarity over those of competition and individual responsibility.

Renewing the Fight to Eliminate Child Poverty

Given the cutbacks to social programs and the rising unemployment and underemployment, it came as no surprise that the incidence of child poverty in Canada had increased from 14.5 per cent in 1989 to approximately 21.3 per cent in 1993 – about one in five children. Furthermore, in Metropolitan Toronto, Canada's largest city, the incidence of child poverty in 1996 had reached an alarming 36 per cent.[122] However, even this deplorable statistic was dwarfed by the *Report of the Royal Commission on Aboriginal Peoples*, released in November 1996, which reported that half of Native children lived in poverty.[123]

When the House of Commons, in November 1989, unanimously passed a resolution 'to seek to achieve the goal of eliminating poverty among Canadian children by the year 2000,' a coalition of social groups banded together as Campaign 2000 to hold the government to its promise. In the run up to the 1997 federal election, Campaign 2000 has released a plan to radically reduce the incidence of child poverty as part of a more comprehensive family policy.

An Investment Fund for Children

Campaign 2000 proposed the establishment of a national fund for the healthy development of all Canadian children, equal to 2 to 2.2 per cent of Canada's gross domestic product, which in 1996 approached $842 billion. The fund would be built up over a five-year period by earmarked taxes on personal income and on businesses and corporations.[124] In terms of programs, Campaign 2000 proposed

- a basic child benefit of $4,200 per annum, which would be approximately four times the existing federal child benefit. Depending on its

design, the program would cost up to $18.5 billion per year, or $13 billion more than was currently being spent on the federal child benefit. A minimum beginning to the enhanced child benefit, as visualized by Campaign 2000, would require an additional $2 billion expenditure. If these figures appear excessive, consider the fact that Canada spends $35 billion per year on OAS and the CPP.
- a supplement for single parents caring full-time for children.
- a comprehensive early childhood and day care program.
- a system to ensure child support payments are received regularly, with a government agency making the payment in cases of default and assuming responsibility for collecting the arrears.
- a youth endowment program that would provide $5,000 per year for up to five years for college and university students. This grant would be subject to a family income test.

A More Pragmatic Approach

The Caledon Institute for Social Policy proposed an integrated federal-provincial child benefit with a dual purpose: not only to direct a more adequate child benefit to all low-income families, both welfare recipients and the working poor, but in so doing 'take children off welfare' and begin a much-needed reform of provincial social assistance programs.[125] The integrated benefit would combine the existing federal child benefit and the provincial payments made on behalf of children in welfare families. Caledon recommended a combined benefit of $3,000 for the first child, $2,500 for the second child, and $2,000 for each additional child in the family. All benefits would be fully indexed to the cost of living, unlike the existing system of federal benefits that is only partially indexed. Provincial welfare benefits are seldom indexed.

Caledon's recommended benefit levels are superior to the existing federal benefits of $1,233 per annum per child under seven and $1,020 per child aged seven to seventeen. Single-parent families would be eligible for an additional $1,400 per annum to replace the equivalent-to-married federal tax credit. In the interest of cost containment, this proposal would also require that the income ceiling below which maximum benefits would be paid be substantially lowered from that currently employed by the federal child benefit, and that the rate at which benefits are retrieved from income above the maximum income ceiling be substantially raised.[126] In other words, this program would be closely targeted to the most needy among low-income families. The additional cost of the integrated benefit was estimated at $2 billion.

There appears to be little chance of Campaign 2000 winning the government's approval for its European-style family policy proposals and the consequent increase in social spending. The Liberal government's first priority since gaining power in 1993 has been deficit reduction, based upon the hotly disputed theory that the cost of government generally, and of social programs in particular, have been the prime cause of the deficit.[127] However, with the government facing an election in 1997, the first priority becomes the retention of office; therefore, some limited relaxation of the purse strings for a variety of social and political purposes – child poverty, youth unemployment, additional tax credits for the disabled, an infrastructure program, and perhaps, fulfilling part of a promise made in 1993, some additional funds for day care – will no doubt take place. The Caledon Institute's spare, North American style of proposal for an integrated benefit may begin with a 'down payment' of from $500 to $600 million.

The new minister of human resources development, Pierre Pettigrew, who replaced Doug Young in October 1996, will have his leadership abilities tested in devising an integrated benefit system that will be acceptable to all the provinces. British Columbia already operates an integrated child benefit system with Ottawa by adding up to $103 per month, per child, for low-income families, with the cheque for the combined benefit coming from Ottawa. After provincial ministers responsible for social assistance met with Pettigrew in early 1997, it was reported that the provinces favoured an integrated benefit that would be administered by them, under 'broad national guidelines.'[128]

What Will Be Our Legacy to the Twenty-First Century?

The Canadian welfare state at the end of the twentieth century stands shakily on the crumbling foundations of large-scale unemployment and underemployment. It has also been battered by unthinking cuts to social programs that have contributed so much to Canada's standard of living. The problem of government deficits has been blamed almost solely on social program spending, yet a blind eye has been turned toward overly (some would say scandalously) generous tax treatment of corporations and wealthy individuals and families.[129]

The welfare state's achievements over the decades since the Second World War have few defenders and innumerable critics from every point on the political spectrum. The difficulty with some of these criticisms is that they often fail to distinguish between the solid advances in social security, such as the substantial drop in the poverty rate among Canada's elderly,[130] and the remnants of the nineteenth-century poor law that we inherited and that still linger. In this respect, one can point to provincial needs-tested social assistance programs, 'workfare' schemes, British Columbia's three-month residence qualification for social assistance applicants who are from out of province, and the ubiquitous food banks, the last word in nineteenth-century paternalism.

Looking back, it seems a little strange to recall that during the 1960s, students of Canadian social policy thought they were leaving the residual model of social welfare behind, to moulder quietly along with the Houses of Industry, Single Men's Relief Departments, work camps for the unemployed, orphanages, soup kitchens, and charity wards in hospitals. While humiliating conditions for the receipt of social assistance benefits remained, even these were thought to be on their way out when experimental programs for a guaranteed annual income were established in the 1970s. Now, two or three decades later, residual forces are rampaging through the country. Cuts to services, if not outright elimination, appear to be the order of the day.

Will Canada's one remaining universal program – medicare – be this century's bequest to the twenty-first century? Although under serious threat, public support remains so strong that all political parties have claimed to be its defender. It is therefore likely to be in place in 2001, and it will make a handsome gift.

Appendixes

Total expenditures on health and social welfare, by level of government, selected fiscal years, 1913-83

Fiscal year	Federal	Provincial	Municipal	Total
	($ millions)			
1913	2.7	4.3	8.2	15.2
1920-1	58.6	22.8	18.8	100.2
1926-7	22.8	18.8	20.7	99.0
1930-1	73.0	52.2	31.5	156.8
1933-4	97.5	75.9	57.1	230.5
1937-8	127.4	127.8	54.4	309.6
1938-9	132.3	123.2	51.6	307.1
1939-40	154.1	114.3	48.9	317.2
1940-1	124.2	87.3	43.6	255.1
1942-3	102.7	89.0	38.3	230.0
1945-6	410.6	120.5	42.6	573.8
1947-8	569.5	179.3	44.8	793.5
1949-50	738.8	274.9	47.4	1,061.1
1951-2	843.0	327.6	59.6	1,230.2
1953-4	1,208.8	386.4	78.4	1,673.7
1955-6	1,346.9	463.3	97.1	1,907.3
1957-8	1,755.1	572.1	112.6	2,439.8
1960-1	2,362.1	885.7	109.0	2,256.8
1962-3	2,683.5	1,097.7	117.3	3,895.5
1964-5	2,969.7	1,376.1	108.2	4,454.0
1966-7	3,243.1	2,017.7	130.0	5,390.8
1968-9	4,450.0	2,725.0	145.0	7,320.0
1969-70	5,190.8	2,943.7	189.6	8,324.2
1970-1	6,278.8	3,443.6	224.0	9,946.6
1971-2	7,230.6	3,971.3	200.8	11,402.8

[continued on next page]

Table A1 [continued]

Fiscal year	Federal	Provincial	Municipal	Total
		($ millions)		
1971-2	7,230.6	3,971.3	200.8	11,402.8
1972-3	8,027.1	4,714.3	273.4	14,014.8
1973-4	10,423.3	5,425.5	231.8	16,080.6
1974-5	12,954.5	6,835.5	286.3	20,076.3
1975-6	15,863.5	8,363.3	373.7	24,600.6
1976-7	17,505.8	9,603.3	427.2	27,536.4
1977-8	20,632.3	10,496.5	449.5	30,978.5
1978-9	22,835.0	11,259.4	501.0	34,572.0
1979-80	24,147.3	12,446.3	651.8	37,245.5
1980-1	27,690.0	15,192.3	736.8	43,646.2
1981-2	31,778.8	17,952.7	893.1	50,624.7
1982-3	40,080.1	20,645.8	763.7	61,489.7

Notes: The term 'health and social welfare' covers all the social security programs discussed in this book with the exception of housing. It also includes certain program costs that have not been discussed — veterans' pension (apart from War Veterans' Allowances) and payments under the Prairie Farm Assistance Act (1939) to farmers in years of crop failure.

From the year 1965-6 on, figures for provincial expenditures include total Quebec expenditures under the shared-cost programs that are now financed partly through tax abatements and adjustment grants under the Special Programs (Interim Arrangements) Act of 1965. These payments are no longer shown as federal expenditures on health and social welfare.

Sources: Government Expenditures on Health and Social Welfare, Canada 1927-1959, Social Security Series, Memorandum no. 16, Table 14, 41; *Brief to the Special Senate Committee on Poverty* by the Department of National Health and Welfare, Table 4, 82; M.C. Urquhart and K.A.H. Buckley, *Historical Statistics* (Toronto: Macmillan 1965), 53. The figures for the years 1969-70 to 1982-3 are supplied through the courtesy of the Department of National Health and Welfare.

Table A2

**Annual average percentage change in the consumer price index
over the previous year, 1915-95**

Year	Percentage change	Year	Percentage change
1915	1.7	1956	1.5
1916	8.5	1957	3.2
1917	18.2	1958	1.7
1918	13.3	1959	1.0
1919	9.8	1960	1.4
1920	15.8	1961	.9
1921	-12.0	1962	1.2
1922	- 8.4	1963	1.7
1923	.2	1964	1.8
1924	- 1.8	1965	2.4
1925	.9	1966	3.7
1926	1.1	1967	3.6
1927	- 1.6	1968	4.0
1928	.2	1969	4.6
1929	1.2	1970	3.3
1930	- .7	1971	2.9
1931	- 9.6	1972	4.8
1932	- 9.1	1973	7.5
1933	- 4.9	1974	10.9
1934	1.8	1975	10.8
1935	.6	1976	7.5
1936	2.0	1977	8.0
1937	3.1	1978	9.0
1938	1.1	1979	9.2
1939	- .8	1980	10.2
1940	4.1	1981	12.5
1941	5.8	1982	10.8
1942	4.7	1983	5.8
1943	1.7	1984	4.4
1944	.7	1985	3.9
1945	.5	1986	4.2
1946	3.4	1987	4.4
1947	9.3	1988	4.0
1948	14.4	1989	5.0
1949	3.0	1990	4.8
1950	2.9	1991	5.6
1915	1.6	1992	1.5
1952	2.4	1993	1.8
1953	1.1	1994	0.2
1954	.6	1995	2.1
1955	.1		

Source: Statistics Canada, *The Consumer Price Index, July 1996*, Cat. 62-001, Table 4, 18.
1981 = 100.

Table A3

Total social security expenditures in Canada for all levels of government, analyzed by selected socioeconomic indicators for fiscal years ending March 31, 1958-9 to 1982-3

Year	Total social security expenditures[a]	GNP	Total current government expenditures[b]	Social security expenditures analyzed		
				Per $100 of GNP	Per $100 of total current government expenditures	Per capita
	($ millions)					
1982-3	61,490	363,815	165,002	16.90	37.27	2,475.13
1981-2	50,632	345,775	142,351	14.64	35.57	2,059.96
1980-1	43,646	308,080	120,656	14.17	36.17	1,796.96
1979-80	37,246	273,398	102,414	13.62	36.37	1,552.87
1978-9	34,572	238,908	91,506	14.47	37.78	1,458.68
1977-8	30,979	215,259	82,157	14.39	37.71	1,319.92
1976-7	27,536	196,626	72,550	14.00	37.96	1,185.74
1975-6	24,601	171,922	64,415	14.31	38.19	1,072.11
1974-5	20,076	151,880	53,251	13.22	37.70	886.81
1973-4	16,081	129,364	42,619	12.43	37.73	720.88
1972-3	14,015	109,251	37,057	12.83	37.82	637.18
1971-2	11,403	97,129	32,490	11.74	35.10	524.05
1970-1	9,947	87,166	28,755	11.41	34.59	462.14
1969-70	8,324	81,369	25,081	10.23	33.19	391.84
1968-9	7,299	74,618	22,153	9.78	32.95	348.41

[continued on next page]

Table A3 [continued]

Year	Total social security expenditures[a]	GNP	Total current government expenditures[b]	Social security expenditures analyzed		
				Per $100 of GNP	Per $100 of total current government expenditures	Per capita
	($ millions)					
1967-8	6,374	67,614	19,434	9.43	32.80	308.76
1966-7	5,329	62,975	16,871	8.46	31.58	262.41
1965-6	4,687	57,061	14,550	8.21	32.21	235.08
1964-5	4,311	51,377	13,185	8.39	32.70	220.22
1963-4	3,962	47,068	12,243	8.42	32.36	206.11
1962-3	3,799	43,521	11,393	8.73	33.34	201.36
1961-2	3,569	40,644	10,775	8.78	33.13	192.74
1960-1	3,286	38,290	10,027	8.58	32.77	180.83
1959-60	3,010	37,452	9,266	8.04	32.49	169.18
1958-9	2,779	35,368	8,696	7.86	31.96	159.68

[a] Total social security expenditures (column 2) are based on individual program information contained in this report, some of which is based on the Financial Management Statistics System from Statistics Canada. Total current government expenditures (column 4) are based on the Statistics Canada System of National Accounts. As a result of the conceptual differences between the two accounting systems, column 7 (derived from columns 2 and 4) should only be used as a rough indicator of trends.

[b] Total current government expenditures (column 4) exclude intergovernmental transfers.

Table A4

Federal social policy tax expenditures, 1992 estimates

	Federal	Federal/Provincial
	($ millions)	
Deductions		
RPP contributions	4,789	7,423
RRSP contributions	3,660	5,673
Non-tax. of RPP interest	9,611	14,896
Non-tax. of RRSP interest	3,273	5,073
Less tax. of withdrawals RPP	4,327	6,707
Less tax. of withdrawals RRSP	813	1,260
Child care expenses	363	563
Treatment of alimony and maintenance payments	437	677
Non-refundable credits		
Age	1,484	2,301
Married	1,147	1,776
Equivalent to married	602	634
Dependent child	405	628
C/QPP contributions	907	1,408
UI premiums	1,145	1,774
Pension income	312	484
Disability	342	530
Medical	232	360
Charitable donations	876	1,358
Tuition fee credit	155	241
Education credit	95	54
Education and tuition fees transferred	147	228
Refundable credits		
Child	2,473	2,473
GST	2,500	2,500
Non-taxation of		
Employer-paid premiums to health plan	906	1,405
GIS and SPA benefits	240	372
Welfare payments	350	543
Workers' compensation payments	767	1,188
Employer-paid premiums for group life insurance	172	266
Veterans' allowances, pensions	27	42

[continued on next page]

Table A4 [continued]

	Federal	Federal/Provincial
	($ millions)	
Veterans' disability pensions	167	258
Employer-paid UI benefits	2,309	3,578
Employer-paid C/QPP premiums	1,189	1,843
RCMP pension/compensation for injury, disability, or death	8	12
Exemption on first $500 of scholarship	7	11
Total social tax spending	36,137	53,278

Sources: Caledon Institute of Social Policy, December 1994; and Canada, *Report of the Standing Committee on Human Resources Development, Security, Opportunities and Fairness: Canadians Renewing Their Social Programs* (Ottawa 1995), 239-40.

Table A5

Selected corporate income tax subsidies, 1989-90

	Cost to Canada ($ millions)	
Item	1989	1990
Reduced tax rate on first $200,000 of profit	2,600	2,100
Reduced tax rate on manufacturing and processing	278	315
Tax credit for scientific research and experimental development	450	548
Partial exclusion of capital gains	1,400	417
Fast write-off for Canadian development expenses	142	156
Fast write-off for Canadian exploration expenses	343	446
Exemption from withholding tax for interest on foreign currency deposits	530	505
Non-taxation of life insurance companies' world profits	100	65
Deductions for meals and entertainment expenses	450	357
Deduction for charitable contributions	82	89
Political contribution tax credit	not reported	not reported
Exemption on tax from international banking centres	not reported	not reported
Deduction of lobbying expenses	not reported	not reported

Source: Ontario Federation of Labour and the Ontario Coalition for Social Justice, *Unfair Shares: Corporations and Taxation in Canada* (Don Mills 1994).

Table A6

Federal, provincial/territorial, and local government expenditures on health[a] and social services[b] for selected fiscal years, 1983-4 to 1995-6

	1983-4	1985-6	1987-8	1989-90	1990-1	1991-2	1992-3	1993-4	1994-5	1995-6
					($ millions)					
Federal										
Health	6,197	7,134	7,462	7,780	7,444	8,048	9,770	8,331	8,895	8,286
Social services	31,778	34,445	37,887	43,210	48,970	55,271	58,869	59,459	57,050	57,276
					($ millions)					
Provincial/ territorial										
Health	22,972	26,471	30,876	37,138	40,128	44,907	44,907	44,925	45,180	n/a[c]
Social services	13,626	15,673	18,7189	21,052	23,891	32,929	32,929	33,916	34,560	
	1983	1985	1987	1989	1990	1991	1992	1993	1994	
					($)					
Local										
Health	2,200,298	2,243,727	2,816,227	2,104,363	3,346,320	3,453,08?	3,567,621	3,662,132	3,577,672	
Social services	1,303,040	1,493,062	1,905,064	2,347,531	2,922,182	4,189,98?	4,924,863	5,437,574	5,570,704	

[a] Health expenditures cover hospital and medical care, preventive care, and related functions.

[continued on next page]

Table A6 [continued]

b   Social services cover eight functions of government, including contributory and non-contributory income-protection plans (C/QPP and old age security); labour force plans such as employment insurance and workers' compensation; family allowances, prior to their termination in 1993, including Quebec's provincial system of family allowances; veterans' benefits; social welfare benefits and services; tax credits and rebates; rebates to home owners to offset municipal taxes; rebates to elderly or disabled people; plus a number of smaller programs. See Statistics Canada, *The System of Government Management* (Ottawa: Minister of Supply and Services 1944), 76-8.

c   As there was no Ontario budget in the spring of 1995, compilation of the 1995-6 data for Ontario and the Canada total was not possible.

Sources: Statistics Canada, *Public Sector Finance, 1995/96* (Ottawa: Ministry of Industry 1996), Cat. 68-212, Table 1.28, 114, and Table 1.32, 166; and *Public Finance, Historical Data 1965/1966-1991/1992* (Ottawa: Minister of Industry, Science and Technology 1992), Cat. 68-512, Table H4, 56-7.

Notes

Preface to the Third Edition

1 See the comments of Edward Luttwak in 'Does America Still Work?' *Harper's Magazine*, May 1996, 35-47. Luttwak, a fellow at the Center for Strategic and International Studies in Washington, DC, along with five other experts discussed the impact of corporations laying off thousands of workers. He noted that the United States was 'rich in GNP but poor in tranquillity' (38), and despite the increase in the value of his shares, he said, 'I would rather earn less, a little less, and be able to park my car without having to fear that I will be murdered' (46).

2 Canada's largest cable company had a policy of adding extra channels to a subscriber's cable service without being asked to do so. Unless subscribers specifically requested not to receive the additional services, they would be billed for them. In 1995 subscribers rebelled en masse, and the company was forced into a public apology and a cessation of its so-called 'negative billing' practice.

3 Frank J. Tester and Peter Kulchyski, *Tammarniit (Mistakes): Inuit Relocation in the Eastern Arctic 1929-63* (Vancouver: UBC Press 1994).

Preface to the Second Edition

1 William H. Beveridge, *Pillars of Security and Other War-Time Essays and Addresses* (London: Allen and Unwin 1943), 98.

Preface to the First Edition

1 Richard M. Titmuss, *Essays on 'The Welfare State'* (London: George Allen and Unwin 1958), 43.

2 In the following discussion on risks to income security and forms of government action to offset them, I wish to acknowledge my debt to Eveline M. Burns, *Social Security and Public Policy* (New York: McGraw-Hill 1956), and L.C. Marsh, *Report on Social Security for Canada*, prepared for the Advisory Committee on Reconstruction (1943; reprint, Toronto: University of Toronto Press 1974).

3 A white paper issued in 1945 committed the federal government to ensuring a high and stable level of income and employment after the war. See Canada, Department of Reconstruction, *Employment and Income with Special Reference to the Initial Period of Reconstruction* (Ottawa 1945).

Chapter 1: The Emergence of Social Security in Canada

1 In the following discussion of the residual and institutional concepts of social welfare, I have made free use of the insights into social welfare history developed by Harold Wilensky and Charles Lebeaux, *Industrial Society and Social Welfare* (New York: Russell Sage Foundation 1958).

2 Richard M. Titmuss, *Commitment to Welfare* (London: George Allen and Unwin 1968), 233.

3 An exponent of these views in Canada is Morris C. Shumiatcher, *Welfare: Hidden Backlash* (Toronto: McClelland and Stewart 1971).

4 L.C. Marsh, 'The Welfare State: Is It a Threat to Canada?' *Proceedings of the Canadian Conference on Social Work* (Ottawa: Canadian Conference on Social Work 1950), 35. See also his excellent discussion of this concept in *Social Welfare and the Preservation of Human Values*, ed. W. Dixon (Vancouver: J.M. Dent and Sons 1957), 37-9.

5 See Chapter 3 for a fuller discussion of this point.

6 John Morgan, 'Social Welfare Services in Canada,' in *Social Purpose for Canada*, ed. M. Oliver (Toronto: University of Toronto Press 1961), 133.

7 Canada, *Report of the Royal Commission on Dominion-Provincial Relations, Book I, Canada: 1867-1939* (Ottawa 1940), 37.

8 Maurice Bruce, *The Coming of the Welfare State* (London: B.T. Batsford 1961), Chapters 3 and 4.

9 In the discussion of the division of powers under the BNA Act and their interpretation by the Judicial Committee of the Privy Council, I am indebted to R.M. Dawson, *The Government of Canada* (Toronto: University of Toronto Press 1962), Chapter 5.

Chapter 2: The Colonial Inheritance

1 The final enactment of a poor law in Elizabeth's reign took place in 1601. But the legislation of 1601 was, for all intents and purposes, a reenactment of legislation deliberated upon and passed three years earlier in 1598. The 1598 statute, the Act for the Relief of the Poore, consolidated and extended poor laws that had been passed earlier in the sixteenth century. The 1598 legislation, with some minor modifications, was reenacted in 1601. See Maurice Bruce, *The Coming of the Welfare State* (London: B.T. Batsford 1961), 20.

2 The poor law of 1598 also emphasized family responsibility – the responsibility of parents to care for their children, for older children to contribute to the care of their parents, and in the final enactment of the poor law in 1601, family responsibility was extended to include grandparents (ibid., 21).

3 See Brian Inglis, *Poverty and the Industrial Revolution* (London: Hodder and Stoughton 1971), 259-67, 352-60; Karl de Schweinitz, *England's Road to Social Security* (New York: A.S. Barnes 1948), 167-8; and Maurice Bruce, *Coming of the Welfare State*, 38-9.

4 For descriptions of English workhouses, see Bruce, *Coming of the Welfare State*, 91-2, and de Schweinitz, *England's Road*, Chapter 7. For descriptions of Canadian counterparts in the colonial period, see J.M. Whalen, 'The Nineteenth Century Almshouse System in St. John County,' *Histoire sociale/Social History* 7 (April 1971):5-27; and Brereton Greenhous, 'Paupers and Poorhouses: The Development of Poor Relief in Early New Brunswick,' *Histoire sociale/Social History* 1 (April 1968):103-28.

5 In the eighteenth century, for example, the citizens of Halifax complained that they were called upon to support more than their share of transient poor from outlying districts as well as having to assist impoverished immigrants who landed in that port city. Accordingly, they received financial help from the colonial government to assist in what was seen as an out-of-the-ordinary situation. See Relief Williams, 'Poor Relief and Medicine in Nova Scotia, 1749-1783,' *Collections of the Nova Scotia Historical Society* 24 (1938):33-56.

6 James M. Whalen, 'Social Welfare in New Brunswick, 1784-1900,' *Acadiensis* 2 (autumn 1972):55-6.

7 For a description of early poor relief practices in Nova Scotia, New Brunswick, and Newfoundland, see Judith Fingard, 'The Relief of the Unemployed Poor in Saint John, Halifax, and St. John's, 1815-60,' *Acadiensis* 5 (autumn 1972):32-54.

8 James M. Whalen, 'Social Welfare in New Brunswick,' 60. Whalen also notes that the general mixed almshouse 'was still very much in evidence in many parts of New Brunswick as late as 1949.'

9 K. Grant Crawford, *Canadian Municipal Government* (Toronto: University of Toronto Press 1968), 39; and Harry M. Cassidy, *Public Health and Welfare Organization in Canada* (Toronto: Ryerson Press 1945), 434.

10 Crawford, *Canadian Municipal Government*, 40; Fingard, 'Relief of the Unemployed Poor,'

33; Judith Fingard, 'The Winter's Tale: Contours of Pre-Industrial Poverty in British America, 1815-1860,' in Canadian Historical Association, *Historical Papers, 1974* (Ottawa 1974), 76; and Peter Neary, '"Traditional" and "Modern" Elements in the Social and Economic History of Bell Island and Conception Bay,' in Canadian Historical Association, *Historical Papers, 1973* (Ottawa 1973), 124.

11 Richard Splane, *Social Welfare in Ontario, 1791-1893* (Toronto: University of Toronto Press 1965), Chapter 3.

12 Ibid., 68.

13 The governors of New France 'took the initiative in paying for the maintenance of foundlings, the control of begging, and the organization of temporary relief committees to give assistance in emergencies, but other matters were left in the hands of the Church.' Elizabeth S.L. Govan, 'The Social Services,' in *Canada,* ed. George W. Brown (Berkeley and Los Angeles: University of California Press 1950), 390. See as well Allana G. Reed, 'The First Poor-Relief System of Canada,' *Canadian Historical Review* 37 (1946):424-31. Reed says 'The church may have supplied hospitals and schools but it was the laymen of Quebec who first took active steps to cope with the needs of the poor' (431).

14 Fingard, 'Winter's Tale,' 76.

15 Ibid. It should also be noted that under British rule no attempt was made to introduce the English poor law into Lower Canada, and the Catholic church continued to expand its activities in the social welfare area. See Govan, 'Social Services,' 390.

16 British North America Act, 1867, British Statutes, 30 Victoria, Chapter 3, Section 92 (7).

17 A. Milton Moore and J. Harvey Perry, Tax Paper no. 6, *Financing Canadian Federation* (Toronto: Canadian Tax Foundation 1953), 5.

18 This latter statement requires some qualification. Harry M. Cassidy noted that Alberta and British Columbia, although not having a poor law, made 'suitable provision for the poor' an obligation of the municipality. See Cassidy, *Public Health and Welfare Reorganization in Canada* (Toronto: Ryerson Press 1945), 44. Richard Splane's *Social Welfare in Ontario* indicates that the Municipal Institutions Act of 1866 made it mandatory for all counties with a population exceeding 20,000 inhabitants to establish a poorhouse within two years (75). Smaller counties were urged to pool their resources and share in the operation of a poorhouse. However, this mandatory provision was removed shortly after Confederation, and the establishment of county poorhouses became *permissible* within four years (80). The movement for a greater measure of public provision for the poor was consequently stillborn.

19 Fingard, 'Winter's Tale,' 76-7.

20 Fingard, 'Relief of the Unemployed Poor,' 35.

21 Ibid.

22 W.L. Morton, 'Victorian Canada,' in *The Shield of Achilles,* ed. W.L. Morton (Toronto: McClelland and Stewart 1968), 312.

23 Fingard, 'Winter's Tale,' 73.

24 Ibid., 68.

25 Fingard, 'Relief of the Unemployed Poor,' 33. Sometimes the immigrant from overseas caused fear and dissension, as in the case of Irish famine immigrants in the 1840s. See G.J. Parr, 'The Welcome and the Wake: Attitudes in Canada West toward the Irish Famine Migration,' *Ontario History* 66 (June 1974):101-13.

26 Parr, 'Welcome and the Wake,' 32.

27 Taken from a report prepared by a committee of the Legislative Assembly, Province of Canada (1849), and cited in Laurence S. Fallis, 'The Idea of Progress in the Province of Canada: A Study in the History of Ideas,' in *Shield of Achilles,* 179. The problem of alcoholism was very real nonetheless, owing to the availability of cheap spirits. Canadians at this time had an unenviable reputation for heavy drinking.

28 Louis Hartz, *The Liberal Tradition in America* (New York: Harcourt, Brace 1955).

29 For example, Kenneth D. McRae, 'The Structure of Canadian History,' in *The Founding of New Societies,* ed. Louis Hartz (New York: Harcourt, Brace, and World 1964).

30 Gad Horowitz, 'Conservatism, Liberalism and Socialism in Canada: An Interpretation,' *Canadian Journal of Economics and Political Science* 32 (1966):143. See as well, by the same

author, *Canadian Labour in Politics* (Toronto: University of Toronto Press 1968), Chapter 1.
31 Arthur R.M. Lower, *Canadians in the Making: A Social History of Canada* (Toronto: Longmans, Green 1958), 96.
32 Horowitz, *Canadian Labour in Politics*, 12.
33 William Christian and Colin Campbell, *Political Parties and Ideologies in Canada* (Toronto: McGraw-Hill Ryerson 1974), 26.

Chapter 3: Saving for a Rainy Day

1 Donald Creighton, *Canada's First Century* (Toronto: Macmillan 1970), 24.
2 In 1871 there were only nineteen urban centres in Canada with a population of over 5,000. By 1891 the number was forty-four, by 1911 seventy-six. Leroy O. Stone, *Urban Development in Canada* (Ottawa: DBS 1967), 69, Table 4.1.
3 Canada, *Report of the Royal Commission on the Relations of Labor and Capital in Canada* (Ottawa 1889), 87 (hereafter cited as the Labor Commission).
4 J.S. Woodsworth, *My Neighbor* (1911; reprint, Toronto: University of Toronto Press 1972), 18.
5 For a brief extract of the 1882 report, see Michael Cross, ed., *The Workingman in the Nineteenth Century* (Toronto: Oxford University Press 1974), 74. Note that in a survey of 465 mills and factories, 173 children under ten were recorded as employees and over 2,000 between the ages of ten and fourteen.
6 Unions were legalized in 1872 by the Canadian Trade Unions Act. It applied only to those trade unions and their members properly registered with the Registrar General of Canada. Unregistered trade unions might still be prosecuted as conspiracies. Accompanying this act was another that weakened its effect – the Criminal Law Amendment Act, 1872, modelled on a British law that made picketing illegal, thus seriously limiting union action. In 1876 this act was repealed, and peaceful picketing became legal. J.E. Cameron and F.J. Young, *The Status of Trade Unions in Canada* (Kingston: Jackson Press 1960), 29.
7 Greg Kealey, ed., *Canada Investigates Industrialism* (Toronto: University of Toronto Press 1973), ix. I am indebted to Kealey's introduction to his abridged version of the royal commission reports and evidence for the following discussion.
8 Ibid., xviii.
9 Labor Commission, *Second Report*, 89. See as well Kealey, *Canada Investigates Industrialism*, 110-11.
10 Labor Commission, *Second Report*, 91.
11 Kealey, *Canada Investigates Industrialism*, 408.
12 Ibid., 105.
13 Labor Commission, *First Report*, 8, and Appendix A, 17.
14 Labor Commission, *Second Report*, 78-9.
15 Ibid., 117.
16 Labor Commission, *First Report*, 8.
17 Labor Commission, *Second Report*, 116.
18 Labor Commission, *First Report*, 8.
19 Ibid., 29.
20 Labor Commission, *Second Report*, 84.
21 For a more complete discussion on workers' compensation legislation, see the next chapter.
22 Kealey, *Canada Investigates Industrialism*, 181.
23 Ibid., 198.
24 Ibid., 204.
25 Ibid., 429.
26 Labor Commission, *Second Report*, 82. For references to union benefit schemes in evidence presented to the commission, see Kealey, *Canada Investigates Industrialism*, 140, 150, 191, 278-9.
27 Kealey, *Canada Investigates Industrialism*, 414, and the Labor Commission, *First Report*, Table of Wages, 187.
28 Labor Commission, *First Report*, Appendix C. The employees had no voice in the operation of the benefit society.

29 Labor Commission, *First Report,* 13.
30 See Kealey, *Canada Investigates Industrialism,* xx. In addition to the recommendations already noted with regard to annuities and the sanitary inspection of houses, the *First Report* also recommended that a government-operated scheme of insurance be instituted to protect the heirs of persons killed in industrial accidents and that the government also invite tenders from private insurance companies to provide insurance for work-related injuries. The commissioners called for improved safety measures for the workforce, particularly on the railroads and Great Lakes shipping. They recommended that factories be inspected more thoroughly and regularly and that only certified engineers be permitted to operate steam boilers. The commissioners recommended that the punishment of child employees by foremen be made a criminal offence; that the system of fining employees be prohibited; and that hours of labour be restricted to ten hours per day, fifty-four hours per week. The commissioners urged that boards of arbitration should be established; that opportunities for technical education be expanded; and that certain laws that weighed heavily on workers be modified or eliminated, such as the Master and Servants Act, the seizure of household property for non-payment of debts, and the practice of charging the debtor with the costs of debt collection (frequently reported as greater than the debt owed). A Bureau of Labour was proposed to compile and publish statistical information on wages, working conditions, and other relevant information.
31 In the following discussion, free use has been made of the insights provided by Elisabeth Wallace, 'The Origin of the Social Welfare State in Canada 1867-1900,' *Canadian Journal of Economics and Political Science* 16 (1950):383-93.
32 The advent of the public school was particularly significant for the education of girls. When families had to bear the costs of educating their children privately, the education of sons tended to be given priority if money for educational purposes was scarce. See Ian E. Davey, 'Trends in Female School Attendance in Mid-Nineteenth Century Ontario,' *Histoire sociale/Social History* 8 (May 1975):253.
33 Judith Fingard, 'Attitudes toward the Education of the Poor in Colonial Halifax,' *Acadiensis* 2 (spring 1973):26. See as well Susan E. Houston, 'Policies, Schools and Social Change in Upper Canada,' *Canadian Historical Review* 53 (1972):249-71.
34 Anthony Platt, 'The Triumph of Benevolence: The Origins of the Juvenile Justice System in the US,' in *Criminal Justice in America,* ed. Richard Quinney (Boston: Little Brown 1975), 370.
35 Ibid., 389. Provincial governments began to enact their own factory acts beginning with Ontario in 1884.
36 This included 80 per cent of labourers, 56 per cent of the artisans, and 59 per cent of the business employees (primarily clerks). Qualifications for municipal elections were less onerous. See Michael B. Katz, *The People of Hamilton, Canada West* (Cambridge: Harvard University Press 1975), 27.
37 The exception to this was in Lower Canada, where from 1809 to 1834 women with the necessary property qualifications could vote.
38 Prince Edward Island granted women the vote in 1922; Quebec women had to wait until 1940. The Dominion of Newfoundland permitted women at the age of twenty-five to vote in 1925. The age qualification was reduced to twenty-one in 1946 (*Report of the Royal Commission on the Status of Women in Canada* [Ottawa 1970], 337).
39 H.W. Arthur, 'Developing Industrial Citizenship: A Challenge for Canada's Second Century,' *Canadian Bar Review* 45 (1967):792.
40 Martin Robin, 'Registration, Conscription and Independent Labour Politics, 1916-1917,' *Canadian Historical Review* 47 (1966):117.
41 Herbert Brown Ames, *The City below the Hill* (Toronto: University of Toronto Press 1972). This work was first published in book form in 1897 following its initial appearance as a series of newspaper articles.
42 Ibid., 7.
43 Charles Booth, *Life and Labour of the People of London* (London: Macmillan 1904). The results of Booth's work, which took ten years to complete, began to appear as early as 1889.

44 Ames, *City below the Hill*, 72.
45 Ibid., 73.
46 Kealey, *Canada Investigates Industrialism*, 234.
47 Ames, *City below the Hill*, 75.
48 Ibid., 76.
49 'If private enterprise does not furnish sufficient opportunity for willing men to provide for their families the absolute necessities of life, during the four cold winter months, then the municipality, by carefully considered relief works conducted at a minimum wage, should come to their assistance' (Ames, *City below the Hill*, 76-7).
50 Ames called for 'legislation that will abolish the rear tenement and the out-of-door closet and will create breathing places for the people' (ibid., 115).
51 Ibid., 107-10.
52 'We may safely fix the limit of decent subsistence at $5.00 per week' (ibid., 68).
53 Ibid., 33.
54 Ibid., 36. This assumes more than one wage earner per family.
55 Terry Copp, *The Anatomy of Poverty* (Toronto: McClelland and Stewart 1974), 32. Ames's poverty line of $5 a week for a family was dangerously low, and the evidence he compiled on death rates supports this contention.
56 For an excellent overview and sampling of issues, see Paul Rutherford, ed., *Saving the Canadian City: The First Phase 1880-1920* (Toronto: University of Toronto Press 1974).
57 Splane, *Social Welfare in Ontario*, 265 ff. In Ontario, prior to 1900, charity was seen as a religious function. This, too, militated against public responsibility for social welfare and accounted for the proliferation of charitable agencies as each denomination attempted to deal with the social welfare problems of its adherents (see Stephen A. Speisman, 'Munificent Parsons and Municipal Parsimony,' *Ontario History* 65 [March 1973]:34-49).
58 Rutherford, *Saving the Canadian City*, 195-208. Urban reform is also the subject of J.S. Woodsworth's *My Neighbor*.
59 For a full account of the social gospel movement in Canada, see Richard Allen, *The Social Passion, Religion and Social Reform in Canada, 1914-28* (Toronto: University of Toronto Press 1971). I am indebted to this work for the following discussion.
60 Stewart Crysdale, *The Industrial Struggle and Protestant Ethics in Canada* (Toronto: Ryerson Press 1961), 19-20.
61 For some idea of the range of social welfare activities conducted by churches at this time, see Woodsworth, *My Neighbor*, Chapter 10.
62 A.E. Smith, 'Cutting Down an Evil Tree,' *Social Service Congress, Report of Addresses and Proceedings* (Toronto: The Social Service Council of Canada 1914), 204-6.
63 G.C. Pidgeon, 'The Church and Labour in British Columbia,' ibid., 46-53.
64 James Simpson, 'The Extension of Social Justice,' ibid., 39-41.
65 W.M. Rochester, 'The Weekly Rest Day and National Well-Being,' ibid., 17-24; Marie Christine Ratte, 'Rescue Work for Girls,' ibid., 222-5; Ven. Archdeacon Cody, 'Why Is It Wrong to Gamble,' ibid., 340-51; and Sara Rowell Wright, 'The W.C.T.U. Programme,' ibid., 322-6.
66 As just one of several examples, J.J. Kelso, 'The Importance of Child Welfare,' ibid., 91-3.
67 Rose Henderson, 'Mothers' Pensions,' ibid., 109-15.
68 For a complete account of the development of old age pensions in Canada (including the development of the Government Annuities Act of 1908), see Kenneth Bryden, *Old Age Pensions and Policy-Making in Canada* (Montreal: McGill-Queen's University Press 1974).
69 Labor Commission, *First Report*, 13.
70 Splane, *Social Welfare in Ontario*, 103. This royal commission report, which Splane describes as 'one of the outstanding documents in the literature of social welfare in Canada' (56), identified poverty and the failure to develop policies and programs in the social welfare area as contributing in a major way to crime and vice in society.
71 Canada, Department of Labour, *Labour Gazette* 1 (October 1900):51-2 (hereafter referred to as *Labour Gazette*).
72 *Labour Gazette* 6 (August 1905):177.
73 Bryden, *Old Age Pensions*, 49.

74 *Canadian Annual Review* (1906), 234, quoting an editorial from the Toronto *Globe* of 23 May 1906. See also 215 ff.
75 Joseph E. Laycock, *The Canadian System of Old Age Pensions,* vol. 1 (PhD diss., University of Chicago School of Social Service Administration 1952), 31.
76 Bryden, *Old Age Pensions,* 52.
77 Wallace, 'Origin of the Social Welfare State,' 387.
78 See evidence of Arthur Laughlen, superintendent, presented to the Ontario Commission on Unemployment, *Report of the Ontario Commission on Unemployment* (Toronto 1916), 234. In the 1880s the Toronto House of Industry's work test involved cutting wood. In their annual report of 1886, the directors noted that because they had experienced difficulty in disposing of the wood, they were forced to discontinue the work test. Apparently they found a market for crushed rock! See 'Charity in Toronto,' *The Workingman in the Nineteenth Century,* ed. Michael S. Cross (Toronto: Oxford University Press 1974), 205-6.
79 Cited in Woodsworth, *My Neighbor,* 63.
80 Alan F.J. Artibise, *Winnipeg: A Social History of Urban Growth, 1874-1914* (Montreal: McGill-Queen's University Press 1975), 188.

Chapter 4: The First Stage of the Modern Era
1 Social insurance is a means by which government is used to guarantee non-discretionary cash payments to offset the effects of well-defined risks to economic security – retirement, sickness or injury, unemployment, pregnancy, or death of a breadwinner. Eligibility relates either to a record of contributions or to covered employment (as in the case of workers' compensation).
2 In my discussion of workers' compensation, I have made free use of the following: Arthur H. Reede, *The Adequacy of Workmen's Compensation* (Cambridge: Harvard University Press 1947); Roy Lubove, *The Struggle for Social Security, 1900-1935* (Cambridge: Harvard University Press 1968); and Michael J. Piva, 'The Workmen's Compensation Movement in Ontario,' *Ontario History* 67 (1975):39-56.
3 Followed by Quebec in 1885 and Manitoba in 1900. Other provinces brought in legislation later. For a brief resume of the first Ontario act, see Michael S. Cross, ed., *The Workingman in the Nineteenth Century* (Toronto: Oxford University Press 1974), 283. For a more detailed discussion, see the *Labour Gazette* (1 November 1900):104-12; and (December):182-92. The enforcement of these acts, in the case of Ontario and Quebec, was criticized by the Royal Commission on the Relations of Labor and Capital. See Labor Commission, *Second Report* (Ottawa 1889), 79, or Greg Kealey, ed., *Canada Investigates Industrialism* (Toronto: University of Toronto Press 1973), 31.
4 This was the Ontario Workmen's Compensation Act of 1886, but as Piva points out it was an employers' liability act rather than a compensation act.
5 The Ontario legislation weakened the force of these defences in a number of special cases: 'namely, where the injury was due to any defect in plant or machinery for which the employer or some person in his service was responsible; the neglect of any person engaged in superintendence; the neglect of any person whose orders the workmen were bound to obey when the injury took place; the act of any fellow-servant done in obedience to any improper or defective rule or instruction of the employer or delegate; and the negligence of any signalman or person in charge of a locomotive and a railway' (*Labour Gazette* 14 [July 1914]:68-70). The legal defence of contributory negligence continued to carry weight.
6 A.F. Young, *Industrial Injuries Insurance* (London: Routledge and Kegan Paul 1964), 59.
7 For a brief discussion of Guyon's work, see Terry Copp, *The Anatomy of Poverty* (Toronto: McClelland and Stewart 1974), 123-6.
8 The *Labour Gazette*'s announcement of the commission in its June 1907 edition makes no mention of Louis Guyon. It simply records that, 'In view of the amount of litigation that has arisen in the past in connection with accidents to workmen and other employees, a special commission ... was appointed ... to enquire into the best means adopted to afford protection to the victims of such accidents' (1385).
9 The commission would not recommend the principle of compulsory insurance unless the

legislature was willing to create a system of state insurance (*Labour Gazette* 9 [April 1909]:1112). See as well the account of this legislation in the 9 October 1909 edition of this same periodical (492-3).

10 Piva reports that between 1900 and 1904 the number of reported industrial accidents in Ontario increased by over 300 per cent. This increase was related, in part, to the buoyant Canadian economy of the first decade in the twentieth century (Piva, 'Workmen's Compensation Movement,' 40).

11 Lubove writes that this view was to be decisively challenged by a study published in 1910 by Crystal Eastman, *Work Accidents and the Law* (New York: Survey Associates). The study, which became a best-seller in the United States, is described by Lubove as 'perhaps the strongest single force attracting public opinion and arousing public conscience concerning this one aspect of wage workers' rights' (*Struggle for Social Security*, 46). I have not come across any reference to this study in Canadian commentary of the time. Piva's article does not mention it, although he notes that with regard to workers' compensation, 'after 1910 the business community underwent a conversion' (56).

12 The commissioner said 'that a compensation law framed on the main lines of the German law with the modifications I have embodied in my draft bill is better suited to this province' (*Labour Gazette* 13 [December 1913]:697).

13 Similar legislation was enacted in Nova Scotia in 1915; British Columbia, 1916; Alberta and New Brunswick, 1918; Manitoba, 1920; Saskatchewan, 1929; Quebec, 1931; Prince Edward Island, 1949; and Newfoundland, 1950.

14 Ontario, Legislative Assembly, *First Report* on Laws Relating to the Liability of Employers, comp. William Ralph Meredith (Toronto 1913), 5.

15 With respect to the evaluation of social security programs, I am utilizing a conceptual framework developed by Winifred Bell ('Obstacles to Shifting from the Descriptive to the Analytic Approach in Teaching Social Services,' *Journal of Education for Social Work* 5 [spring 1969]:5-19).

16 Although farm work was one of the more hazardous occupations, farmers resisted coverage under the compensation laws, and they had the necessary voting power in all provinces to back their stand. For an explanation of the farmers' position, see British Columbia, *Report of the Commissioner, Hon. Gordon McG. Sloan, The Workmen's Compensation Act and Board*, 1952 (Victoria), 30-1.

17 Reede, *Adequacy of Workmen's Compensation*, 175. British Columbia's waiting period was three days; the State of Washington's law had no waiting period.

18 Estimating the adequacy of these sums in terms of maintaining the health and decency of a family is difficult in the absence of data on living costs. However, in 1914 the city of Toronto established a minimum wage for its male employees of $15 per week, something over $60 per month. The maximum allowable benefit under workers' compensation for a widow with four or more children was $40 (see H.C. Hocken, 'The New Spirit in Municipal Government,' in *Saving the Canadian City: The First Phase 1880-1920*, ed. Paul Rutherford (Toronto: University of Toronto Press 1974), 205.

19 It is possible to argue that these allowances would prevent families from having to turn to municipal poor relief for assistance; in any case, the strictness of the means test for poor relief would have rendered them ineligible. But one wonders how dependent these families were on relatives, neighbours, and private charities when faced with emergency expenditures.

20 The first annual report of the Ontario Workmen's Compensation Board indicated that 17,033 notices of accidents had been received in the first year of operation. Of that number, 9,829 accidents were compensated for, and at the year's end only 1,117 cases remained unadjudicated. Of 682 persons permanently injured, 140 were under twenty-one, 2 were eleven, 1 was thirteen, 6 were fourteen, 14 were fifteen, and 21 were sixteen. Of those receiving benefits in the first year, 7,472 were male employees and 128 were female ('Report of the Ontario Workmen's Compensation Board for the Year 1915,' *Labour Gazette* 16 [July 1916]:1430-1).

21 Grant M. Osborn, *Compulsory Temporary Disability Insurance in the United States* (Homewood, IL: Richard D. Irwin 1958), 4.

Chapter 5: The Social Impact of the First World War

1 One measure of this change – the value of manufactured goods exported from Canada to Britain – increased from $8 million in 1913-14 to $339 million in 1917-18 (C. Stacey, 'The Twentieth Century,' in *Canada,* ed. George W. Brown [Berkeley and Los Angeles: University of California Press 1950], 135).
2 See Chapter 6.
3 'Before World War I the number of divorces granted in Canada represented less than one per 1,000 of the yearly number of marriages. After the war, however, there was a definite upward trend. In 1918 there were 118 divorces granted in Canada. Ten years later this fig-ure had multiplied seven times and in the period between the 1931 and 1941 census there was an increase of 239 per cent in the total number of divorces granted' (*Canada Year Book,* 1970/71, 320, and *Canada Year Book,* 1942, 130).
4 I am indebted to Roy Lubove's *The Struggle for Social Security 1900-1935* (Cambridge: Harvard University Press 1968) for some of his insights into the development of mothers' pensions.
5 Rose Henderson's speech on mothers' pensions to the Social Services Congress in 1914 (referred to in Chapter 3) is one of many indications that Canadians were closely follow-ing American developments. Henderson raised the idea earlier in 1912 at a meeting of the Trades and Labour Congress held in Guelph, Ontario. This is mentioned briefly in *Social Welfare* 1, no. 7 (1919):157.
6 *Labour Gazette* 15 (April 1915):1183.
7 A.W. Coone, 'The Child as an Asset,' *Social Welfare* 1, no. 2 (1918):36.
8 'These Little Ones,' ibid., 39.
9 British Columbia, *Report on Mothers' Pensions* (Victoria 1920), T5 (hereinafter referred to as *Report on Mothers' Pensions*).
10 These ideas are discussed in the *Report on Mothers' Pensions* and in an article by Peter Bryce, 'Mothers' Allowances,' *Social Welfare* 1, no. 6 (1919):131-2. See as well in the same issue J. Howard T. Falk, 'Mothers' Allowances,' 131, where the idea of the recognition of the wid-owed mother as the new 'civil service' is put forward. Unfortunately, Falk's ideas are marred by his moralizing about unmarried mothers, the wives of men in prison, widows with male boarders, and so forth.
11 Bryce, 'Mothers' Allowances,' 131.
12 Some of this story is recounted in the *Labour Gazette* 14 (May 1914):1286. It is interesting to note that in the west, where private charity did not have the same foothold because of the relative newness of settlement, women's groups petitioned their provincial govern-ments directly and expressed the unequivocal view that a woman left alone with children to raise had a claim on the state. This direct approach to the government, the relative absence of established private agencies to provoke opposition, and the contribution of women in settling the west probably helped to account for the fact that Manitoba (1916), Saskatchewan (1917), and Alberta (1919) were the first Canadian provinces to implement mothers' pensions.
13 *Report on Mothers' Pensions,* T4, and 'Canadian Cavalcade,' *Supplement to Child and Family Welfare* 11, no. 1 (1935):23.
14 Lubove, *Struggle for Social Security,* 103.
15 'Mothers' Allowances,' *Labour Gazette* 20 (August 1920):940.
16 British Columbia, *First Annual Report of the Superintendent of Neglected Children and Mothers' Pensions, for the Year Ending November 30, 1920* (Victoria 1921), 5.
17 *Report on Mothers' Pensions,* T6.
18 *First Annual Report of the Superintendent of Neglected Children,* 5.
19 *Report on Mothers' Pensions,* T5.
20 Wilfred Rasmussen, 'An Evaluation of the Mothers' Allowances Programme in British Columbia' (MSW thesis, University of British Columbia 1950), 87.
21 Ibid., 105 ff.
22 *Report on Mothers' Pensions,* T6-7.
23 *Statutes of British Columbia, 1920,* An Act to Provide Pensions for Mothers, Chapter 61, 319-21.

24 Rasmussen, 'Evaluation,' 124-6.
25 Tamara K. Hareven, 'An Ambiguous Alliance: Some Aspects of American Influences on Canadian Social Welfare,' *Histoire sociale/Social History* 3 (April 1969):82-98.
26 British Columbia, Provincial Secretary, Civil Service Commission, *Report on the Administration of Mothers' Pensions in British Columbia 1920-1 to 1930-1: Summary of Findings and Recommendations,* typescript, n.d., 21.
27 Ibid., 1.
28 Ibid., 49.
29 Whitton called for restrictions on the inclusion of divorced and unmarried mothers and one-child families, and her report criticized the lack of skilled, centralized supervision and direction. Ibid., 42-5 and 26.
30 Ibid., 49.
31 Ibid., 17.
32 Ibid. In 1931 a group of influential and reactionary British Columbia businessmen were appointed to inquire into provincial finances. This committee (the Kidd Committee) recommended draconian cuts in most public services. The Whitton Report provided them with what they considered as indisputable evidence of mismanagement and waste in the social services. See British Columbia, *Report of the Committee Appointed by the Government to Investigate the Finances of British Columbia* (Victoria 1932), 37. For the impact of the Kidd Committee's report on social services, see Harry M. Cassidy, *Public Health and Welfare Organization in Canada* (Toronto: Ryerson Press 1945), 58, 63, and 179.
33 Ibid., 5. This point was also given great play by the Kidd Committee's report (37).
34 Rasmussen, 'Evaluation,' 128, and *Child and Family Welfare* 8, no. 5 (1933):56. There was strong criticism voiced by women's groups and others in BC over the government's cutbacks and denial of applications.
35 'The Canadian Conference on Child Welfare,' *Social Welfare* 8, no. 1 (1925):4-6.
36 'Executive Director's Thirteenth Annual Report to the Council,' *Child and Family Welfare* 9, no. 1 (1933):11. This criticism of public welfare is seen, as well, in the remarks of the council's president, Dr. Charles Morse, K.C., prepared for the fifteenth annual meeting of the council (2 May 1935), when he referred to 'ultra-modern' forms of social assistance, 'hastily developed in our newer areas with little appreciation of the administrative machinery required to safeguard such services from wholesale abuse and protect the tax payer from impossible burdens,' *Child and Family Welfare* 11, no. 1 (1935):4.
37 Cited in Cassidy, *Public Health and Welfare Reorganization,* 396. For a more complete account of relief standards in Saint John, see 'Saint John Agency Surveys Relief Families,' *Canadian Welfare Summary* 15, no. 1 (1939):46-50.
38 A.E. Grauer, 'Public Assistance and Social Insurance: A Study Prepared for the Royal Commission on Dominion-Provincial Relations' (Ottawa 1939), 43.
39 Until the Second World War, Natives were excluded from federal and provincial social security programs. As late as 1966 only three provinces included Native women in their programs of mothers' allowances. Welfare services for Natives tended to develop independently under the aegis of the Indian Affairs branch of the federal government.
40 Rasmussen, 'Evaluation,' 35.
41 Ibid., 38.
42 Ibid., 40-4.
43 L.C. Marsh, *Report on Social Security for Canada,* prepared for the Advisory Committee on Reconstruction (Ottawa 1943), 25.
44 Ruth Harvey, 'The Expansion of Social Services to Meet the Needs of Men and Women in the Armed Forces,' *Proceedings of the Ninth Canadian Conference of Social Work* (Winnipeg 1944), 116-18.
45 British Columbia was an exception in this regard. The allowance for each child was $7.50.
46 *Report on the Administration of Mothers' Pensions in British Columbia, 1920-1 to 1930-1,* 45, 47-8.
47 Kenneth Bryden, *Old Age Pensions and Policy-Making in Canada* (Montreal: McGill-Queen's University Press 1974), 88-92. See as well 'Grants to Needy Mothers in Quebec,' *Canadian Welfare Summary* 14, no. 4 (1938):45.

48 The term 'public assistance' refers to those income security programs that provide benefits on the basis of an individual needs or means test.

49 Saskatchewan and British Columbia paid 100 per cent of the costs of administration and allowances at the outset; Alberta and Ontario paid 100 per cent of the costs of administration and 50 per cent of the costs of allowances, requiring the municipality where the mother and her family resided to pay the other 50 per cent; Manitoba divided the financing in the same way, but the municipality's share was raised by a general levy on all municipalities without regard to the residence of the family being assisted. This reduced the tendency of municipalities refusing to refer a fatherless family to the program as a means of avoiding their share of the costs. It also meant that the burden of costs on municipalities was more equitably shared (see W.C. Kierstead, 'Mothers Allowances in Canadian Provinces,' *Social Welfare* 7, no. 91 [1925]:175-80).

Chapter 6: The 1920s

1 'The Maritime Provinces failed to recover from the brief post-war slump and subsided into a seemingly chronic depression' (Donald Creighton, *Canada's First Century* [Toronto: Macmillan 1970], 180).

2 'Conditional grants were first used in 1913 when federal assistance to the provinces for agricultural instruction was granted for a ten-year period. As part of the reconstruction program at the close of the war, similar grants were provided for assistance to highways, technical education, control of venereal disease, and maintenance of employment offices' (Canada, *Report of the Royal Commission on Dominion-Provincial Relations, Book 1, Canada: 1867-1939* [Ottawa 1940], 131).

3 Creighton, *Canada's First Century*, 194.

4 'Public welfare' is used here to cover mothers' allowances, unemployment relief, child welfare services, institutional care for special groups, support for hospitals, and medical care for the indigent (*Report of the Royal Commission on Dominion-Provincial Relations, Book 1*, 128).

5 Margaret S. Gould, 'A Standard of Health and Decency as a Living Wage,' *Social Welfare* 8, no. 9 (1926):220-2.

6 League for Social Reconstruction, *Social Planning for Canada* (Toronto: Thomas Nelson and Sons 1935), 6.

7 Terry Copp, *The Anatomy of Poverty* (Toronto: McClelland and Stewart 1974), 43.

8 There were also many 'reconstruction study groups,' including the Canadian Reconstruction Association, consisting mainly of employers whose special objectives were efficiency in production and the expansion of trade and commerce; the Canadian Problems Committee, a Winnipeg group of students; and the Canadian National Reconstruction Groups, with headquarters in Montreal, which attempted to act as a clearing house for the recommendations and studies of all other groups (see *Social Welfare* 1, no. 4 [1919]: 76).

9 My brief description of the farmers' platform does not do it justice. For a full, contemporary analysis, see Salem G. Bland, 'The Farmer's Platform, I,' *Social Welfare* 1, no. 5 (1919):101-2; 'II,' 1, no. 6 (1919):145 ff.; 'III,' 1, no. 8 (1919):183-4, 197; 'IV,' 1, no. 9 (1919):213-14, 218. For a listing of the major planks in the platform, see 'The Farmers' Platform, 1918,' in *Canadian History in Documents, 1763-1966*, ed. J.M. Bliss (Toronto: Ryerson Press 1966), 255-8.

10 Stuart M. Jamieson, *Times of Trouble: Labour Unrest and Industrial Conflict in Canada, 1900-66* (Ottawa: Information Canada 1971), 170.

11 The agenda of the Trades and Labour Congress also included free education and textbooks, less government by order-in-council, an end to child labour, and other items. See the address of Tom Moore, president of the TLC, to a Social Welfare Congress in Toronto in January 1919, reprinted in *Social Welfare* 1, no. 7 (1919):155-7.

12 The British Labour Party's postwar agenda rested on the following principles: the highest good of all the people as the ideal and test of social legislation and institutions; the right of the child to be well born, well developed, well reared, and well educated; a single standard for both sexes in politics, morals, and economic opportunity; the application of Christian principles to industrial relations; a living wage, an eight-hour day where possible, and the weekly rest day; the conservation of natural resources and public utilities for the people's benefit; the honourable getting and the equitable distribution of welfare and

its administration in trust for the public good; and universal peace (*Social Welfare* 1, [1918]:5).

13 Veronica Jane Strong-Boag, *The Parliament of Women: The National Council of Women in Canada, 1893-1929*, National Museum of Man, Mercury Series (Ottawa 1976), 290. See also John H. Thompson, 'The Beginning of Our Regeneration,' in *Prophecy and Protest*, ed. S.D. Clark, J. Paul Grayson, and Linda M. Grayson (Toronto: Gage Educational 1975), 97-101.

14 For an example of a women's platform developed within the 400,000-member National Council of Women in 1920, see 'National Action for Canada's Women,' *Social Welfare* 2, no. 7 (1920):179. Concerns indicated in this platform include political purity, prohibition, more equality before the law, equal pay for equal work, an end to sexual discrimination in employment, the right of the worker to bargain collectively, minimum wage laws, and the eight-hour day. See also 'The Canadian Reconstruction Association's Programme for Canadian Women,' *Social Welfare* 1, no. 7 (1919):174-5.

15 W.L. Morton, *The Kingdom of Canada* (Toronto: McClelland and Stewart 1963), 433.

16 R. MacGregor Dawson, *William Lyon Mackenzie King*, vol. 1 (Toronto: University of Toronto Press 1959), 300.

17 W.L. Mackenzie King, *Industry and Humanity* (Toronto: Thomas Allen 1918), 354.

18 Canada, 'Report of the Royal Commission to Enquire into Industrial Relations in Canada together with a Minority Report,' contained in the appendix to Canada, National Industrial Conference, *Official Report of Proceedings and Discussions* (Ottawa 1919), 6.

19 J. Russell Harris, 'Impressions of the National Industrial Conference,' *Social Welfare* 2, no. 2 (1919):41.

20 With the exception of the program of veterans' benefits, the old age pension plan, and the limited housing initiatives, plus a number of conditional grant programs (see note 2 above).

21 'The Statement of the Methodist General Conference,' *Social Welfare* 1, no. 8 (1919):186-7.

22 A mental hygiene movement with both negative and positive qualities developed at the war's end. The war's psychiatric casualties focused attention on the care and treatment of the mentally ill, a positive step. At the same time, a negative factor was the attention given to the problem of 'feeblemindedness,' a generic term used to cover all types of mental disability. The mentally disabled were blamed for contributing to the bulk of crime, prostitution, pauperism, alcoholism, illegitimacy, et cetera. This led to an emphasis on segregating the mentally disabled in institutions – a trend that we are only beginning to remedy (see C.M. Hincks, 'Feeblemindedness in Canada,' *Social Welfare* 1, no. 2 [1918]:29-30).

23 The Canadian National Institute for the Blind was established in 1918 (see Grace Worts, 'The Canadian National Institute for the Blind,' *Social Welfare* 9, no. 3 [1926]:318-19).

24 The *Canadian Child Welfare News* (May-July 1924), 2, noted that one-third of the men presenting themselves for service overseas in World War One were physically unfit; that 80 per cent of this number owed their condition to defects that could have been remedied in childhood.

25 Lubove's analysis of the emergence of social work indicates that in the 1920s the profession became increasingly focused on 'inner need' as opposed to 'outer need' (a reference to social work's concentration on the psychological aspects of individual and family problems contrasted with more broad-scale measures of social intervention) (Roy Lubove, *The Professional Altruist* [Cambridge: Harvard University Press 1965], Chapter 4).

26 Elisabeth Wallace, 'The Origin of the Social Welfare State in Canada, 1867-1900,' *Canadian Journal of Economics and Political Science* 16 (1950):387.

27 Agnes M. Machar, 'Outdoor Relief in Canada,' *Proceedings of the National Conference of Charities and Correction, 1897* (Boston: G.H. Ellis 1898), 240.

28 Ontario, *Report of the Ontario Commission on Unemployment* (Toronto 1916).

29 Canada, Parliament, House of Commons, *Debates*, 1921, 2. For an excellent review of public opinion on unemployment insurance in Canada in 1921, see B.M. Stewart, 'Canadian Opinion on Unemployment Insurance,' *Social Welfare* 3, nos. 10-11 (1921):272-5.

30 A.E. Grauer, 'Public Assistance and Social Insurance: A Study Prepared for the Royal Commission on Dominion-Provincial Relations' (Ottawa 1939), 17.

31 M.K. Strong, *Public Welfare Administration in Canada* (Chicago: University of Chicago Press 1930), 132.

32   Dorothy King, 'Unemployment Aid (Direct Relief),' in *Canada's Unemployment Problems,* ed. L. Richter (Toronto: Macmillan 1939), 64.

33   J.S. Woodsworth, 'Parliament as a Social Welfare Agency,' *Social Welfare* 10, no. 11 (1928):255-6, 262. See as well Canada, Parliament, House of Commons, Select Standing Committee on Industrial and International Relations, *Report, Proceedings and Evidence* (Ottawa 1928).

34   Kathleen Derry and Paul H. Douglas, 'The Minimum Wage in Canada,' *Journal of Political Economy* 30 (April 1922):155-88.

35   Jamieson, *Times of Trouble*, 158.

36   Minimum wage acts to protect women from exploitation were passed beginning in Manitoba and British Columbia in 1918; Quebec and Saskatchewan in 1919; Nova Scotia in 1920, but not put into effect until 1930; Ontario 1920; Alberta 1922; New Brunswick 1936; and Newfoundland 1947. Minimum wage acts were amended to include male employees in British Columbia in 1925; Manitoba and Saskatchewan in 1934; Alberta and New Brunswick in 1936; Ontario and Quebec in 1937; and Newfoundland in 1947. *Labour Gazette* 50 (September 1950):1439.

37   Frank Whittingham, *Minimum Wages in Ontario* (Kingston: Queen's University 1970), 4.

38   'Minimum Cost of Living Budgets in Canada,' *Labour Gazette* 19 (August 1919):862.

39   Whittingham, *Minimum Wages in Ontario*, 5.

40   For a comprehensive history of old age pensions in Canada, see Kenneth Bryden, *Old Age Pensions and Policy-Making in Canada* (Montreal: McGill-Queen's University Press 1974).

41   Although the committee received evidence to the effect that $520 per year was the minimum income required by a single female factory operative to support herself, the maximum yearly pension for the elderly was set at $240.

42   In 1926-7 a dollar a day was deemed the minimum amount compatible with subsistence living for an aged, single person. It was roughly calculated that the basic pension would provide two-thirds of this amount and that the pensioner's own resources, which the committee referred to somewhat optimistically as 'outside income,' would provide the other third. Therefore, the basic allowance was fixed at $20 per month or a maximum of $365 per year, allowing for outside income of up to $10 per month or $125 per annum (Canada, Parliament, Senate and House of Commons, Joint Committee of the Senate and House of Commons on Old Age Security, *Proceedings and Evidence,* 29 May 1950, 112).

43   Bryden, *Old Age Pensions*, 77.

44   H. Blair Neatby, *William Lyon Mackenzie King, Vol III (1924-32)* (Toronto: University of Toronto Press 1963), 126.

45   'The Quebec government bluntly stated that province would not adopt any old age pension scheme' (Neatby, *Mackenzie King*, 109).

46   Grauer, 'Public Assistance and Social Insurance,' 15.

47   See Bryden's account of this episode, 69ff.

48   The precedent for setting up a grant-in-aid program had been established by a series of joint federal-provincial ventures beginning in 1913 when the Dominion, in conjunction with the provinces, initiated a program for extending agricultural education and improving agricultural production. In this first type of grant-in-aid program, very little was required of the province in the way of meeting standards or making any specific financial contribution. Other grant-in-aid programs followed – the 1918 agreement for the setting up of provincial employment offices and the 1919 program for building highways. This latter plan was significant for the fact that for the first time in any grant-in-aid program, the federal government insisted on the province meeting a minimum standard. In the same year, a federal grant-in-aid program to assist vocational training set a requirement that the provinces must contribute as much of their own money as they received from Ottawa. With the Old Age Pension Act of 1927, we see the first of a number of federal grant-in-aid programs in the welfare field calling for provincial contributions and with some overall standards of administration (see D.V. Smiley, *Conditional Grants and Canadian Federalism* [Toronto: Canadian Tax Foundation 1963]).

49   In the 1930 federal election R.B. Bennett pledged that the federal government would take

over the entire cost of old age pensions, thus enabling those provinces that felt they could not afford their share of the existing scheme to be covered. However, by 1930 the Depression had struck, and all levels of government were hard pressed financially. Bennett 'honoured his pledge to the extent of assuming 75 per cent of the cost of pensions' (Bryden, *Old Age Pensions*, 74).

50 J.E. Laycock, 'New Directions for Social Welfare Policy,' in *The Prospect of Change*, ed. Abraham Rotstein (Toronto: McGraw-Hill 1965), 308. See as well Bryden, *Old Age Pensions*, 71-4.

51 Joseph E. Laycock, *The Canadian System of Old Age Pensions*, vol. 1 (PhD diss., University of Chicago School of Social Service Administration 1952), 100.

52 L.C. Marsh, *Report on Social Security for Canada* (1943; reprint, Toronto: University of Toronto Press 1975), 71. Indians as defined by the Indian Act were excluded from the provisions of the Old Age Pension Act.

53 However, some provinces still imposed a much stricter means test than others (see Bryden, *Old Age Pensions*, 101).

54 Laycock, *Canadian System of Old Age Pensions*, vol. 2, 331-2.

55 Smiley, *Conditional Grants and Canadian Federalism*. See also J.A. Corry, *Difficulties of Divided Jurisdiction* (Ottawa: Royal Commission on Dominion-Provincial Relations 1940).

56 Canada, Parliament, House of Commons, Select Standing Committee on Industrial and International Relations, *Report, Proceedings and Evidence* (Ottawa 1929).

57 See as well the editorial 'Family Allowance,' *Social Welfare* 11, no. 7 (1929):147.

58 Commenting on the fact that the Child Welfare Committee of the League of Nations had received a special report on the value of family allowances where they had been tried, the *Canadian Child Welfare News* noted: 'The system being entirely foreign to present Canadian and United States practice will doubtless arouse considerable interest among social workers on this side of the water' (2, no. 2 [1926]:9). The references to the United States, as apparently parallelling Canada without any qualification, are noteworthy.

59 *Labour Gazette* 29 (December 1929):1364. For the reference to the Trades and Labour Congress of Canada's convention, see *Labour Gazette* 29 (September 1929):1011.

60 *Labour Gazette* 32 (August 1932):861-2.

61 The exception to this statement is the inclusion of family allowances as a necessary ingredient of a more equitable wage system in the 'most comprehensive treatise on the Canadian economy from a socialist point of view' (Research Committee of the League for Social Reconstruction, *Social Planning for Canada* [Toronto: Thomas Nelson and Sons 1935], 373-4).

62 A.E. Grauer, *Housing: A Study Prepared for the Royal Commission on Dominion-Provincial Relations* (Ottawa 1939), 34-5.

63 Ibid., 37.

Chapter 7: The Depression Decade

1 Harry M. Cassidy, *Social Security and Reconstruction in Canada* (Toronto: Ryerson Press 1943), 50. See as well L.C. Marsh, A.G. Fleming, and C.F. Blackler, *Health and Unemployment* (Toronto: Oxford University Press 1938).

2 An attempt was made to revive one escape route. In 1932 a scheme for settling families on the land was inaugurated with federal financial assistance, and cost-sharing agreements were worked out with all provinces except Prince Edward Island. The federal government paid one-third of the costs of relocation, up to a maximum of $600 per family, with the remaining two-thirds shared by the provinces and municipalities concerned. The plan was restricted to families who otherwise would be drawing direct relief. The Rowell-Sirois Report was critical of these colonization schemes: 'Many of the recent colonization schemes ... have been done with such lack of intelligent direction that new depressed areas are being created' (*Report of the Royal Commission on Dominion-Provincial Relations*, Appendix 6, A.E. Grauer, 'Public Assistance and Social Insurance' [Ottawa 1939], 51).

3 For a description of the treatment of transients, notably the single male, during the Depression, read 'The Menace of Single Men,' in *The Dirty Thirties: Canadians in the Great*

Depression, ed. Michiel Horn (Toronto: Copp Clark 1972), 306 ff., and Barry Broadfoot, *Ten Lost Years* (Toronto: Doubleday 1973).

4 *Report of the Royal Commission on Dominion-Provincial Relations, Book I, Canada: 1867-1939* (Ottawa 1940), 162.

5 One of the best factual summaries of public assistance policy in Canada during the 1930s is to be found in Grauer, 'Public Assistance and Social Insurance,' 81 ff. For an excellent analysis of the problems involved in trying to administer unemployment work projects and unemployment relief in Ontario in the early years of the Depression, see Harry M. Cassidy, *Unemployment and Relief in Ontario* (Toronto: J.M. Dent and Sons 1932). Also valuable is Marsh, Fleming, and Blackler, *Health and Unemployment.* See as well 'The Morass of Relief,' in *Dirty Thirties,* ed. Horn, 251-304, and James H. Gray, *The Winter Years* (Toronto: Macmillan 1966).

6 Cassidy, *Unemployment and Relief in Ontario.*

7 Ibid., 144.

8 See Cassidy's discussion of the built-in inefficiencies of work-for-relief projects, ibid., 150-2.

9 The exception was New Brunswick, which in 1936 discontinued direct relief and concentrated on work-for-relief programs.

10 Toronto's House of Industry was an example of an agency that issued relief-in-kind. Hampers of groceries were made up for families of various sizes and in amounts to last for one or two weeks. No choices were permitted, and the agency defended its policy on the grounds of economy and nutrition. The agency purchased food in bulk quantities, and it claimed that it was able to provide food orders at less cost than the individual would pay in retail outlets. Cassidy, on the other hand, presented evidence in his study of relief policy in Ontario that indicated only a marginal difference in the cost of an adequate minimum weekly food budget for a family of five purchased through retail outlets in Toronto in 1931 ($6.75) from the cost of a similar food budget supplied by the House of Industry ($6.50). Furthermore, the House of Industry admitted that families had problems with food spoilage as a result of not having proper storage for the bulk supplies provided in the hampers (see Cassidy, *Unemployment and Relief in Ontario,* 185).

11 'Family Problems in Relief,' *Child and Family Welfare* 9, no. 2 (1933):30. The executive secretary of the Family Welfare Association of America was reported as saying that 'social workers are convinced that the more choice that they can give those who receive relief and the more they can let them plan their own expenditures the more they foster a feeling of responsibility and worthwhileness.'

12 'Shall We Have Cash Relief?' *Child and Family Welfare* 9, no. 5 (1934). Businessmen supported the idea of cash relief, particularly those who were not in the grocery business! C.L. Burton, president of the Robert Simpson Company, called for cash relief in an interview with the *Financial Post,* 30 September 1933. See an account of this interview in 'The Cash Dole – Best Way Out?' *Child and Family Welfare* 9, no. 4 (1933):56-8. *Child and Family Welfare* referred to Burton's opinion as 'a startling statement.' (Burton was a member of the governing board of the Canadian Council on Child and Family Welfare.)

13 Alma Lawton, 'Relief Administration in Saskatoon during the Depression,' *Saskatchewan History* 22, no. 1 (1969):41-59.

14 'Ontario's New Relief Policy,' *Child and Family Welfare* 12, no. 3 (1935):53.

15 Grauer, 'Public Assistance,' 37.

16 There was some attempt at standardization at the provincial level, as, for example, under the administration of the Saskatchewan Relief Commission (see Blair Neatby, 'The Saskatchewan Relief Commission, 1931-34,' *Saskatchewan History* 2, no. 2(1950):41-56.

17 Grauer, 'Public Assistance,' 37.

18 The land settlement scheme (see note 2 above) and the federally assisted Youth Training Scheme (1937) may be seen as exceptions. For some details on the Youth Training Scheme, see Grauer, 'Public Assistance,' 22.

19 The scale of economic dependency caused the private charitable agencies to question another 'received truth.' Traditionally, they had claimed sovereignty over all services to families, including the provision of material aid or direct relief. This position was part of their long-standing opposition to the expansion of public welfare, though seldom

acknowledged as such. During the 1930s they came to the belated recognition that only the government could meet the cost of direct relief. In 1934 the Canadian Council of Child and Family Welfare, in consultation with its member agencies, issued a policy statement that declared that the responsibility for direct relief should be considered an essential public service ('Relative Responsibilities – Public and Private Services in the Family Field,' *Child and Family Welfare* 10, no. 2 [1934]:28-9).

20   A.H. Birch, *Federalism, Finance and Social Legislation* (Oxford: Clarendon Press 1955), 184. For more background, see W.H. McConnell, 'The Genesis of the Canadian "New Deal,"' *Journal of Canadian Studies* 4, no. 2 (1969):19-36.

21   Birch, *Federalism, Finance and Social Legislation*. A more recent view is that Prime Minister Bennett's disenchantment with laissez-faire as a policy lodestar was evident two to three years before his famous series of radio talks to the public in January 1935. Bennett began to consider a system of unemployment insurance as early as 1931. By 1933 he was preparing legislation (enacted by the end of 1934) to assist hard-pressed farmers, marking a degree of federal activity in the agricultural field 'that would have been unheard of ten years earlier' (J.R.H. Wilbur, 'R.B. Bennett: Social Reformer,' in *Dirty Thirties*, ed. Horn, 591). See as well Harry M. Cassidy's contemporary article, 'Unemployment Insurance for Canada,' *Queen's Quarterly* 38 (1931):306-34. Cassidy indicates that Bennett announced his interest in unemployment insurance earlier than indicated by Wilbur, on 29 April 1931 (308).

22   The Weekly Rest in Industrial Undertakings Act, the Minimum Wages Act, the Limitation of Hours of Work Act, the Employment and Social Insurance Act, the Dominion Trade and Industry Commission Act, and amendments to the Criminal Code of Canada dealing with unfair trade practices. Two earlier statutes, the Farmers' Creditors Arrangement Act and the National Products Marketing Act, are also considered to be part of the 'New Deal' legislation (see McConnell, 'Genesis of the Canadian "New Deal"').

23   For a contemporary analysis of this legislation, see L. Richter, 'The Employment and Social Insurance Bill,' *Canadian Journal of Economics and Political Science* 1, no. 3 (1935):436-48; and in the same volume see W.J. Couper, 'A Comment from the Point of View of American Opinion' (448-56), in which the American unemployment insurance legislation of 1935 is contrasted with the Canadian plan.

24   Calgary *Herald*, 5 January 1935, 2

25   'Bill Number 8,' *Child and Family Welfare* 10, no. 6 (1935):1-21.

26   F.R. Scott, 'The Privy Council and Mr. Bennett's "New Deal" Legislation,' *Canadian Journal of Economics and Political Science* 3 (1937):237.

27   See McConnell, 'Genesis of the Canadian "New Deal,"' and Birch, *Federalism, Finance and Social Legislation*, 185.

28   Birch, *Federalism, Finance and Social Legislation*, 191. See as well H. Blair Neatby, *William Lyon Mackenzie King, Vol III (1924-32)* (Toronto: University of Toronto Press 1976), 199-200.

29   The commissioners recommended that a 'clear line should be drawn between employable and unemployable,' but acknowledged some of the administrative difficulties that made a 'clear line' all but impossible to define (Canada, *Report of the Royal Commission on Dominion-Provincial Relations, Book II, Recommendations*, 25).

30   Ibid., 44.

31   The grants were to be calculated by determining for each province the expenditures that would be necessary if a normal Canadian standard of government services was provided and the revenue that would be provided by each province imposing a taxation load of normal severity. If the provinces were left with a deficit, a national adjustment grant would make it up. See J.A. Maxwell, *Recent Developments in Dominion-Provincial Fiscal Relations in Canada*, Occasional Paper 25 (New York: National Bureau of Economic Research 1943), 6.

32   Luella Gettys published a study of Canadian conditional grants in which she came to the conclusion that federal-provincial discord was a product of weak administrative practices – primarily the lack of strong central supervision. *The Administration of Canadian Conditional Grants* (Chicago: Public Administration Service 1938).

33   The Canadian Welfare Council, *The Rowell-Sirois Report and the Social Services in Summary* (Ottawa: Canadian Welfare Council 1940).

34 Ibid., 22.

35 'Whither in Welfare Organization?' *Canadian Welfare Summary* 14, no. 5 (1939):52.

36 Bessie Touzel, 'Two Points of View on Social Security,' *Social Worker* 12, no. 4 (1944):3-8. See as well L.C. Marsh, *Report on Social Security for Canada* (1943; reprint, Toronto: University of Toronto Press 1975), 105 ff.

37 'The Union Nationale Party was formed in the early thirties out of a union of former Conservatives, former Liberals and a number of independent Nationalists. It was a protest against the unemployment, falling incomes and economic hardships resulting from the depression ... It was a party of radical Nationalism, with a program of economic and social reform similar in most respects to Roosevelt's New Deal in the United States. Once in power, however, the Union Nationale, while retaining its Nationalist features, soon forgot most of its radical economic politics and took a sharp turn to the right' (Herbert J. Quinn, 'The Union Nationale Party,' *Canadian Forum* 35 [May 1955]:29-30).

38 A partial list of the studies completed by Marsh and other scholars at McGill includes the following: L.C. Marsh, *Employment Research* (Toronto: Oxford University Press 1935); L.C. Marsh, A.G. Fleming, and C.F. Blackler, *Health and Unemployment* (Toronto: Oxford University Press 1938); L.C. Marsh, *Canadians In and Out of Work* (Toronto: Oxford University Press 1940); G.V. Haythorne and L.C. Marsh, *Land and Labour: A Social Survey of Agriculture and the Farm Labour Market in Central Canada* (Toronto: Oxford University Press 1941). Harry Cassidy's work includes *Unemployment and Relief in Ontario, 1929-32* (Toronto: J.M. Dent and Sons 1932); with F.R. Scott, *Labour Conditions in the Men's Clothing Industry* (Toronto: T. Nelson 1935); as well as Cassidy's two definitive books on social security in Canada – *Social Security and Reconstruction in Canada* (Toronto: Ryerson Press 1943) and *Public Health and Welfare Reorganization in Canada* (Toronto: Ryerson Press 1945). Marsh and Cassidy were close friends up to the time of the latter's death in 1951. It is not generally known that Cassidy initiated the first draft of *Social Planning for Canada* and that Marsh did the comprehensive editing of the final version.

39 Canada, Parliament, House of Commons, *Debates*, 4 March 1930, 248. See also the *Debates* for 20 March 1930, 804.

40 Walter S. Woods, *Rehabilitation* (Ottawa 1953), 389-95.

41 Ibid.

42 For details, see R.G. Young and R.I. Brown, *Income Maintenance Measures in Canada, Program Descriptions* (Ottawa: Department of National Health and Welfare 1965), 19.

43 See Canada, Parliament, House of Commons, Special Committee on Social Security, *Minutes of Proceedings and Evidence,* 6 July 1943, 630-8 and 689-95.

44 Canada, Dominion Bureau of Statistics, *Canada Year Book* (Ottawa 1946), 798.

45 For a discussion of medical care for the unemployed in the 1930s, see Marsh, Fleming, and Blackler, *Health and Unemployment,* Chapter 21.

46 As early as 1914 Saskatchewan municipalities began to put doctors on salary to provide basic medical care for ratepayers. The scarcity of population in some parts of the Prairies made it difficult to attract doctors who depended on a fee-for-service basis for their livelihood, and the idea of a 'municipal doctor' with a salary paid by the municipality took hold (Canada, *Royal Commission on Health Services, Book 1*). See as well Charlotte Whitton, *Social Work and the People's Health* (Ottawa: The Canadian Welfare Council 1936), and Grauer, 'Public Assistance.'

47 British Columbia, Department of the Provincial Secretary, *Summary of the Health Insurance Act,* mimeographed (Victoria 1936).

48 *Report of the Lieutenant-Governor's Committee on Housing Conditions in Toronto* (Toronto: Hunter-Ross 1934), 115. In the same year a similar study was published in Montreal under the sponsorship of the Board of Trade and the Civic Improvement League. It was one of the first reports on housing in Canada to relate the need for low-rental housing to the distribution of income in the city.

49 Cited in R.E.G. Davis, 'Housing Legislation in Canada,' *Canadian Welfare* 28 (15 December 1952):12.

50 Ibid.

51 Advisory Committee on Reconstruction, IV, *Housing and Community Planning, Final Report*

of the Subcommittee (the Curtis Report), 24 March 1944 (Ottawa 1946). See Chapter 1, 27-8.

Chapter 8: The Second World War

1 Wilfred Eggleston, 'Canada at the End of the War,' *Queen's Quarterly* 12 (1945):360.
2 Harry M. Cassidy, *Social Security and Reconstruction in Canada* (Toronto: Ryerson Press 1943), 3.
3 Richard M. Titmuss, 'War and Social Policy,' in *Essays on 'The Welfare State'* (London: Allen and Unwin 1958).
4 'The record seems clear that the primary purpose of the Unemployment Insurance Act of 1940 was the positive one of establishing and maintaining an effective National Employment Service' (Canada, *Report of the Committee of Inquiry into the Unemployment Insurance Act* [Ottawa 1962], 20).
5 J.W. Pickersgill, *The Mackenzie King Record,* vol. 1 (Toronto: University of Toronto Press 1960), 61.
6 Jacobus TenBroek and R.B. Wilson, 'Public Assistance and Social Insurance – A Normative Evaluation,' *UCLA Law Review* 1 (April 1954):241.
7 J.L. Granatstein, *Canada's War: The Politics of the Mackenzie King Government 1939-1945* (Toronto: Oxford University Press 1975), 252-4.
8 The supplement was payable to a man whose wife was wholly or mainly dependent on him, a married woman with a dependent husband, or a widow or widower with dependent children under sixteen.
9 Granatstein, *Canada's War,* 254.
10 The committee's functions were eventually transferred to a new Advisory Committee on Reconstruction (see Granatstein, *Canada's War,* 257). There were a number of committees working on various aspects of postwar planning in addition to the Committee on Post-War Reconstruction. The General Advisory Committee on Demobilization and Rehabilitation, composed of civil servants, began work in 1940 on plans for the return to civilian life of members of the armed forces. The House of Commons set up its own Special Committee on Reconstruction and Re-establishment in March of 1942. The Committee on Health Insurance, composed of civil servants but with much organized consultation of the medical profession, began work in 1941. An Economic Advisory Committee, composed of senior civil servants, was concerned with all matters of wartime economic policy, and eventually set up its own reconstruction planning body (see Granatstein, *Canada's War,* 254-7).
11 Sir William Beveridge, *Social Insurance and Allied Services* (New York: Macmillan 1942), 6.
12 Ibid., 158.
13 Pickersgill, *Mackenzie King Record,* 433-4.
14 L.C. Marsh, *Report on Social Security for Canada* (1943; reprint, Toronto: University of Toronto Press 1975), xx. For a review of Marsh's extensive background in social welfare research, see Donald Bellamy and Allan Irving, 'Pioneers,' in J.C. Turner and Francis J. Turner, eds., *Canadian Social Welfare* (Don Mills: Collier Macmillan 1981), 27-48.
15 Eugene Forsey, 'Social Security for Canada,' *Canadian Unionist* 16, no. 11 (1943):274.
16 'Canada Gets in Step on Social Insurance,' *Financial Counsel,* 17 March 1943.
17 'The Welfare State,' *Canadian Business* 21 (April 1943):14. See also Hugh H. Wolfenden, 'Social Security – The Ideas of Beveridge and Others,' *Industrial Canada* 44, no. 8 (1943):76-80.
18 Forsey, 'Social Security,' 274-5.
19 *Labour Gazette* 42 (October 1943):1452.
20 George F. Davidson, 'The Marsh Report on Social Security for Canada,' *Canadian Welfare* 19, no. 1 (1943):3-6.
21 For a description of the work of this committee, see Margaret McWilliams, 'Women in the Post-War World,' *Canadian Welfare* 19, no. 3 (1944):3-7, 37-40.
22 In replying to this criticism, Marsh told a large public meeting in Montreal that 'Santa Claus did not require that a man be sick or lose his job before he was given a present, nor did Santa Claus ask for contributions and taxes as a preliminary for making a gift' (Montreal *Gazette,* April 1943).

23   Charlotte Whitton, *The Dawn of Ampler Life* (Ottawa: Macmillan 1943), iii.
24   Marsh considered the 'living wage' concept illogical: 'there is no reason why a man who has a large family should get a larger wage or salary than someone performing the same work, who happens to be unmarried or to have no children at all' (Marsh Report, 57). He maintained that the proper approach to the problem of intolerably low wages 'is to raise the efficiency of the worker ... either through training or education, or by placing him in an environment where his efficiency will be improved' by improving both working and living conditions. The disadvantages of the living wage had also been pointed out by an Australian royal commission in 1919. The commission found that if wage levels were based on the needs of a typical family with two or three children, the national expenditure on wages would exceed the total produced wealth of Australia. Furthermore, thousands of non-existent wives and children would have been provided for, yet the financial problems of a family with more than three children would remain. The commissioners, accordingly, recommended a system of family allowances. See George F. Davidson, 'Family Allowances: An Installment on Social Security,' *Canadian Welfare* 20, no. 3 (1944):5.
25   Income tax became effective at $660 for persons with no dependants and $1,200 for persons with one dependant. This provision alone, it was estimated, would exclude nearly half the population from coverage in 1944 (see George F. Davidson, 'The Whitton and Marsh Proposals – A Comparison and a Contrast,' *Canadian Welfare* 19, no. 7 [1944]:13).
26   *Public Health and Welfare Reorganization in Canada* (Toronto: Ryerson Press 1943). This book was published prior to the release of the Marsh Report.
27   Harry M. Cassidy, *Public Health and Welfare Reorganization in Canada* (Toronto: Ryerson Press 1945), 23.
28   Whitton argued that the use of the social assistance type of program was preferable to social insurance because it was more in keeping with Canada's cultural and constitutional background, and, accordingly, 'of more practical value.' Furthermore, she considered the 'automatic payment of insurance benefits along traditional European lines' to be less favourable than an 'improved, humane and adequately integrated system of social assistance at need, adjusted with understanding, help and service to meet each individual case' (*Dawn of Ampler Life*, 15, 45).
29   In 1944 the federal government reluctantly introduced conscription for overseas service. Opposition to this measure in Quebec returned arch-nationalist Maurice Duplessis and his Union Nationale Party to power in Quebec City the same year. This assured that the Marsh Report, which had recommended a dominant role for the federal government in planning a national social security system, would be buried.
30   'Social Security and the Canadian Constitution,' *Economist*, 19 June 1943, 792. The *Economist* was repeating a popular conservative belief at this time, a precursor to the 'trickle down' theory, that a high national income automatically takes care of poverty and related concerns.
31   Pickersgill, *Mackenzie King Record*, 634.
32   'Still No Plan,' *Canadian Forum* 23, no. 1 (1944):278.
33   Canada, Parliament, House of Commons, *Debates*, 1944, 2.
34   'A Post-War Programme for the US,' *International Labour Review* 47 (1943):450-65.
35   J.A. Maxwell, *Recent Developments in Dominion-Provincial Fiscal Relations in Canada*, Occasional Paper 25 (New York: National Bureau of Economic Research 1948).
36   Students of ecology may be interested to learn that a major report on conservation and resources projects was published at the same time as the Curtis Report, as the full employment counterpart of the Housing and Planning Report. This was long before 'ecology' or the 'resources crisis' became headlines (see A.H. Richardson, *The Ganaraska Watershed* [Toronto 1944]).
37   Albert Rose, *Canadian Conference on Housing*, 'Canadian Housing Policies,' Background Paper no. 2, mimeographed (Ottawa: Canadian Welfare Council, June 1968).
38   Dorothy Stepler, 'Family Allowances for Canada,' *Behind the Headlines* 3, no. 2 (1945).
39   Ibid., 11.
40   Charlotte Whitton, 'The Family Allowance Controversy in Canada,' *Social Service Review* 18 (December 1944):413-32. Allowances were to be reduced for the fifth child by $1; for

the sixth and seventh by $2; and for the eighth and additional children by $3. 'The government's justification for these lower grants is that it costs relatively less to maintain them because they fall heir to the cast-off clothes, books and toys of their older brothers and sisters' (Harry M. Cassidy, 'Family Allowances in Canada,' *Proceedings of the National Conference of Social Work* [New York: Columbia University Press 1945], 170).

41 Stepler, 'Family Allowances for Canada,' 29.

42 Ibid., 4.

43 'A Year's Progress Reviewed,' *Canadian Unionist* 18, no. 5 (1944):109-10.

44 In October 1943 *Canadian Welfare* noted that opinion on the advisability of family allowances divided social workers into two camps: 'A number opposed, but on the whole a larger group in support' ('Children's Allowances – Pro or Con?' *Canadian Welfare* 19, no. 5 [1943]:1). Support grew rapidly. See 'Family Allowances,' *Social Worker* 13, no. 2 (1944):1-6. The Canadian Association of Social Workers supported family allowances in its *Brief on the Marsh Report*, submitted to the Dominion Advisory Committee on Social Services in March 1944; see as well the three-part series of articles by George F. Davidson, 'Family Allowances: An Instalment on Social Security,' *Canadian Welfare* 20, no. 3 (1944):2-6; no. 4 (1944):6-11; and no. 5 (1944):11-17.

45 The payments varied according to age: for children under 5, $5 per month; from 6 to 9 years, $6; 10 to 12 years, $7; 13 to 15, $8 (Cassidy, 'Family Allowances in Canada,' 170). See as well note 40 above. The rates Marsh suggested (based on cost-of-living studies) were up to 4 years, $5 per month; 5 to 9 years, $6.50 per month; 10 to 12 years, $8 per month; 13 to 14 years, $10 per month; and 15 to 16 years, $12.50 per month (Marsh Report, 204)

46 Whitton, 'Family Allowance Controversy,' 420.

47 'This did not mean that all Conservatives – or indeed all others – were converted. During the succeeding months there was intermittent criticism by certain newspapers, mainly Conservative in persuasion' (Cassidy, 'Family Allowances in Canada,' 173).

48 Universal programs provide benefits to large sections of the public generally on the basis of age or status – that is, allowances to all children or medical care to all citizens. In Canada, where these universal programs involve cash benefits related only to age and residence, they are also termed 'demogrants.'

49 Does the beginning of family allowances in Canada owe something to the influence of philosophical Tory values in our background? It is significant that the United States, with its history shaped by liberal-bourgeois values, is the one industrially advanced country in the world without a system of family allowances. The debate between Whitton and Lebel in 1929 and 1932 and the fight in the Liberal cabinet over the 1944 legislation illustrate the presence of both Tory and liberal-bourgeois values.

50 T.H. Kewley, *Social Security in Australia* (Sydney: University Press 1965), 194.

51 'Social Work Looks at Parliament,' *Canadian Welfare* 24, no. 8 (1949):20-1.

52 Eggleston, 'Canada at the End of the War,' 358.

53 A.H. Birch, *Federalism, Finance and Social Legislation* (Oxford: Clarendon Press), 195.

54 The grant was to be either equal to the revenue the provinces had collected from the tax fields in 1940, or if the provinces preferred, an amount equal to the net cost of debt service in 1940 (less their revenue from succession duties) (see Maxwell, *Recent Developments*).

55 Canada, Dominion-Provincial Conference on Reconstruction, *Proposals of the Government of Canada* (August 1945), 7.

56 Quoting from the federal brief: 'The proposals which we desire to advance for the consideration of this Conference are designed, when fitted into place in the whole Dominion-Provincial scheme of things, to fill the three main gaps in our present system. Health Insurance, National Old Age Pensions and Unemployment Assistance, combined with health and welfare measures already adopted ... will meet the main needs' (Conference on Reconstruction, *Proposals of the Government of Canada*, 27).

57 The idea may have originated closer to home. Bryden reports that the CCF advocated a universal pension on retirement during the 1930s (*Old Age Pensions and Policy-Making in Canada* [Montreal: McGill-Queen's University Press 1974], 108).

58 F.R. Scott, 'Labour Learns the Truth,' *Canadian Forum* 26, no. 304 (1946):29-30.

59 Maxwell, *Recent Developments,* 36.

60 'Congress Representation on Health Services Legislation,' *Canadian Unionist* 16, no. 11 (1944): 266.

61 A decade later, in 1955, when Ontario was considering a provincial hospital insurance plan, the commercial insurance representatives reverted to their customary policy position of criticizing public health insurance as an attack on free enterprise. The industry's spectacular success in selling sickness and accident insurance policies in the 1950s was seen as the principal reason for the change. By 1949 the Canadian Medical Association had also changed its position. It continued to endorse the principle of health insurance but 'withdrew its support of plans organized and financed by government' (Malcolm G. Taylor, *Health Insurance and Canadian Public Policy* [Montreal: McGill-Queen's University Press 1978], 22-33, 254).

62 Vancouver *Province,* 8 January 1975, 5, interview with the Hon. Paul Martin.

Chapter 9: The 1950s

1 Tom Kent, *Social Policy for Canada* (Ottawa: Policy Press 1962), Chapter 2.

2 For evidence of this renewed interest, see ibid.

3 The financing formula for the universal pension involved earmarked taxes in the form of a 2 per cent sales tax, a 2 per cent corporation tax, and a 2 per cent tax on individual incomes up to a $3,000 ceiling. In 1959 the conservatives increased the 2-2-2 formula to 3-3-3, with a maximum personal income tax set at $90 per year, up from $60. In 1963 the Liberals raised the personal income tax portion to 4 per cent, and in 1966 the tax was applied on the first $6,000 of personal income, or a maximum of $240 per year. These increases generally followed an increase in the pension. In 1972 the earmarked tax was eliminated for individuals and corporations but retained as part of a revised federal sales tax. During the twenty years that Canadians paid this tax, enough money was collected to pay both the cost of OAS and the GIS. See Statistics Canada, *Social Security: National Programs 1976,* 285. See also Kenneth Bryden, *Old Age Pensions and Policy-Making in Canada* (Montreal: McGill-Queen's University Press 1974), 206-11, for a discussion of the regressive nature of this financing formula. Earmarked taxes are defined as 'the practice of designating specific revenues to the financing of specific public services' (Irving J. Goffman, *Some Fiscal Aspects of Public Welfare in Canada* [Toronto: Canadian Tax Foundation 1965], 70).

4 Canada, Parliament, Senate and House of Commons, Joint Committee on Old Age Security, *Report* (Ottawa 1950).

5 The federal government agreed to share in 50 per cent of the cost of allowances for the disabled; it continued its policy, established in 1927, of paying 75 per cent of the cost of allowances for the blind.

6 Canada, Dominion Bureau of Statistics and Department of National Health and Welfare, *Canadian Sickness Survey, 1950-51,* Special Compilation no. 6, Permanent Physical Disabilities (National Estimates) (Ottawa 1955), 11.

7 As discussed in earlier chapters, the Royal Commission on Dominion-Provincial Relations had recommended full federal responsibility for this category of need in 1940, as had the Marsh Report in 1943. This same idea was included in the federal government's 'Green Book' proposals of 1945. In March 1941 the federal government terminated its unemployment relief grants to the provinces, which had been in effect since 1930. Many provinces followed this example by ending their support of municipal relief programs. This left a potentially sizeable number of Canadians without income protection in the event of unemployment, particularly as some municipalities refused to help the able-bodied unemployed. In the 1950s, for the first time since the Depression, 'soup-lines' began to appear in some of the major cities (see 'The Employable Unemployed,' *Canadian Welfare* 30 [February 1955]:1).

8 The council recommended that provinces be required to provide an adequate level of assistance as a condition of federal sharing, a recommendation that was not acted upon. Canada, Parliament, Senate, 'Brief of the Canadian Welfare Council,' 1240-74, in Special Committee on Manpower and Employment, *Proceedings* (Ottawa 1961).

9   However, general revenue, drawn from more progressive taxation, is to be preferred to sales taxes that are usually regressive (and hence less redistributive) in character.

10   Credit should be given to the CCF government of Saskatchewan. It pioneered the first universal hospital insurance program in Canada in 1946, which served as a model for the federal legislation for a national system that followed in the 1950s. For the most complete detailing of the development of health insurance in Canada, see Malcolm G. Taylor, *Health Insurance and Canadian Public Policy* (Montreal: McGill-Queen's University Press 1978).

Chapter 10: The 1960s

1   This was necessary because under the BNA Act, as amended, the federal Parliament could only enact legislation in respect to old age pensions. This did not include survivor, death, or disability benefits. Ottawa required a further amendment to cover these additional categories in the CPP. Quebec cooperated fully in agreeing to the amendment but with the proviso that provincial rights to legislate in the pensions area remained paramount.

2   In addition to retirement benefits and disability pensions, there were benefits for dependent children of deceased plan members and for children of disabled persons, pensions to surviving spouses, and lump-sum death benefits to defray funeral expenses. Contributions were first collected in 1966, and partial retirement pensions were first paid in 1967, survivor benefits and lump-sum death benefits in 1968, and disability benefits in 1970. The ten-year transition period ended in January 1976, allowing full benefits to commence (Kenneth Bryden, *Old Age Pensions and Policy-Making in Canada* [Montreal: McGill-Queen's University Press 1974], 133). Benefits are taxable, and contributions were tax deductible until the 1980s, when the deduction became a tax credit. Ottawa's original plan called for a pension of 20 per cent of insurable earnings at age seventy, but reduced if taken between sixty-five and sixty-nine, and for surviving widows a pension at sixty-five.

3   The Royal Commission on the Status of Women recommended that (a) both the Canada and Quebec Pension Plans be amended so that the spouse who remains at home can participate in the plan, and (b) the feasibility be explored of (i) crediting to the spouse remaining at home a portion of the contributions of the employed spouse and those contributions made by the employer on the employed spouse's behalf, and (ii) on an optional basis, permitting the spouse at home to contribute as a self-employed worker (Canada, *Report of the Royal Commission on the Status of Women in Canada* [Ottawa: Information Canada 1970], 40).

4   Bryden, *Old Age Pensions*, 206.

5   This was also made necessary because the Canada and Quebec Pension Plans required ten years to mature, that is, to pay benefits at the maximum rate.

6   The maximum monthly amount of the supplement was reduced by $1 for each full $2 a month of additional income other than the old age security pension.

7   As an option, provinces could retain the categorical programs or phase them out gradually. A third alternative was the provision for opting out of the shared-cost arrangement altogether under the provisions of the Established Programs (Interim Arrangements) Act of 1965, in which the province would receive compensating 'tax room' and equalization grants.

8   Canada, Parliament, House of Commons, *Debates*, 5 April 1965, 5.

9   Canada, Report of the Special Senate Committee on Poverty, *Poverty in Canada* (Ottawa: Information Canada 1971), 168.

10   Canada, *Welfare in Canada: The Tangled Safety Net*, A Report by the National Council of Welfare, November 1987.

11   *Poverty in Canada*, 73.

12   Canada, *Royal Commission on Health Services*, vol. 1 (Ottawa 1964).

13   The costs of dental care, prescription drugs (except for hospital patients), and optometrists' services remained outside the plan, a serious omission for lower-income families.

14   Some authorities, such as A.W. Johnson, refer to four principles, leaving out reference to

the fifth principle (see *Social Policy in Canada: The Past as It Conditions the Present*, Studies in Social Policy [Ottawa 1987], 15). However, the National Council of Welfare lists five in *Medicare: The Public Good and Private Practice* (Ottawa: Minister of Supply and Services 1982), 14-15; so does Monique Begin, a former minister of national health and welfare (1979-84), in her stimulating account of the fight to save accessibility, the fifth principle (see *Medicare: Canada's Right to Health* [Ottawa: Optimum Publishing 1987] 54).

15 The task force recommended that all urban residential land be developed and marketed by municipalities and that the federal government provide loans for this purpose; that housing programs directed solely at the poor be discontinued; that housing subsidies be paid to people rather than to buildings; and that cooperative and non-profit housing schemes be given greater encouragement. Hellyer resigned his cabinet post in protest over the federal government's lack of action on his proposals. His departure 'propelled the government into action,' and by June 1969 Parliament passed housing legislation that incorporated some of the recommendations of the task force. An analysis of the work of the task force and the opposition it engendered is contained in Lloyd Axworthy, 'The Housing Task Force: A Case Study,' in *The Structures of Policy-Making in Canada,* ed. G. Bruce Doern and Peter Aucoin (Toronto: Bryant Press 1971).

16 Only a brief summary of the report was issued by the CMHC. The authors subsequently arranged for the report to be published (see Michael Dennis and Susan Fish, *Programmes in Search of a Policy: Low Income Housing in Canada* [Toronto: A.M. Hakkert 1972]).

17 In 1968 Arthur Block, chair of the United Community Services housing committee, Vancouver, accused the federal government of a serious misdirection of public funds for housing over the previous twenty years. He charged that since 1954 an average of only 3.4 per cent of federal funds for mortgages had gone to low-income groups (*Vancouver Sun,* 8 November 1968).

18 Andrew Armitage, *Social Welfare in Canada* (Toronto: McClelland and Stewart 1975), 125.

19 Michael Wheeler, 'Politics and Housing,' *Community Welfare Planning Council Letter* 1, no. 41 (August 1969).

Chapter 11: Stemming a Residual Tide

1 This figure was said to represent the cost of 'non-deferrable expenses' for short-term unemployment. Benefits now became taxable and contributions tax deductible, but taxing benefits brought the 67 per cent figure down to an average of 60 per cent. Under the new act, qualifying conditions for benefits were eased depending upon the national and regional rates of unemployment. The act also stipulated that the federal government would contribute to the cost of benefits in any year in which the national unemployment rate exceeded 4 per cent, a policy the government would soon regret. See Canada, House of Commons, *Minutes of Proceedings and Evidence of the Standing Committee on Labour, Manpower and Immigration, Respecting the White Paper on Unemployment Insurance,* 29 October 1970, 7:5-7:6.

2 Canada, Parliament, House of Commons, *Debates,* 5 April 1965, 5. Some other measures promised included regional development, reemployment and training of workers, redevelopment of rural areas, and new opportunities for young Canadians. Many of these ideas sprang from a Liberal Party social policy conference in 1960. See Tom Kent, *Social Policy for Canada* (Ottawa: Policy Press 1962), chapter 9.

3 The principal reports include Economic Council of Canada, *Fifth Annual Review* (Ottawa 1968); *Social Policies for Canada, Part I* (Ottawa: Canadian Welfare Council 1969); *Social Security for Canada 1973* (Ottawa: Canadian Council on Social Development 1973); Canada, Report of the Special Senate Committee, *Poverty in Canada* (Ottawa: Information Canada 1971); Ian Adams, William Cameron, Brian Hill, and Peter Penz, *The Real Poverty Report* (Edmonton: M.G. Hurtig 1971); Quebec, Report of the Commission of Inquiry on Health and Social Welfare, *Income Security,* 3 vols., 1971; Canada, *Report of the Royal Commission on the Status of Women in Canada* (Ottawa: Information Canada 1970).

4 The Senate committee also recommended that the Canada Assistance Plan be retained for the delivery of social services and to meet financial needs for the under-forty group. See *Poverty in Canada,* xv-xvi.

5 Canada, Royal Commission on Taxation, *Report,* 6 vols. (Ottawa) 1966, (the Carter Commission). For brief comments on the Carter Commission, see National Council of Welfare, *Statement on Income Security,* Ottawa, April 1971, 15-16; *Real Poverty Report,* 139-51, 204-13; *Poverty in Canada,* 46-7.

6 In 1971 a family of four would be entitled to a basic guarantee of $4,100 per annum. Each additional dollar of earned income would reduce the guaranteed amount by 60 cents. The break-even point in this example – that is, when the basic guarantee would be taxed completely away – occurs when the family head earns around $6,900 (*Real Poverty Report,* 95).

7 The Quebec commission recommended that the income-tested supplement to OAS be increased to equal stage two of the GSAP. It also recommended that benefits under the QPP be increased and that the workers' compensation program be extended. See Canadian Council on Social Development, *Social Security for Canada 1973,* 109-14.

8 What would a *defensible* degree of inequality involve? The reader is referred to W.G. Runciman, *Relative Deprivation and Social Justice* (Berkeley and Los Angeles: University of California Press 1966).

9 Economic Council of Canada, *Fifth Annual Review,* 122.

10 Senate Committee, *Poverty in Canada,* 35.

11 Adams et al., *Real Poverty Report,* section 11.7, 68-74.

12 Economic Council of Canada, *Fifth Annual Review,* 121.

13 *Report on the Royal Commission on the Status of Women,* 320.

14 The royal commission recommended, as a first step toward a guaranteed annual income for all Canadians, that it first be paid to all one-parent families headed by women.

15 Women and social security policy is comprehensively discussed in Kevin Collins, *Women and Pensions* (Ottawa: Canadian Council on Social Development 1978).

16 Senate Committee, *Poverty in Canada,* ix. The 'misguided' element of the quotation, in my view, is the suggestion that social assistance costs were so out of control that they threatened to 'suffocate' the taxpayer. This was a favourite theme of neoconservatives who wanted to see sharp cutbacks in such programs. Canada's social program costs were modest compared to other developed nations.

17 The maximum retirement benefits under the Canada Pension Plan were to be raised, as were the flat-rate benefits for disabled contributors and widows, plus a new benefit providing a flat-rate payment of $80 per month for wives of disabled contributors under sixty-five with dependent children to support. The improvements in social assistance were to be worked out in consultation with the provinces. Areas in which improvement would be sought included expanded day care centres and homemaker services, special needs of the handicapped and disabled, and employment opportunities for social assistance recipients. The proposed changes to the Canada Pension Plan were badly needed; unfortunately, they were not proceeded with. The changes to the old age security and the guaranteed income supplement programs were, on the other hand, 'rushed through Parliament before Canadians had time to consider or react to them' (Donald Bellamy, 'Welfare,' *Canadian Annual Review,* 1970, 466).

18 Dennis Guest, 'If We Keep Family Allowances,' *Canadian Welfare* 45, no. 3 (1969):14-16.

19 *The Family Income Security Plan* (Ottawa: Canadian Council on Social Development 1971), 23.

20 Richard M. Titmuss, *Essays on 'The Welfare State'* (London: Allen and Unwin 1958). See his essay entitled 'The Social Division of Welfare.'

21 Economic Council of Canada, *Sixth Annual Review* (Ottawa 1969), 110.

22 Family and youth allowances were to be raised from $6, $8, and $10 per month to $16 for children under the age of twelve and $20 for children twelve to seventeen (and attending school). Families with incomes over $4,500 would receive diminishing amounts and, at a family income of $10,000 (higher for large families), some would lose benefits entirely. Family allowances had been raised only once since 1945 and had lost two-thirds of their value. The proposed increases would have restored them to their 1945 purchasing power, and their value at the time was less than that recommended by the Marsh Report. As an antipoverty strategy, the proposed new allowances failed to make the grade. See Canadian Council on Social Development, *Social Security for Canada 1973,* 36; National Council of

Welfare, *Statement on Income Security*, 18; and Johnson, *Social Policy in Canada: The Past as It Conditions the Present*, Studies in Social Policy (Ottawa 1987), 22.

23 National Council of Welfare, *Statement on Income Security*, 3.

24 The American academic community was awash with learned papers on the impact of automation on the workforce and the possibility of and necessity for some type of guaranteed annual income. See, for example, Robert Theobald, ed., *The Guaranteed Income: Next Step in Socioeconomic Evolution?* (New York: Anchor Books 1967). Furthermore, a number of demonstration projects testing the feasibility of GAI were launched in the US and Canada.

25 See the letter to the province of Quebec from William A. Dyson, one of the commissioners of the Castonguay-Nepveu Commission, arguing that the traditional economy was failing to produce enough jobs for those looking for work. Therefore, it was the economy that needed to change, not the unemployed, and too much attention to work incentives is 'unnecessarily demeaning, and all too frequently [is] implicitly punitive.' Province of Quebec, Report of the Commission of Inquiry on Health and Social Welfare, *Income Security*, vol. V (1971), 163-6.

26 Richard Simeon, 'Conflicts and Contradictions: Contemporary Strains in Canadian Federation,' *Conference on Social Development in a Pluralist Society, Proceedings* (Ottawa: Canadian Council on Social Development 1977).

27 See Maxwell Cohen's commentary on Edward McWhinney's 'Federalism, Constitutionalism, and Legal Change: Legal Implications of the "Revolution" in Quebec,' in *The Future of Canadian Federalism*, ed. P.A. Crepau and C.B. MacPherson (Toronto: University of Toronto Press 1965), 175.

28 Donald Smiley, 'Public Administration and Canadian Federalism,' *Canadian Public Administration* 7 (September 1964): 373.

29 Canada, *Dominion-Provincial Conference, 1960* (Ottawa 1960), 90-1.

30 Ibid., 85.

31 Ibid., 130.

32 Smiley, 'Public Administration,' 379.

33 E.R. Black and A.C. Cairns, 'A Different Perspective on Canadian Federalism,' *Canadian Public Administration* 9 (March 1966): 35.

34 In 1939 federal, provincial, and municipal governments shared almost equally in total government expenditure in Canada. Under wartime pressure, the federal share rose to 87 per cent in 1944. By 1963 the federal share had dropped to 46 per cent, while the provincial share was up to 26 per cent and the municipal share 38 per cent. It was estimated that if there were no major changes in defence spending and no major reallocations of functions between governments, each level of government would be spending about one-third of the total by 1980. Given provincial responsibility for municipalities, such a trend would put two-thirds of the total government expenditure in Canada under provincial jurisdiction (ibid.).

35 Ibid.

36 D.V. Smiley, 'Federalism,' in Mel Watkins, ed., *Handbooks to the Modern World* (New York: Facts on File 1993), 249.

37 Johnson, *Social Policy in Canada*, 15.

38 Canada, *Income Security and Social Services* (Ottawa 1969).

39 In the past a province that refused to take part in a cost-sharing agreement was penalized by the fact that although its citizens contributed toward the costs of the program in other provinces through their income tax, they received no benefits. The federal government proposed in another of the Working Papers on the Constitution, *Federal-Provincial Grants and the Spending Power of Parliament*, that where a province remains outside a program on which there has been general consensus, the federal government would find some mechanism for returning the money that would have been spent in the province under the terms of the program to the *people* of the province rather than to their provincial government.

40 *Canadian Annual Review*, 1971, 56-7.

41 See W.A.J. Armitage, 'The Emerging Realignment of Social Policy – A Problem for Federalism,' *Canadian Welfare* 47, no. 5 (1971): 4-5, 30; and Smiley, 'Federalism,' 48-9.

42 *Canadian Annual Review*, 1971, 51.

Chapter 12: Unfinished Business

1 Canada, Minister of National Health and Welfare, *Working Paper on Social Security in Canada* (Ottawa, April 1973), 2. According to Keith Banting, Lalonde and his deputy 'went into Cabinet with a document containing specific policy proposals; they came out with a document full of principles and observations, but virtually no policy content.' Thus, the paper was neither white nor green and emerged instead with an orange cover, and was referred to as 'the Orange Paper.' K. Banting, 'The Way Beavers Build Dams,' in K. Banting and K. Battle, eds., *A New Social Vision for Canada*, School of Policy Studies, Queen's and the Caledon Institute of Social Policy, Ottawa, 1994, 133.

2 Under the terms of the original 1944 Family Allowance Act, it was Parliament's intention that taxpayers who received a family allowance for their children should not receive the full benefit of tax relief for those children under the Income Tax Act (see Canada, Parliament, House of Commons, *Debates*, 27 June 1946, 2915). In the taxation year 1945, 'the effect of the Income Tax Act was that married persons with incomes of $3,000 or over had to return an amount equal to all of the family allowances they received' (average earnings of employees in manufacturing industries in 1945 amounted to $1,538 for production worker and $2,191 for supervisory or office employees). In 1947 the Income Tax Act was amended again 'so as to make the deduction for a child eligible for family allowances less than the deduction for a child not so eligible. The effect of this was that the parent of a child eligible for the allowance would gain financially by claiming the allowances' (see Canada, Department of National Health and Welfare, *Income Maintenance Measures in Canada, Program Descriptions*, comp. R.G. Young and R.I. Brown [Ottawa 1965], 25). A double benefit for income tax payers with dependent children between sixteen and seventeen was allowed under the provisions of the Youth Allowances Act (1964). Allowances were not taxable, and tax exemptions for this age group of dependent children were not reduced (ibid., 27).

3 Quebec and Alberta took advantage of this option. In the case of Alberta, rates were varied according to the age of the child, and in Quebec rates varied according to the number of children in a family and their ages (see Statistics Canada, *Social Security National Programs* [Ottawa: Ministry of Industry, Trade, and Commerce 1976], 201-12).

4 The community employment strategy was soon relegated to a series of small demonstration projects; the social insurance strategy produced changes in benefits and policy in the Canada and Quebec Pension Plans that were undoubtedly already in process – for example, changes in the YMPE were inevitable – although the review may have had the effect of speeding up the timetable for change. The 'federal-provincial' strategy appeared to be little more than a restatement of familiar jurisdictional positions by the two levels of government.

5 The Canadian Council on Social Development noted that 'The scale of the Community Employment Strategy envisaged in the working paper appears to be small and ... is directed toward the severely disadvantaged only.' Canadian Council on Social Development, *Social Security for Canada 1973* (Ottawa: CCSD 1973), 177. A more focused critique can be found in the National Council of Welfare, *Incomes and Opportunities*, Ottawa, November 1973, 7-16.

6 Canadian Council on Social Development, *Social Security for Canada 1973*, 177. See as well Eric Shragge's critique of the Community Employment Strategy in *Canadian Welfare* 51 (March-April 1975):22-4.

7 Another amendment removed the earnings test for people aged sixty-five to seventy from the Canada Pension Plan. This was the so-called retirement test: if a pension was claimed before seventy, the pensioner could only earn up to $900 a year without affecting the pension.

8 In addition, a new program under the Old Age Security Act called the Spouse Allowance was enacted in 1975 to provide an income-tested allowance to men or women aged sixty to sixty-four who were married to recipients of old age security. This was a program largely oriented toward women. For a critique of this program, see Kevin Collins, *Women and Pensions* (Ottawa: Canadian Council on Social Development 1978), 106 ff.

9 Donald Rumball, 'CLC Misses Target with Proposals for Canada Pension Plan,' *Labour Gazette* 75 (April 1975):214-19.

10 This provision was included in the QPP in 1977, but Ontario's opposition prevented CPP's adoption of the same stipulation until 1983, at which time the amendment was back-dated to 1978. The lobbying by private insurance companies, many of which had their head offices in Toronto, was thought to be the principal reason for Ontario's footdragging.

11 Joan C. Brown, *How Much Choice? Retirement Policies in Canada* (Ottawa: Canadian Council on Social Development 1975), xix-xx.

12 Canada, Department of National Health and Welfare, *Income Security for Canadians* (Ottawa 1970), 47.

13 Cited in Rumball, 'CLC Misses Target,' 218.

14 'Muddled Pension Picture Means Poverty,' Vancouver *Province,* 27 November 1975.

15 Some provinces had attempted to develop programs that included the working poor: Saskatchewan, in 1974, developed the Family Income Plan, which provided payments to low-income families with dependent children (see Graham Riches, 'FIP Flops,' *Perception* 1, no. 6 [1978]: 42).

16 Canada, *Working Paper,* 9.

17 Canadian Council on Social Development, *Social Security for Canada 1973,* 177.

18 William H. Beveridge, *Full Employment in a Free Society* (London: Allen and Unwin 1944), 36.

19 The social security review issued a background paper to the public entitled *Income Support and Supplementation* in February 1975. Six possible options for a support and supplementation plan were discussed. The most favoured option is outlined here.

20 See *Guide to the Guaranteed Income* (Ottawa: National Council of Welfare, March 1976), 14 ff.

21 Some suggested national standards were 'provision for appropriate differentiation between general support or guaranteed income levels for families of different sizes and with different needs, including differences due to disabilities and age; provision for special or emergency assistance to families for whom the general support levels, or the general support scheme, are from time to time found to be insufficient; provision for increasing the general support or guaranteed income levels as the cost of living rises; provision that, when the family begins to earn an income, not all the earnings would be treated as a substitute for or a replacement of support payments; provision that, as family earnings increased as a result of more regular employment, and began to approach the support or guarantee levels, increased work incentives would be provided ... ; provision that all family income would be taken into account when determining the level of support ... required; provision for common technical requirements in the provincial guaranteed income plans including the definitions of income, the determination of what constitutes a family unit, the setting of accounting periods, the establishment of enforcement requirements, and the exchange of information between governments; provision for a proper appeal system for persons seeking or receiving support; provision for ensuring that the beneficiaries in each province are made aware of the contributions being made toward the income and employment plan by Canadian taxpayers as a whole' (Marc Lalonde, *The Next Major Steps in Reforming Canada's Social Security System,* statement to the Conference of Federal and Provincial Ministers of Welfare, February 1975, 8-9).

22 National Council of Welfare, *Support/Supplementation: Who Will Benefit?* (Ottawa 1976), 32.

23 The National Council of Welfare cited a study prepared for the Economic Council of Canada in 1972, which found that 'while government expenditure programs may contribute to the redistribution of income ... the tax system as a whole does nothing to contribute to this goal.' National Council of Welfare, *Bearing the Burden: Sharing the Benefits* (Ottawa, March 1978), 4.

24 The exception was the services for the vocational rehabilitation of the disabled, for which there was federal cost-sharing beginning in 1952.

25 National Council of Welfare, *The Federal Government and Social Services* (Ottawa, March 1978), 5.

26 Ibid., 7.

27 *Communiqué,* Meeting of Federal and Provincial Ministers of Welfare, Ottawa, 3-4 February 1976, 1.

28 Ibid.
29 National Council of Welfare, *Federal Government and Social Services,* 8-9.
30 In November 1978, in the course of parliamentary debate on family allowances, the minister of national health and welfare, Monique Begin, made the following comment: 'Canadians in general receive $25.68 per child every month. Alberta has a somewhat different program, but Quebec has a completely different system about which we were not consulted' (Canada, Parliament, House of Commons, *Official Report of Debates,* 29 November 1978, 1638). Quebec varied its family allowances according to the number of children in the family. By lowering the benefit for the first child and increasing it in steps for the second, third, fourth, and subsequent children, a steep acceleration of benefit was achieved (i.e., $12 for the first child; $18 for the second; $28 for the third; and $31 for the fourth and any additional children). This would be a potent antipoverty policy for larger families. See Statistics Canada, *Social Security: National Programs* (Ottawa: Supply and Services 1976), Table B, 211. Alberta arranged for Ottawa to pay the allowances by age: ages 0 to 6, $15; 7 to 11, $19; 12 to 15, $25; and 16 to 17, $28 (ibid., Table C. 212).
31 *Canadian Annual Review,* 1976, 39.
32 National Council of Welfare, *Federal Government and Social Services,* 8.
33 H. Philip Hepworth, 'Federal Proposals for Contributing to the Financing of Personal Social Services,' mimeographed (Ottawa: Canadian Council on Social Development 1977), 5.
34 Canada, Department of Health and Welfare, *Summary of the Principal Components of the Social Services Bill* (Ottawa 1977), 2.
35 National Council of Welfare, *Federal Government and Social Services,* 12. Estimates of federal per capita contributions by province in 1977 were British Columbia $22, Alberta $17, Saskatchewan $20, Manitoba $28, Ontario $16, Quebec $32, New Brunswick $17, Nova Scotia $17, Prince Edward Island $29, and Newfoundland $19. Shifrin made an interesting observation with reference to Ontario, which spent an estimated $16 per capita on social services in 1977-8: 'The extra $5 per capita that the federal government is offering (beginning in 1979), represents a 30 per cent increase in a social services budget that Ontario plans to increase next year by only six per cent. The balance will simply be a windfall gain for the provincial treasury.' *NAPO-INFO* 4, no. 5, 6.
36 National Council of Welfare, *Federal Government and Social Services,* 13.
37 Hepworth, 'Federal Proposals,' 8.
38 Maurice Kelly, 'The New Social Services Legislation – What Next?' *Social Worker* 45, no. 4 (1977): 159.
39 Canada, Parliament, House of Commons, *Official Report of Debates,* 17 November 1978, 1225, and 21 November 1978, 2341. Social services would continue to be financed under the provisions of the Canada Assistance Plan.
40 *Vancouver Sun,* 25 August 1978. The minister also announced a $20 per month increase in the guaranteed income supplement program.
41 National Council of Welfare, *The Refundable Child Tax Credit: What It Is ... How It Works* (Ottawa, August 1978), 1.
42 *Vancouver Sun,* 1 September 1978.
43 Ibid. This was just one of a series of amendments to the UI Act – five in just over ten years – all aimed at cutting back on the presumed 'generosity' following from the act's 1971 revisions. The minister and his officials made much of the abuse of the system, obscuring a more fundamental problem of growing unemployment.
44 *Vancouver Sun,* 2 September 1978.
45 Ibid.

Chapter 13: Social Security in the 1980s

1 Canada, Parliament, House of Commons, *Official Report of Debates,* 12 December 1979, 2283.
2 See *Unemployment Insurance: Another Victim of the '80s* (Ottawa: Canadian Centre for Policy Alternatives 1981).
3 When the Liberals regained power in 1980 they established a Task Force on Unemployment

Insurance within the Department of Employment and Immigration, which called for even further restrictions on unemployment insurance benefits. See *Unemployment Insurance in the 1980s,* Ottawa, 1981. According to observers such as Soderstrom, 'Unemployment Compensation: A Different View,' in *Unemployment Insurance: Another Victim of the '80s,* 48-61, the task force ignored Canada's 'chronic shortage of decent jobs.'

4 Bill C-6, passed by Parliament, replaced a provision in the Old Age Security Act that had cut off a spouse's allowance six months after the death of the older spouse with the same benefit continuing on a basis of need. This amendment also removed a provision that suspended old age security benefits to anyone sent to prison for more than ninety days. Such a provision also penalized the prisoner's wife, if she was receiving spouse's allowance, because that allowance was being suspended at the same time (*Canadian Annual Review,* 74).

5 Canada, National Council of Welfare, *Pension Primer: A Report by the National Council of Welfare on the Retirement Income System* (Ottawa, April 1984), 11.

6 *Debates,* 22 October 1979, 462. The National Council of Welfare recommended that the spouse's allowance be replaced by an income-tested benefit equal to the combined OAS/GIS benefit to all people between the ages of sixty and sixty-four, regardless of their marital status (National Council of Welfare, *Pension Reform* [May 1984], 47).

7 Tax deductions reduce taxable income; tax credits reduce the amount of tax an individual or business has to pay.

8 The mortgage tax credit was 25 per cent of mortgage interest up to a ceiling of $5,000 (maximum credit $1,250). The plan was to be phased in over four years, one-quarter of the maximum credit in the first year, one-half in the second, three-quarters in the third, and the full $1,250 in the fourth. In addition, a flat-rate property tax credit of $250 phased in over four years, worth $62.50 in the first year, $125 in the second, $187 in the third, and $250 in the fourth and subsequent years. See *Debates,* 19 November 1979, 1461-9, and Janet McClain, 'The Saga of Mortgage Deductibility,' *Perception* 3, no. 2 (1979):34-5. McClain's analysis of the proposed measure indicated that the largest number of home owners across Canada (using 1976 statistics) were within the $10,000 to $15,000 family income range. The average annual amount spent on mortgage interest and taxes was approximately $970 in 1976. Under the Conservative tax credit plan, the maximum average tax savings to a family would be $262 in the fourth year but a mere $34 plus the property tax credit, yielding total tax savings in the first year of a 'paltry' $97.00. McClain then compared these benefits with households in the over $30,000 income range and found a significant difference in level of benefit. The maximum tax savings for this income group in the fourth year would be $591 and in the first year approximately $148, a 100 per cent difference.

9 Some provincial governments in the late 1970s provided shelter allowances for senior citizens: Nova Scotia, New Brunswick, Quebec, Manitoba, and British Columbia. Manitoba also offered help to families. See the Economic Council of Canada's *Twentieth Annual Review* (1983), 73-9, for details.

10 Richard M. Titmuss, *Essays on 'The Welfare State'* (London: Allen and Unwin 1958), 34-55.

11 Canada, National Council of Welfare, *The Hidden Welfare System* (Ottawa 1976); see as well from the same organization *Bearing the Burden Sharing the Benefits* (March 1978), and *The Hidden Welfare System Revisited* (March 1979).

12 *Hidden Welfare System Revisited,* 7.

13 Canada, Department of Finance, *Report on Integration of Social Program Payments into the Income Tax System,* November 1978 Budget Paper.

14 Canada, Department of Finance, *Government of Canada Tax Expenditure Account,* (Ottawa 1979). For a critique of this report, see Edward Tamagno, 'Comparing Direct Spending and Tax Spending,' *Canadian Taxation* 1, no. 4 (winter 1979).

15 Tamagno, 'Comparing Direct Spending and Tax Spending,' 43.

16 *Debates,* 14 April 1980, 4-5.

17 The November 1981 budget introduced the Canada Mortgage Renewal Plan whereby people who were faced with spending in excess of 30 per cent of their gross income on house payments because they had to renew a mortgage were permitted to defer payment of the

interest with the federal government guaranteeing the interest deferred (see Canadian Tax Foundation, *The National Finances, 1982-83,* 6).

18 Michael Prince, 'The Liberal Record,' *Perception* 8, no. 1 (1984):23-5.

19 J.E. Pesando and S.A. Rea, *Public and Private Pensions in Canada: An Economic Analysis* (Toronto: University of Toronto Press 1977); Quebec, *COFIRENTES+* (Quebec City 1977); Keith H. Cooper and Colin C. Mills, *Canada at the Pension Crossroads* (New York: Research Foundation of Financial Executives Institute 1978); Social Planning Council of Metropolitan Toronto, *Old Age Insecurity* (Toronto 1978); Canada, Senate, The Report of the Special Senate Committee on Retirement Age Policies, *Retirement without Tears* (Canadian Government Publishing Centre 1979); Economic Council of Canada, *One in Three: Pensions for Canadians to 2030* (Canadian Government Publishing Centre 1979); Social Planning Council of Metropolitan Toronto, *Pensions: Passport to Poverty* (Toronto 1979); Canada, Federal Task Force on Retirement Income Policy, *The Retirement Income System in Canada: Problems and Alternative Policies for Reform,* The Lazar Report, 2 vols. (Canadian Government Publishing Centre 1980); Ontario, Report of the Royal Commission on the Status of Pensions in Ontario, *A Plan for the Future,* 10 vols. (Toronto 1980); National Action Committee on the Status of Women, Pensions Committee, 'Women and Pensions: A Discussion Paper' (1981), mimeographed, 17 pp.; Canada, Department of National Health and Welfare, *Proceedings, National Pensions Conference, Ottawa, March 31, April 1 and 2, 1981* (Minister of Supply and Services 1981); Canadian Centre for Policy Alternatives, *Pensions: Public Solutions vs. Private Interest,* Proceedings of the CCPA Conference on Pensions, March 1981, Montreal (Ottawa: Canadian Centre for Policy Alternatives 1982); British Columbia, *Developing a Pension Policy for the Future* (Victoria 1982); Canada, *Better Pensions for Canadians* (Ottawa: Health and Welfare Canada 1982) (The Green Paper); Canada, House of Commons, *Report of the Parliamentary Task Force on Pension Reform* (Ottawa 1983).

20 See, for example, R.M. Macintosh, 'The Great Pension Fund Robbery,' *Canadian Public Policy* 2, no. 2 (1976):257-61, and Geoffrey N. Calvert, *Pensions and Survival – The Coming Crisis of Money and Retirement* (Toronto: Maclean-Hunter 1977). For a contrasting view, see National Council of Welfare, *Financing the Canada Pension Plan* (Ottawa, December 1982).

21 Canada, Minister of Health and Welfare, *Retirement Age,* Background Paper to the Brief Presented to the Special Senate Committee on Retirement Age Policies by the Minister of National Health and Welfare, 14 December 1978 (revised April 1979), 18-19.

22 The Economic Council of Canada believed this point to be misleading because the public expenditure on the old is estimated to be roughly three times that on the young. However, most costs of child care are borne privately by families, while most costs of the care of the elderly are borne publicly. Therefore, the dollars saved on fewer children will offset some of the additional costs incurred on behalf of the elderly. *One in Three,* 25.

23 The 1980s began with three years of double-digit inflation, beginning in 1980 with a rate of 12.2 per cent, 12.5 per cent in 1981, and 10.8 per cent in 1982. In 1983 the rate dropped to 5.8 per cent and below 5 per cent in 1984.

24 National Council of Welfare, *Sixty-Five and Older* (Ottawa: Minister of Supply and Services 1984), 24. For a concise summary of provincial supplements and financial aid to the elderly, see National Council of Welfare, *Pension Primer.*

25 National Pensions Conference, *Proceedings,* 43.

26 Council on the Status of Women, *As Things Stand* (Ottawa: CACSW 1983), 89.

27 National Council of Welfare, *Pension Reform* (Ottawa: Minister of Supply and Services 1984), 1. See as well *One in Three,* 6.

28 It is also possible, following Richard M. Titmuss, to see Canada's retirement system as consisting of forms of social welfare in that all three owe their development in the modern era to public policy and subsidy. The programs in the public sector may be viewed as part of the traditional structure of *social welfare* benefits; those in the private sector are either examples of *occupational welfare* benefits (the employer-sponsored pension plans) or *fiscal welfare* benefits (those provisions within the Income Tax Act that encourage individuals to save for their retirement). See Titmuss, 'The Social Division of Welfare,' in *Essays on 'The Welfare State.'*

29 For brief histories of the development of the private pension sector in Canada, see the

Lazar Report, vol. 2, 'The Development of the Retirement Income System in Canada,' by Hart D. Clark, and British Columbia, *Developing a Pension Policy*, 2-3.

30 *Better Pensions for Canadians*, 19, and National Council of Welfare, *Pension Primer, 1996*, 36-40.
31 *Old Age Insecurity*, 32.
32 Anyone could make contributions to an RRSP of up to $3,500 per annum if the contributor belonged to an employer-sponsored pension plan, and up to $5,500 if he or she was not a plan member (*Better Pensions for Canadians*, 7).
33 *Proceedings*, 29.
34 Ibid., 33-4.
35 Vesting refers to the member's right, on termination of employment before retirement, under a pension plan to all or part of the benefit that has accrued, both the employer's contribution and his or her own. The benefit is often payable as a deferred pension upon retirement. Most of the studies of Canadian pensions offer a glossary to help the reader through the complex terminology. The National Council of Welfare's *A Pension Primer* is an example.
36 Portability refers to the arrangements for the transfer of members' pension credits to the pension plan of their next employer when they change jobs.
37 *Retirement without Tears*, 59. In 1977 the average private pension was $2,885 per year.
38 The most startling example was the allegation of fraud against 'a number' of recipients of the guaranteed income supplement by Claude Castonguay before the National Pensions Conference. Mr. Castonguay said 'that a number of the recipients of the Guaranteed Income Supplement have set their affairs in order often with the help of their children, in such a way as to make it easier to qualify for this program. For this reason, one must be cautious in interpreting broad statistics' on the incidence of low income among old age pensioners (*Proceedings*, 27).
39 Ibid., 26.
40 Ibid., 26, 79.
41 British Columbia, *Developing a Pension Policy for the Future*, 9-10. This study, in discussing the relationship between pre- and post-retirement income, argues that it is unrealistic to expect 100 per cent of pre-retirement income as a pension because by the age of sixty-five many Canadians have paid off their mortgage, have educated their children, and are significant net savers. 'It is not logical to expect a retirement income system to provide benefits for the purpose of permitting continued significant savings after retirement.' But no one on the other side of the issue was suggesting this. The Canadian Labour Congress, for example, said that a desirable standard of pension adequacy would be 75 per cent of pretax income before retirement (*Proceedings*, 15).
42 *Proceedings*, 58.
43 *Retirement Income System in Canada*, vol. 1.
44 *Retirement without Tears*, 14-15.
45 *COFIRENTES+*, cited in P. Kumar and A.M.M. Smith, *Pension Reform in Canada: A Review of the Issues and Options* (Kingston: Industrial Relations Centre 1981), 41.
46 *Proceedings*, 69-70.
47 *Retirement Income System in Canada*, vol. 1, 242.
48 Louis Erlichman, 'An Expanded Public Pension Plan and Collective Bargaining,' in Canadian Centre for Policy Alternatives, *Pensions: Public Solutions vs. Private Interest*, 171.
49 *Proceedings*, 20. For the least ambiguous statement from a union representative to the conference, see the comments of Vincent Dagenais, economist and union adviser from Quebec, 77-8.
50 Richard Denton, 'The Political Economy of Pensions: The Political and Economic Framework of the Canadian Pension System,' in Canadian Centre for Policy Alternatives, *Pensions: Public Solutions vs. Private Interest*, 68.
51 Titmuss, *Essays*, 216.
52 Denton, 'Political Economy of Pensions,' 74.
53 'Pension Policy Remains a Puzzler,' Vancouver *Province*, 9 June 1982.
54 National Council of Welfare, *Pension Reform*, 31. See as well *Proceedings*, 55-7.

55 The Ontario Royal Commission rejected proposals for expanding the Canada Pension Plan but proposed a compulsory plan for all workers in Ontario. The plan would be fully funded with private sector control of pension funds. The plan would be portable within the province and, in time, between provinces. The program, to be known as the Provincial Universal Retirement System (PURS), would not begin to pay benefits until the year 2028. To assist current pensioners and people retiring before 2028, the commission recommended a special inflation tax credit to protect that part of the pensioner's income that was non-indexed. A fully funded plan is one that at any particular time has sufficient assets to provide for the payment of all pension and other benefits required of it. For comment and summary of the Ontario report, see Michael Mendelson, 'The Haley Report: An Old Age Insecurity Program,' in Canadian Centre for Policy Alternatives, *Pensions: Public Solutions vs. Private Interest,* 126-9, and Louis Ascah, 'Recent Pension Reports in Canada: A Survey,' *Canadian Public Policy* 10, no. 4 (1984):415-28.

56 Canada, House of Commons, *Report of the Parliamentary Task Force on Pension Reform,* Ottawa, 1983.

57 The following discussion on homemaker pensions is based upon the CACSW publication *As Things Stand,* 89-91, and Canada, National Council of Welfare, *Better Pensions for Homemakers* (Ottawa, May 1984).

58 Canada, Department of Finance, *Action Plan for Pension Reform* (Ottawa, February 1984).

59 The GIS program was also amended to guarantee recipients of partial old age security pensions the same minimum income as other elderly Canadians (ibid., 13).

60 The *proposed* amendments to the C/QPP included ending the practice of terminating survivor benefits upon remarriage; extending the division of pension credits on marriage breakdown to legal separations and the breakdown of common-law relationships; automatic pension splitting when the younger spouse reaches sixty-five; and annual earnings on which pension contributions and benefits are based to be raised to the level of average industrial wages by January 1987. The following items would require more discussion with the provinces: an increase in the disability benefits paid under C/QPP; an increase in the number of years of low-income earnings that can be omitted in calculating benefits; increased flexibility in the age of eligibility for pension benefits; and further discussion on the financing of the C/QPP.

61 The proposed federal minimum standards for private pensions would have covered all future pensions, including deferred benefits. Private plans would be required to index their benefits by 60 per cent of the change in the consumer price index, subject to an annual maximum of 8 per cent CPI increase. Vesting and portability would be handled by required vesting after two years in the plan. When employees leave a job, they would be able to take their vested benefits with them or leave them to continue to grow in the pension plan. The portability aspect was to be accomplished in one of three ways: leaving total pension entitlements with the former employer as a deferred benefit, to be available on retirement; transferring accumulated contributions and vested benefits to a locked-in Registered Pension Account, forming a new individual pension plan for the mobile worker, or transferring the credits to the pension plan of a new employer (if the latter was willing); employees may transfer their own contributions and interest to an RPA and leave the remaining pension entitlement with the former employer as deferred benefit, to be available on retirement.

The treatment of women workers and spouses was to be improved under private plans in a number of ways: by requiring survivor benefits to be paid even if the widowed spouse remarries; survivor benefits were to be mandatory in all plans at no less than 60 per cent of the level received by the deceased spouse; survivor benefits would be required before retirement – that is, younger survivors (typically those under age sixty) would be given a lump sum transferable to an RPA; older survivors would receive an immediate survivor pension or its equivalent; pension credits and pensions-in-pay would normally be split equally on marriage breakdown; pension benefits would be equal for male and female employees retiring under identical circumstances; membership in a private plan would become compulsory for anyone over the age of twenty-five who was a full-time employee where the employer offered a plan for a particular occupational group; regular part-time workers would also be covered if they had at least three years of service, were twenty-five years or older, and provided they had worked at least 50 per cent of the normal work period. Standards with regard to disclosure to members of the details of their accrued benefits and accumulated contributions were also to be strengthened.

62 The Hon. Emmett M. Hall, *Canada's National-Provincial Health Program for the 1980's* (Ottawa: Department of National Health and Welfare 1980).

63 *Health Services Review '79*, Press Release, Ottawa, 3 September 1980, 2.

64 'Doctors are paid by each province's medical insurance plan according to an established schedule of fees for insured services. Because they are dissatisfied with the level of payments received under the fee schedules, in recent years a sizeable number of doctors in several provinces have been charging patients an amount over and above the approved rate. This practice is commonly known as extra-billing, though terms such as "balance billing" and the absurd euphemism "patient participation" are sometimes used to mean the same thing' (Canada, National Council of Welfare, *Medicare: The Public Good and Private Practice* [Ottawa 1982], 25).

65 The medical profession's arguments in support of extra-billing are summarized by Pran Manga, *The Political Economy of Extra Billing* (Ottawa: Canadian Council on Social Development 1983), 13.

66 Canada, House of Commons, Parliamentary Task Force on Federal-Provincial Fiscal Arrangements, *Fiscal Federalism in Canada* (Ottawa 1981), 112.

67 Ibid.

68 Robert Evans, *Hiding behind Medicare: Health Care Funding in the BC Budget*, BC Economic Policy Institute, Paper No. P-84-6 (March 1984), 16.

69 Hall, *Canada's National-Provincial Health Program*, 10.

70 Ibid., 11.

71 *Fiscal Federalism in Canada*, 108.

72 Evans, *Hiding behind Medicare*, 19.

73 National Council of Welfare, *Medicare*, 22-3.

74 A study of extra-billing by Ontario physicians, conducted by G.L. Stoddard and C.A. Woodward and commissioned by Mr. Justice Hall's review, showed that patients with lower incomes were more likely to reduce the use of a doctor's services or delay treatment owing to extra charges (*Canada's National-Provincial Health Program*), 24-5.

75 Manga, *Political Economy of Extra Billing*, 13.

76 Ibid., 13-14. A striking example of the abuse of advanced medical technology and procedures was the claim that fully half of all the heart bypass operations in the United States were unnecessary (see Thomas A. Preston, 'Marketing an Operation,' *Atlantic Monthly* [December 1984]):32-7.

77 Manga, *Political Economy of Extra Billing*, 17.

78 *Canada's National-Provincial Health Program*, 23, 41, 42.

79 Authorized hospital charges were a form of user fee collected from the hospital patient in some provinces. They generally take the form of a per diem charge, and certain groups are exempted. Three provinces and one northern territory also bill their residents for health care premiums, which are generally flat-rate charges for single people and families. Mr. Justice Hall refrained from recommending the abolition of premiums and authorized hospital charges 'at this time,' but he left no doubt in the minds of his readers that when the economy improved these regressive, inequitable, and inefficient forms of taxation should be phased out. For a description of the various charges in the provinces and territories in 1981-2, see the National Council of Welfare, *Medicare*.

80 *Fiscal Federalism in Canada*, 97-8.

81 Canada, Minister of National Health and Welfare, *Preserving Universal Medicare* (Ottawa 1983).

82 'Poll Says No to Extra Charges,' *Vancouver Sun*, 12 September 1983.

83 *Canada Health Act*, 32-3 Elizabeth II, Chapter 6, Section 3.

84 This was the situation in May 1982 as reported by the National Council of Welfare in *Medicare* (38). However, by 1990, the council reported that only two provinces, BC and Alberta, continued to collect premiums, 'a policy that unfairly burdens low and moderate

income families.' National Council of Welfare, *Health, Health Care and Medicare* (Ottawa: Minister of Supply and Services 1990), 38.

85 Monique Begin, minister of health and welfare, 'Address to the Colloque Juridique,' Montreal, 9 March 1984, mimeographed, 8 pp., 5.

86 A more balanced approach to health policy involving health care, protection, and promotion was discussed in a speech delivered by the minister of health and welfare, Monique Begin, on 9 May 1984, where she cited the ideas of Professor Philip Lee of the University of California ('Health: The Canadian View,' Brock Chisholm Memorial Lecture 1, 3). See also the National Council of Welfare's 1982 report, *Medicare*, which details the poverty and ill health, 16-23.

87 Canada, Department of Finance, *A New Direction for Canada: An Agenda for Economic Renewal* (Ottawa 1984), 77.

88 Canada, Minister of National Health and Welfare, *Child and Elderly Benefits, Consultation Paper* (Ottawa 1985), 11.

89 Department of Health and Welfare, *Child and Elderly Benefits* (1985).

90 For example, the federal white paper *Income Security for Canadians* (1970), the orange paper of 1973, and the development of the child tax credit in 1979 were all instances when attempted or completed restructuring of family allowances was carried on in isolation from other types of child benefit.

91 The consultation paper also pointed out that even with providing these increases to the refundable child tax credit, there were additional savings to the federal government of $80 million from the first option and $130 million from the second. Provinces would also experience 'windfall savings' of $330 million for the first option and $150 million for the second. This was because both levels of government would receive large increases in tax revenue from the elimination of the child tax deduction in the first case, and partial elimination in the second. Ottawa would be using its savings to increase the child tax credit, but the 'windfall' to provincial revenues would carry no such obligations. *Consultation Paper,* 13.

92 Jonathan R. Kesselman, 'Credits, Exemptions and Demogrants in Canadian Tax-Transfer Policy,' *Canadian Tax Journal* 27, no. 6 (1979):653-88, and 'Family Allowances: How to Save and Pay to All,' *Financial Post,* 11 December 1983.

93 M. Mendelson, *The Administrative Cost of Income Security Programs: Ontario and Canada* (Toronto: Ontario Economic Council 1979).

Chapter 14: A Sombre Anniversary

1 A.W. Johnson, *Social Policy in Canada: The Past as It Conditions the Present* (Institute for Research on Public Policy 1987), 26.

2 Furthermore, as Kitchen points out, the federal government *saved* money from this restructuring – $170 million in fiscal 1978-9, $36 million in 1979-80, and $45 million in 1980-1. Brigitte Kitchen, 'The Refundable Child Tax Credit,' *Canadian Taxation* 1, no. 3 (1979):44-51.

3 The intent of the 'six and five' program was to restrain increases in indexed benefits as well as public sector wages to 6 per cent in 1983 and 5 per cent in 1984. The RCTC and GIS were not included, and in fact both were raised in value. But as the inflation rate fell sharply from 10.8 per cent in 1982 to 5.8 per cent in 1983 and to 4.4 per cent in 1984, the effect on indexation was negligible. Full indexation resumed in 1985.

4 There was some Liberal support for a return to a full employment policy in a 1981 report of a parliamentary task force, *Employment Opportunities in the 80's* (the Allmand Report), which deplored the Liberal government's drift away from a policy of full employment.

5 William H. Beveridge, *Full Employment in a Free Society* (London: Allen and Unwin 1944), 36.

6 Stephen McBride, 'The Employment Policy of the Mulroney Government: Implications for the Provinces,' 3rd Conference on Provincial Social Welfare Policy, April, 1984, cited in A. Armitage, *Work and Welfare*, mimeographed, 29.

7 Lars Osberg, *The Future of Work in Canada: Selected Policy Options* (Ottawa: Canadian Council on Social Development 1988), 1.

8 Linda McQuaig, *Behind Closed Doors* (Markham, ON: Viking 1987).
9 For a sampling of these submissions, see *The Other Macdonald Report,* ed. Daniel Drache and Duncan Cameron (Toronto: James Lorimer 1985).
10 Ibid., x.
11 'Economic Ills, Who's to Blame?' *Vancouver Sun,* 24 January 1992.
12 Mel Hurtig, *The Betrayal of Canada* (Toronto: Stoddart 1991). For a labour point of view, see Canadian Union of Public Employees, 'Free Trade: Worse than Anyone Ever Imagined,' *The Facts on Free Trade* 13, no. 2 (1992):13-18. See as well Jim Sinclair, ed., *Crossing the Line* (Vancouver: New Star Books 1992).
13 Economic Council of Canada, *Good Jobs, Bad Jobs* (Ottawa: Minister of Supply and Services 1990). The Council identified four types of non-standard employment, but I have selected the two most common types for discussion.
14 Ibid., ix.
15 Gordon Ternowetsky, 'Profits and Jobs: Who Wins, Who Loses,' *Perception* 10, no. 5 (1987):39-42.
16 Marjorie Griffin Cohen, 'The Lunacy of Free Trade,' in Sinclair, ed., *Crossing the Line,* 23.
17 Michael Mendelson, 'Maintaining an Independent Social Policy,' *Perception* 12, no. 4 (1988):9-11.
18 Maude Barlow of the Council of Canadians has argued that the provisions of the FTA prevented the Ontario NDP government from keeping one of their election promises – to institute public auto insurance. Barlow argues that when the new NDP government moved to bring in auto insurance, American private insurance companies promptly filed claims for compensation for over $600 million. Total compensation to Canadian and American companies could have reached as much as $2 billion. Such claims are legal under FTA, which requires that governments offer prior consultation plus compensation to any private firm that is about to be displaced by the creation of a public enterprise. The government's plans were shelved. Maude Barlow, 'The Road Back,' in Sinclair, ed., *Crossing the Line.* Tom Walkom, author of *Rae Days,* a careful analysis of Ontario's first NDP government, says that 'according to those on the inside, the decision not to proceed with public insurance stemmed not from fear of the FTA but from a reluctance to countenance job losses and start-up costs' (personal correspondence).
19 David Ross and Richard Shillington, *Background Documents on Social Reform: Work and Income in the Nineties* (Ottawa: Canadian Council on Social Development 1986), 3. This same paper also lists business and community sector criticisms of the social security system – the results of a series of forums throughout the country. Business criticisms echo the government's view but add the cost to small business of payroll taxes – C/QPP, UI, and workers' compensation. Community sector criticisms are more numerous and encompass the government's economic policy – that is, its failure to promote full employment; failure to develop a fair tax system; failure to deal with the inequitable distribution of income; as well as complaints about inadequate benefit levels in various income security programs.
20 Even the government's friends in the business community failed to support this move. The finance department had suggested that the GIS portion of the old age pension be 'double-indexed' as compensation for the partial indexing of OAS, but this was vetoed by cabinet as too expensive.
21 Canada lacks an effective political constituency in support of universal family allowances. Allan Moscovitch, '"Slowing the Steamroller": The Federal Conservatives, the Social Sector and Child Benefits Reform,' in *How Ottawa Spends, 1990-91,* ed. Katherine A. Graham (Ottawa: Carleton University Press 1990).
22 'If the actual deficit as a proportion of GNP is compared with deficits at the end of World War II, it need not be considered out of control ... The increase in the deficit is due more to decreased revenue than increased expenditures' (Jean-Bernard Robichaud, 'Canada Can Afford Its Ideals,' Working Paper no. 6, *Work and Income in the Nineties* [Ottawa: Canadian Council on Social Development 1986], 13). There is also the tendency on the part of politicians to encourage the average Canadian to view the finances of government as no different than those of a private individual or business firm. See Ruben Bellan, 'The Big

Lie,' *Vancouver Sun,* 14 February 1991. For some observations of how big business contributes to the deficit, see Larry Brown, 'Smokescreen Economics,' *Perception* 13, no. 3
(1989):20-2, and Barry George, 'Taxing Questions,' *Perception* 14, no. 3 (1990):46.

23 One reason for not moving to a tax credit may have been that federal officials felt that the
resulting tax windfall for the provinces would not be used for the benefit of families with
children (Moscovitch, ' "Slowing the Steamroller" ').

24 Canada, House of Commons, *Minutes and Proceedings of the Legislative Committee on Bill C-
80,* evidence of Ken Battle, president of the Caledon Institute of Social Policy, 16 June
1992. This, of course, was not generally understood by the public – 'social policy by
stealth.'

25 The RCTC was to be increased over three years to $524 per child, per annum, from the
then current $367. The first raise to $454 would take effect in the 1986 taxation year; $489
in 1987; and $524 in 1988, plus full indexing. The partial-indexing formula would be
applied beginning in 1989. The reduction in the 'turnover point' – the point at which the
tax credit begins to reduce by 5 cents for every dollar of additional income – would also
be partially indexed beginning in 1986. The tax exemption for child dependants was lowered from $710 per child, per annum, to $560 in the 1987 taxation year; to $470 in 1988;
and in 1989 to an amount equal to the annual FA benefit. At that time, the deduction
would be subject to the partial indexation formula. To make some sense out of the foregoing maze of numbers (such mazes being a prime characteristic of 'selective' programs),
see National Council of Welfare, *Giving and Taking: The May 1985 Budget and the Poor*
(Ottawa: Supply and Services, July 1985).

26 These estimates of tax liabilities were predicated on the higher RRSP deductions available
in 1986 as outlined in the 1985 budget. Instead of rising from $3,500 to $15,500 over five
years, as originally planned, the RRSP tax deductions were phased in more slowly so that
the $15,500 limit would not be reached until 1996. However, the criticism of the impact
of these tax deductions is still valid because the Department of Finance officials and the
minister of finance would know the implications of their initial recommendations.

27 Family allowances were fully indexed beginning in 1974. The C/QPP was indexed from
the outset although limited to 2 per cent a year until 1974, when it was fully indexed. The
OAS was fully indexed in 1972, the GIS in 1973. In 1973 the federal government also
indexed the personal income tax system to ensure that taxpayers would not face higher
taxes simply because of inflation-linked wage increases. Social assistance rates in the
provinces are not indexed to the cost of living (except in Quebec). Most provinces use an
ad hoc system to increase rates – a policy of neglect. Canada, Department of National
Health and Welfare, *Inventory of Income Security Programs in Canada, July 1985,* 72-3, 104.

28 National Council of Welfare, *Help Wanted: Tax Relief for Canada's Poor,* revised (Ottawa:
Supply and Services, November 1989), 3.

29 National Council of Welfare, *Social Spending and the Next Budget* (Ottawa: Supply and
Services, April 1989), 5.

30 Canada, House of Commons, *Minutes and Proceedings of the Legislative Committee on Bill C-
80,* evidence of Ken Battle.

31 Economic Council of Canada, *Annual Review,* 1986, 34.

32 Recommended for conversion to tax credits were the basic personal, age, married or equivalent, and the child tax exemption. In addition, deductions for C/QPP, UI premiums, medical expenses, disability deductions, pension income, charitable donations, tuition fees,
and educational expenses were all recommended for conversion to tax credits.

33 An authority on tax law had this to say about the capital gains exemption: 'This subsidy
program is highly inequitable: over 45 per cent of the $500 million spent annually on this
program is received by the richest 1 per cent of taxpayers. The richest 10 per cent receive
over 80 per cent of the subsidy. Yet only 1 or 2 per cent of the subsidy is received by people who have made a truly risky investment. The vast percentage of the subsidy is received
by people realizing profits on the sale of real estate or blue-chip securities' (Neil Brooks,
'Formula for Tax Fairness,' *The Facts on Free Trade* 13, no. 1 [1991]:10). Criticisms such as
this may have moved the government to announce in the 1992 budget that the capital

gains exemption 'would be directed toward more productive investments.' The exemption would no longer be applicable to capital gains accrued on real estate after February 1992 (*Budget, 1992*), 23.

34 National Council of Welfare, 'Testing Tax Reform,' a brief presented to the House of Commons Standing Committee on Finance and Economic Affairs, 4 September 1987.

35 National Council of Welfare, *Help Wanted*. This study provides a detailed assessment of the impact of the GST on different levels of income.

36 To review the debate over day care would take this chapter too far afield. A good introduction to the debate can be found in National Council of Welfare, *Child Care: A Better Alternative* (Ottawa: Supply and Services, December 1988). See as well Susan Phillips, 'Rock-a-Bye Brian: The National Day Care Strategy,' in Graham, ed., *How Ottawa Spends*, 165-208. When the federal election of 1988 was called, the Canada Child Care Act was being discussed in the Senate. The government promised to reintroduce the bill following the election, but the project was abandoned.

37 The *White Paper on Tax Reform* initially proposed a $65 tax credit to replace the CTE. The House of Commons Standing Committee on Finance and Economic Affairs expressed concern at the erosion of child benefits as a result of this move and the partial indexing of benefits and turnover points, and suggested the tax credit be augmented by a credit of $130 for the third and subsequent children. This suggestion was accepted, and the tax credits became effective in the 1988 taxation year. See Moscovitch, ' "Slowing the Steamroller," ' 186.

38 National Council of Welfare, *Child Care*, 16.

39 National Council of Welfare, *The 1989 Budget and Social Policy* (Ottawa: Supply and Services, September 1989), 12.

40 A major national survey undertaken by the Southam newspaper group concluded that 24 per cent of adults are illiterate. Eight per cent are totally illiterate, and 16 per cent are functionally illiterate (lacking the skills to understand written material encountered in daily life). See Richard Wiler, 'The National Crisis in Literacy: Why Four to Five in Twenty Adults Can't Read,' *Perception* 13, no. 2 (1989):29.

41 Canada, Department of National Health and Welfare, *Inventory of Income Security Programs in Canada*, January 1988, Table 3.3a, 37. In 1987, out of a total of 2.2 million tax filers claiming the child tax credit, 1.6 million claims were allowed. This seems to be an improvement in take-up until one realizes that there were over 3.6 million families with children receiving family allowances. See *Inventory of Income Security Programs in Canada*, July 1990, 40, 43.

42 Canada, Department of Health and Welfare, *The Child Benefit*, A White Paper on Canada's New Integrated Child Tax Benefit, n.d., 5. Quebec's system of provincial family allowances would not be changed as a result of the new child benefit. André Bourbeau, income security minister, said parents would continue to receive the provincial family allowance of $10.17 per month for the first child, $14.25 for the second, $17.82 for the third, and $21.35 for the fourth and subsequent children. This program cost the provincial government $586 million. The federal family allowance benefit in Quebec paid $22.30 per month for the first child, $33.25 for the second, and $83.02 for the third and subsequent children. A child over the age of twelve received an additional $8.56 per month. Quebec is the only province with a pro-natalist policy, which was raised to particular prominence in the province's 1988 budget, when the finance minister announced Allowances for Newborn Children – $500 for the birth or adoption of the first child, $1,000 for the second child, and $6,000 for the third or subsequent child. These benefits are not available to families on social aid. See 'Federal Baby-Bonus Plan Won't Affect Quebec Plan,' Montreal *Gazette*, 27 February 1992, and Canada, Department of Health and Welfare, *Inventory of Income Security Programs in Canada*, July 1990, 47.

43 To qualify for the *earned* income supplement, a family had to have earned income of at least $3,750. The amount of the supplement increased at 8 per cent for every $100 of earned income above $3,750. An earned income of $10,000 qualified for the full $500 payment, which remained at the $500 level until earned income reached $20,521, when it was reduced at 10 per cent for every $100 of earned income over the $20,521 ceiling.

The basic child benefit had a turnover point of $25,921, and net family income over that would reduce the benefit at the rate of 5 per cent for families with two or more children and at 2.5 per cent for families with one child. Canada, House of Commons, *Minutes and Proceedings of the Legislative Committee on Bill C-80,* 15 July 1992.

44 *Vancouver Sun,* 15 July 1992.

45 Lise Corbeil of the National Anti-Poverty Organization made this point on CBC Radio, July 1992.

46 Canada, House of Commons, *Minutes and Proceedings of the Legislative Committee on Bill C-80,* evidence of Ken Battle.

47 The six-member commission was headed by Claude Forget, a former professor of economics and member of the Quebec National Assembly from 1973 to 1981 who served as minister of social affairs from 1971 to 1973. His five other commissioners included two labour leaders, a former CEO of Ford Motors of Canada, and a CEO of a large forestry company.

48 This American innovation is known as 'experience rating.' The Macdonald Commission thought it a good idea, but the Forget Commission considered it of doubtful benefit and did not recommend it. Labour unions, by and large, opposed the idea.

49 In addition to the minority report by the two labour members, a third commissioner registered his objections to 'annualization,' a main recommendation of the report (Forget Report, 421). Therefore, the report had a bare 50 per cent of its members fully supporting the recommendations.

50 Reinhard A. Hohaus, cited in Eveline Burns, *Social Security and Public Policy* (New York: McGraw Hill 1957), 36.

51 The majority report's criticisms of the UI administration – its heavy-handed bureaucracy, the complexity of regulations – were well founded. It was unfortunate that some of the report's ideas in this area were shelved along with the rest of the report. See Chapter 10 of the report.

52 Dennis Guest, 'Canadian and American Income Security Responses to Five Major Risks: A Comparison,' in *Free Trade and Social Policy,* ed. Glenn Drover (Ottawa-Montreal: Canadian Council on Social Development 1988), 95.

53 Cited in Michael Lynk, 'Labour Law Erosion,' *The Facts on Free Trade* 10, no. 2 (1988):75.

54 Canadian Council on Social Development, 'Canada's Social Programs Are in Trouble,' Ottawa, published for the Campaign against Bill C-69, October 1990, 5.

55 'BC Wants Court Fight over Ottawa Cash Cuts,' *Vancouver Sun,* 27 February 1990.

56 See 'Canada's Social Programs Are in Trouble,' which listed forty-one community organizations opposed to the bill.

57 Canada, Department of Health and Welfare, *Inventory of Income Security Programs in Canada,* January 1987, 8.

58 National Council of Welfare, *Funding Health and Higher Education: Danger Looming,* spring 1991, 21.

59 Canada, Minister of Finance, *Budget,* 26 February 1991, 71.

60 National Council of Welfare, *Funding Health and Higher Education,* 22-3. The federal government will save an estimated $97.6 billion in EPF payments between 1986-7 and the year 2000 (18).

61 The terms 'welfare' and 'social assistance' are used interchangeably. They refer to provincial social assistance programs, the last public safety net for Canadians with no other resources. The federal government shares the cost of these programs through the Canada Assistance Plan.

62 Eric Shragge, 'Welfare Reform, Quebec Style,' in *Unemployment and Welfare: Social Policy and the Work of Social Work,* ed. G. Riches and G. Ternowetsky (Toronto: Garamond Press 1990), 126.

63 Ibid., 129; and Graham Riches, 'Welfare Reform and Social Work Practice: Political Objectives and Ethical Dilemmas,' in Riches and Ternowetsky, eds., *Unemployment and Welfare,* 110.

64 Riches, 'Welfare Reform,' 114.

65 The financial assistance provided by the PWA program contained three components: a

supplement to employment income; reimbursement of approximately 55 per cent of eligible day care expenses; and a housing allowance where applicable. In addition, families enrolled in the PWA program did not have to pay provincial income tax. Canada, Department of Health and Welfare, *Inventory of Income Security Programs in Canada,* July 1990, 47-8.

66 Canadian Council on Social Development, 'Impressions,' *Perception* 10, no. 1 (1986):3.

67 C. Wright Mills, *The Sociological Imagination* (New York: Grove Press 1959), 8 ff.

68 Ibid.

69 This same confusion between personal troubles and public issues was seen at the federal level with the Canadian Jobs Strategy program, which ran from 1985 to 1989, when it was supplanted by yet another plan, the Labour Force Development Strategy. Both focus on the supply of labour to the neglect of the job supply. For a discussion of the Canadian Jobs Strategy, see Michael J. Prince and Jim J. Rice, 'The Canadian Jobs Strategy: Supply Side Social Policy,' in Graham, ed., *How Ottawa Spends,* 247-88; for a review of its successor, see Rianne Mahon, 'Adjust to Win? The New Tory Training Initiative,' in Graham, ed., *How Ottawa Spends 1990-91,* 50-72; and for a solid critique of the Canadian Jobs Strategy, see Patricia Daenzer, 'Policy and Program Responses of the 1980s: The National Training Program and the Canadian Jobs Strategy,' in Riches and Ternowetsky, eds., *Unemployment and Welfare,* 65-90.

70 Beveridge, *Full Employment,* 254.

71 The initial target group were people in need aged 60 to 64, who were married to low-income OAS/GIS recipients. However, single, separated, or divorced people in the same age and income bracket were denied coverage, as were a low-income married couple, both in the 60 to 64 age group. These regulations were being challenged in the courts under Section 15 of the Charter of Rights and Freedoms. Canadian Union of Public Employees, *The Facts on Free Trade* 11, no. 2 (1989):37.

72 Beginning 1 January 1987 people could claim a reduced pension at any time between the ages of 60 and 70. Claiming a pension before the standard retirement age of 65 would mean a reduced pension of one-half of 1 per cent for every month before a person's 65th birthday. Conversely, waiting until age 70 would mean an enhanced pension using the same formula.

73 By 1989, pension credit splitting remained the exception rather than the rule in Canada. As of June 1989, only 20,482 applications for pension splitting had been submitted since the option became available in 1987. Over this same time period, there were half a million divorces in Canada, not counting divorces in Quebec, that could have led to credit splitting under the QPP (National Council of Welfare, *A Pension Primer* [Ottawa: Supply and Services 1989], 32).

74 The increases specified indicated a gradually increasing contribution rate from 1987 to 2011. The rate for 1987 was set at 1.9 per cent for the employee, 1.9 per cent for the employer, and 3.8 per cent for the self-employed. The rate schedule was reviewed and raised again in 1991 from 2.3 per cent each from employee and employer, to eventually reach a combined rate of 9.1 per cent by the year 2011. Identical contribution rates will apply to the QPP for at least five years. Although paying a contribution rate of 4.5 per cent on the insurable portion of wages in the year 2011 may seem high, the Canadian worker will still be paying far less than people covered by more mature social insurance systems, such as those in Europe or the United States. In the United States, for example, American workers were, in the early 1990s, paying 7.65 per cent of insurable earnings up to $55,500 in 1992. In Canada, the 1992 contribution rate was 2.4 per cent on a year's maximum pensionable earnings of $32,300.

75 Michael J. Prince, 'From Meech Lake to Golden Pond: The Elderly, Pension Reform and Federalism in the 1990s,' in *How Ottawa Spends, 1991-92,* ed., Frances Abele (Ottawa: Carleton University Press 1991), 329.

76 'Quilting Odd Jobs Together New Way of Making Ends Meet,' *Vancouver Sun,* 2 September 1992, citing a report prepared for Statistics Canada.

77 National Council of Welfare, *A Pension Primer,* 42-3.

78 Ibid., 47.

79 The council suggested that the reduction rate be raised from 50 per cent to 63 per cent for single pensioners and to 60 per cent for couples.

80 National Council of Welfare, *Pension Reform* (Ottawa: Supply and Services 1990), 28. Better pensions would require higher contributions, but the council suggested that the cost of improved pensions could be offset by charging premiums on the worker's total wage rather than on wages up to what is roughly equivalent to the average wage. See ibid., 73.

81 National Council of Welfare, *Women and Poverty Revisited* (Ottawa: Minister of Supply and Services 1990), 103.

82 Canada, Health and Welfare, *Income Security Programs, Monthly Statistics,* June 1992, 13.

83 Stephen Hume, 'As PM Preens, Canada's Children Go Hungry,' *Vancouver Sun,* 5 October 1990.

84 As a result of the deeper recession in 1990-1, the percentage of children in poverty had moved closer to 20 per cent. 'Ottawa's Contribution to Child Welfare Not Impressive, Activist Groups Say,' *Vancouver Sun,* 1 October 1991; and 'Two Million Needed Food Aid,' ibid., 17 March 1992.

85 'Child Poverty Scandalous, All-Party Panel of MPs Told,' *Vancouver Sun,* 31 October 1991.

86 'Ottawa's Contribution.'

87 Phillips, 'Rock-a-Bye Brian,' 165-208.

88 When the value-added GST was introduced in 1991, the government increased the refundable sales tax credit to $100 for each child and $275 for adults. The turnover point, above which the credit is reduced, was to rise to $24,800 in 1991 (up from $18,000 under the old federal sales tax in 1990). This refundable credit is paid quarterly, whereas formerly it was paid once a year. The National Council of Welfare said that the enhanced credit will reduce but not remove the sales tax burden from most poor families and individuals (*Help Wanted*).

89 'Child Poverty Scandalous.'

90 '$500-Million Federal Program Called a "Band-Aid,"' *Vancouver Sun,* 5 May 1992.

91 National Council of Welfare, *Help Wanted,* 31.

92 According to J.K. Galbraith, lowering interest rates and slashing social programs do nothing to promote economic recovery ('Galbraith Says Public Works Needed Today,' *Vancouver Sun,* 8 August 1992).

93 Brooks, 'A Formula for Tax Fairness,' 7-12.

94 Child Poverty Action Group and the Social Planning Council of Metropolitan Toronto, *Unequal Futures: The Legacies of Child Poverty in Canada* (Toronto 1991).

95 I am indebted in this initial section to Nelson Wiseman, 'The Folly of Constitutional Reform,' in *'English Canada' Speaks Out,* ed. J.L. Granatstein and Kenneth McNaught (Toronto: Doubleday 1991).

96 Desmond Morton, *Confederation: A Short History of Canada's Constitution* (Toronto: Umbrella Press 1992), 33.

97 Statements such as 'the Constitution Act of 1982 was imposed on Quebec against its will' are 'like all myths worthy of the name, a half truth. This Act was endorsed, indeed formulated, by the province's democratically elected representatives in the federal House of Commons' (J. Stefan Dupré, 'Canada's Political and Constitutional Future: Reflections on the Belanger-Campeau Report and Bill 150,' in Granatstein and McNaught, eds., *'English Canada' Speaks Out,* 67-8.

98 A.W. Johnson, formerly a senior Ottawa bureaucrat, wrote that the opting-out arrangement would mean that in the future 'every premier and every provincial minister of finance would have a no-lose incentive for opting out: they would be compensated by the federal government whether or not they conformed with the norms and standards of the proposed national program. They would be in a position to get at least some "free money" for other objectives simply by mounting a less costly program and they would avoid any real accountability for the spending of the "equivalent compensation" they got from the federal government' ('A National Government in a Federal State,' in *Constitutional Politics,* ed. Duncan Cameron and Miriam Smith [Toronto: James Lorimer 1992], 84-5).

99 See, as examples, Patrick Grady, *The Economic Consequences of Quebec Sovereignty* (Vancouver: Fraser Institute 1991); the nine studies commissioned by the Belanger-

Campeau Commission; Toronto Dominion Bank, Department of Economic Research, 'Developments in Canada's Constitution: An Analysis of the Meech Lake Accord,' 1990; David Varty, *Who Gets Ungava?* (Vancouver: Varty and Company 1991).

100 In fact, as any changes to national institutions called for unanimity rather than the existing 7/50 formula, this meant that each province had a veto.

101 The idea of entrenching social rights in the new Constitution was never a part of the federal proposals. In fact, the subject had to be 'forced into the discussions on the constitution' at the third constitutional conference in Montreal in February 1992 at the initiative of Ontario and its premier, Bob Rae ('Social Charter Thrust to Centre,' *Globe and Mail*, 5 February 1992).

102 David Shugarman, 'The Social Charter,' in Cameron and Smith, eds., *Constitutional Politics*, 158. See also Martha Jackman, 'When a Social Charter Isn't,' *Canadian Forum* 70, no. 808 (April 1992):8-10.

103 Nationally, 54.2 per cent voted against the accord and 44.8 per cent voted for it. Only Newfoundland, Prince Edward Island, New Brunswick, and the Northwest Territories approved the deal with decisive majorities. Ontario voted 'yes' 49.8 per cent and 'no' 49.6 per cent. All other provinces and the Yukon voted no (*Maclean's*, 2 November 1992, 13).

104 Duncan Cameron, 'October 26, 1992: A Symposium on the Outcome of the National Vote,' *Canadian Forum* 71, no. 815 (December 1992):12.

105 Kari Levitt, 'Requiem for a Referendum,' *Canadian Forum* 71, no. 815 (December 1992):13.

106 Mel Watkins, 'A Flawed Process,' *Canadian Forum* 71, no. 815 (December 1992):14.

107 The clearest explanation of what asymmetrical federalism would mean is provided by A.W. Johnson, who would transfer certain of Parliament's powers to the Quebec National Assembly but 'provide that wherever Parliament cannot constitutionally legislate in Quebec (the areas transferred), Quebec MPs and Senators can no longer legislate in the rest of Canada, through Parliament. They would simply lose their power to speak or to vote on specific measures that could not, constitutionally, apply in Quebec. This would not apply to Appropriation Acts or taxation measures; they have to do with the ensemble of government functions. As to the specific measures themselves (in respect of which Quebec's MPs and Senators could not participate), the government would have to find support for its measures from among the MPs and Senators from other provinces. If the government failed, and were defeated on its measures, that defeat would not be treated as a non-confidence vote. The consequence of this approach to constitutional reform is, of course, striking. The people of Quebec would have more constitutional powers through their provincial government than would the people of the other provinces, but they would enjoy correspondingly less power than the others, through their MPs and Senators in Parliament ... Taken together, however, the constitutional power that would be exercised by Quebeckers would be equal to those enjoyed by Canadians elsewhere. No special status for anyone, in short' (Johnson, 'A National Government in a Federal State,' 90-1). However, asymmetrical federalism becomes more complex if Aboriginals are recognized as a third nation with asymmetrical allocation of powers and entitlements. See Frank Cunningham, 'Democracy and Three-National Asymmetry,' *Canadian Forum* 71 no. 815 (December 1992):14.

108 A separate referendum was held in Quebec following rules that the rest of Canada would have done well to emulate. The Quebec National Assembly laid down rules that promoted equal treatment of both sides of the issue, including equal amounts of money for advertising. In other provinces the 'yes' side had the resources of the federal government to promote its position while the 'no' side had to raise its own funds, which made the 'no' victory all the more impressive. See Levitt, 'Requiem,' 13.

109 Senator Jacques Herbert made the 'ramming' charge ('Commons Curtails Debate on Child Benefits,' *Vancouver Sun*, 10 October 1992).

110 To add to the appearance of growing harmonization, the one controversial addition to the new child benefit package, effective January 1993, was a $500 supplement to low-income families with work-related income (which violates the much-repeated pledge of Conservatives that they wish to see help directed to the neediest). This type of benefit is also found in the United States.

111 Finance minister Mazankowski announced a number of economy measures in a mini-budget, 2 December 1992. A total of $8 billion was chopped from the budget, a third of which was taken from the UI account by reducing the benefit paid from 60 to 57 per cent of insurable earnings and by denying benefits to workers fired for misconduct or who quit their jobs. A wage freeze for all federal employees, including elected officials, was also announced. See 'Unemployed Bear Third of Budget Cuts,' *Vancouver Sun,* 3 December 1992. The percentage of unemployed Canadians who qualify for UI benefits has dropped significantly since 1986, when almost 85 per cent of the unemployed qualified. In October 1992, the *Vancouver Sun* reported that '2.5 years of recession combined with tighter UI eligibility rules have resulted in the proportion of unemployed collecting benefits falling to 60 per cent' ('Fall Brings Surge in Bankruptcies, Growing Tab for Jobless Benefits,' 29 October 1992). This pushes the Canadian UI system closer to the American system, in which the percentage of American unemployed who qualified for UI was described by the Economic Council of Canada (1987 *Annual Review*) as 'extraordinarily low – about one in four.'

112 BC health minister Elizabeth Cull, giving evidence before a Commons legislative committee studying Bill C-91, a Patent Protection Bill, said that 'extended patent protection will drive drug prices up to American levels, which are 35 per cent higher than Canada's' ('Cull Warns of Frightening Costs from Proposed Drug Legislation,' *Vancouver Sun,* 1 December 1992). Ralph Nader, the American consumer advocate, said, 'The target for the giant health care industries in the United States is to subvert, if not destroy both the compulsory pricing system for drugs and elements of the universal health insurance system.' He also stated that the powerful US drug and hospital lobby wants to do away with the Canadian medicare system and drug care system because these are being proposed as models for US reform of its health care system. See 'Americans Killing Medicare, Nader Says,' *Vancouver Sun,* 3 December 1992.

113 'Training, Not Benefits, Bank's Key to Unlocking Jobless Yoke,' *Vancouver Sun,* 11 December 1992.

114 In a 1992 report prepared by Statistics Canada comparing the costs and outcomes of health care in Canada and the United States, it was indicated that Canadians have a lower rate of infant mortality, lower rates of most chronic diseases, and greater life expectancy for both men and women. See 'Medicare Reported Healthier Here than US,' *Vancouver Sun,* 30 October 1992.

115 'Raising Our Children ... out of Poverty,' Canadian Council on Social Development, *Overview* 7, no. 1 (1989).

116 Phillips, 'Rock-a-Bye-Brian,' 194.

117 'No Magic Wand to Dispel Woes, Mulroney Says,' *Vancouver Sun,* 17 November 1992.

Chapter 15: Debating the Future of Social Security

1 In 1993, a few months prior to the general election, the Conservative Party elected a new leader, opinion polls having shown that Brian Mulroney's popularity had plummeted beyond hope of recovery – a victim of the severe recession of 1991-2. Kim Campbell, the party's choice for leader and prime minister, assumed her office in June 1993 and began planning for a federal election to be held later that year.

2 Therese Jennisen, 'Farewell to Welfare? A Review of Benoit Bouchard's Speech to the OECD,' *Canadian Review of Social Policy* 31 (spring 1993):85. The plans for social security reform developed by the Conservative government (but never made public) bear a striking similarity to those that eventually appeared under the aegis of its Liberal successor: the concern for labour supply, the idea of tailoring job training to the individual, the general concern for cost containment, and designing programs to take care of the 'most vulnerable.' One can only assume that the senior civil servants in the Department of Finance, who were said to be neoconservative in outlook, simply handed the homework they did on social program reform for the Conservatives to the new Liberal government, which found it to its liking.

3 Under the Mulroney government, Employment and Immigration Canada was the department responsible for unemployment insurance. When Kim Campbell became prime

minister, she reduced the number of government departments, and Employment, Immigration Settlement, and Unemployment Insurance were incorporated into a new department called Human Resources and Labour. When the Liberals took over in 1993, Citizenship and Immigration Canada was made responsible for immigration; unemployment insurance became the responsibility of the renamed Human Resources Development Canada.

4 Canada, House of Commons, *Notes for an Address by the Honourable Lloyd Axworthy, Minister of Human Resources Development,* Ottawa, 31 January 1994.

5 Human Resources Development Canada, *Improving Social Security in Canada: A Discussion Paper,* October 1994, 9. This document is also referred to as the Green Paper.

6 The government had already announced the cancellation of a UI premium rate increase scheduled for 1995 in December 1993. The rate was to be frozen at $3.07 per $100 of insurable earnings, the 1994 rate. The budget, however, rolled the rate back to $3.00 per $100 of insurable earnings. The employer's rate would be correspondingly reduced. Effective April 1994, the maximum duration of UI claims for new beneficiaries was to be reduced (determined in part by the employee's work history); effective July 1994, the minimum entrance requirement was increased to twelve weeks from ten; the benefit rate for new beneficiaries was to be adjusted from the existing 57 per cent of insurable earnings to a new two-part rate structure – claimants with dependants and low earnings (below one-half the maximum insurable earnings limit of $780 per week) would receive 60 per cent of their insured earnings and other claimants 55 per cent, although government officials admitted that only 15 per cent of the unemployed would qualify for the higher rate. To improve fairness, the government planned to amend provisions of the Unemployment Insurance Act relating to workers who quit their jobs voluntarily or were fired for misconduct. Canada, Department of Finance, *The Budget Plan,* February 1994, 36-7, and Human Resources Development Canada, *Proposed Changes to the Unemployment Insurance Program,* February 1994, and *The Budget Speech,* 22 February 1994, 10-11.

7 National Council of Welfare, *The Canada Assistance Plan: No Time for Cuts* (winter 1991), 23.

8 Members of the expert committee were Ken Battle, president of the Caledon Institute of Social Policy; John Fryer, former union executive; Patrick Johnson, formerly executive director of the Canadian Council on Social Development; Arthur Kroeger, university chancellor, former federal civil servant; Aidea Landry, lawyer and businesswoman; Judith Maxwell, economist; Lorna Marsden, university president; Alice Nakamura, professor of finance and management science; John D. O'Leary, president of Frontier College; Guylaine Saucier, chartered accountant and company director; Brian J. Stock, CEO and company director; Joseph B. Stern, economist; Michel Vennat, company director; David Zussman, president of a research firm.

9 Canada, House of Commons, Report of the Standing Committee on Human Resources Development, *Security, Opportunities and Fairness: Canadians Renewing Their Social Programs,* Ottawa 1995.

10 'Social Reforms Take a Back Seat,' *Globe and Mail,* 31 January 1995.

11 Human Resources Development Canada, *Improving Social Security in Canada,* referred to as the green paper or the discussion paper. There were also a number of supplementary papers issued providing additional background information: *The Context of Reform; From Unemployment Insurance to Employment Insurance; Reforming the Canada Assistance Plan; Income Security for Children; Child Care and Development; Persons with Disabilities; Employment Development Services;* and *Federal Support to Post-Secondary Education.*

12 Canada, Minister of Human Resources Development, *Context of Reform: A Supplementary Paper,* 3.

13 Ibid., 2.

14 Ibid., 8.

15 Osberg reported that the recession of 1991-2 had 'created a generalized surplus of labour in almost all skill categories' ('Micro Transitions and Macro Policy in a Federal State,' in Elisabeth B. Reynolds, *Income Security in Canada: Changing Needs, Changing Means* [Montreal: Renouf Publishing Company 1993], 89).

16 Patricia Daenzer, 'Policy and Program Responses in the 1980s: The National Training Program and the Canadian Jobs Strategy,' in *Unemployment and Welfare: Social Policy and the Work of Social Work*, ed. G. Riches and G. Ternowetsky (Toronto: Garamond Press 1990), 66.

17 Judith Maxwell, 'Globalizations and Family Security,' in *Family Security in Insecure Times*, Canadian Council on Social Development (Ottawa 1993), 41.

18 When Chrysler Canada hired 1,000 new workers to staff the third shift at its Windsor minivan plant in 1994, almost 30 per cent of those employed had degrees, said Chrysler official Walt McCall. See 'GM Job Seekers Need High School Diploma to Gain Employment,' *Vancouver Sun*, 13 January 1995.

19 A better explanation might be found in the following quotation: 'The microelectronic revolution of the 1980s has overturned [the] basic relationship between employment and output and threatens devastating effects on employment levels. This is because microelectronics permit an exponential rise in output, together with an exponential fall in input such as energy, capital and labour. We have thus reached a stage where output can be increased with a continual reduction of input, especially of labour' (David N. Ashton, *Unemployment under Capitalism* [Brighton: Harvester Press 1986], 42).

20 Diana Ralph, 'What Do Canadians Really Think about the Social Security Review?' *Canadian Review of Social Policy* 34 (winter 1994):59-71.

21 'Taxing Firms with High Layoff Rates Being Considered,' *Vancouver Sun*, 26 February 1994.

22 Parliamentary Standing Committee on Human Resources Development, *Report*, 263.

23 Ralph, 'What Do Canadians,' 61-2.

24 Bernard Casey, 'Employment Promotion,' in *The Social Dimension: Employment Policy in the European Community*, ed. Michael Gold (London: MacMillan 1993), 172-83.

25 Bruce Little, 'Monetary Policy Worsened Recession, Caused Living Standards to Slip, Economist Says,' *Globe and Mail*, 29 May 1995.

26 Minister of Human Resources Development, *Employment Development Services: A Supplementary Paper* (Ottawa 1994), 16.

27 Susan Carter and Chris Clark, 'A Critique of Social Security Reform Proposals,' *Perception* 18, no. 2 (1994):9.

28 Richard Mackie, 'Quebec Unions Pan Axworthy Reforms,' *Globe and Mail*, 5 November 1994.

29 Eric Beauchesne, 'Target Welfare State, Investor Group Urges,' *Vancouver Sun*, 25 January 1994.

30 Eric Beauchesne, 'UI System Tops Budget Woes, Report Claims,' *Vancouver Sun*, 12 January 1994.

31 Human Resources Development Canada, *From Unemployment Insurance to Employment Insurance* (Ottawa 1994), 62 and Tables B1 and B2.

32 The G-7 is composed of the United States, France, the UK, Germany, Italy, Canada, and Japan, and the average of their UI wage replacement rate is 49 per cent (not including Canada). The average replacement rate of the ten countries surveyed is 59.6 per cent. The finance department manages to be both technically correct and widely misleading.

33 A.B. Atkinson and G.V. Mogensen, eds., *Welfare and Work Incentives: A North European Perspective* (Oxford: Clarendon Press 1993), 296-7. The type of careful research and even more careful conclusions of Atkinson's work in Europe and Corak's research in Canada on work incentive and social welfare benefits throw into doubt the claims of the Fraser Institute that the Canadian UI system 'with its generous access and benefits has artificially boosted Canada's jobless rate by three or four per cent' ('Streamline UI Programs New Finance Minister Urged,' *Vancouver Sun*, 14 December 1993).

34 Miles Corak, 'Unemployment Insurance, Work Disincentives and the Canadian Labour Market: An Overview,' in *Unemployment Insurance: How to Make It Work*, C. Green et al., C.D. Howe Institute (Ottawa: Renouf Publishing Company 1994), 140. Corak, who reviewed the Canadian research on the relationship between unemployment rates and UI benefits, also pointed out that there was no evidence to suggest that the decision to quit a job was influenced by the availability of UI (148). Nor did he find a strong relationship between generosity of benefits (weekly benefit payments and duration) and the probability of being a more frequent claimant (147). Nevertheless, the Conservative government amended the UI legislation in 1993 to deny, outright, benefits to those who quit their jobs

without good cause. Previously, quitting a job would mean a period of disqualification, as is common in Europe. In this regard, Canada has aligned its social policy with that of the United States, where all but four states have a disqualification clause.

35 According to Corak, 'there are no detailed examinations in the Canadian empirical litera-ture of the effect of UI on the behaviour of firms' (ibid., 133).

36 'Companies That Lay Off Employees ... Government Study,' *Vancouver Sun,* 21 December 1994.

37 Human Resources Development Canada, *Proposed Changes to the UI Program,* February 1994, 2.

38 'Job-Creation Scheme "Absurd,"' *Vancouver Sun,* 12 March 1994.

39 Human Resources Development Canada, *From Unemployment Insurance to Employment Insurance,* 20.

40 Richard M. Titmuss, *Social Policy: An Introduction,* ed. Brian Abel-Smith and Kay Titmuss (London: Allen and Unwin 1974), 31.

41 Saskatchewan will be the first province in Canada to require employers to pay benefits to part-time workers. The new labour code will require companies with more than twenty employees to pay their part-time workers all benefits, primarily medical, dental, and life insurance, that are paid to full-time workers. The benefits would be pro-rated to the hours worked. The Canadian Federation of Independent Business was not pleased, arguing that this will further retard job creation. 'Saskatchewan First Province to Force Benefit Payments to Part-Time Workers,' *Vancouver Sun,* 12 March 1994.

42 Human Resources Development Canada, *Child Care and Development,* Ottawa 1994, 2.

43 Ecumenical Coalition for Economic Justice, *Reweaving Canada's Social Programs: From Shredded Safety Net to Social Solidarity,* Toronto 1993, 67.

44 Human Resources Development Canada, *Child Care and Development.*

45 Minister of Human Resources Development, *Report of the Advisory Group on Working Time and the Distribution of Work* (Ottawa: Supply and Services, December 1994).

46 Penelope Leach, *Children First* (New York: Knopf 1994).

47 Richard Titmuss, an ardent foe of means tests for the basics of life because of the implied personal failure involved, saw nothing wrong with means-tested university grants. Such an application would demonstrate ambition, not failure; therefore no personal humilia-tion is invoked (personal conversation).

48 The International Labour Office (ILO), Geneva, sees the fundamental purpose of social security as 'giving individuals and families the confidence that their level of living and quality of life will not, in so far as it is possible, be greatly eroded by any social or economic eventuality' (*Into the Twenty-First Century: The Development of Social Security* [Geneva: ILO 1984], 19).

49 National Council of Welfare, *Incentives and Disincentives to Work* (autumn 1993), 52-3.

50 In 1981, a Special Parliamentary Committee on the Disabled recommended a compre-hensive national disability insurance program for people both in and out of the workforce (Canada, House of Commons, Special Committee on the Disabled and Handicapped, *Obstacles,* 1981). This idea was rejected at the time by the Liberal government. Terry Ison, an Ontario law professor, has for a number of years advocated a comprehensive system that would merge 'all existing plans such as Workers' Compensation, auto insurance ben-efits, compensation for victims of crime, private individual and group long-term disabil-ity plans, Canada Pension Plan disability benefits, and sickness benefits under Unemployment Insurance, to eliminate duplication, inequity and the inefficiencies of multiple administrations. The plan would provide an indexed income replacement up to a maximum and would be funded through a combination of employer-employee contri-butions, a tax on gasoline and motor vehicles, a tax on hazardous activities, and through general government revenue. It would also allow for an integrated and systematic approach to rehabilitation, a key element that would help stabilize costs' (Leon Muscynski, *Alternatives to Welfare* [Ontario: Social Assistance Review Committee, March 1987], 24).

51 Rodney S. Haddow, *Poverty Reform in Canada 1958-78* (Montreal and Kingston: McGill-Queen's University Press 1993).

52 The total cost of the demonstration project in New Brunswick and British Columbia (the Self-Sufficiency Project) is $70 million, and it will run for nine years (it began in 1992). Cost of administration will be $38.5 million with $30 million in income supplements. Those recruited for the pilot project (entry is voluntary, but potential recruits are randomly selected) will, if they find a low-wage job, have their wage doubled, up to a maximum, but they move off social assistance and are totally responsible for themselves. A report in 1994 indicated that if a single mother in British Columbia takes a full-time $7 per hour job, her income will be doubled to $24,870. This supplement continues for three years, by which time the worker may have advanced in her job to the point where the supplement is no longer required.

53 Sheila B. Kamerman and Alfred J. Kahn, *Mothers Alone: Strategies for a Time of Change* (Dover, MA: Auburn House Publishing 1988), 82.

54 The province of Quebec hopes to have legislation in place by the end of 1995 that will permit the province to deduct child support payments automatically from parents' paycheques, whether they are in default or not. The government estimated that child-support orders are in default about 55 per cent of the time. This high rate of non-compliance is undoubtedly a reflection of the severe unemployment situation in that province ('Child Support to Be Taken from Cheques,' *Vancouver Sun,* 29 October 1994).

55 Since July 1989, the period of time has expanded to 450 days. For the first 360 days the system compensates about 90 per cent of income loss for most parents. Later days are compensated at a flat rate. See Bjorn Gustafsson and N. Anders Klevmarken, 'Taxes and Transfers in Sweden: Incentive Effects on Labour Supply,' in Atkinson and Mogensen, eds., *Welfare and Work Incentives,* 103.

56 Jonathan Murphy, 'Analysing the Poverty of Christopher Sarlo,' *Perception* 17, no. 2 (1993):19-21.

57 Kammerman and Kahn, *Mothers Alone,* 219.

58 ILO, *Into the Twenty-First Century,* 23.

59 Four models were offered for the first approach: Model 1A would provide significant increases in CTB benefits for all families with incomes less than $25,000, but with maximum benefits concentrated on those families with incomes of less than $15,000. Such a program could provide a maximum benefit of $2,500 per annum for the first child, $2,000 for the second, and $1,500 for the third and each subsequent child. There would be 'significant reallocation' from families with incomes of $45,000 and over. The additional net cost of this model would be $1 billion. Model 1B would provide enhanced benefits to a wider group (all families below the $45,000 range) with a net cost of $2 billion. Model 1C was more economical. Benefit increases would be less generous and more targeted, and the net cost would be $800 million. Model 1D would have zero net cost – it would involve increased benefits to the lowest-income families (probably those with incomes less than $15,000), and all the money would be reallocated from families above a cut-off figure (which was not specified). The WIS would be merged in each of the four models with the CTB (*Income Security for Children,* 14).

60 The advantages of this plan, according to the supplementary paper, were that removing children's benefits from the welfare system would strengthen the work incentive for their parents (15), a design element lacking in the first model.

61 'New Pact Urged to Combat Poverty,' *Vancouver Sun,* 7 March 1995.

62 Neil Brooks, 'Tax Breaks for the Rich,' *Canadian Dimension* (January/February 1994): 9. Brooks's recommendations for a more progressive income tax system were discussed in Chapter 14.

63 Beth Gorham, 'Spend Smarter to Make Benefits Better, Group Says,' *Vancouver Sun,* 11 March 1994.

64 Richard Shillington, 'The Tax System and Social Policy Reform,' in Jane Pulkingham and Gordon Ternowetsky, eds., *Remaking Canadian Social Policy: Social Security in the Late 1990s* (Halifax: Fernwood Publishing 1996), 100-11.

65 This idea was the brainchild of economist James Tobin and was endorsed by the Canadian Centre for Policy Alternatives, the Council of Canadians, and the Canadian Labour Congress. Finance Minister Martin said the idea was 'theoretically quite attractive' but

impractical because currency speculators would have little difficulty avoiding it by operating through tax havens. Tobin disputed this and said 'These transactions occur through banks and mostly big banks ... and they're not going to move their operations to the Cayman Islands' (Eric Beauchesne, 'Tax Aimed at Whacking Speculators "Won't Fly,"' *Vancouver Sun*, 30 May 1995).

66 No changes were to be made in major transfer programs for 1995-6, but in 1996-7 the new Canada Social Transfer will be $2.5 billion less than what would have been paid under the CAP and EPF programs. In 1997-8, the Canada Social Transfer will be cut by a further $4.5 billion to $25.1 billion. The two territories will have their entitlements frozen at the 1994-5 levels, and the following year the expenditure base in the formula will be reduced by 5 per cent for each territory. *Budget Speech* (1995), 19.

67 According to the finance minister, the provinces would no longer have to put up with the following irritants as a result of the new block-funded arrangement: the provinces would not be subject to rules stipulating which expenditures are eligible for cost-sharing; provinces could pursue their own 'innovative' approaches to social program reform; and the expense of administering cost-sharing (the reporting requirements and so on) would be eliminated. See Canada, Minister of Finance, *Budget 1995*, February 1995.

68 Richard Splane, letter to the editor, *Globe and Mail*, 22 April 1995. Formerly, Splane was an assistant deputy minister in the Department of Health and Welfare, Ottawa, and one of the architects of the Canada Assistance Plan.

69 Bruce Little, 'Transfer Cut Not a Threat: Study,' *Globe and Mail*, 15 November 1995, and 'Municipalities Fear Offloaded Debt,' *Vancouver Sun*, 1 March 1996.

70 National Council of Welfare, *The 1995 Budget and Block Funding* (Ottawa: Minister of Supply and Services 1995), 22-3, and Sherri Torjman, 'Is CAP in Need of Assistance?' in Keith Banting and Ken Battle, eds., *A New Social Vision for Canada? Perspectives on the Federal Discussion Paper on Social Security Reform* (Ottawa and Kingston: Caledon Institute of Social Policy and School of Policy Studies, Queen's University, 1994), 99-113. In November 1995, the BC government announced it would impose a three-month residence requirement on all new applications for social assistance, in defiance of the one remaining welfare standard accompanying the new CHST block funding. Ottawa replied with a threat to withhold $47 million in transfer payments. The province estimated that its residence requirement would save $25 million, which still left a substantial $21 million penalty. The BC government claimed it was receiving more than its share of unemployed from other provinces, where welfare rates had been slashed. Cynics said the NDP government, facing an election in 1996, was aiming to undercut the Liberal opposition, which was expected to have a 'get tough on welfare' plank as part of its platform. The NDP won the election, but narrowly.

71 Mark Kennedy, 'UI Reform Package Being Greeted with Little Fanfare, Proponents Say,' *Vancouver Sun*, 9 May 1996.

72 Ibid.

73 The basic UI premium rate was reduced from $3.00 per $100 of insured earnings to $2.95, effective 1 January 1996. This modest cut in premiums was accompanied by a major cut in the maximum insurable earnings from $815 to $750 per week. This reduced the maximum benefit from $448 to $412 per week. This, according to the government, maintained the 55 per cent ratio of benefit to insured earnings, although labour representatives claimed that benefits would be less than half of previous insured earnings. Alan Freeman and Edward Greenspon, 'Ottawa to Cut UI Premiums,' *Globe and Mail*, 23 November 1995; and Nancy Riche, Executive Vice-President CLC, Ottawa, 'Unemployment Insurance [letter to the editor],' *Globe and Mail*, 1 April 1996. The maximum duration of benefits was reduced from fifty to forty-five weeks, but only a minority would qualify for the maximum owing to a 'work component' introduced in the 1994 budget, which counts not only the number of weeks of insured employment but the length of attachment to the workforce in calculating the number of weeks of paid benefit. Canada, Human Resources Development, *Proposed Changes to the Unemployment Insurance Program*, February 1994, 4-5.

74 A minimum of twenty-six weeks of insured employment would be required by these three categories.

75 Under the 'intensity rule,' people who claim more than twenty weeks of benefits in the past five years will receive a 1 per cent reduction in their benefits, and an additional 1 per cent reduction for each subsequent claim. The intensity rule will only reduce the benefit by a maximum of 5 per cent, or to 50 per cent of insured earnings. The family income supplement will be gradually phased in and will be linked to the child tax benefit and the working income supplement.

76 The government estimated that 420 to 700 hours were the equivalent of twelve to twenty weeks at thirty-five hours per week. It was thought this higher qualification would encourage young people to remain in school longer or take job training.

77 Described by the government as a 'strengthened clawback,' the new rules stipulated that for those who have claimed less than twenty-one weeks of benefit in the past five years, the clawback will only begin at incomes above $48,750. A maximum of 30 per cent of benefits potentially can be clawed back. However, for those with a longer history of claims over a five-year period, from 50 to 100 per cent of benefits could be retrieved, beginning with incomes of $39,000. 'This provision will discourage unnecessary use of the system by workers with levels of income substantially above the average.' Human Resources Development Canada, *Employment Insurance: A Guide to Employment Insurance, July 1976*, 11.

78 In press releases, Human Resources Development Canada mentioned five 'active employment benefits': *wages subsidies,* provided to employers who give jobless Canadians work experience leading to permanent employment; *earnings supplements,* a temporary wage top-up to encourage individuals to get back into the workforce; *self-employment assistance,* practical help for people who wish to start their own business; *job creation partnerships,* providing jobs and community-based work experience in projects that contribute to local economic growth; and *skills, loans, and grants,* provincially approved financial support for unemployed workers to acquire occupational skills leading to reemployment.

79 Ken MacQueen, 'Much-Maligned UI Contributes to the Nation's Collective Welfare,' *Vancouver Sun,* 15 January 1996.

80 Nancy Riche, 'In Defence of Unemployment Insurance,' *Globe and Mail,* 18 December 1995. Nancy Riche is vice-president of the Canadian Labour Congress.

81 Eric Beauchesne, 'UI Payments Drop to Five-Year Low, Ottawa Says,' *Vancouver Sun,* 30 November 1995.

82 'Few Impressed with Looming UI Adjustments,' *Vancouver Sun,* 24 November 1995.

83 The National Council of Welfare reports that 69 per cent of tax filers with taxable returns and incomes of $50,000 or more took advantage of RRSPs in 1993, with an average contribution of $5,155. Only 23 per cent of tax filers with incomes under $10,000 put money into RRSPs, and their average contribution was only $1,115. *Pension Primer 1996*, Table 10, 43.

84 Monica Townson, *The Social Contract for Seniors in Canada: Preparing for the 21st Century,* Advisory Council on Aging, March 1984, 11.

85 'Keep Paws Off Pension, Ottawa Warned,' *Vancouver Sun,* 15 June 1995. The argument of the Conference Board of Canada that any move toward social equity will damage economic growth was also used by Conservatives in 1966 against the Carter Commission on Taxation's appeal for greater equity in the tax system. But this argument has even longer historical roots. In the 1840s, when Edwin Chadwick, the noted English social reformer, investigated the issue of child labour and found very young children working for long hours in mines and factories, he met with a similar response, according to historian Maurice Bruce: 'Coal-owners and manufacturers regarded all interference as unnecessary and ruinous and believed it would force them out of business.' See Bruce, *The Coming of the Welfare State* (London: B.T. Batsford 1961), 58.

86 'Ottawa Must Hack Spending Much More,' *Vancouver Sun,* 7 October 1994.

87 Townson, *Social Contract,* 35.

88 A bizarre footnote to the announcement of his particular policy change was revealed in

the book *Double Vision: The Inside Story of Liberals in Power*, published in November 1996, which revealed that Martin argued strongly to be allowed to introduce his seniors benefit plan in his 1995 budget. The prime minister, anticipating the Quebec referendum on independence scheduled for later in the year, saw it as politically risky and vetoed the idea. The spectre of Solange Denis hung in the air. Almost as a form of exorcism, Martin arranged a highly secret visit to Denis, explained the new seniors benefit, and won her approval. It is doubtful if he told her, as one of the so-called winners in the new arrangement, that her pension would be increased by a munificent $120 per annum. But Chrétien remained adamant: changes to the old age security program would have to wait until after the referendum. Edward Greenspon and Anthony Wilson-Smith, *Double Vision: The Inside Story of Liberals in Power* (Toronto: Doubleday Canada 1996), 261, 371.

89 Canada, Department of Finance, *Budget Speech*, 6 March 1996, 12-14. A single pensioner with no other sources of income would receive $ll,420 a year from the new seniors benefit – $120 a year more than the estimated value of the OAS/GIS pension in 2001. The seniors benefit will be reduced by 50 cents for every dollar of other income until it is reduced to $5,160 a year (when other income amounts to $15,000 per annum). The amount of $5,160 per year is the same as the estimated OAS pension in 2001. The seniors benefit will be protected from further decreases until outside income reaches $25,921, at which point it will be reduced by 20 cents on every additional dollar of other income. The new benefit will be taxed away completely when other income reaches $51,721. The maximum seniors benefit for a couple will be $18,440, $120 per year more than the estimated value of OAS/GIS for a couple in 2001. This amount will be reduced 50 cents for every dollar of other income until it is reduced to $10,320 (requiring outside income of about $20,000). When outside income reaches $25,921, the benefit will again reduce at the rate of 20 cents for every dollar of additional income until it disappears when household income, other than the seniors benefit, reaches $77,521. National Council of Welfare, *A Guide to the Proposed Seniors Benefit*, Ottawa, 1996, 3-5.

90 Canada, *The Seniors Benefit: Securing the Future*, Ottawa, 6 March 1996, 7. During the referendum, the prime minister, alarmed at the prospect that Quebec might vote for independence, promised his Quebec audiences that current pensioners would not be affected by any proposed changes to the pension system, and the new seniors benefit honours that pledge.

91 *Guide to the Proposed Seniors Benefit*, 2-3.

92 Linda McQuaig, *Shooting the Hippo: Death by Deficit and Other Canadian Myths* (Toronto: Viking 1995).

93 Canada, Department of Finance, *An Information Paper for Consultations on the Canada Pension Plan*, Released by the Federal, Provincial, and Territorial Governments of Canada, Ottawa, February 1996. Although released on the agreement of the two levels of government, the *Information Paper* appears to be the work of federal finance department officials. There was no agreement reached by the two levels of government at the time the paper was released as to what course of action should be taken.

94 Ian Jack, 'CPP Increases Inevitable: Experts,' *Globe and Mail*, 16 November 1995, provides a brief account of a conference held in Toronto, sponsored by the Fraser Institute. The chief actuary of the CPP, Bernard Dussault, said that 'doom and gloom predictions about the plan going bankrupt are silly.'

95 Alan Freeman, 'Major Reform of Canada Pension Plan Urged,' *Globe and Mail*, 8 January 1996.

96 Alan Freeman, 'Wind Down CPP, Think-Tank Urges,' *Globe and Mail*, 3 January 1996. A Ponzi scheme is a fraudulent investment scheme to cheat unwary investors. Small returns to initial investors are paid from money supplied by later victims of the hoax. Pay-as-you-go pension plans, which are found throughout the industrial world, including the United States, are backed by the government with its power to tax. To compare this arrangement with a Ponzi scheme is nonsensical.

97 Canadian Centre for Policy Alternatives, 'It's a Myth that the Canada Pension Plan Is Broke,' *Vancouver Sun*, 25 January 1996.

98 The Canadian Union of Public Employees charged that promotion of the public consul-

tation process was 'essentially non-existent' and criticized the 'closed door' meetings held by federal and provincial ministers on the CPP in 1995 without consultation with workers, even though CUPE said 'we volunteered to meet and discuss our views.' Canadian Union of Public Employees, 'Hands Off Our Public Pension Plan', *The CUPE Submission to the Canada Pension Plan Consultation Panel*, 1.

99 Bruce Little, 'Keep CPP Benefits, Panel Told,' *Globe and Mail*, 16 April 1996, and Barrie Mckenna, 'Politicians Hit Road for Pension Review,' *Globe and Mail*, 15 April 1996.

100 Presentation on behalf of the Canadian Labour Congress by Dick Martin, Secretary-Treasurer, to the Joint Panel of the Governments of Canada and Ontario, on the Review of the CPP Contribution Rate, 14 April 1996, 4 pp. The panel was chaired by David Walker, MP, and it appeared that he was the only permanent member, as provincial representatives joined the panel when it arrived in each province or territory and dropped off when it left their jurisdiction. The panel also visited Montreal, where common problems with the QPP were discussed with provincial representatives. Eric Beauchesne, 'Elderly Worry about Pension Reforms,' *Vancouver Sun*, 13 April 1996.

101 National Council of Welfare, *A Pension Primer* (Ottawa: Minister of Supply and Services 1996).

102 Grant Schellenberg, 'Diversity in Retirement and the Financial Security of Older Workers,' in Pulkingham and Ternowetsky, eds., *Remaking Canadian Social Policy*, 151-69. Schellenberg reports that in 1971, 74.1 per cent of men in the age group 60-4 were in the labour force; in 1994 the figure was 47.2 per cent; in the age group 55-9, the comparable figures were 84.9 and 72.7 per cent. For women in the 60-4 age group, 29.1 per cent were in the labour force in 1972, and this figure declined to 25.3 per cent in 1994; in the 60-4 age group, 38.7 per cent in 1971 and 49.2 per cent in 1994. The statistics for women may be skewed by the greater tendency for women to work outside the home since the Second World War.

103 'The government of Ontario was especially aggressive in pushing disability cases from its social assistance welfare rolls over to the Canada Pension Plan ... and mounted a special drive to identify such social assistance clients. Other provinces followed suit ... Private sector companies ... began to use the CPP disability system ... Private insurance companies also stepped up their pressure on disability claimants to apply to the CPP. One letter sent as recently as last September [1995] to a 45-year old claimant by Equitable Life Insurance said the claimant would lose part of his monthly disability cheque of about $1,700 if he did not apply to the CPP for disability benefits ...' Terence Corcoran, 'CPP Disability Scam', *Globe and Mail*, 13 January 1996.

104 Alan Freeman 'CPP Reports Decline in Disability Payouts,' *Globe and Mail*, 11 January 1996.

105 The *Information Paper* has three suggestions for cost-cutting in this area: reduce CPP disability benefits to those also in receipt of workers' compensation benefits; tighten eligibility requirements by requiring contribution for four of the last six years as opposed to the existing two out of the last three years; and convert the disability benefit to an actuarially reduced retirement pension at sixty-five, rather than paying the normal retirement benefit, which means that someone who retired early, on disability, receives a full pension at sixty-five. *Summary, Information Paper for Consultations on the Canada Pension Plan*, Ottawa, 19-20.

106 Cited by Dorothy Lipovenko, 'Women Would Feel CPP Changes Most,' *Globe and Mail*, 16 February 1996.

107 The 15.3 per cent combined contribution rate in 1995 is on earnings up to $61,200 (US), which yielded a maximum annual pension of $14,388 (US) compared to the CPP maximum of $8,724 per annum (1996). In the American presidential election year of 1996, neither candidate for the two major parties was claiming that a 'crisis' existed in the American public pension system. Monica Townson, 'Our Aging Society: Preserving Retirement Incomes into the 21st Century,' presentation to a public pension forum organized by the Trade Union Research Bureau and the Social Planning and Research Council of BC, Vancouver, 15 June 1996, 4.

108 Union support for the government in Quebec is conditional on the Parti Québécois demonstrating its commitment to progressive legislation. This means that a combination

of Quebec, Saskatchewan, and British Columbia could veto any regressive moves against the CPP. This information was given at a recent meeting in Toronto, where a prominent Quebec Union leader spoke. The Public Pension Forum, Vancouver, 15 June 1996.

109 Rheal Seguin, 'Quebec May Double Pension Payments,' *Globe and Mail*, 14 June 1996.

110 Edward Greenspon, 'Finance Minister Won't Push Pension Plan Agenda on BC,' *Globe and Mail*, 3 October 1996. Ottawa called Petter's idea 'a delaying tactic.'

111 Edward Greenspon, 'UI Premium Reduction Assailed,' *Globe and Mail*, 20 November 1996.

112 The Congressional Budget Office, Washington, DC, prepared a study that indicated that a Canadian-style system in the United States would reduce medical spending by $114 billion by 2003 and still cover all Americans. Such a system would eliminate the need for much of the existing private health insurance. 'Canada-Style Health System Called Cost Saver,' *Vancouver Sun*, 18 December 1993.

113 'Taming "Monster" Not Warts and All,' *Vancouver Sun*, 23 March 1995.

114 'Manning Would Stop Ottawa Funding of "Non-Essential Medicine,"' *Vancouver Sun*, 6 April 1995.

115 'Health Study Points Way to Save Billions,' *Vancouver Sun*, 18 January 1995.

116 'Province to Steer Doctors Away from Using "Cadillac" Drugs,' *Vancouver Sun*, 26 August 1995.

117 Michael Rachlis and Carol Kushner, *Strong Medicine: How to Save Canada's Health-Care System* (Toronto: Harper Collins 1994), 79.

118 The comments on a two-tier system by Dr. Evans come from an interview by Jane Coutts, 'MDs Support Injection of Private Money,' *Globe and Mail*, 27 December 1996.

119 Some examples are Stanley Aronowitz, *The Jobless Future: Sci-Tech and the Dogma of Work* (Minneapolis: University of Minnesota Press 1994); and Jeremy Rifkin, *The End of Work: The Decline of the Global Labor Force and the Dawn of the Most Market Era* (New York: Putnam 1995). Mr. Rifkin predicts 80 per cent unemployment within thirty years. Canadian contributions to this issue include Bruce O'Hara, *Working Harder Isn't Working: How We Can Save the Environment, the Economy and Our Sanity by Working Less and Enjoying Life More* (Vancouver: New Star Books 1993). Mr. O'Hara advocates an end to overtime and a four-day week as a possible solution to mass unemployment. See also Armine Yalnizyan, T. Ran Ide, and Arthur J. Cordell, *Shifting Time: Social Policy and the Future of Work* (Toronto: Between the Lines 1994), and Human Resources Development Canada, *Report of the Advisory Group on Working Time*.

120 Richard J. Barnet, 'The End of Jobs,' *Harper's*, September 1993.

121 Yves Vaillancourt, 'Remaking Canadian Social Policy: A Quebec Viewpoint,' in Pulkingham and Ternowetsky, eds., *Remaking Canadian Social Policy*, 81-99.

122 Ken Battle and Sherri Torjman, 'Desperately Seeking Substance: A Commentary on the Social Security Review,' in Pulkingham and Ternowetsky, eds., *Remaking Canadian Social Policy*, 52-66, and Jane Gadd, 'Poverty Hits One-Third of Children in Toronto,' *Globe and Mail*, 14 January 1997.

123 Elizabeth Aird, 'Young Indians Face Bleak Future, Commission Finds,' *Vancouver Sun*, 22 November 1996.

124 The income tax rate would be 0.5 per cent on gross income above $10,000, 1 per cent on gross income above $50,000, and 2 per cent on gross income above $100,000. A capital tax was recommended for corporations. The use of gross income as a tax base would make the tax more progressive because it is based on income before the many deductions and credits are applied, which tends to render the Canadian tax system much less progressive than it might be. Similarly, the coalition felt that a capital tax on corporations would yield more income than one that merely taxed profit. Jane Gadd, 'Child Poverty Benefit Urged,' *Globe and Mail*, 16 November 1996; and 'Child Poverty: Is the Solution More Taxes?' *Vancouver Sun*, 29 November 1996.

125 By paying the integrated benefit to children of all low-income parents, regardless of the source of their income, the new benefit would replace the social assistance payment for child support. Provincial authorities would then be responsible for setting support rates for couples or single parents, and any children involved would be 'off welfare.' This idea was first advanced by Leonard Marsh in 1943.

126 Ken Battle and Leon Muszynski, *One Way to Fight Child Poverty* (Ottawa: Caledon Institute for Social Policy, Renouf Publishing 1995).

127 The reader is referred once again to McQuaig's excellent book *Shooting the Hippo.*

128 Jane Gadd, 'Tax Credit to Target Child Poverty,' *Globe and Mail*, 14 January 1997. The broad national guidelines have not, as of mid-January 1997, been agreed to.

129 See *Unfair Shares: Corporations and Taxation in Canada*, April 1994. This thirty-seven-page publication, issued by the Ontario Federation of Labour and Ontario Coalition for Social Justice, provides details of Canadian corporations paying little or no tax, Canadian corporations owing $5 million or more in deferred taxes, and a list of selected corporate income tax subsidies (see Appendix Table A5). Of the 266 corporations listed, 134 had an income tax rate of 0 per cent. Of the remaining 132 corporations, the highest tax rate was 18 per cent. With regard to the generous tax concessions to wealthy families, in May 1996 the auditor-general of Canada revealed that in 1985 and again in 1991, a wealthy Canadian family was given permission by Revenue Canada and the Department of Finance to move $2 billion in assets to the United States from a family trust without paying capital gains tax. The resulting loss in tax revenue was estimated at between $500-$700 million. Family trusts are used by wealthy people to shield assets from capital gains tax for up to twenty-one years. Taxes are collected, in theory, when assets are removed or the trust is wound up. The auditor-general was highly critical of both the 'secret advance rulings' granted in this case and the lack of documentation. Tax expert Neil Brooks of Osgoode Hall law school called the Revenue Canada rulings 'outrageous.' Alan Freeman, 'Auditor Seeks Changes to Capital Gains Law,' *Globe and Mail*, 16 May 1996; Alan Freeman, 'Mystery Trust Was Bronfmans,' *Globe and Mail*, 16 May 1996; Canadian Press, 'Challenge to Bronfman Trust Tax Deal,' *Vancouver Sun*, 10 September 1996. This tax loophole was subsequently closed.

130 One group of the elderly still lacks adequate protection. Elderly women, aged seventy-five or older, living on their own stand a 40 per cent chance of living below the poverty line, according to a Statistics Canada study. The $120 per year increase in proposed new seniors benefit is not likely to be of much help. Lipovenko, 'Elderly Women at Risk.'

Bibliography

Books

Abele, Frances, ed. *How Ottawa Spends 1991-92*. Toronto: James Lorimer 1991
Adams, Ian, et al. *The Real Poverty Report*. Edmonton: M.G. Hurtig 1971
Allen, Richard. *The Social Passion: Religion and Social Reform in Canada, 1914-1928*. Toronto: University of Toronto Press 1971
Ames, Herbert Brown. *The City below the Hill*. 1897. Reprint. Toronto: University of Toronto Press 1972
Armitage, Andrew. *Social Welfare in Canada*. Toronto: McClelland and Stewart 1975
Artibise, Alan F.J. *Winnipeg: A Social History of Urban Growth 1874-1914*. Montreal: McGill-Queen's University Press 1975
Ashton, David N. *Underemployment under Capitalism*. Brighton: Harvester Press 1986
Atkinson, A.B., and G.V. Morgensen, eds. *Welfare and Work Incentive: A North European Perspective*. Oxford: Clarendon Press 1993
Banting, Keith G. *The Welfare State and Canadian Federalism*. Kingston: McGill-Queen's University Press 1982
Bercuson, D., J.L Granatstein, and W.R. Young. *Sacred Trust?* Toronto: Doubleday 1986
Beveridge, William H. *Full Employment in a Free Society*. London: Allen and Unwin 1944
–. *Social Insurance and Allied Services*. New York: Macmillan 1942
Birch, A.H. *Federalism, Finance and Social Legislation*. Oxford: Clarendon Press 1955
Bliss, J.M., ed. *Canadian History in Documents, 1763-1966*. Toronto: Ryerson Press 1966
Broadfoot, Barry. *Ten Lost Years*. Toronto: Doubleday 1973
Brooke, Jeffrey. *Breaking Faith: The Mulroney Legacy of Deceit, Destruction and Disunity*. Toronto: Key Porter Books 1992
Bruce, Maurice. *The Coming of the Welfare State*. London: B.T. Batsford 1961
Bryden, Kenneth. *Old Age Pensions and Policy-Making in Canada*. Montreal: McGill-Queen's University Press 1974
Burns, Eveline M. *Social Security and Public Policy*. New York: McGraw-Hill 1956
Calvert, Geoffrey N. *Pensions and Survival – The Coming Crisis of Money and Retirement*. Toronto: Maclean-Hunter 1977
Cameron, D., and M. Smith, eds. *Constitutional Politics*. Toronto: James Lorimer 1992
Cameron, Duncan, and Mel Watkins, eds. *Canada under Free Trade*. Toronto: James Lorimer 1993
Campbell, Bruce. *Moving in the Wrong Direction: Globalization, the North American Free Trade Agreement and Sustainable Development*. Ottawa: Canadian Centre for Policy Alternatives 1993
Canadian Centre for Policy Alternatives. *Unemployment Insurance: Another Victim of the '80s*. Ottawa: Canadian Centre for Policy Alternatives 1981
Canadian Council on Social Development. *Family Security in Insecure Times*. Ottawa: n. p. 1993 Cassidy, Harry M. *Public Health and Welfare Reorganization in Canada*. Toronto:

Ryerson Press 1945
–. *Social Security and Reconstruction in Canada*. Toronto: Ryerson Press 1943
–. *Unemployment and Relief in Ontario*. Toronto: J.M. Dent and Sons 1932
Christian, William, and Colin Campbell. *Political Parties and Ideologies in Canada*. Toronto: McGraw-Hill Ryerson 1974
Cooper, Keith H., and Colin C. Mills. *Canada at the Pension Crossroads*. New York: Research Foundation of Financial Executives Institute 1978
Copp, Terry. *The Anatomy of Poverty: The Condition of the Working Class in Montreal, 1897-1929*. Toronto: McClelland and Stewart 1974
Crawford, K. Grant. *Canadian Municipal Government*. Toronto: University of Toronto Press 1968
Creighton, Donald. *Canada's First Century*. Toronto: Macmillan 1970
Cross, Michael, ed. *The Workingman in the Nineteenth Century*. Toronto: Oxford University Press 1974
Crysdale, Stewart. *The Industrial Struggle and Protestant Ethics in Canada*. Toronto: Ryerson Press 1961
Dawson, R.M. *The Government of Canada*. Toronto: University of Toronto Press 1962
–. *William Lyon Mackenzie King*. Vol. 1. Toronto: University of Toronto Press 1959
Dennis, Michael, and Susan Fish. *Programs in Search of a Policy: Low Income Housing in Canada*. Toronto: A.M. Hakkert 1972
Doern, J. Bruce. *How Ottawa Spends, 1981*. Toronto: James Lorimer 1981
Drache, D., and D. Cameron, eds. *The Other Macdonald Report*. Toronto: James Lorimer 1985
Eisner, Robert. *The Misunderstood Economy*. Boston: Harvard Business School Press 1994
Gettys, Luella. *The Administration of Canadian Conditional Grants*. Chicago: Public Administration Service 1938
Gold, Michael, ed. *The Social Dimension: Employment Policy in the European Community*. London: Macmillan 1993
Graham, Katherine A., ed. *How Ottawa Spends, 1988-89*. Ottawa: Carleton University Press 1988
–. *How Ottawa Spends, 1989-90*. Ottawa: Carleton University Press 1989
–. *How Ottawa Spends, 1990-91*. Ottawa: Carleton University Press 1990
Granatstein, J.L. *Canada's War: The Politics of the Mackenzie King Government 1939-1945*. Toronto: Oxford University Press 1975
Granatstein, J.L., and K. McNaught, eds. *'English Canada' Speaks Out*. Toronto: Doubleday 1991
Gray, James H. *The Winter Years*. Toronto: Macmillan 1966
Green, Christopher, et al. *Unemployment Insurance: How to Make It Work*. C.D. Howe Institute; Ottawa: Renouf Publishing 1994
Haddow, Rodney S. *Poverty Reform in Canada 1958-78: State and Class Influence on Policy Making*. Montreal: McGill-Queen's University Press 1993
Hall, Hon. Emmett M. *Canada's National-Provincial Health Program for the 1980's*. Ottawa: Department of National Health and Welfare 1980
Hartz, Louis. *The Liberal Tradition in America*. New York: Harcourt Brace 1955
Heckscher, Gunnar. *The Welfare State and Beyond*. Minneapolis: University of Minnesota Press 1984
Horn, Michiel, ed. *The Dirty Thirties: Canadians in the Great Depression*. Toronto: Copp Clark 1972
Horowitz, Gad. *Canadian Labour in Politics*. Toronto: University of Toronto Press 1968
Inglis, Brian. *Poverty and the Industrial Revolution*. London: Hodder and Stoughton 1971
International Labour Organization. *Into the Twenty-First Century: The Development of Social Security*. Geneva: ILO 1984
Jamieson, Stuart M. *Times of Trouble: Labour Unrest and Industrial Conflict in Canada, 1900-1966*. Ottawa: Information Canada 1971
Johnson, Andrew F., Stephen McBride, and Patrick J. Smith. *Continuities and Discontinuities: The Political Economy of Social Welfare and Labour Market Policy in Canada*. Toronto: University of Toronto Press 1994

Kamerman, Sheila B. and Alfred J. Kahn. *Mothers Alone: Strategies for a Time of Change.* Dover, MA: Auburn House Publishing 1988

Katz, Michael B. *The People of Hamilton, Canada West.* Cambridge: Harvard University Press 1975

Kealey, Greg. *Canada Investigates Industrialism.* Toronto: University of Toronto Press 1973

Kent, Tom. *Social Policy for Canada.* Ottawa: Policy Press 1962

Kewley, T.H. *Social Security in Australia.* Sydney: Sydney University Press 1965

King, W.L. Mackenzie. *Industry and Humanity.* Toronto: Thomas Allen 1918

Kumar, P., and A.M.M. Smith. *Pension Reform in Canada: A Review of the Issues and Options.* Kingston: Industrial Relations Centre 1981

Kuttner, Robert. *The Economic Illusion: False Choices between Prosperity and Social Justice.* New York: Houghton Mifflin 1984

Leach, Penelope. *Children First.* New York: Knopf 1994

League for Social Reconstruction. Research Committee. *Social Planning for Canada.* 1935. Reprint. Toronto: University of Toronto Press 1975

Lower, Arthur R.M. *Canadians in the Making: A Social History of Canada.* Toronto: Longmans, Green 1958

Lubove, Roy. *The Professional Altruist.* Cambridge: Harvard University Press 1965

–. *The Struggle for Social Security 1900-1935.* Cambridge: Harvard University Press 1968

McBride, Stephen, and John Shields. *Dismantling a Nation: Canada and the New World Order.* Halifax: Fernwood Publishing 1993

McCallum, John, ed. *A Social Charter for Canada?* Toronto: C.D. Howe Institute 1992

McGregor, F.A. *The Fall and Rise of Mackenzie King: 1911-1919.* Toronto: Macmillan 1962

McQuaig, Linda. *Behind Closed Doors: How the Rich Won Control of Canada's Tax System – and Ended up Richer.* Markham, ON: Viking 1987

–. *Shooting the Hippo: Death by Deficit and Other Canadian Myths.* Toronto: Viking 1995

Manga, Pran. *The Political Economy of Extra Billing.* Ottawa: Canadian Council on Social Development 1983

Marsh, L.C. *Canadians In and Out of Work.* Toronto: Oxford University Press 1940

–. *Report on Social Security for Canada.* 1943. Reprint. Toronto: University of Toronto Press 1975

Marsh, L.C., A.G. Fleming, and C.F. Blackler. *Health and Unemployment.* Toronto: Oxford University Press 1938

Mendelson, M. *The Administrative Cost of Income Security Programs: Ontario and Canada.* Toronto: Ontario Economic Council 1979

Menning, Richard. *Poverty and Incentives.* London: Oxford University Press 1984

Menzies, Heather. *Women and the Chip.* Montreal: Institute for Research on Public Policy 1981

Moore, M., and J.H. Perry. *Financing Canadian Federation.* Toronto: Canadian Tax Foundation 1953

Morton, Desmond. *Confederation: A Short History of Canada's Constitution.* Toronto: Umbrella Press 1992

Morton, W.L. *The Kingdom of Canada.* Toronto: McClelland and Stewart 1963

–, ed. *The Shield of Achilles.* Toronto: McClelland and Stewart 1968

Myrdal, Alva. *Nation and Family.* New York: Harper 1941

Neatby, H. Blair. *William Lyon Mackenzie King, Vol III (1924-32).* Toronto: University of Toronto Press 1963

O'Hara, Bruce. *Working Harder Isn't Working: How We Can Save the Environment, the Economy and Our Sanity by Working Less and Enjoying Life More.* Vancouver: New Star Books 1993

Osborn, Grant M. *Compulsory Temporary Disability Insurance in the United States.* Homewood, IL: Richard D. Irwin 1958

Pesando, J.E., and S.A. Rea. *Public and Private Pensions in Canada: An Economic Analysis.* Toronto: University of Toronto Press 1977

Piven, Frances Fox, and Richard A. Cloward. *Regulating the Poor: The Functions of Public Welfare.* Toronto: Random House 1971

Reynolds, Elisabeth E. *Income Security in Canada: Changing Needs, Changing Means.* Institute for Research on Public Policy; Montreal: Renouf Publishing Company 1993

Riches, Graham, and Gordon Ternowetsky, eds. *Unemployment and Welfare: Social Policy and the Work of Social Work.* Toronto: Garamond Press 1990

Richter, L., ed. *Canada's Unemployment Problems.* Toronto: Macmillan 1939

Room, Graham, ed. *Towards a European Welfare State?* Bristol: J.W. Arrowsmith 1991

Rutherford, Paul, ed. *Saving the Canadian City: The First Phase 1880-1920.* Toronto: University of Toronto Press 1974

Sinclair, Jim, ed. *Crossing the Line.* Vancouver: New Star Books 1992

Smiley, Donald V. *Conditional Grants and Canadian Federalism.* Toronto: Canadian Tax Foundation 1963

Social Service Congress. *Report of Addresses and Proceedings.* Toronto: The Social Service Congress of Canada 1914

Splane, Richard. *Social Welfare in Ontario, 1791-1893.* Toronto: University of Toronto Press 1965

Stone, Leroy O. *Urban Development in Canada.* Ottawa: Dominion Bureau of Statistics 1967

Strong, M.K. *Public Welfare Administration in Canada.* Chicago: University of Chicago Press 1930

Struthers, James. *The Limits of Affluence: Welfare in Ontario, 1920-1970.* Toronto: University of Toronto Press 1994

Titmuss, Richard M. *Commitment to Welfare.* London: George Allen and Unwin 1968

–. *Essays on 'The Welfare State.'* London: George Allen and Unwin 1958

–. *Social Policy: An Introduction.* London: Allen and Unwin 1974

Van Parijs, Philippe, ed. *Arguing for a Basic Income.* London: Verso 1992

Walkom, Thomas. *Rae Days.* Toronto: Key Porter Books 1994

Whitton, Charlotte. *The Dawn of Ampler Life.* Toronto: Macmillan 1943

Wilensky, Harold L., and Charles N. Lebeaux. *Industrial Society and Social Welfare.* New York: Russell Sage Foundation 1958

Woodsworth, J.S. *My Neighbor.* Toronto: The Missionary Society of the Methodist Church 1911

Yalnizyan, Armine, et al. *Shifting Time: Social Policy and the Future of Work.* Canadian Centre for Policy Alternatives; Toronto: Between the Lines 1994

Young, A.F. *Industrial Injuries Insurance.* London: Routledge and Kegan Paul 1964

Zakuta, Leo. *A Protest Movement Becalmed.* Toronto: University of Toronto Press 1964

Articles

Arthur, H.W. 'Developing Industrial Citizenship: A Challenge for Canada's Second Century.' *Canadian Bar Review* 45 (1967):786-830

Ascah, Louis. 'Recent Pension Reports in Canada: A Survey.' *Canadian Public Policy* 10, no. 4 (1984):415-28

Barnet, Richard J. 'The End of Jobs.' *Harper's*, September 1993, 47-52

Bell, Winifred. 'Obstacles to Shifting from the Descriptive to the Analytical Approach in Teaching Social Services.' *Journal of Education for Social Work* 5 (spring 1969):5-19

Bellamy, Donald. 'Welfare.' *Canadian Annual Review* (1970):464-75

'Bill Number 8.' *Child and Family Welfare* 10, no. 6 (1935):1-21

Black, E.R., and A.C. Cairns. 'A Different Perspective on Canadian Federalism.' *Canadian Public Administration* 9 (March 1966):27-44

Bland, Salem. 'The Farmer's Platform.' *Social Welfare* 1, no. 5 (1919):101-2 (continued in three subsequent issues)

Brooks, Neil. 'A Formula for Tax Fairness.' *The Facts* 13, no. 1 (1991):7-12

–. 'Tax Breaks for the Rich.' *Canadian Dimension*, January-February 1994, 6-9

Brown, Larry. 'Smokescreen Economics.' *Perception* 13, no. 3 (1989):20-2

Bryce, Peter. 'Mothers' Allowances.' *Social Welfare* 1, no. 6 (1919):131-2

Burns, Eveline, M. 'Social Security Plans of the USA.' *Public Affairs* 6, no. 4 (1943):190-4

Cameron, Duncan, et al. 'October 26, 1992: A Symposium on the Outcome of the National Vote.' *Canadian Forum*, December 1992, 12-19

Canadian Cavalcade 1920-1935. Supplement to *Child and Family Welfare* 11, no. 1 (1935)

Canadian Council on Social Development. 'Impressions.' *Perception* 10, no. 1 (1986):3

Canadian Union of Public Employees. 'Free Trade: Worse than Anyone Ever Imagined.' *The Facts on Free Trade* 13, no. 2 (1992):13-18

Carrier, Jean-Guy. 'The Crombie Interview.' *Perception* 3, no. 3 (1980):24-7

Carter, Susan, and Chris Clark. 'A Critique of Social Security Reform Proposals.' *Perception* 18, no. 2 (1994):8-9

Cassidy, Harry M. 'The Canadian Social Services.' *Annals of the American Academy of Political and Social Sciences* 253 (1947):190-201

–. 'Family Allowances in Canada.' *Proceedings of the National Conference of Social Work*. New York: Columbia University Press 1945

–. 'Unemployment Insurance for Canada.' *Queen's Quarterly* 38 (1931):306-34

'Children's Allowances – Pro or Con?' *Canadian Welfare* 19, no. 5 (1943):1

Davey, Ian E. 'Trends in Female School Attendance in Mid-Nineteenth Century Ontario.' *Histoire sociale/Social History* 8 (1975):238-54

Davidson, George F. 'Family Allowances, An Instalment on Social Security.' *Canadian Welfare* 20, no. 3 (1944):11-14

–. 'The Marsh Report on Social Security for Canada.' *Canadian Welfare* 19, no. 1 (1943):3-6

–. 'The Whitton and Marsh Proposals – A Comparison and a Contrast.' *Canadian Welfare* 19, no. 7 (1944):11-14

Davis, R.E.G. 'Housing Legislation in Canada.' *Canadian Welfare* 28 (December 1952):17-26

Deaton, Richard. 'The Political Economy of Pensions: The Political and Economic Framework of the Canadian Pension System.' In Canadian Centre for Policy Alternatives, *Pensions: Public Solutions vs. Private Interest*

Derry, K., and Paul H. Douglas. 'The Minimum Wage in Canada.' *Journal of Political Economy* 39 (1922):155-88

Erlichman, Louis. 'An Expanded Public Pension Plan and Collective Bargaining.' In Canadian Centre for Policy Alternatives, *Pensions: Public Solutions vs. Private Interest*

Falk, Howard T. 'Mothers' Allowances.' *Social Welfare* 1, no. 6 (1919):131

'Family Allowances.' *Social Welfare* 11, no. 7 (1929):147

'Family Allowances.' *Social Worker* 13, no. 2 (1944):1-6

'Family Problems in Relief.' *Child and Family Welfare* 9, no. 2 (1933):29-30

Findlay, Peter C. 'Social Welfare in Canada: The Case for Universality.' CCASW, *Review 83*

Fingard, Judith. 'Attitudes toward the Education of the Poor in Colonial Halifax.' *Acadiensis* 2, no. 2 (1973):15-42

–. 'The Relief of the Unemployed Poor in Saint John, Halifax and St. John's, 1815-60.' *Acadiensis* 5, no. 1 (1972):32-54

–. 'The Winter's Tale: Contours of Pre-Industrial Poverty in British America, 1815-60.' In Canadian Historical Association, *Historical Papers* (1974):65-94

Forsey, Eugene. 'Social Security for Canada.' *Canadian Unionist* 16, no. 11 (1943):274-5

George, Barry. 'Taxing Questions.' *Perception* 14, no. 3 (1990):46

Gilbert, Neil. 'From Entitlements to Incentives: The Changing Philosophy of Social Protection.' *International Social Security Review* 45, no 3 (1992):5-10

Gould, Margaret S. 'A Standard of Health and Decency as a Living Wage.' *Social Welfare* 8, no. 9 (1926):220-2

Govan, Elizabeth S.L. 'The Social Services.' In *Canada*, ed. George W. Brown. Berkeley: University of California Press 1950

Greenhous, Brereton. 'Paupers and Poorhouses: The Development of Poor Relief in Early New Brunswick.' *Histoire sociale/Social History* 1 (1968):102-28

Guest, Dennis. 'If We Keep Family Allowances.' *Canadian Welfare* 46 (May-June 1969):14-15

–. 'Social Policy in Canada.' *Social Policy and Administration* 18, no. 2 (1984):130-47

–. 'Three Social Policy Issues for the '70's.' *Canadian Welfare* 46, no. 4 (1970):12-15

Hareven, Tamara K. 'An Ambiguous Alliance: Some Aspects of American Influences on Canadian Social Welfare.' *Histoire sociale/Social History* 3 (1969):82-98

Harris, J. Russell. 'Impressions of the National Industrial Conference.' *Social Welfare* 2, no. 2 (1919):39-42

Harvey, Ruth. 'The Expansion of the Social Services to Meet the Need of Men and Women in the Armed Forces.' In *Proceedings of the Ninth Canadian Conference of Social Work*, 116-18. Winnipeg: Canadian Conference on Social Work 1944

Heclo, Hugh. 'Toward a New Welfare State?' In *The Development of Welfare States in Europe and America*, ed. Peter Flora and Arnold J. Heidenheimer. New Brunswick, NJ: Transaction Books 1981

Hepworth, H. Philip. 'Federal Proposals for Contributing to the Financing of Personal Social Services.' Mimeographed. Ottawa: Canadian Council on Social Development 1977

Hincks, C.M. 'Feeblemindedness in Canada.' *Social Welfare* 1, no. 2 (1918):29-30

Horowitz, Gad. 'Conservativism, Liberalism and Socialism in Canada: An Interpretation.' *Canadian Journal of Economics and Political Science* 32 (1966):143-71

Houston, Susan E. 'Politics, Schools and Social Change in Upper Canada.' *Canadian Historical Review* 53, no. 3 (1972):249-71

Hudson, Robert B. 'The Evolution of the Welfare State: Shifting Rights and Responsibilities for the Old.' *International Social Security Review* 48, no. 1 (1995):3-17

Jackman, Martha. 'When a Social Charter Isn't.' *Canadian Forum*, December 1991, 8-10

Jennisen, Therese. 'Farewell to Welfare? A Review of Benoit Bouchard's Speech to the OECD.' *Canadian Review of Social Policy* 31 (spring 1993):84-8

Kamerman, S.B., and Alfred Kahn. 'Family Policy and the Under-3's: Money, Services and Time in a Policy Package.' *International Social Security Review* 47, no. 3 (1994):39-44

–. 'Income Transfers, Work and the Economic Well-Being of Families with Children: A Comparative Study.' *International Social Security Review* 3 (1982):345-82

Kesselman, Jonathan R. 'Family Allowances: How to Save and Pay to All.' *Financial Post*, 11 December 1983.

Kierstead, W.C. 'Mothers' Allowances in Canadian Provinces.' *Social Welfare* 7, no. 9 (1925):175-80

King, W.L. Mackenzie. 'Labour and the War.' *Labour Gazette* 42 (November 1942):56; and 43 (March 1943):309

Kitchen, Brigitte. 'Politics Affecting Family Income.' CCASW, *Review 83*

–. 'The Refundable Child Tax Credit.' *Canadian Taxation* 1, no. 3 (1979):44-51

Lawton, Alma. 'Relief Administration in Saskatoon during the Depression.' *Saskatchewan History* 22, no. 1 (1969):41-59

Lewis, Jane. 'Eleanor Rathbone and the Family.' *New Society*, 27 January 1983

McClain, Janet. 'The Saga of Mortgage Deductibility.' *Perception* 3, no. 2 (1979):34-5

McConnell, W.H. 'The Genesis of the Canadian "New Deal."' *Journal of Canadian Studies* 4, no. 2 (1969):19-36

Machar, A.M. 'Outdoor Relief in Canada.' In *Proceedings of the National Conference of Charities and Correction*. Toronto: G.H. Ellis 1897; and Boston: G.H. Ellis 1898

Macintosh, R.M. 'The Great Pension Fund Robbery.' *Canadian Public Policy* 2, no. 2 (1976):257-61

McRae, Kenneth D. 'The Structure of Canadian History.' In *The Founding of New Societies*, ed. Louis Hartz. New York: Harcourt, Brace, and World 1964

Marsh, L.C. 'The Welfare State: Is It a Threat to Canada?' In *Proceedings of the Canadian Conference on Social Work 1950*. Ottawa: Canadian Conference on Social Work 1950.

Melchers, Ronald. 'The Cap on CAP.' *Perspectives* 14, no. 4 (1990):19-23

Mendelson, Michael. 'The Haley Report: An Old Age Insecurity Program.' In Canadian Centre for Policy Alternatives, *Pensions: Public Solutions vs. Private Interest*

Morgan, John S. 'The Social Services in Canada.' In *Social Purpose for Canada*, ed. M. Oliver. Toronto: University of Toronto Press 1961

Morgan, John S., and Albert Rose. 'The Unfinished Business in Social Security.' *Social Worker* 33 (July 1965):182-9

Murphy, Jonathan. 'Analyzing the Poverty of Christopher Sarlo.' *Perception* 17, no. 2 (1993):19-22

Nash, Walter. 'Social Security in New Zealand.' *Public Affairs* 7, no. 2 (1944):78-82

Neary, Peter. '"Traditional" and "Modern" Elements in the Social and Economic History of Bell Island and Conception Bay.' *Historical Papers* (1973):105-36

Neatby, Blair. 'The Saskatchewan Relief Commission, 1931-34.' *Saskatchewan History* 2, no. 2 (1950):41-56

'Ontario's New Relief Policy.' *Child and Family Welfare* 12, no. 3 (1935):52-3

Parr, G.J. 'The Welcome and the Wake: Attitudes in Canada West toward the Irish Famine Migration.' *Ontario History* 66 (1974):101-13

Piva, Michael J. 'The Workmen's Compensation Movement in Ontario.' *Ontario History* 67 (1975):39-56

Platt, Anthony. 'The Triumph of Benevolence: The Origins of the Juvenile Justice System in the United States.' In *Criminal Justice in America*, ed. Richard Quinney. Boston: Little, Brown 1975

Prince, Michael. 'The Liberal Record.' *Perception* 8, no. 1 (1984):23-5

Quinn, H.J. 'The Union Nationale Party.' *Canadian Forum*, May 1955, 29-30

Ralph, Diana. 'What Do Canadians Really Think about the Social Security Review?' *Canadian Review of Social Policy* 34 (winter 1994):59-71

Reed, Allana G. 'The First Poor-Relief System of Canada.' *Canadian Historical Review* 37, no. 4 (1946):424-31

'Referendum File.' *Maclean's*, 2 November 1992, 12-14

'Relative Responsibilities – Public and Private Services in the Family Field.' *Child and Family Welfare* 10, no. 2 (1934):28-9

Report of the Secretary-General. 'Developments and Trends in Social Security 1990-92.' *International Social Security Review* 45, no. 4 (1992):7-64

Riches, Graham. 'FIP Flops.' *Perception* 1, no. 6 (1978):42

Richter, L. 'The Employment and Social Insurance Bill.' *Canadian Journal of Economics and Political Science* 1 (1935):436-48

Robin, Martin. 'Registration, Conscription and Independent Labour Politics, 1916-1917.' *Canadian Historical Review* 47 (1966):101-18

Robinson, David. 'Putting Sand in the Wheels of Currency Speculators: The Tobin Tax.' *Canadian Perspectives* (summer 1995):9-10

Rose, Albert. 'Canadian Housing Policies.' *Canadian Conference on Housing*. Background Paper no. 2. Mimeographed. Ottawa: Canadian Welfare Council, June 1968

Rumbold, Donald. 'C.L.C. Misses Target with Proposals for Canada Pension Plan.' *Labour Gazette* 75 (April 1975):214-19

'Saint John Agency Surveys Relief Families.' *Canadian Welfare Summary* 15, no. 1 (1939): 46-50

Scott, F.R. 'Labour Learns the Truth.' *Canadian Forum* 26, no. 3 (1944):3-9

–. 'The Privy Council and Mr. Bennett's New Deal.' *Canadian Journal of Economics and Political Science* 3 (1937):234-41

'Shall We Have Cash Relief?' *Child and Family Welfare* 9, no. 5 (1934):5-7

Shifrin, Leonard. 'Federalism and Flexibility.' *NAPO-INFO* 4, no. 5:6

Shragge, Eric. 'Community Employment Programs: Relief, Regulation or Service to People?' *Canadian Welfare* 51 (March-April 1975):22-4

–. 'The New Welfare Workhouse.' *Perception* 15, no. 1 (1991):32-5

Smiley, Donald. 'Public Administration and Canadian Federalism.' *Canadian Public Administration* 7 (1964):371-88

'Social Security and the Canadian Constitution.' *Economist*, 19 June 1943, 792

'Social Work Looks at Parliament.' *Canadian Welfare* 24, no. 8 (1949):20-1

Speisman, Stephan A. 'Munificent Parsons and Municipal Parsimony.' *Ontario History* 65 (1973):34-49

Stepler, Dorothy. 'Family Allowances for Canada.' *Behind the Headlines* 3, no. 2 (1945):1-31

Stewart, B.M. 'Canadian Opinion on Unemployment Insurance.' *Social Welfare* 3 (1921):272-5

'Still No Plan.' *Canadian Forum*, March 1944, 278

Tamagno, Edward. 'Comparing Direct Spending and Tax Spending.' *Canadian Taxation* 1, no. 4 (1979):42-5

TenBroek, Jacobus, and R.B. Wilson. 'Public Assistance and Social Insurance – A Normative Evaluation.' *UCLA Law Review* (1954):237-302

Ternowetsky, G. 'Profits and Jobs: Who Wins, Who Loses.' *Perception* 10, no. 5 (1987):39-42

'The Canadian Conference on Child Welfare.' *Social Welfare* 8, no. 1 (1925):4-6

'The Cash Dole – Best Way Out?' *Child and Family Welfare* 9, no. 4 (1933):56-58

'The Statement of the Methodist General Conference.' *Social Welfare* 1, no. 8 (1919):186-7

Touzel, Bessie. 'Two Points of View on Social Security.' *Social Worker* 12, no. 4 (1944):3-8

Wallace, Elisabeth. 'The Origin of the Social Welfare State in Canada 1867-1900.' *Canadian Journal of Economics and Political Science* 16 (1950):389-93

Whalen, James M. 'The Nineteenth Century Almshouse System in St. John County.' *Histoire sociale/Social History* 7 (1971):5-27

–. 'Social Welfare in New Brunswick, 1784-1900.' *Acadiensis* 2, no. 1 (1972):54-64

Wheeler, Michael. 'Politics and Housing.' *Canadian Welfare Planning Council Letter* 1 (August 1969)

Whitton, Charlotte. 'The Family Allowances Controversy in Canada.' *Social Service Review* 18 (1944):413-32

–. 'Security for Canadians.' *Behind the Headlines* 3, no. 6 (1943):1-8

Wiler, Richard. 'The National Crisis in Literacy: Why Four to Five in Twenty Adults Can't Read.' *Perception* 13, no. 2 (1987):29-32

Williams, Relief. 'Poor Relief and Medicine in Nova Scotia, 1749-1783.' *Collections of the Nova Scotia Historical Society* 24 (1938):33-56

Wolfenden, Hugh H. 'Social Security – The Ideas of Beveridge and Others.' *Industrial Canada* 44, no. 8 (1943):76-80

Woodsworth, J.S. 'Parliament as a Social Welfare Agency.' *Social Welfare* 10, no. 11 (1928): 255-62

Worts, Grace. 'The Canadian National Institute for the Blind.' *Social Welfare* 9, no. 3 (1926): 318-19

Young, Margot. 'Pensions and Equality.' *The Facts on Free Trade* 11, no. 2 (1989):35-7

Government Reports and Publications

British Columbia. Department of the Provincial Secretary. 'Summary of the Health Insurance Act, 1936.' Mimeogaphed. 6 April 1936

–. Department of the Provincial Secretary. Civil Service Commission. 'Report on the Administration of Mothers' Pensions in British Columbia 1920-1 to 1930-1: Summary of Findings and Recommendations.' Typescript, n.d.

–. *Developing a Pension Policy for the Future*. Victoria 1982

–. Report of the Commissioner, Hon. Gordon McG. Sloan. *The Workmen's Compensation Act and Board*. Victoria 1952

–. *Report of the Committee Appointed by the Government to Investigate the Finances of British Columbia*. Victoria 1932

–. *Report on Mothers' Pensions*. Victoria 1920

–. Superintendent of Neglected Children and Mothers' Pensions. 'First Annual Report.' Victoria 1921

Canada. *Action Plan for Pension Reform*. Ottawa 1984

–. *Better Pensions for Canadians*. Ottawa: Health and Welfare Canada 1982

–. *Child and Elderly Benefits Consultation Paper*. Ottawa 1985

–. *Child Care and Development: A Supplementary Paper*. Ottawa 1994

–. *Consensus on the Constitution*. Charlottetown, 28 August 1992. Final Text

–. Department of Finance. *Report on Integration of Social Program Payments into the Income Tax System*. November 1978

–. Department of Finance. *The Budget Plan*. February 1994

–. Department of Finance. *Budget Speech*. 22 February 1994

–. Department of Finance. *Budget Speech*. 27 February 1995

–. Department of Finance. *Facing Choices Together*. February 1994

–. Department of Labour. *The Labour Gazette*

–. Department of National Health and Welfare. *The Child Benefit*. A White Paper on Canada's New Integrated Child Tax Benefit, n.d.

–. Department of National Health and Welfare. *Government Expenditures on Health and Social*

Welfare, Canada 1927 to 1959. Ottawa 1961
–. Department of National Health and Welfare. *Income Maintenance Measures in Canada, Program Descriptions.* Comp. R.G. Young and R.I. Brown. Ottawa 1965
–. Department of National Health and Welfare. *Income Security for Canadians.* Ottawa 1970
–. Department of National Health and Welfare. *Income Security Programs Monthly Statistics.* June 1992
–. Department of National Health and Welfare.'The Next Major Steps in Reforming Canada's Social Security System.' Statement by the Hon. Marc Lalonde to the Conference of Federal and Provincial Ministers of Welfare. Ottawa, February 1975
–. Department of National Health and Welfare. *Summary of the Principal Components of the Social Services Bill.* Ottawa 1977
–. Department of National Health and Welfare. *Working Paper on Social Security in Canada.* Ottawa 1973
–. Department of Reconstruction. *Employment and Income with Special Reference to the Initial Period of Reconstruction.* Ottawa 1945
–. Dominion Bureau of Statistics and Department of National Health and Welfare. *Canadian Sickness Survey 1950-51.* Special Compilation no. 6, Permanent Physical Disabilities (National Estimates). Ottawa 1955
–. *Dominion-Provincial Conference 1960, Ottawa, July 25, 26, 27, 1960.* Ottawa 1960
–. Dominion-Provincial Conference on Reconstruction. *Proposals of the Government of Canada.* Ottawa 1945
–. Economic Council of Canada. *Fifth Annual Review.* Ottawa 1967
–. Economic Council of Canada. *Good Jobs, Bad Jobs.* Ottawa: Supply and Services 1990
–. Economic Council of Canada. *Living Together: A Study of Regional Disparities.* Ottawa: Ministry of Supply and Services 1978
–. Economic Council of Canada. *The New Face of Poverty.* Ottawa: Supply and Services, July 1992
–. Economic Council of Canada. *On the Mend.* Twentieth Annual Review. Ottawa: Minister of Supply and Services 1983
–. Economic Council of Canada. *One in Three: Pensions for Canadians to 2030.* Ottawa: Canadian Government Publishing Centre 1979
–. Economic Council of Canada. *Twenty-First Annual Review, 1984.* Ottawa: Supply and Services 1984
–. Economic Council of Canada. *Twenty-Third Annual Review, 1986.* Ottawa: Supply and Services 1986
–. Economic Council of Canada. *Twenty-Eighth Annual Review, 1991.* Ottawa: Supply and Services 1991
–. Employment and Immigration. *Unemployment Insurance in the 1980s.* Ottawa: Minister of Supply and Services 1981
–. *Employment Development Services: A Supplementary Paper.* 1994
–. Federal-Provincial Social Security Review. *Background Paper on Income Support and Supplementation.* Published under the authority of the Federal-Provincial Conference of Ministers of Welfare, February 1975
–. Federal Task Force on Retirement Income Policy. *The Retirement Income System in Canada: Problems and Alternative Policies for Reform.* The Lazar Report. 2 vols. Ottawa: Canadian Government Publishing Centre 1980
–. *From Unemployment Insurance to Employment Insurance: A Supplementary Paper.* 1994
–. *Government of Canada Tax Expenditure Account.* Ottawa 1979
–. Health and Welfare Canada. *Inventory of Income Security Programs in Canada July 1990.* Ottawa: Minister of Supply and Services 1991
–. *Health, Welfare and Labour.* Reference Book for the Dominion-Provincial Conference on Reconstruction, 1945
–. Human Resources Development Canada. *Improving Social Security in Canada: A Discussion Paper.* October 1994
–. *Income Security for Children: A Supplementary Paper.* 1994
–. *Inventory of Income Security Programs in Canada.* Ottawa 1985, 1987, 1988, and 1990

–. *Legislative Committee on Bill C-80.* Ottawa, 18 June 1992
–. Minister of Finance. *A New Direction for Canada: An Agenda for Economic Renewal.* Ottawa 1984
–. Minister of Finance. *Where Your Tax Dollars Go.* Ottawa, February 1990
–. Minister of Finance. *White Paper on Tax Reform.* Ottawa 1987
–. Minister of National Health and Welfare. *Preserving Universal Medicare.* Ottawa 1983
–. National Employment Commission. 'Final Report.' Ottawa 1938
–. Parliament. House of Commons. Advisory Committee on Reconstruction. *Housing and Community Planning, Final Report of the Sub-Committee, March 24, 1944.* Ottawa 1946
–. Parliament. House of Commons. *Minutes and Proceedings of the Legislative Committee on Bill C-80.* Ottawa, 18 June 1992
–. Parliament. House of Commons. *Minutes of Proceedings and Evidence of the Standing Committee on Labour, Manpower and Immigration Respecting the White Paper on Unemployment Insurance.* Ottawa: Information Canada 1970
–. Parliament. House of Commons. *Notes for an Address by the Honourable Lloyd Axworthy, Minister of Human Resources Development.* 31 January 1994
–. Parliament. House of Commons. *Official Report of Debates.*
–. Parliament. House of Commons. *Proceedings and Evidence of the Standing Committee on Finance and Economic Affairs.* 4 September 1987
–. Parliament. House of Commons. *Report of the Advisory Committee on Reconstruction.* Ottawa 1943
–. Parliament. House of Commons. Report of the Standing Committee on Human Resources Development. *Security, Opportunities and Fairness: Canadians Renewing Their Social Programs.* Ottawa 1995
–. Parliament. House of Commons. *Reports of the Parliamentary Task Force on Pension Reform.* Ottawa 1983
–. Parliament. House of Commons. Select Standing Committee on Industrial and International Relations. *Minutes of Proceedings and Evidence.* Ottawa 1926, 1927, 1928
–. Parliament. House of Commons. Special Committee on Social Security. Advisory Committee on Health Insurance. *Health Insurance: Report.* Ottawa 1943
–. Parliament. House of Commons. Special Committee on Social Security. *Minutes of Proceedings and Evidence.* Ottawa 1943
–. Parliament. Senate and House of Commons. Joint Committee on Old Age Security. *Report.* Ottawa 1950
–. Senate and House of Commons. Parliamentary Task Force on Federal-Provincial Fiscal Arrangements. *Fiscal Federalism in Canada.* Ottawa 1981
–. *Persons with Disabilities: A Supplementary Paper.* 1994
–. *Proceedings, National Pensions Conference, Ottawa, March 31, April 1 and 2, 1981.* Ottawa: Minister of Supply and Services 1981
–. *Reforming the Canada Assistance Plan: A Supplementary Paper.* 1994
–. *Report of the Advisory Group on Working Time and the Distribution of Work.* Ottawa: Supply and Services, December 1994
–. *Report of the Commission of Inquiry on Unemployment Insurance* (The Forget Report). Ottawa 1987
–. *Report of the Royal Commission on Dominion-Provincial Relations, Book I, Canada, 1867-1939.* Ottawa 1940; and *Book II, Recommendations.* Ottawa 1940
–. *Report of the Royal Commission on Dominion-Provincial Relations.* Appendix 6. A.E. Grauer. 'Public Assistance and Social Insurance.' Ottawa 1940; and by the same author, *Housing,* a study prepared for the Royal Commission on Dominion-Provincial Relations. Ottawa 1939
–. *Report of the Royal Commission on the Relations of Labor and Capital in Canada.* Ottawa 1889
–. *Report of the Royal Commission on the Status of Women in Canada.* Ottawa: Information Canada 1970
–. *Report of the Royal Commission to Enquire into Industrial Relations in Canada together with a Minority Report.* Contained in the appendix to Canada, National Industrial Conference, 1919, *Official Report of Proceedings and Discussions.* Ottawa 1919

–. *Report on Social Security for Canada*. Prepared for the Advisory Committee on Reconstruction, House of Commons, Special Committee on Social Security, Session 1943, by L.C. Marsh. Republished as a historical document by the University of Toronto Press, 1975

–. *Retirement Age*. Ottawa 1979

–. *Royal Commission on Health Services, Vol. 1*. Ottawa 1964

–. Senate. The Report of the Special Committee on Retirement Age Policies. *Retirement without Tears*. Ottawa: Canadian Government Publishing Centre 1979

–. Special Senate Committee on Poverty. *Poverty in Canada*. Ottawa: Information Canada 1971

–. Statistics Canada. *Social Security, National Programs*. Ottawa: Minister of Industry, Trade and Commerce 1976

–. *The Context of Reform: A Supplementary Paper*. 1994

–. Working Paper on the Constitution. *Income Security and Social Services*. Ottawa 1969

Ontario. Commission on Laws Relating to the Liability of Employers to Make Compensation to Their Employees for Injuries Received in the Course of Their Employment. *Final Report*. 2 vols. Toronto 1912-13

–. Legislative Assembly. *Report of the Ontario Commission on Unemployment*. Toronto 1916

–. Ministry of Community and Social Services, Report of the Social Assistance Review Committee. *Transitions*. Toronto: Queen's Printer of Ontario 1988

–. *Report of the Commissioners Appointed to Enquire into the Prison and Reformatory System of the Province of Ontario, 1891*. Toronto: Warwick and Sons 1891

–. *Report of the Lieutenant Governor's Committee on Housing Conditions in Toronto*. Toronto: Hunter-Ross 1934

–. Report of the Royal Commission on the Status of Pensions in Ontario. *A Plan for the Future*. 10 vols. Toronto 1980

Quebec. *COFIRENTES+*. Quebec City 1977

–. Commission of Inquiry on Health and Social Welfare. *Income Security*. Government of Quebec, 1971

–. *Social Insurance Commission*. Quebec: Minister of Labour 1933

–. *White Paper on the Personal Tax and Transfer System*. Quebec 1984

Miscellaneous Reports and Unpublished Material

Armitage, A. *Work and Welfare*. Mimeographed. 1989

Brown, Joan C. *How Much Choice? Retirement Policies in Canada*. Ottawa: Canadian Council on Social Development 1975

Caledon Institute of Social Policy. *Federal Social Policy Agenda*. September 1993

Canada Health Survey. *The Health of Canadians*. Ottawa: Minister of Supply and Services 1981

Canadian Centre for Policy Alternatives. *Pensions: Public Solutions vs. Private Interest*. Ottawa: Canadian Centre for Policy Alternatives 1982

Canadian Council on Child and Family Welfare. *Report on the Administration of Mothers' Pensions in British Columbia 1920-21 to 1930-31*. Supplement to *Child and Family Welfare*, May 1932

Canadian Council on Social Development. 'Canada's Social Programs Are in Trouble.' 1990

–. *The Family Income Security Plan*. Ottawa: Canadian Council on Social Development 1971

–. *Social Security for Canada, 1973*. Ottawa: Canadian Council on Social Development 1973

Canadian Tax Foundation. *The National Finances, 1982-83*

Canadian Union of Public Employees. *The Facts on Free Trade* 10, no. 2 (1988)

Canadian Welfare Council. *The Rowell-Sirois Report and the Social Services in Summary*. Ottawa: Canadian Welfare Council 1940

–. *Social Policies for Canada, Part I*. Ottawa: Canadian Welfare Council 1969

Child Poverty Action Group and Social Planning Council of Metropolitan Toronto. *Unequal Futures: The Legacies of Child Poverty in Canada*. Toronto 1991

Collins, Kevin. *Women and Pensions*. Ottawa: Canadian Council on Social Development 1978

Communiqué. Meeting of Federal and Provincial Ministers of Welfare, Ottawa, 3-4 February 1976

–. Meeting of Federal and Provincial Ministers of Welfare, Ottawa, 1-2 June 1976

Ecumenical Coalition for Social Justice. *Reweaving Canada's Social Programs: From Shredded Safety Net to Social Solidarity.* Toronto 1993

Evans, Robert. *Hiding behind Medicare: Health Care Funding in the BC Budget.* BC Economic Policy Institute, March 1984

Golfman, Irving J. *Some Fiscal Aspects of Public Welfare in Canada.* Toronto: Canadian Tax Foundation 1965

Gray, Gratton. 'Social Policy by Stealth.' *Policy Options,* March 1995, 17-29

Hess, Melanie. *An Overview of Social Policy.* Ottawa: Canadian Council on Social Development 1993

Johnson, A.W. *Social Policy in Canada: The Past as It Conditions the Present.* The Institute for Research on Public Policy. Ottawa 1987

Laycock, J.E. *The Canadian System of Old Age Pensions.* PhD diss., University of Chicago School of Social Service 1952

Lui-Gurr, Susanna, et al. *Making Work Pay Better than Welfare: An Early Look at the Self-Sufficiency Project.* Social Research and Demonstration Corporation. October 1994

Maxwell, J.A. *Recent Developments in Dominion-Provincial Fiscal Relations in Canada.* Occasional Paper 25. New York: National Bureau of Economic Research 1948

Muszynski, Leon. *Alternatives to Welfare.* Ontario Social Assistance Review Committee. March 1987

National Action Committee on the Status of Women. Pensions Committee. 'Women and Pensions: A Discussion Paper.' 1981

National Council of Welfare. *Bearing the Burden, Sharing the Benefits.* Ottawa 1978

–. *Better Pensions for Homemakers.* Ottawa 1984

–. *The Canada Assistance Plan: No Time for Cuts.* (Winter 1991)

–. *Child Care: A Better Alternative.* Ottawa: Supply and Services, December 1988

–. *The Federal Government and Social Services.* Ottawa: National Council of Welfare, March 1978

–. *Financing the Canada Pension Plan.* Ottawa 1982

–. *Funding Health and Higher Education: Danger Looming.* (Spring 1991)

–. *Giving and Taking: The May 1985 Budget and the Poor.* Ottawa: Supply and Services, July 1985

–. *Guide to the Guaranteed Income.* Ottawa: National Council of Welfare 1976

–. *Help Wanted: Tax Relief for Canada's Poor.* Revised Version. Ottawa: Supply and Services, November 1989

–. *The Hidden Welfare System.* Ottawa 1976

–. *The Hidden Welfare System Revisited.* Ottawa 1979

–. *Incentives and Disincentives to Work.* (Autumn 1993)

–. *Medicare: The Public Good and Private Practice.* Ottawa 1982

–. *The 1989 Budget and Social Policy.* Ottawa, September 1989

–. *The 1995 Budget and Block Funding.* (Spring 1995)

–. *A Pension Primer.* Ottawa: Supply and Services 1989

–. *Pension Primer: A Report by the National Council of Welfare on the Retirement Income System.* Ottawa, April 1984

–. *Pension Reform.* Ottawa: Minister of Supply and Services 1984

–. *Pension Reform.* Ottawa: Supply and Services, February 1990

–. *The Refundable Child Tax Credit: What It Is ... How It Works.* Ottawa: National Council of Welfare 1978

–. *Sixty-Five and Older.* Ottawa: Minister of Supply and Services 1984

–. *Social Spending and the Next Budget.* Ottawa: Supply and Services, April 1989

–. *Support/Supplementation: Who Will Benefit?* Ottawa: National Council of Welfare 1976

–. *Welfare Reform.* (Summer 1992)

–. *Women and Poverty Revisited.* Ottawa: Supply and Services 1990

Osberg, Lars. *The Future of Work in Canada: Selected Policy Options*. Ottawa: Canadian Council on Social Development 1986

Perspective Canada. Ottawa: Information Canada 1974

Perspective Canada II. Ottawa: Minister of Supply and Services 1977

Rasmussen, Wilfred. 'An Evaluation of the Mothers' Allowances Programme in British Columbia.' MSW thesis, University of British Columbia, 1956

Robichaud, Jean-Bernard. 'Canada Can Afford Its Ideals.' Working Paper no. 6, *Work and Income in the Nineties*. Ottawa: Canadian Council on Social Development 1986

Robinson, David. *Standing on Guard for Canada's Social Programs*. Council of Canadians. March 1995

Ross, David. *Canadian Fact Book on Poverty*. Ottawa: Canadian Council on Social Development 1975

Ross, David P., and Richard Shillington. 'Background Documents on Social Reform.' *Work and Income in the Nineties*. Ottawa: Canadian Council on Social Development 1986

Simeon, Richard. 'Conflicts and Contradictions: Contemporary Strains in Canadian Confederation.' In Conference on Social Development in a Pluralist Society, *Proceedings*. Ottawa: Canadian Council on Social Development 1977

Social Planning Council of Metropolitan Toronto. *Old Age Insecurity*. Toronto 1978

–. *Pensions: Passport to Poverty*. Toronto 1979

Townson, Monica. *The Social Contract for Seniors in Canada: Preparing for the 21st Century*. Ottawa, National Advisory Council on Ageing. March 1994

Unfair Share: Corporations and Taxation in Canada. Don Mills, The Ontario Federation of Labour and the Ontario Coalition for Social Justice. April 1994

Index

Set in Stone by Val Speidel

Printed and bound in Canada by Freisens

Copy-editor: Randy Schmidt

Proofreader: Dallas Harrison

Indexer: Patricia Buchanan